Building a Classical Music Library

Bill Parker

Jormax Publications
Minneapolis, Minnesota

Library of Congress Cataloging-in-Publication Data

Parker, Bill.
    Building a classical music library / Bill Parker. -- 3rd ed.,
fully rev.
        p.   cm.
    Includes index.
    ISBN 0-9641332-0-2
    1. Music--Discography.   2. Music appreciation.   I. Title.
    ML 156.2.P25   1994
    016.78'0266--dc20   94-36266
                                                              CIP
                                                               MN

First printing: October 1994

Printed in the United States of America

98 97 96 95 94   6 5 4 3 2 1

Cover by *Circus Design*
Interior by *Mori Studio*

Table of Contents

Acknowledgments

This book was made possible with the publishing expertise of Bob Morris, and the support of Jeff and Sandy Abrams, with cheering from Jordan and Max.

Along the way I had invaluable help from Rex Levang, who assisted me in research, and from Tim Hartz, Mark Webb, and Judy Gilats, who advised and assisted in computer applications.

Introduction

Never believe the saying that one has to hear music many times to understand it. It is utter nonsense, the last refuge of the incompetent.
—*Frederick Delius*

For Delius, one of the greatest English composers, classical music was not a forbidding or difficult subject, it was "the expression of a poetical and emotional nature." So it has always been for me, and I urge you to keep that definition in mind whenever you pore through this book.

Nothing can substitute for listening to the music itself, not any verbal descriptions or exhortations that I or anyone else can conjure up. It is just as true, however, that you do not have to labor over listening to music to feel you have gotten something worthwhile out of it.

There is nothing wrong with studying music theory and history; it will enhance and deepen your enjoyment. But if you have ordinary intelligence and some interest in the subject, the essentials will embed themselves in your psyche in short order. You may not know the technical name for what is happening in all the music you hear, but if the composer has done a good job you will get the point. After all, music supposedly is a language that goes beyond words, so why worry about words?

What Is Classical Music?

For many people, the word "classical" suggests music that is relaxing. You have probably heard it said, "I can't listen to that classical stuff—it puts me to sleep." For others, it means music that is stiff and formal, music that you can't dance to. For yet others it signifies music written in and for other cultures and times, not theirs, and therefore music which is not understandable and of no interest.

I hope in the course of your explorations you will come to believe that none of the above are true. There is quiet classical music, to be sure, but one would be hard pressed to sleep through Tchaikovsky's *1812 Overture*. If you think classical music has no beat, try Ravel's *Boléro*. And although it was often written originally for wealthy aristocrats, classical music today is the universal property of everyone, thanks to its increasing use in films and commercials, and its ready availability on recordings.

Actually, the term "classical" is somewhat misleading to begin with. More precisely, it should refer to the period of about 1750-1820, the age of Haydn and Mozart and early Beethoven. The way to keep its two uses apart is to notice that when the specific era is denoted, it is spelled with a capital "C." Generically (with a small "c"), "classical" is a loose term for music that has the cachet of history and respectability. Nowadays it could apply to Beatles songs as well as to the Bruckner symphonies.

But for our purposes, and in the common usage, we are referring to what might better be called "art music"—works of music that are deliberately written down (i.e., composed) by professional musicians in an acknowledged tradition that can be traced just like a genealogy from the late Middle Ages and Renaissance to the present, from the masses of Guillaume de Machaut to the cantatas of Bach, from the piano concerti of Mozart to the tone poems of Franz Liszt, and from the ballets of Stravinsky to the symphonies of Górecki.

It is music that ultimately rests on a set of academic rules—no matter how often the rules are transgressed—regarding melody, harmony, rhythm, tempo, and other technical devices. And above all (and what sets it apart emotionally from other types of music) is its relative sense of philosophical distance. It is designed to last beyond the present moment. It is meant to be not only listened to, but concentrated on.

Another term for it is "concert music"—that is, music you deliberately go into a room or hall to sit down and pay attention to. It is not intended for dancing or marching (although there are very often dances and marches in it), or even for putting yourself to sleep or waking yourself up (although no one can stop you from putting it to whatever use you like.) Its real purpose is to either make you feel deeply, think deeply, or both. If you can accept these as conditions for liking classical music, you are ready to make a stab at it.

To do that, you don't need to sign up for a university course. This book may give you a push, but ultimately you have to rely on your own ears to communicate with your own brain. Listening to the beauty and variety of classical music over a period of time is its own education. Beethoven once said his music was written "from the heart, to the heart." If music is good, whatever style or period it represents, it will find its way into a willing heart and brain.

In this book you will not find terms such as "exposition," "development," or "recapitulation." These are technical classical music terms that you need to know to perform the music, or to analyze it if you go on to the advanced stages of study, but they are absolutely irrelevant for acquiring a real love and instinctive understanding of the music. More important are your inner qualities of inquisitiveness, compassion, and courage. Don't be afraid of classical music. Read a little, listen a lot, and you will have your reward.

Finally, remember that classical music is not intrinsically "better" than other kinds of music. Jazz, folk music, and rock are legitimate forms of artistic expression, but they have different emotional and philosophical aims. There is a type of music for every temperament. If you find classical music is not for you, there should be no shame in it. At the same time, if you enjoy classical music, you are not authorized to use your tastes to bludgeon your friends, or to place yourself above them. Centuries of association with wealthy patrons has given classical music an undeserved reputation as "highfalutin'" and obnoxious. "There is room in the world," said Delius, "for all kinds of music to suit all tastes."

The Purpose of This Book

This book is not written, as I feel some guides to classical music are, from one aficionado to another. I have tried to avoid speaking a "secret language," striving for plain English instead. So many music books sound to me like music professors writing for colleagues down the hall. Others are patronizing and embarrassing for grownups to read. What I have tried to do is write a book on classical music and its recordings that a real human being, a person of average intelligence but without a degree in music, can read with profit and comfort, yet without shame.

I have not included a glossary because I have tried to explain any specialized terms as they occur in the narrative. If I have neglected any it is because I hope their meaning will be fairly clear from the context. In any case, I do not think people like to read glossaries, or to have to interrupt their reading to constantly look up unfamiliar terms.

In selecting the composers and their works I have tried not to be shallow, but I have emphasized breadth over depth. I wanted to touch on as wide a spectrum—from the Middle Ages to recent times—as I could without abandoning the principle that I should stick to the proven classics.

Already a friend has berated me for omitting Olivier Messiaen while including Arthur Honegger. I can only say I have a reason for everything I do. In this case I agree with Charles Osborne, who has written that "Messiaen is clearly not in the mainstream of contemporary composition, wherever that stream may be wandering, but has made a safe place for himself in one of its backwaters." (*The Dictionary of Composers,* 1981) Of course, no two people would ever do a book like this exactly the same way, and I do not claim my selection is right and others are wrong.

I am merely satisfied that I have come close to what I intended to do: to cover as wide a spectrum as the paper allotted to me could hold, to avoid musicological jargon, to make the composers come to life as real humans as best I could, to suggest the emotions most people have when they hear the various works of music, and to recommend recordings that have wide consensus as to their merits.

When Sir Neville Marriner endorsed my first edition fourteen years ago, he wrote, "Parker is positive; this is a slim volume of suggestions, not derogatory comparisons." The book is not quite so slim today, but I have kept the maestro's compliment firmly in mind. Just as then, I have tried not to waste ink on invective. My purpose is not to show how I can trash my nemeses and *bêtes noires* (although I have let my opinions and prejudices show through when it seemed appropriate), but to point out good things that listeners may like.

Since there are countless new recordings coming out every year, record recommendations date fairly quickly. Fortunately, classical recordings are somewhat insulated from obsolescence, since (1) the repertory changes only very slowly over long timespans, and (2) the acknowledged greatest recordings tend to stay in print and to retain their status as classics over a period of many years.

Still, recordings come and go, and even as we go to press wonderful new things are coming on line, and great old ones are either disappearing or being reissued with new cata-log numbers or on new labels. Keep these things in mind if you use these listings in your shopping; your record store clerk will help sort out what is still in print and what is not. All I can guarantee is that every record listed here was in print when I typed it into my computer.

How the Recordings Were Selected

Only standard compact discs are listed in this book. No attempt is made to distinguish other formats, as they are either nearly extinct or have not yet become widely accepted. Music cassettes still exist, but they are such a small proportion of the classical music catalog that I thought listing them would add little if anything to the book.

My goal was to list neither too few nor too many discs. Some books give as few as one recommendation per work; this implies to many readers that only one worthwhile record-ing exists of each piece, and if the record store is out of that one the shopper should skulk home disappointed. Others give so many, with so many qualifications, that sorting through them can make it seem that the purpose of such a book—to narrow choices down—is being defeated.

My view is that there are three principal things a buyer might be looking for: the best-sounding recording, the greatest performance, or the best price (or, of course, any combi-nation of these). For each work of music I have looked for an outstanding recording in each of these three categories. Sometimes there have been more than one in each, of approximately equal value. Sometimes one recording encompasses two or, rarely, three of the criteria, as when a budget recording is the best performance as well. Sometimes I could not in good conscience list any recording for one of the criteria, as when there simply is not a good budget recording. I have chosen not to list a mediocre performance just because it is cheap, or a brilliant digital recording of an inferior artist.

If a recording is not listed it may be out of print, or it may just not have fit the arbi-trary (but consistent) criteria I set for myself. Many fine recordings are not listed in this book because they have "non-basic" couplings (they contain oddly matched pieces) or are excessively expensive when another version essentially as good exists with better couplings or a better price.

As an example of a great recording that is not listed, I can cite the Brahms First Symphony on Chesky Records, conducted by Jascha Horenstein. It is a wonderful perfor-mance, and the Chesky label specializes in restoring the sonics of great recordings of the recent past (in this case 1962). But it is a high-priced label, the recording is analog, and the coupling is a rather odd one—the *Bacchanale* from Wagner's *Tannhäuser*. In my judgment, Bruno Walter's recording, though just as old, is just as good or better, and much cheaper; Claudio Abbado's recent digital one is less expensive and has a Brahms coupling instead of Wagner (the antithesis, many would say, of Brahms); and Günter Wand's performance, newer in sound (and an even greater performance, many would say), is available in a mid-priced set of the complete Brahms symphonies. As far as I am concerned, my three criteria of great sound, great performance, and great pricing are adequately covered without including the Chesky recording, which will in addition be harder to find in stores than the other discs, since generally only specialty shops and the largest stores carry the label.

My intent is not to insult Chesky, a wonderful label (and their recording of the Sibelius Second Symphony *is* included), but to insist that fine as the disc is, it does not fit the criteria I have chosen for a first-time choice for the beginning collector as well as some others. If you love the Brahms First, and get one or more of the records I have listed, or your store just does not have them and you have plenty of money, please *do* buy the Horenstein recording! You will not be making a mistake by any means. I cannot, however, list every good recording ever made in the confines of this book, nor can I guarantee that one not listed is good or bad. All I can do is say with confidence that all those which are listed have a great deal going for them, and you will not, I hope, have to regret purchasing any one of them.

As for my judging of the recordings themselves, it is based primarily on the common consensus among critics. I do read, and have read for many years, the reviews in all the leading music magazines and other publications judging recordings, and get a sense of what recordings are widely admired and which are not. In addition, I have been in the record business and/or classical radio broadcasting for more than thirty years, and am keenly aware, often by osmosis, of what is happening in classical recordings. I keep copious and detailed notes on all the pieces that I cover in my book, on all the recordings of them, in and out of print, on their changing labels and numbers, and on whatever else is relevant.

And, of course, there is my personal judgment; but I never allow this to overrule the general consensus. If there is a recording that only I like, it is not listed in this book. And there are a few recordings here that I don't like, but list anyway because everybody else likes them. There are no marginal choices here; all are "central" selections. To be listed, a disc must give good value all around, fulfill the criteria for an excellent first purchase, be fairly easy to find, not be unduly expensive, not give a highly controversial view of the music. Much safer than that a record cannot be.

How to Interpret the CD Listings

The recordings are listed in approximate descending order of desirability, with digital recording given preference if all else is approximately equal. Since I do not intend to list any inferior or questionable recordings at all, just because a CD is last on the list does not mean it is far less valuable than the top item; it only means that for a hypothetical "average" buyer I think it might be slightly less optimal than items above it. It might be a greater performance than one higher on the list, but more expensive. Many fine points often determine the sequence, and I don't advise giving it too much weight in your considerations. In the brief evaluations preceeding each set of listings I try to indicate the major differences among the recordings at hand.

For each recording, the soloist's last name is given first (if there is a soloist), followed by the conductor's last name, then the name of the orchestra or other ensemble. Next is the name of the record label (occasionally preceeded by a generic album title, if any, in quotation marks), followed by the selection number and number of discs in a set (if more than one) in parentheses.

Next, the "pedigree" of the recording is given in brackets, if definitively known by me. The "pedigree," also known as the Spars Code, is the three-letter code showing on virtually all compact discs to indicate (1) whether the original master was analog or digital, (2) whether or not that master has been digitally remastered for this release, and (3) the current format. Thus, [DDD] means the recording is digital from the first step to the last; [ADD] means the original analog master has been digitally remastered for issue on compact disc; [AAD] means the original analog master has not been digitally remastered for issue on compact disc. (The final letter will always be a "D," since a compact disc is by definition a digital format.)

You may presume in virtually all cases that if no pedigree is given, the recording is analog, whether remastered or not. When there is no pedigree listed, it usually means that the manufacturer does not list the pedigree in the standard Schwann Opus catalog; in most cases I have preferred to let this alone.

All recordings are stereo unless specifically marked (mono) after the pedigree; I have allowed only a tiny number of monophonic recordings into this book, as most do not fulfill the criteria for a first purchase. Later on, as an in-depth collector, you may wish to acquire many great performances which are in older sound—but not, usually, the first time around.

If there are additional pieces on the disc besides the featured item, a plus sign (+) will appear and be followed by their titles. If no composer is given, the additional pieces are by the composer under discussion. I have tried to indicate changes in artists for coupled works if it clarifies the description.

Finally, if the description ends there, it indicates the disc is designed to sell at full price, that is, a list price of thirteen dollars or more. If the list price is lower, I add the designation (mid-price) if the list is nine to twelve dollars, and (budget) if the list is eight dollars or lower.

Following is a sample listing of an imaginary CD which shows all the features explained above:

Parker, Bourbon Symphony Orchestra. "Tales from the Crypt," Rusty Dagger Records 911 (2) [AAD] (mono) + *Ale and Farewell,* Variations on "Scots Wha' Hae wi' Wallace Bled" (with Fisher conducting); Gorgonzolla: Mad Scene from *Clair de Loony* (mid-price)

About "Super Budget" Recordings

This book discusses in detail only recordings that have list prices of about six dollars or more; the great majority are at least eight dollars. But there is another kind of compact disc being carried in many stores these days, known in the trade as the "super budget." These discs retail at five dollars or less, and often are treated as "in and out" or "promotional" merchandise; that is, they appear in mass quantities, sell for a limited period, and then disappear.

Generally these are recordings by artists with no name recognition, or from countries with no copyright laws or where the economy is distressed (often in Eastern Europe) and masters are available very cheaply, and so on. Whatever the reason, the record company has little or no expense involved with recording costs, royalties, or advertising, and it is possible for them to sell the discs at a very low price.

Most of these recordings are actually 100% digital [DDD] and are manufactured with the same quality standards as high-priced discs. Very few of them are returned to stores as defective; fewer than normal, in fact, since when they *are* defective, people are more likely to use them as coasters, considering their price.

It is true that most of these performances fall short of the genius or inspired level. Still, some of them are excellent, and even when they are not they may make a reasonably acceptable introduction to a piece of music which you may wish to replace later with a greater artist. In any case, I did not think it a good use of space to discuss the merits of individual super-budget discs. I assume that it is when you are considering spending larger amounts of money that you are most likely to look for the detailed information and guidance this book provides.

About Technology

An article in *Insight* magazine dated March 28, 1988, noted that "The demise of the long-playing record is at hand, some say, but such forecasts may be rash. True, some stores have cut orders of vinyl and grant more space to compact discs, but records won't vanish, except perhaps from classical bins." A record executive was quoted as predicting that customers would not be able to buy LPs in five years, but the article treated this as exaggeration.

Unless you have been in a galaxy far, far away for the last five years, you know that the record executive was too generous. Long before his deadline, LPs were virtually extinct, and not just in the classical bins. An article in the St. Paul *Pioneer Press* dated June 21, 1991 (three years and a month after the foregoing prognosis) asked, "Buy any good records lately? Probably not. Major 'record' companies have virtually stopped selling them in the United States, and few retailers carry them."

The little silvery wafer that finally drove the vinyl LP into the Jurassic period was the compact disc, or CD. (May I plead plaintively for you to spell it "disc?" The spelling "disk" is reserved for computer disks—or, more properly, diskettes.)

The CD was designed to be a format, or carrier, for digital recordings. (The term "digital" refers to a computerized technology for recording which was introduced to the public in 1982.) Unlike the previous standard system, in which sound waves were mechanically inscribed on wax or plastic, the digital system converts the sound waves to numerical values. These are expressed as electrical pulses which are magnetically recorded onto tape. When the CD is manufactured, the numerical values are decoded back into the sounds (music) which they represent. This process involves no friction and so eliminates the background of noise, or "tape hiss," inevitable with the old analog system; it also eliminates the need for artificial compression of the music, thus capturing the full dynamic range of a performance. Besides all this, digital recording can guarantee accuracy of pitch (eliminating "flutter" and "wow"), and greatly lower distortion.

The compact disc, unlike the vinyl LP, does not wear out from repeated plays, as there is no physical contact between the laser beam which reads and reflects the encoded information on the disc and the disc itself. The old stylus tracked the LP from the outer edge inward at a constant speed of thirty-three and one-third revolutions per minute; the laser reads the CD from the center out, at speeds varying from five hundred rpm near the center to two hundred rpm near the outer edge. Compact discs also completely eliminate pops and ticks and the other assorted noises endemic to LPs, and hold about fifty percent more music in a much smaller space.

Despite these advantages, there are listeners who insist that they prefer the sound of analog recordings, even with their little noises and distractions. They say the sound is "warmer," and there is no reason to doubt or dismiss the claim; all hearing is subjective to begin with, and in listening to recordings we can grow fond of what we are most used to, whether it is the newest-fangled invention or not. It is even more clearly true that there was a black, liquid beauty to the old LP, and one could experience a certain comfort in watching it spin on the turntable. Nowadays, the CD is rather disconcertingly swallowed up by the player and not seen again till the concert is over. And although the music is no longer compressed, the artwork is; I don't think I will ever enjoy looking at a CD cover as much as an LP sleeve.

Ironically, the worst charge levelled against digital recordings is that they are *too* clear and undistorted—extraneous sounds such as the player's throat-clearings, or even the fingers striking the keys, can suddenly become intrusive on a CD. Many early CDs were marred by such oddities, but as time passes the sound engineers learn to compensate for these.

It is important to remember that while digital technology has eliminated noise and distortion and expanded dynamic range and frequency, the real point of a recording is not technology. It is *music*. An expensive camera does not guarantee a great photograph. It is the photographer who has to manipulate the camera artistically. In the recording studio there are many factors besides digital technology that affect the final product, such as microphone placement and tonal balance, and above all, the quality of the musicians who are playing.

There is no point in buying a new digital recording of a lousy performance when you can get a beautifully produced analog recording of a great artist that has been well reprocessed digitally. Many buyers make the mistake of refusing to consider anything but an all-digital [DDD] recording, regardless of the many complex considerations that go into a great disc. That is why I have tried in this book to include all-digital recordings only when they are testaments of really good music making, and why I have included many analog recordings that are so good you would be foolish to pass them up just because they are not all-digital.

When my previous record guide was published in 1984, compact discs were still very new, most recordings were still available on vinyl LP, and no one was sure whether the new technology would really become the standard or not. Now, ten years later, there are rumors and rumblings of even newer technologies. Sony has introduced the mini disc (MD), and Philips the digital compact cassette (DCC). A couple of years ago these formats were seen as possibly posing a serious challenge to the CD, but that has not happened. An even earlier threat, digital audio tape (DAT), became a staple tool of radio stations and professional recording studios, but never caught on with the general public. It seems that CD, after a bit of a slow start and a couple of pauses, has settled in to be the standard home audio format for a while yet, and the hesitations customers once had about investing in it have pretty much evaporated.

Lately, however, there has been a concern about evaporation in another sense: almost from the beginning of the CD era there has been a rumor afloat that in a matter of a few years the music on a disc will fade out to silence. Nobody could prove this or disprove it, because no CD was presumably old enough to start decaying. In the spring of 1994, however, there were confirmed reports of some discs eroding. The latest information would seem to indicate, however, that the phenomenon is limited to a small percentage of discs made prior to about 1991 involving a particular chemical reaction among ingredients used in one nonstandard manufacturing process. As of this writing, there does not appear to be any mass degradation looming on the horizon.

Finally, this is a book about classical music and its recordings, not audio equipment, and so I am afraid I can't go into detail here about CD players and related technologies. For that (as well as to learn about such things as passacaglias and Picardy thirds) you will just have to get another book.

The Middle Ages and Renaissance

Since very little contemporary concert music has won a wide audience in the past thirty or forty years (except possibly for some of the current "minimalist" music), the gap has been filled by a renewed interest in very old music—the songs and dances and chants whose authors, as often as not, are unknown, but which form the basis for all Western classical music.

Gradually we have learned that these works are not only historically important, but also direct in expression and delightful to listen to. In response to this, record companies have issued hundreds of recordings of the pre-Bach repertoire.

A collective rubric for the tonal works created in Europe from about A.D. 800 to 1600 is "Early Music," though some writers extend this term (quite unreasonably, I think) to include composers as late as Mozart, who died in 1791. Much of this music is anonymous in origin, and has come down to us through oral tradition, or in a written form whose authenticity is very much in doubt. And what this music actually sounded like is often a topic of acrimonious dispute.

None of this music is part of what is considered the standard modern concert repertoire. If you attend an evening of the Boston Symphony or the Los Angeles Philharmonic, you may hear Bach, Mozart, Beethoven, Brahms, Berlioz, or Stravinsky on the program; you will not hear any troubadour songs, Gregorian chants, or Renaissance dances (unless re-orchestrated by Respighi). For these you must seek out occasional special recitals, often in museum galleries.

Nevertheless, a few names stand out with whom any person interested in these early times should become familiar. A generous selection of them and some of their most representative compositions are offered in this chapter, along with a few collections that attempt to honor in some small fashion that most prolific of all composers, "Anonymous."

Gregorian Chant (fl. ca. 600-1150)

This music, intended for use in the liturgy of the Roman Catholic Church, evolved from the psalm-singing and intoned rituals of the Jewish temple, with additional influences from Greek and Roman choral traditions. The four original church modes seem to have been taken over from the secular modes of the Greeks in about the fourth century A.D. It took another seven centuries before our modern system of musical notation was developed, so the early chants were either handed down orally or transmitted by a rather inexact system of signs called "neumes," whose quaint and pretty diamond shapes we admire in medieval manuscripts.

There were actually several different styles of chanting in the earliest days, but the system attributed to Pope St. Gregory I (540-604), with the addition of four new modes, became dominant throughout Christendom. The pure original style of singing this music (also known as "plainsong") degenerated over the centuries, but since the 1830s the Benedictine monks of the Abbey of Solesmes, France, have succeeded with admirable scholarship in restoring this ancient art to its first glory.

With its monodic melody, unhampered by either barlines or harmonization, Gregorian chant is ideally suited to its intended function of suggesting an austere and mystical beauty not of this earth. Ironically, it has all but disappeared from the liturgy of the Church today, while it has found new favor with many as an accompaniment to such activities as painting and Zen meditation.

In the spring of 1994 the impossible happened: a recording of chants sung by the Choir of the Benedictine Monastery of Santo Domingo de Silos in Spain became a sales phenomenon. Starting out as a favorite early-morning album of a radio disc jockey, it garnered unprecedented media attention for such an item, getting reviews and interviews on *Good Morning America,* the *Tonight Show,* the *Today Show, Newsweek,* you name it. It hit the pop charts and was being merchandised in many record stores right beside the latest rock albums. Would old Pope Gregory be pleased or appalled?

Less media-savvy, but more musically sophisticated, are the choir of monks from the Abbey of Saint-Pierre de Solesmes, directed by Dom Gajard, who have made about twenty fine recordings demonstrating their rigorous adherence to the highest standards of Gregorian chant performance. Excellent singing is also preserved in recordings by the Neideraltaicher Scholaren and the Schola Hungarica.

Santo Domingo de Silos Monks. "Chant," EMI 62735 [DDD]
Monastic Choir of St. Peter's Abbey, Solesmes.
    Gregorian Sampler I, Paraclete 629-1
    Gregorian Sampler II, Paraclete 629-2, or
    I and II in one 2-CD set, Paraclete 829
Ruhland, Neideraltaicher Scholaren. Sony 53899 [DDD]
Schola Hungarica. "From Evening to Evening with Gregorian Chant," Hungaroton 31086 [DDD]

Medieval Collections

What historians call the High Middle Ages and musicians the Gothic Era (ca. 1150-1450) is a period rich in the development of secular song and dance music. There are the chivalrous lyrics of the Troubadours, Trouvères, and Minnesingers—wandering minstrels with evocative names such as Bernard de Ventadorn and Walther von der Vogelweide. And there are countless irresistible little dances for instruments such as the nakers, rommelpot, cow horn and clappers.

Sacred music also evolved further in this period, with the appearance of polyphonic choral compositions; in these, two or more melodies were sung simultaneously to create a richer and more varied effect than the old plainsong. Polyphony was in effect an intermediate stage between the monody of chant and the development of modern harmony.

A classic survey is the three-record set "Music of the Gothic Era" by the Early Music Consort of London, directed by David Munrow, excerpts of which have been re-issued on CD. The Hilliard Ensemble has a nice collection of medieval English songs and church music called "Sumer is Icumen In," as well as a disc of Troubadour songs. Joel Cohen's Boston Camerata has made many cleverly conceived recordings, including "A Medieval Christmas" and the authentic original of "Tristan et Iseult."

Recently the Martin Best Mediaeval Ensemble from England has contributed some highly interesting material, both sacred and secular. From France, the virtuosic Clemencic Consort has produced several volumes of the original settings of the *Carmina Burana*, more familiar to many from the modern cantata setting by Carl Orff.

Another outstanding group specializing in medieval music is Sequentia, from Cologne, Germany, whose accomplishments are crowned by a complete recording of the remarkable *Ordo Virtutum*, or "Play of the Virtues," by the abbess Hildegard of Bingen (1098-1179). She is well served also by The Gothic Voices on their splendid album, *A Feather on the Breath of God*.

The Gothic Voices score also with "Music for the Lion-Hearted King," melodies from the time of the Crusades, which are represented as well on one of David Munrow's fine survey albums.

Two other recordings I can't leave out are Phillip Pickett's New London Collective performing pilgrim songs and dances on *The Pilgrimage to Santiago*, and *Ars Magis Subtiliter* by Ensemble P.A.N., an anthology of late fourteenth century music.

Munrow, London Early Music Consort. *Music of the Gothic Era*, DG Archiv 415292 [ADD]

Hillier, Hilliard Ensemble. *Sumer is Icumen In*, Harmonia Mundi 901154

Hillier, Hilliard Ensemble. *Proensa* (Troubodour songs), ECM 21368 [DDD]

Cohen, Boston Camerata. *A Medieval Christmas*, Nonesuch 71315 [ADD] (mid-price)

Cohen, Boston Camerata. *Tristan et Iseult*, Erato 45348

Martin Best Medieval Ensemble. *Songs of Chivalry*, Nimbus 5006

Clemencic Consort. *Carmina Burana* (sel.), Harmonia Mundi 90335

Sequentia. Hildegard von Bingen: *Ordo Virtutum*, Editio Classica 77051 [DDD] (mid-price)

Kirkby, Page, Gothic Voices. Hildegard von Bingen: *A Feather on the Breath of God,* Hyperion 66039 [DDD]

Page, Gothic Voices. *Music of the Lion-Hearted King,* Hyperion 66336 [DDD]

Munrow, London Early Music Consort. *Music of the Crusades,* London Jubilee 430264 [ADD] (mid-price)

Pickett, New London Collective. *The Pilgrimage to Santiago,* L'Oiseau-Lyre 433148 (2) [DDD]

Ensemble P.A.N. *Ars Magis Subtiliter,* New Albion 021 [DDD]

Renaissance Collections

The Renaissance Period (ca. 1450-1600) in music corresponds to the great flowering of secular and humanist ideals in Europe after the fall of Constantinople to the Turks and the subsequent flight of Eastern scholars to the West, which resulted in the rediscovery of much long-lost literature and philosophy. Secular works gained even more attention from composers. Huge repertoires were built up for solo instruments such as the lute and virginals. Splendid brass music was written for processions at the royal courts. Little proto-orchestras, such as "consorts of viols," came into being. Secular part-songs, particularly the Italian madrigals, became larger, more complex, and infinitely richer, as heard in the cosmic-sounding masses of Palestrina, Byrd, and Victoria.

The first four albums listed below provide excellent overviews of Renaissance music by the four principal nationalities involved in creating music at this period: Spain, England, France, and Italy.

Renaissance sacred music is represented in an anthology from the Eton Choirbook of England, performed by The Sixteen.

Most other anthologies are of secular music, including those listed by the Ulsamer Collegium, Calliope, the Atrium Musicae de Madrid, the Waverly Consort, the Broadside Band, and the Deller Consort. Each of these fine ensembles has a unique perspective on Renaissance music, as well as distinguished musicality.

Hill, Westminster Cathedral Choir. *Treasures of the Spanish Renaissance,* Hyperion 66168 [DDD]

Hillier, Hilliard Ensemble. *The Old Hall Manuscript* (early English Renaissance music), Angel 54111 [DDD]

Page, Gothic Voices. *The Service of Venus and Mars* (French motets and Mass movements), Hyperion 66238 [DDD]

Thomas, London Pro Musica. *A Florentine Carnival,* IMP PCD 825 [DDD] (mid-price)

Christophers, The Sixteen. *Rose and the Ostrich Feather,* Collins 1314 [DDD]

Ragossnig, Ulsamer Collegium. *Dance Music of the Renaissance,* DG Archiv 415294 [ADD]

Calliope. *Calliope Dances: A Renaissance Revel,* Nonesuch 79039 [DDD]

Paniagua, Atrium Musicae de Madrid. *Musique Arabo-Andalouse,* Harmonia Mundi 90389

Jaffee, Waverly Consort. 1492: *Music from the Age of Discovery,* EMI 54506

Barlow, Broadside Band. *English Country Dances,* Saydisc 393 [DDD]

Deller Consort. *Shakespeare Songs and Consort Music.* Harmonia Mundi 190202

William Byrd (1543-1623)

Byrd was a devout Catholic whose musical genius protected him in an England where Catholics were ruthlessly persecuted. His royal patron, Queen Elizabeth, pointedly ignored his religious views. In gratitude, he created some of the greatest masterpieces of English Protestant church music, including *The Great Service.* For many years Byrd was a close associate of Thomas Tallis, the "father of English Cathedral music." The Queen granted the pair a joint license which allowed them to virtually monopolize music publishing.

Byrd also contributed significant instrumental music, including some 140 pieces for the virginals (an early keyboard instrument whose repertoire is now often performed on the harpsichord). These are widely anthologized in two famous collections, *Ladye Nevell's Virginal Booke* and the *Fitzwilliam Virginal Book.* William Byrd is often considered the most versatile composer of his time, and the first great genius of the keyboard.

Choral Music

The Tallis Scholars and the Winchester Cathedral Choir both have outstanding recordings of the Latin Masses for 3, 4, and 5 Voices, but at full price. If you are willing to forego the Mass for 3 Voices, you can save a pretty penny with the Oxford Camerata recording at budget price.

Phillips, Tallis Scholars. Gimell 345

Hill, Winchester Cathedral Choir. Argo 430164 [DDD]

Summerly, Oxford Camerata. Naxos 8.550574 [DDD] (budget)

Consort Music

A fine introductory selection is found on a disc by the British group Fretwork, paired with the *Lachrimae* of John Dowland.

Fretwork. Virgin Classics 59539 [DDD]

John Dowland (1563-1626)

A younger contemporary of William Byrd, Dowland was England's other most famous Elizabethan composer. After a visit to Paris at age seventeen, he converted to Catholicism, but fared less well in the Virgin Queen's favor than Byrd. As a result he spent considerable time abroad, moping, as was his wont, in the courts of Brunswick and Denmark.

His reputation for melancholy was so pervasive that he adopted as his motto "Semper Dowland Semper Dolens" ("Always Dowland, Always Sorrowing"). It is no surprise that among his best-known titles are "Flow my tears," "I saw my lady weep," "In darkness let me dwell," and "Forlorn hope." One of his texts reads: "My wailing Muse her woeful work begins, sounding nought but sorrow, grief and care." Not a party animal perhaps, but a touching poet.

He was a master of the lute, and more importantly, the song with lute accompaniment. His sensitivity in matching words and music has carried his reputation as one of the greatest song writers down to the present day.

Lachrimae, or Seven Teares

This unique instrumental work calls for five viols and a lute to play seven pavans (slow dances), each beginning with a sorrowful descending figure, and covering the gamut of weeping including "teares, and sighes, and grones." An additional fourteen pieces in the collection abandon the "lachrimae" motif; a few of them are actually quite cheerful! The British group Fretwork handily couple this work with samples of consort music by William Byrd.

Fretwork. Virgin Classics 59539 [DDD]

Lute Music

Guitarist/lutenist Julian Bream is legendary for his performances of this music, but at this writing his Dowland album seems not to be available except in a twenty-eight-disc (!) set; therefore for the time being let us opt for the estimable recital by Ron McFarlane of twenty-eight dances and fantasias (not discs!).

McFarlane. Dorian 90148 [DDD]

Lute Songs

These have been stylishly and beautifully recorded complete by Anthony Rooley's Consort of Musicke. The "Third and Last Book of Songs or Aires" (1603) makes a fine introduction.

Rooley, Consort of Musicke. L'Oiseau-Lyre 430284

Giovanni Gabrieli (ca. 1554/57-1612)

Gabrieli, about whose life little is known, became the most important composer of grandiose ceremonial music in Renaissance Italy. As organist of St. Mark's, Venice, following the death of his uncle and teacher, Andrea, he had free rein to compose in an ornate and brilliant style. Contemporary visitors to the church described being overwhelmed by the antiphonal pealings of organ and brass echoing back and forth across the chancel. Late in life Gabrieli became the teacher of Heinrich Schütz, who was to become known as the "father of German music" and the greatest German composer before Bach. Gabrieli's music fell into oblivion for centuries, being revived only in recent years.

Canzoni for Brass

These short, gleaming pieces work well on either modern or historical brass instruments. The Empire Brass "and friends" have done a smashing digital recording of selected works by Gabrieli and a few of his contemporaries, using modern brass. On period instruments, Andrew Parrott's London Cornett and Sackbut Ensemble provide a fascinating contrast.

Organist E. Power Biggs is joined by the Edward Tarr Brass Ensemble, the Gregg Smith Singers, and the Texas Boys' Choir for a classic Gabrieli potpourri which includes seven each of brass canzoni, organ intonations, and motets, plus three mass movements and a sonata, all recorded at St. Mark's Basilica in Venice, where Gabrieli held forth in life. It was a marvelous recording project for 1967, but it would be better if CBS/Sony issued it at mid-price.

A similar celebratory album, in modern sound, is provided by the Gabrieli Consort and Players in an album which reconstructs a coronation mass using music by both Andrea and Giovanni Gabrieli. Here you at least get digital sound for full price.

Empire Brass and Friends. Telarc 80204 [DDD]
Parrott, Taverner Consort Choir and Players. Angel 54265
Biggs, Edward Tarr Brass Ensemble, Gregg Smith Singers, Texas Boys' Choir. *The Glory of Venice/Gabrieli in San Marco*, CBS 42645 [ADD]
McCreesh, Gabrieli Consort and Players. *A Venetian Coronation* 1595, Virgin Classics 59006 [DDD]

Josquin des Pres (ca. 1440-1521)

Considered almost universally by his colleagues to be the greatest composer in the world around the year 1500, Josquin's long life produced a large number of masterpieces, mostly sacred works such as masses and motets. He commanded large salaries and was sought after by princes and kings, one of whom chafed that Josquin would compose "only when it suits him, not when you wish." His mature works exhibited an admirable balance among the elements of euphonious sound, formal symmetry, vigor of expression, and fresh imagination. They were regarded respectfully everywhere as models of composition.

We think of him today as a Frenchman, but that is scarcely cosmopolitan enough for one who had a Flemish upbringing, spent the better part of forty years in Milan and Rome, and maintained close contacts with the court of the Holy Roman Emperor. He won the praise of the author Rabelais, and of Martin Luther, who called him "the master of notes—they have to do what he wants." His tomb was destroyed during the French Revolution along with other hated symbols of the past; his music survives undefiled.

Masses and Motets

The inimitable Tallis Scholars have made musically precise, tonally lustrous recordings of some of Josquin's masses, with interesting historical notes. A selection of representative motets is sung with apt period style by the Chapelle Royale Chorus, directed by Philippe Herreweghe.

A footnote: in searching catalogues for this composer's works, keep in mind that some sources alphabetize him under "D," others under "J"—though none under "P." It is not quite certain whether or not des Pres (or Despres, or des Prez) should be considered a surname in the modern sense, or if he is just "Little Joe from Picardy." I lean towards the latter.

Phillips, Tallis Scholars. Gimell 009 [DDD]
Herreweghe, La Chapelle Royale Chorus. Harmonia Mundi 901243

Orlandus Lassus (ca. 1532-1594)

Lassus was a close counterpart to Josquin des Pres one century later, and could be considered his direct musical descendant in the field of counterpoint. Though less of a melodist than the earlier master, Lassus compared favorably in form, fecundity, energy, and attention to detail. He even had similar name problems: born in Mons (now part of Belgium), he was christened Roland de Lassus; from a sojourn in Rome (as master of music at the Basilica of St. John Lateran) he gained the alternate spelling of Orlando di Lasso. His name shows up in various catalogues under either "D" or "L."

Along with Palestrina he dominated his era, and was the last great composer of the Flemish School. Emperor Maximilian II granted him a patent of nobility, Pope Gregory II created him a Cavalier of St. Peter. When he died, in Munich, of depression and fatigue, all Europe mourned him as the Belgian Orpheus, and the Prince of Music.

Madrigals and Motets

The best introduction to Lassus is currently an album of assorted madrigals and motets by the Alsfelder Vocal Ensemble. Their singing is expert and beautiful, although one might wish more variety of texture, as everything is sung by the full chorus. But this quibble is offset by the moderate price.

Helbich, Alsfelder Vocal Ensemble. Teldec Das Alte Werk 93685 [ADD] (mid-price)

Claudio Monteverdi (1567-1643)

Born in Cremona, Italy, Monteverdi showed an early aptitude for music and by age twenty-three was employed as a string player in the court of Mantua, where he worked for over two decades, beginning composition of the madrigals which were to represent the core and paradigm of his creative life. Ever an experimenter, Monteverdi added instrumental accompaniments to the traditionally a capella choral works. Singlehandedly he created the first true orchestra. Eventually his efforts made it possible for the madrigal to evolve into the cantata. He became the first genius of opera, creating *Orfeo* only seven years after the form was invented, and producing one of the greatest of all operas, *The Coronation of Poppea*, at the age of seventy-five.

Monteverdi was to Italian Renaissance music what Michelangelo was to its visual art. In 1613 he took over the most coveted post in his country: music director of St. Mark's in Venice. During the next thirty years he accomplished the miracle of metamorphosing from the last great composer of the Renaissance to the first great composer of the Baroque era. During his long and highly productive life he suffered often from depression, especially for several years after the death of his wife. In 1630 he took ordination as a priest.

The scope and inspiration of his music mark him as one of the greatest composers of the seventeenth century, and one of the greatest of all time. The intense beauty of his melodies, his forceful expression of emotion and humanity, make his music seem astonishingly modern even today.

L'Incoronazione di Poppea

For an example of Monteverdi's great operas most record guides start with his first, *La Favola d'Orfeo*. Although it is obviously historically important, *The Coronation of Poppea*, his last opera, written when in his seventy-fifth year, is infinitely richer and more interesting in every way, and is far more likely to make you sit up and understand why this very ancient composer is still so alive. It has pageantry, intrigue, tragedy, comedy, and it's completely amoral—the evil Nero and his conniving wife Poppea are triumphant at the end. But they win us over by singing one of the most sublime love duets of any opera ever written.

There have been several fine recordings of this work, but the Hickox version seems the obvious choice at this writing, having a fine cast and gorgeous sound, and the whole long extravaganza makes it onto three discs instead of the usual four.

Hickox, City of London Baroque Sinfonia, Auger, Leonard, Jones, Hirst, Bowman, Reinhart. Virgin Classics 59524 (3) [DDD]

Madrigals

Raymond Leppard recorded the complete madrigals for Philips a generation ago; these volumes were true classics of the catalog, but only one volume is currently in print, and one might be better advised to move up to the similar project by the Consort of Musicke. Their approach is more up-to-date in musicological terms, and the sound is digital. As an introduction I suggest the disc which contains the "love" (as opposed to "war") half of Book 8, which includes one of Monteverdi's most perfect madrigals, the "Lamenta della ninfa." Another possibility is William Christie's album of selections from Books 7 and 8.

Rooley, Consort of Musicke. *Madrigals of Love,* Virgin Classics 59621 [DDD]
Christie, Les Art florissants. Harmonia Mundi 1901068

Vespro della Beata Vergine (Vespers of 1610)

This long and magnificent choral paean of evening prayers to the Virgin Mary has had a surprising number of complete recordings, most notably by John Eliot Gardiner and his English Baroque Soloists, who cast aside timidity and reservation to show this as the gloriously dramatic work it can be.

Gardiner, English Baroque Soloists, London Monteverdi Choir, His Majesties Sagbutts and Cornetts, Chance, Terfel, Monoyios, Pennicchi, Tucker, Robson, Naglia, Miles. DG Archiv 429565 (2) [DDD]

Giovanni Pierluigi da Palestrina (ca. 1525-1594)

He was in some ways the diametric opposite of his fellow Italian Renaissance composer Claudio Monteverdi—Palestrina had almost no interest in innovation or musical revolution. Far from indulging in the vivid expression of human emotion, he reserved his creativity for flights of spiritual ecstasy. He had no interest in instruments or vertical harmony; his great compositions are all a capella and represent the culmination of the polyphonic style. They may sound over-refined to some listeners, but there is no denying the purity and power of Palestrina's seamless "cathedrals in sound." He wrote nearly a thousand such works, many of them commissioned by princes, potentates, and popes.

Missa Papae Marcelli

This melodically and harmonically beautiful mass written for Pope Marcellus, clear and noble in its lineaments, has long been the most famous and beloved of Palestrina's more than one hundred masses. Among several fine recordings, those by the Tallis Scholars and the Westminster Cathedral Choir come first to mind.

Phillips, Tallis Scholars. Gimell 339 [AAD] + Allegri: *Miserere*
Hill, Westminster Cathedral Choir. Hyperion 66266 [DDD] + other works by Palestrina

Michael Praetorius (1571-1621)

Like Monteverdi, Praetorius spanned the Renaissance and Baroque periods. He was the youngest son of a Protestant pastor who had studied directly under Martin Luther. During his relatively short life he dedicated himself mainly to the composing and publishing of Lutheran church music, producing more than 1,200 chorales (the Reformation-era counterparts to the medieval Catholic plainsong). Ironically, Praetorius is remembered today mostly for his delightful instrumental settings of secular French dances, giving some credence perhaps to the medieval adage that "the Devil has the best tunes."

Terpischore

Published in 1612, this collection of seventy-eight merry, lilting, foot-stomping dances sounds as fresh today as four centuries ago. No particular instruments are specified in the score, but all reputable performers now employ a colorful array of authentic period fiddles, winds, and percussion. Philip Pickett's New London Consort provides a rainbow of sonorities for thirty-three representative dances on one CD. On another, David Munrow's Early Music Consort of London offers earlier recordings of fewer dances, but at lower price, and with a sampling of the composer's choral works.

Pickett, New London Consort. L'Oiseau-Lyre 414633 [DDD]
Munrow, London Early Music Consort. Angel Studio 69024 [ADD] + Motets (mid-price)

Thomas Tallis (ca. 1505-1585)

When he was buried at Greenwich, Tallis was recommended to eternity by some verses on a tombstone no longer extant:

Enterred here doth ly a worthy Wyght
Who for long Tyme in Musick bore the Bell:
His Name to shew, was Thomas Tallys hyght,
In honest vertuous Lyff he dyd excell.

Prophetic, perhaps, in fixing his musical fame in the past, for he has the dubious distinction of being better known as part of another composer's title rather than on his own merits. For years, the *Fantasia on a Theme by Thomas Tallis* (by Ralph Vaughan Williams) was the only way most people were reminded of him, and one might wonder why a theme so haunting did not sooner spark curiosity about his own works.

He was an organist at Waltham Abbey when Henry VIII shut down the monasteries in 1540. Like his friend and colleague William Byrd, he made his peace with necessity and joined the King's own Chapel Royal, where he composed music and played the organ through the reigns of three more Tudors: Edward VI, Mary, and Elizabeth I. He and Byrd were granted a monopoly of music paper and printed music by the staunchly Protestant Elizabeth, for which they thanked her by dedicating a major printed collection of their hymns and motets. The fact that she graciously ignored the ill-disguised Catholicism of two of her best composers has justified her nickname of Good Queen Bess, at least among music lovers.

Tallis wrote much music for the Anglican service, but ironically, most of it is lost and his surviving works are principally in Latin, including two settings of *The Lamentations of Jeremiah,* and the sixteen motets dedicated to the Queen. His works are distinguished by dark sonorities and thick textures. They are richly expressive, although limited in range by an emphasis on sombre and melancholy emotions.

His long career encompassed nearly all of the 16th century. We know of no tragic or dramatic incidents in his life, or whether any personal losses contributed to his morose muse, but his very personal idiom has guaranteed him a place in the pantheon of great composers which no one, and nothing, can take away. As his tombstone concluded:

As he dyd lyve, so also did he dy,
In mild and quyet sort (O! happy Man).
To God ful oft for Mercy did he cry,
Wherefore he lyves, let Death do what he can.

Church Music

The Tallis Scholars offer a beautifully sung selection of 6 anthems, plus the astounding forty-part motet *Spem in Alium,* a tour de force if there ever was one. This is the ultimate in polyphonic composition: the music is laid out for eight choirs singing simultaneously, each having five separate melodic lines. The piece begins with each of the forty parts entering one by one, and then singing together at a dramatic point in the text with a breathtaking change of harmony.

Phillips, Tallis Scholars. Gimell 006 [DDD]

Tomas Luis de Victoria (ca. 1549-1611)

The most famous Spanish composer of the High Renaissance, Victoria spent more than twenty years in Rome; some believe he studied with Palestrina, although that influence may have been only indirect. Whatever the case, there is no denying a flavor in Victoria's music that evokes the sombre Spanish court of Philip II and his forbidding palace, the Escorial. His religious music combines a dark mystical intensity with the unbending severity of the Inquisition. There is also often a sense of drama—some say melodrama—that is totally absent from the ethereal music of Palestrina.

Requiem Mass

In its striking blend of seriousness and serenity, this work projects a galvanizing and granitic strength. Hearing it, one cannot argue with those who draw parallels between Victoria's music and the religious paintings of his contemporaries, El Greco and Velazquez. Both the Tallis Scholars and the Winchester Cathedral Choir offer stunning performances of this unique work, the former ethereal, the latter dramatic.

Phillips, Tallis Scholars. Gimell 012 [DDD] + A. Lobo: *Funeral Motet for Philip II of Spain*
Hill, Winchester Cathedral Choir. Hyperion 66304 [DDD]

The Baroque Era
(ca. 1600-1750)

Several qualities distinquish the Baroque era, and the dictionary is the best place to begin. "Baroque: anything extravagantly ornamented, especially something so ornate as to be in bad taste." Lovers of Baroque music will be offended by the second half of the definition, but keeping the possibility in mind can serve as a useful corrective when examining this music.

A great expansion of instrumental resources around 1600, particularly through the creative efforts of Claudio Monteverdi (see preceding chapter), led to a decline of interest in the purely vocal style. Art music grew larger and louder. Changing political events led to a growing patronage of the arts by the nobility, who favored grandiosity in all things.

The Catholic Church, battered by the Lutheran Reformation, lost much of its influence in the arts; the emphasis on polyphony gave way to homophony, a texture in which a single melody predominates, accompanied by subordinate harmonies. The old church modes faded from the scene, generally replaced by a new system of tonality based on "keys," major and minor; at the end of the period, J. S. Bach threw all his weight on the "modern" side with the publication of his *Well-Tempered Clavier,* a demonstration both practical and artistic of the new system's superior technical potential.

While adventurers were exploring and colonizing the world beyond Europe, musicians were busily creating new and more complex forms in which to express their ideas. The concerto and "concerto grosso," the dance suite, the sonata, the cantata, and the oratorio all were new in the 1600s—as was opera, perhaps the most influential form of all. Monteverdi, again, was the main force behind the success of this form, whose vivid portrayal of dramatic conflict insinuated itself into most of the other forms, not excepting the Mass. But by the end of the Baroque era, most composers interested in vocal music had stopped writing Masses and were concentrating on the theater.

Whatever the form, sacred or secular, ornate grandeur is the hallmark of the Baroque style. It is virtually impossible to miss. You can "drop a needle" on just about any piece of Baroque music, by any composer from any country, and its "Baroqueness" is immediately identifiable. It is this fact which leads its detractors to dismiss much of it as "musical wallpaper." It is true that a huge amount of Baroque music was written rapidly, under commission, and according to formula. Telemann's *Tafelmusik,* Handel's *Water Music,* and thousands more were composed to order as background music for some sybaritic king's dinner party or Sunday outing. Genius, however, will out. Bach and Couperin, Scarlatti and Purcell conformed to the rigid rules of their time, but they were able to bend the system to their wills, and create from its raw materials music that still stuns the senses, engages the intellect, and often, in its rather extroverted way, touches the heart.

A rebirth of popular interest in Baroque music has occurred over the last thirty years thanks largely to a return to the use of period instruments, and a renewed scholarly attention to authentic performance traditions. Many current recordings adhere to these ideals, a fact frequently reflected in the recommendations.

Tomaso Albinoni (1671-1750)

Albinoni was not really a very important composer, but his one "hit," emasculated as it is, is so big we can't leave him out. He was born in Venice just seven years before his neighbor, the far more significant Antonio Vivaldi (q.v.). Eldest son of a prosperous paper manufacturer, he did not even claim to be more than a dilettante for the first half of his life. Nevertheless, Bach admired much of his work and even "borrowed" some of it as grist for his own mill.

Adagio for Strings and Organ

Ironically, Albinoni provided only the seed from which his "masterpiece" sprouted. A twentieth-century Italian, Remo Giazotto, took a fragment of Albinoni's music and worked it into a full-length pseudo-Baroque Adagio. This magnificent forgery shows up on innumerable recordings, the best being those by Karajan, Marriner, Münchinger, Paillard, and I Musici—not necessarily in that order. All contain other Baroque favorites, including the Pachelbel *Canon* on all four discs.

> **Karajan, Berlin Philharmonic.** DG 420718 [DDD] (mid-price)
> **Marriner, Academy of St. Martin-in-the-Fields.** Angel 47391
> **Münchinger, Stuttgart Chamber Orchestra.** London 411973 [DDD]
> **Paillard Chamber Orchestra.** RCA 65468 [DDD]
> **I Musici.** Philips 420718 [ADD] (mid-price)

Johann Sebastian Bach (1685-1750)

Along with Mozart and Beethoven, Bach is one of the leading candidates for Greatest Composer. He is the hands-down winner among performing musicians, who appreciate more than the general public the solid professionalism behind his art. All his life he was the grudging "most obedient servant" of one princely or clerical employer or another, being required to churn out occasional and functional pieces by the hundreds. Despite this he seemed constitutionally incapable of shoddy work, insisting on filling his compositions with deep ideas, sonic splendors, or heartwrenching emotions, as his muse dictated.

Like many composers of his time, Bach came from a family which had produced musicians as if they were tradesmen through several generations. His biography produces no very colorful events, no titillating scandals—unless you are obsessed, as many seem to be, by the fact that his two wives bore him a total of twenty children. Far more amazing than that is the fact that three of them became excellent composers in their own right. Bach did spend about a month in jail once, but only because he had irritated one of his royal employers over his desire to take a better-paying job elsewhere.

Many of his contemporaries spoke of his being stubborn and difficult. He once compared the playing of one of his bassoonists to a nanny-goat, and barely escaped being drawn into a duel. He was a perfectionist, yet was quick to praise those he admired. As a young man he walked more than two hundred miles to hear the great Buxtehude play the organ. He liked the instrumental music of the Italians, especially Vivaldi, and paid them the ultimate compliment of rewriting some of their works in his own style. And he was a sincere family man: he nurtured his musical sons, compiled a remarkable genealogy of his musical ancestors and collected their manuscripts, and wrote a delightful collection of pieces for his second wife to play, the *Anna Magdalena Bach Notebook*.

Bach's death in 1750 has stood ever since as the marker ending the Baroque era. It was he who fulfilled its ideals and burst its limits. After him, most composers felt there was nothing more to be done in the old style, and new ideas began to evolve. The reaction was so severe that Bach's music itself seemed to disappear almost overnight. Not until 1829, when the twenty-year-old Felix Mendelssohn conducted a highly successful performance of the *St. Matthew Passion,* did Bach's music start its slow march back into the affections of the public. Even at that, it was only in the 1960s that it had truly a vigorous revival among musicians and on records.

On purely musical grounds, and in terms of the Baroque parameters, Bach's music is considered virtually a model of perfection. Marvelous in its logic, it is highly favored by intellectuals; Bach was Albert Einstein's favorite composer. Most of it is noble and serious in tone, and there is a certain weightiness even in the movements based on popular songs and dances. Some listeners find Bach's approach overly severe and are uncomfortable with the often hymn-like sonorities and the music's measured Teutonic tread; but no one denies the awesome intelligence which must have been necessary to create works of such complexity and power.

Brandenburg Concerti (6). S.1046/51

Commissioned by the Margrave of Brandenburg, these six concerti blend French, Italian and German stylistic elements into a colorful mix of courtly entertainment music that has remained, with Handel's *Water Music* and Vivaldi's *The Four Seasons,* the most popular orchestral music of the Baroque. Each concerto allows a different instrument(s) of the ensemble to have a starring role.

On period instruments, Pinnock leads the pack, at least in digital, with Harnoncourt coming up a lively second with a recording thirty years old and still cooking. All of the best versions on modern instruments are analog: Marriner, Leppard, and Richter.

> **Pinnock, The English Concert.** #1-3, DG Archiv 410500 [DDD]; #4-6, DG Archiv 410501 [DDD]
>
> **Harnoncourt, Vienna Concentus Musicus.** Teldec Das Alte Werk 77611 (2) [ADD] (mid-price)
>
> **Marriner, Academy of St. Martin-in-the-Fields.** #1-3, Philips 400076 [ADD]; #4-6, Philips 400077 [ADD]
>
> **Leppard, English Chamber Orchestra.** #1-3, Philips Silver Line 420345 [ADD]; #4-6, Philips Silver Line 420346 [ADD] (mid-price)
>
> **Richter, Munich Bach Orchestra.** DG Archiv 427143 (2) [ADD] + two other concerti (mid-price)

Cantatas

Bach wrote about three hundred of these Lutheran church pieces for soloists, chorus, and orchestra, of which some two hundred survive. Some of the favorite short pieces by Bach, such as "Jesu, Joy of Man's Desiring," "Sheep May Safely Graze," and "Sleepers Wake" come from the cantatas.

One of the great recordings projects of all time has been that of the Leonhardt Consort and the Vienna Concentus Musicus, who have been turning out the complete Bach cantatas for several years in scholarly volumes. Below is listed a very representative volume to see if you like it. Also given are two single digital discs at full price and budget which give two complete cantatas each in excellent performances, and as a more condensed introduction to Bach's choral music in general, a recent disc of great choruses from the cantatas, the *Passions,* the *Christmas Oratorio,* and the Mass in B Minor.

> **Leonhardt Consort, Harnoncourt, Vienna Concentus Musicus.** Cantatas 5-8, Teldec Das Alte Werk 42498 (2) [DDD] (mid-price)
>
> **Gardiner, English Baroque Soloists, Monteverdi Choir.** Cantatas 140, 147, DG Archiv 431809 [DDD]
>
> **Failoni Chamber Orchestra, Budapest and Hungarian Radio Choirs.** Cantatas 80, 147, Naxos 8.550642 [DDD] (budget)
>
> **Gardiner, English Baroque Soloists, Monteverdi Choir.** *"Jesu, Joy of Man's Desiring": Great Bach Choruses,* DG Archiv 439885 [DDD]

Concerti (7) for Harpsichord. S.1052/8

These are among the earliest masterpieces of music for keyboard instrument with orchestral accompaniment. Bach wrote them during a break from his church music duties, while directing a group called the Collegium Musicum. These were students and Leipzig townspeople who got together to play in a local coffeehouse.

Actually, it appears that virtually all these concertos are Bach's transcriptions from earlier works, such as violin or wind pieces, which are now lost. They are noted for the technical virtuosity of the "outer" movements (1 and 3) and the soulful expressiveness of the slow middle movements.

Trevor Pinnock's performances with The English Concert are the acknowledged standards for these works on historical instruments. The same forces play the no less enjoyable Bach concertos for 2, 3, and 4 harpsichords, works which may well have had their premieres by Bach himself, playing with his sons.

On modern instruments—which may indeed seem peculiar with the harpsichord holding center stage—the best versions are those by Igor Kipnis with Neville Marriner conducting, and by Raymond Leppard both soloing and conducting and with Andrew Davis joining him in the double, triple, and even quadruple concerti.

Sorry, there simply are no digital versions worth recommending over these three analogs. Stop worrying, they sound fine.

Pinnock, English Concert. DG 415991 (# 1, 2, 3), DG 415992 (# 4, 5, 6) [ADD]

Kipnis, Marriner, London Strings. Odyssey 45616 (2) [ADD] (budget)

Leppard, A. Davis, English Chamber Orchestra. Philips 422497 and 426084 [ADD] (mid-price)

Concerti (2) for Violin, S.1041/2; Concerto in D Minor for 2 Violins, S.1043

These are the first great violin concerti in European history. They are packed with beautiful themes, clever details of construction, and opportunities for bravura display. That is what great violin concerti have striven for ever since. The "double" concerto is especially beloved for its ravishing slow movement.

All three can fit conveniently on one CD, so look for a good version that does not split them over two or more discs. For period instruments, try La Petite Bande with Sigiswald Kuijken, available at an attractive price, Schroeder and Hirons with Hogwood conducting, or Standage and Wilcock led by Pinnock. For modern instruments, try Mutter and Accardo as violinists for a digital version, or Grumiaux and Krebbers from the previous (analog) generation. There are dozens of other decent performances, but these continue to stand out for their special beauties and insights.

Kuijken, La Petite Bande. Editio Classica 77006 [DDD] (mid-price)

Schroeder, Hirons, Hogwood, Academy of Ancient Music. L'Oiseau-Lyre 400080 [DDD]

Standage, Wilcock, Pinnock, The English Concert. DG Archiv 410646 [DDD]

Mutter, Accardo, English Chamber Orchestra. Angel 47005 [DDD]

Grumiaux, Krebbers, DeWaart, Philharmonia Orchestra. Philips 420700 [ADD] + Double Concerto for Violin and Oboe in D Minor, S.1060 (mid-price)

Harpsichord Music

Listed below are some of the more famous of Bach's numerous solo works for harpsichord (or often, originally, clavichord), and some of their best and most representative recordings.

Chromatic Fantasy and Fugue in D Minor, S.903

Rousset (harpsichord). L'Oiseau-Lyre 433054 [DDD] + Partita in B Minor, S.831, 4 Duets, S.802-5, Italian Concerto

Goldberg Variations, S.988

Pinnock (harpsichord). DG Archiv 415130 [ADD]
Gould (piano). Sony 38479 [ADD] (mid-price)
A. Schiff (piano). London 417116 [DDD] (mid-price)

Italian Concerto in F, S.971

Rousset (harpsichord). L'Oiseau-Lyre 433054 [DDD] + Partita in B Minor, S.831, 4 Duets, S.802-5, Chromatic Fantasy and Fugue in D Minor
Pinnock (harpsichord). "The Harmonious Blacksmith," DG Archiv 413591 [DDD] + short favorites by Handel, Couperin, Rameau, Scarlatti and others

Well-Tempered Clavier, S.846-893

Gilbert (harpsichord). DG Archiv 413439 (4) [DDD]
Moroney (harpsichord). Harmonia Mundi 901285/88 (4) [DDD]
Gould (piano). CBS 42266 (3) [AAD]
A. Schiff (piano). Book I, London 414388 (2) [DDD]; Book II, London 417236 (2) [DDD]

Instrumental Music—Miscellaneous

Bach wrote a considerable variety of pieces for solo instruments or for small ensembles. Aside from the English Suites and French Suites (whose names mean nothing anyway!), most of these look rather boringly generic in the catalogs, what with an endless litany of suites, partitas, sonatas, and trio sonatas. A prudent approach might be to focus on an already favored instrument and try one of Bach's more famous works written for it. If you already have a taste for a specific artist, indulge it as well. To get you started, here are some of the best-known works along with favored artists.

Lute Music

Bream (tr. guitar). RCA 5841
Isbin (tr. guitar). Virgin Classics 59503 [DDD]
Kirchhof (Baroque lute). Sony Vivarte 45858 (2)

Sonatas (3) and Partitas (3) for Solo Violin, S.1001-1006

Perlman. Angel 49483 (2) [DDD]
Grumiaux. Philips Duo 438736 (2) [ADD] (mid-price)
Milstein. DG 423294 (2) [ADD] (mid-price)
S. Kuijken. Editio Classica 77043 (2) [ADD] (mid-price)

Suites (6) for Solo Cello, S.1007-1012

(The legendary Pablo Casals recorded the Cello Suites in the 1930s. Every serious collector will want these recordings, still in print, but it is perhaps better to begin with something more recent.)

Fournier. DG 419359 (2) [ADD] (mid-price)
Starker. Mercury 432756 (2) [ADD] (mid-price)
Ma. CBS 37867 (2) [DDD]

Magnificat in D. S.243

A joyful choral Christmas classic, the *Magnificat* takes its text (in Latin) from the story of the angel's revelation to Mary that she will bear the Savior, and her poetic response, "My soul shall magnify the Lord." The work has complex textures and demands careful choral singing to avoid becoming a jumble.

Preston, Academy of Ancient Music, Christ Church Cathedral Choir. L'Oiseau-Lyre 414678 [ADD] + Vivaldi: *Gloria* in D, R.589
Hickox, Collegium Musicum 90. Chandos 0518 [DDD] + Vivaldi: Gloria in D, R.589

Mass in B Minor, S.232

This pinnacle of Bach's vocal and sacred music is in many ways a paradox. The composer spent more than fifteen years cobbling it together from bits and pieces of earlier works, polishing it into a veritable treatise of choral composition. There is no record of its performance as a complete work, since its curious construction fits neither the Catholic nor Protestant liturgy. It is difficult to deny the theory that Bach wrote it out of pure idealism, heedless of its impracticality, much as some believe Shakespeare wrote *Hamlet,* which is twice as long as Elizabethan plays were allowed to be. In any case, it is not only Bach's greatest choral work, but one of the greatest ever written by anyone. And some would agree with the Swiss critic Nageli, who as early as 1817 called it the "greatest work of music of all ages, and of all peoples."

The leading recent recordings in terms of performance and sonics are those conducted by John Eliot Gardiner, Peter Schreier, and Richard Hickox. Otto Klemperer's classic set from the 1960s is a fine budget alternative, as is Leonhardt's period instrument version at mid-price.

> **Gardiner, English Baroque Soloists, Monteverdi Choir.** DG Archiv 415514 (2) [DDD]
> **Schreier, Dresden State Orchestra, Leipzig Radio Choir.** Philips 432972 (2) [DDD]
> **Hickox, Collegium Musicum 90 Chorus and Orchestra.** Chandos 0533/4 (2) [DDD]
> **Klemperer, New Philharmonia Orchestra, BBC Chorus.** Angel Studio 63364 (2) [ADD] (mid-price)
> **Leonhardt, La Petite Bande.** Editio Classica 77040 (2) [ADD] (mid-price)

Organ Music

The Philips label once issued an LP box of the complete organ works of Bach played by Wolfgang Rübsam; it contained twenty-five records! This is no longer in print, and only the most serious collector would want it, but highlights were reissued on CD. This too now seems to have disappeared, but the budget Naxos label has managed to collar Mr. Rübsam into making a splendid sampler disc of Bach organ music. It, like all those listed at full price below, contains Bach's most famous organ piece, the Toccata and Fugue in D Minor, S.565.

A few years after Rübsam, the English organist Peter Hurford recorded the complete Bach organ works for CD; these are still available [ADD], but you must buy them in 2- or 3-CD full-price sets. There was a Hurford sampler disc, but like Rübsam's it seems to have disappeared. No doubt it is a conspiracy.

Alain. Erato Bonsai 45922 (mid-price)
Biggs. Great Organ Favorites, CBS 42644 [ADD]
Curley. Favorite Organ Works of Bach, London Jubilee 430746
[DDD] (mid-price)
Fox. RCA Victrola 7736 [ADD] (budget)
Kee. Chandos 0527 [DDD]
Koopman. DG 427801 [DDD]
Rübsam. Naxos 8.550184 [DDD] (budget)

St. Matthew Passion, S.244

For many listeners, four hours of solemn music telling the grim story of Christ's suffer-ings may seem daunting. Perhaps being a devout Christian helps to undertake the project, but anyone might be affected by the powerful drama that Bach creates from his mighty polyphonic arsenal. This is not mere pious reflection, but a wrenching enactment of the Gospel story, alternately heartrending and consoling. Musically, it is astounding in that despite the vast canvas, the painting is not done in broad strokes, but is finely etched down to the minutest detail. It has been called a compendium of all the techniques of composi-tion which preceded it.

For those preferring period instruments and style, John Eliot Gardiner leads a vivid performance rated first by many critics among digital versions, but hard on his heels is Philippe Herreweghe, whose recording features a particularly eloquent Evangelist in Howard Crook. Peter Schreier, a fine tenor and conductor, pulls off a magnificent stunt by singing the Evangelist and conducting the best digital performance on modern instru-ments. Otto Klemperer's beloved 1961 analog version is thankfully available on CD.

Gardiner, English Baroque Soloists, Monteverdi Choir. DG Archiv
427648 (3) [DDD]
Herreweghe, Chapelle Royale Orchestra, Ghent Collegium Vocale.
Harmonia Mundi 901155/57 (3) [DDD]
Schreier, Dresden State Orchestra, Leipzig Radio Choir. Philips 412527
(3) [DDD]
Klemperer, Philharmonia Orchestra. EMI 63058 (3) [ADD] (mid-price)

Suites (4) for Orchestra, S. 1066/9

Sometimes also listed as "Overtures," these Suites are uniformly fine, though No. 3 is best known since it contains the beloved "Air on the G String." Along with the Brandenburg Concerti, these constitute the "easiest" Bach listening.

John Eliot Gardiner's superlative recording seems unaccountably to have vanished from the American catalog, leaving the period instrument field to Christopher Hogwood and Sigiswald Kuijken, the latter at mid-price even though digital. On modern instruments, János Rolla directs a fine digital performance, while Neville Marriner, though analog, is hard to resist, being the only complete recording on a single disc and at mid-price besides. Another alternative is to purchase the attractive anthology by I Musici, containing only the second suite, but including the Albinoni *Adagio* (q.v.), Pachelbel's *Canon*, and attractive works by Corelli and Handel—a dignified introduction to the Baroque.

Hogwood, Academy of Ancient Music. L'Oiseau-Lyre 417834 (2) [DDD]
Kuijken, La Petite Bande. Editio Classica 77008 (2) [DDD] (mid-price)
Rolla, Franz Liszt Chamber Orchestra. Hungaroton 31018 (2) [DDD]
Marriner, Academy of St. Martin-in-the-Fields. London Jubilee 430378 [ADD] (mid-price)
I Musici. Suite No. 2 only, Philips 420718 [ADD] + Albinoni: *Adagio*, Pachelbel: *Canon*, Corelli: *Christmas* Concerto, Handel: Harp Concerto (mid-price)

Arcangelo Corelli (1653-1713)

Corelli was an elegant Italian composer of wealthy family, whose works for violin or strings were among the most popular in the eighteenth century. He seems to have enjoyed a life of almost unlimited luck and success, even though there were others who could play or conduct better than he. For nearly twenty-five years he was paid handsomely by the wealthy Pietro, Cardinal Ottoboni, to serve as his private music director. When Corelli died, rich and in possession of a fabulous art collection, the Cardinal saw to it that he was buried in an elaborate tomb in the Pantheon of Rome. His very Baroque monument can still be seen there.

Concerti Grossi (12), op. 6

By far Corelli's most famous works, these tuneful and colorful short concerti rival Handel's wonderful set (also op. 6) in popularity. Period instrument groups seem to take to them with alacrity; versions conducted by Trevor Pinnock and Nicholas McGegan are particularly notable. The Guildhall String Ensemble stand out on modern instruments, and the most famous of the set of twelve, No. 8, the "Christmas" concerto, can be had alone with other Baroque favorites on the I Musici anthology disc.

Pinnock, The English Concert. DG 423626 (2) [DDD]
McGegan, Philharmonia Baroque Orchestra. #1-6, Harmonia Mundi 907014; #7-12, Harmonia Mundi 907015

Guildhall String Ensemble. RCA 60071 (2)
I Musici. No. 8 only, Philips 420718 [ADD] + Albinoni: *Adagio,* Pachelbel:
Canon, Bach: Orchestral Suite No. 2, Handel: Harp Concerto (mid-price)

François Couperin (1668-1733)

Known as "le grand," Couperin was only the most famous of a dozen musicians in his family who contributed to French music in the seventeenth and eighteenth centuries. The Great François is principally remembered for his works for harpsichord, including twenty-seven suites ("ordres") of dance movements with picturesque titles. Another collection, *L'Art de toucher le clavecin,* offers detailed instructions on how to play the instrument, including not only proper posture but also the correct way of making affecting grimaces.

At the young age of twenty-five he was appointed by the Sun King, Louis XIV, to the post of organist in the Royal Chapel at Versailles. For years he was music teacher to the king's children. He was the first composer to insist that his music be played exactly as written, without further embellishment or improvisation. His frequent use of markings such as "gracious, naive, tender, breezy" seems to reflect his own charming character no less than the spirit of his times. When he died, his post as royal harpsichordist (by then under Louis XV) was inherited by his daughter, last of a distinguished line.

Harpsichord Music

All twenty-seven "ordres" have been recorded by Kenneth Gilbert, a splendid achievement. The beginning collector, however, may well wish to sample a single disc, such as those played by Skip Sempé, or William Christie and Christophe Rousset (together). If even that is too much to contemplate, a tantalizing taste is available on Trevor Pinnock's wonderful anthology disc, "The Harmonious Blacksmith."

These pieces are full of wit and refinement, and they established a tradition of understatement which became one of the fundamentals of French music thereafter.

Sempé. Selections, Deutsche Harmonia Mundi 77219 [DDD]
Christie, Rousset. Selections, Harmonia Mundi 901269 [DDD]
Pinnock. "The Harmonious Blacksmith," DG Archiv 413591 [DDD] +
Bach: *Italian Concerto,* short pieces by Handel, Rameau, Scarlatti and others

George Frideric Handel (1685-1759)

Handel is universally considered to be, along with J.S. Bach, the greatest Baroque composer. Ironically, though they were both Germans, and born in the same year, the two masters never met. Even odder, Handel nevertheless became close friends with several other famous composers, including Telemann and Domenico Scarlatti.

A child prodigy, Handel spent his early twenties studying in Italy. He became adept at the "Italian Style," putting it to good use after his move in 1711 to London, where for several years he composed and produced highly successful Italian operas. Handel's official patron, the Elector of Hanover, succeeded to the English throne in 1714 as George I, providing the composer with one of the most fortuitous job opportunities in history.

Handel remained in England for the rest of his life, becoming a citizen and anglicizing his name—though, as you can see above, without perfect aptness. The British rage for Italian operas waned in the 1730s, and Handel moved on to other things, such as his great religious oratorios. His later years were plagued by ill health, including blindness and a severe stroke, afflictions which he bore with characteristic dignity. When he died, he was given a state funeral in Westminster Abbey.

Handel was often described as stubborn and autocratic. "He disdained," we are told, "to teach his art to any but princes," and reputedly could swear in five languages. At the same time he possessed a lively—if somewhat caustic—wit, and as often as not was given to impromptu turns of kindliness. Altogether, an oddly endearing character, his comically corpulent frame invariably clad in the most costly garments, and topped off by an enormous white wig which, a contemporary critic claimed, when things were going well at a performance, had "a certain nod, or vibration" of its own.

Handel's music makes a fascinating contrast to Bach's. Less profoundly thought through, it nevertheless can make a more immediate impact, and the melodies are more singable—less "instrumental"—than Bach's. Before consigning Handel to second place in the Baroque, as many musicologists do today, we might pause to remember Mozart saying he "strikes like a thunderbolt," and Beethoven calling him "the greatest, ablest composer that ever lived."

Concerti Grossi (12), op. 6

In Europe, these tuneful, glowingly orchestrated pieces are almost as popular as Bach's *Brandenburg Concerti.* For some reason they are not so well known in America. You only impoverish yourself by not knowing them.

There are several fine digital sets, which divide neatly into three categories. Best in class are Pinnock for period instruments, Iona Brown on modern instruments but with period style, and Turovsky for all-out modern-instrument exhilaration.

Pinnock, The English Concert. DG Archiv 410897/9 (3) [DDD]
Brown, Academy of St. Martin-in-the-Fields. Philips 410048 (3) [DDD]
Turovsky, I Musici di Montreal. Chandos 9004/6 (3) [DDD]

Concerti (16) for Organ

Although Bach remains the most famous (and copious) composer of solo organ music, Handel was the inventor of the organ concerto, pitting the instrument brilliantly against a battery of strings and winds. There is no "churchiness" in this organ music, as you can verify by sampling, for instance, the scintillating Concerto No. 13, nicknamed "The Cuckoo and the Nightingale."

An ideal sampler disc for this repertoire features organist Simon Preston with the English Concerto conducted by Trevor Pinnock in concerti nos. 2, 9-11, and 13.

Preston, Pinnock, The English Concert. DG Archiv 431708 [DDD]

Messiah

If Bach's Mass in B Minor and *St. Matthew Passion* are the musician's usual top choices for greatest choral works, we still need not apologize for adoring the people's choice in sacred music. The Bach may be both more intellectual and truly spiritual, but Handel's *Messiah* is more infectiously celebratory, more hummable. Though its text is in English, its musical manner is unapologetically Italian, abandoning Teutonic brooding in favor of joyful extroversion. If there is anything in all music that makes you want to leap to your feet and cheer more than the "Hallelujah Chorus," I cannot think of it. And yes, Handel really wrote it all in three weeks. (This happened before television.)

There is absolutely no composition of comparable length and scope that has had more recordings. There are several different editions of the score, so that whether you select "traditional" or "authentic" performances you may run into sections that sound rather different from the version you hear at your local church each Christmas; be prepared to keep an open mind.

John Eliot Gardiner leads the pack, by common consent, among period-instrument versions; many critics consider it the finest *Messiah* ever recorded, "period" (excuse the pun). Very nearly as fine, however, are those conducted by Trevor Pinnock, Christopher Hogwood, and Martin Pearlman.

If you would rather stick with the traditional full-bore approach, Sir Colin Davis's impeccably musical analog recording from the 1960s is the classic, now at mid-price; Sir Charles Mackerras offers a very respectable runner-up, also a mid-price analog; and outstanding digital versions emanate from Sir Georg Solti and Robert Shaw.

Gardiner, English Baroque Soloists, Monteverdi Chorus. Philips 411041 (3) [DDD]
Pinnock, The English Concert. DG Archiv 423630 (2) [DDD]

Hogwood, Academy of Ancient Music. L'Oiseau-Lyre 411858 (3) [DDD]
Pearlman, Boston Baroque. Telarc 80322 (2) [DDD]
C. Davis, London Symphony Orchestra and Chorus. Philips Duo 438356 (2) [ADD] (mid-price)
Mackerras, English Chamber Orchestra, Ambrosian Singers. EMI 62748 (2) [ADD] (mid-price)
Solti, Chicago Symphony Orchestra and Chorus. London 414396 (2) [DDD]
Shaw, Atlanta Symphony Orchestra and Chamber Choir. Telarc 80093 (2) [DDD]

Royal Fireworks Music/Water Music

The first is brilliant trumpet-and-drums music to celebrate the signing of a peace treaty, the second outdoorsy winds-and-strings music to accompany King George's royal barge cruises up and down the Thames. They appear so often together on recordings that they are difficult to separate; there are complete versions, and complete suites, and individual suites, and selections put together helter-skelter. How much you should get on a disc is a function of how much you enjoy either or both.

For the *Royal Fireworks Music* alone:

Pinnock, The English Concert. DG Archiv 431707 [DDD] + *Alexander's Feast,* 2 Concerti Grossi from Op. 6
Fennell, Cleveland Symphonic Winds. Telarc 80038 [DDD] + Bach, Holst

For the *Water Music* alone:

Pinnock, The English Concert. DG Archiv 410525 [DDD]
Gardiner, English Baroque Soloists. Philips 434122 [DDD]
McGegan, Philharmonia Baroque Orchestra. Harmonia Mundi 907010 [AAD]

For suites from each, together on one disc:

Marriner, Academy of St. Martin-in-the-Fields. Argo 414596 [ADD]
Hogwood, Academy of Ancient Music. L'Oiseau-Lyre 400059 [ADD]

Johann Pachelbel (1653-1706)

An eminent organist in the generation before Bach, some of Pachelbel's relatives were his students. He was not, however, a significant composer. Most of his works are considered prolix, repetitive, and uninspired. His name is omitted from several standard dictionaries of composers. All the more amazing then that one tiny piece, the "*Canon* in D," revised, augmented, and reorchestrated by other hands, has in recent years become possibly the most popular, most often played and recorded classical composition in the world!

Canon in D

Originally scored for three violins and continuo, the "celebrated *Canon*" is now ordinarily heard in a version for string orchestra. Part of its mass appeal is surely that it is repetitive; its clear "beat" and hypnotically undulating melody have a powerfully relaxing effect. Some listeners claim it recalibrates their biorhythms, or puts them in touch with higher harmonies.

The *Canon* in D has become such a cult item that people have developed fierce loyalties to one or another performance, and refuse to listen to any competitors. One label has even put out an album called "Pachelbel's Greatest Hit," containing several different versions of this one piece, so it can be listened to over and over in slightly different versions without changing records.

With dozens of recordings to choose from, much depends on what other music comes in your package (the *Canon* itself is only about seven minutes long). Some of the most reliable conductors to look for are Karajan, Marriner, and Münchinger, along with the conductor-less group I Musici. But it must be stressed that the performance which really made the *Canon* a blockbuster, quite apart from its initial film appearance as the "theme" of *Ordinary People*, was that conducted by Jean-Francois Paillard. At any one time it seems to be available in several packagings with varying companion pieces.

Paillard Chamber Orchestra. RCA 65468 [DDD] + Albinoni: *Adagio,* selections by nine other Baroque composers

Paillard Chamber Orchestra, various other artists (including Cleo Laine! What next?). "Pachelbel's Greatest Hit," RCA 60712 (nine versions) (mid-price)

Karajan, Berlin Philharmonic Orchestra. DG 413309 [DDD] + Albinoni: *Adagio,* short works by Bach, Gluck, Mozart, and Vivaldi

Marriner, Academy of St. Martin-in-the-Fields. Angel 47391 + Albinoni: *Adagio,* short works by Bach, Boccherini, Fauré, Grieg, Mendelssohn, Mozart, and Tchaikovsky

Münchinger, Stuttgart Chamber Orchestra. London 411973 [DDD] + Albinoni: *Adagio,* other Baroque favorites

I Musici. Philips 420718 [ADD] + Albinoni: *Adagio,* Bach: Orchestral Suite No. 2, Corelli: *Christmas Concerto,* Handel: Harp Concerto (mid-price)

Henry Purcell (1659-1695)

Purcell lived a life almost exactly as brief as Mozart's, and in some ways it was almost as brilliant. He wrote an extraordinary amount of quality music in that short span, and took his place in music history as the greatest native English composer during more than two centuries.

Born into a musical family, Purcell (pronounced PUR-cell) early became a chorister, then a composer to the Chapel Royal, and a little later on, organist for Westminster Abbey. Although adept at writing organ and harpsichord pieces, odes and anthems, songs and sonatas, it was in theater music that he excelled.

We could call him the first great English opera composer except that his stage works are not what we would call operas today. Handel, with his full-blown Italianate operas, was a generation away from arriving on the London scene, and until then the English seemed most reluctant to fully embrace such a foreign art form. They were more likely to use the term "masque" than "opera" to describe a pastiche of music, dancing, talking, and singing that is closer to what we would call "incidental music."

Whatever it was, it was a stunning visual and auditory entertainment, and though few of the masques are staged today, we can relive their splendor quite vividly through recordings.

Purcell remained more talked about than heard for many decades after his death. The first rush of revival began after Benjamin Britten in the twentieth century used one of Purcell's haunting harpsichord themes as the basis for his *Young Person's Guide to the Orchestra* (alternate title: *Variations on a Theme by Henry Purcell*). A second spurt of interest followed the dramatic use of Purcell's *Funeral Music for Queen Mary* in the film *A Clockwork Orange.* The latter music was played not only at Queen Mary's funeral, and in the classic movie, but also at Purcell's own untimely obsequies in Westminster Abbey.

Dido and Aeneas

This is Purcell's masterpiece—his greatest theater work and the one closest to a true opera. Although it is now more than three hundred years old, it is still often performed and has had an amazing number of recordings. Those conducted by Trevor Pinnock and Raymond Leppard are the most admired at the moment, the latter featuring soprano Jessye Norman as Dido, the ill-fated Queen of Carthage, whose final lament "When I am laid in earth" has never been surpassed for noble poignancy.

Pinnock, The English Concert. DG Archiv 427621 [DDD]
Leppard, English Chamber Orchestra. Philips 416299 [DDD] (mid-price)

In addition, there is a very fine single-disc anthology which gives a good overview of Purcell's range:

Christie, Les Arts florissants; A. Deller, Deller Consort; London Baroque.
"Prelude Baroque VII," Harmonia Mundi 290807

Jean-Philippe Rameau (1683-1764)

Rameau acquired a reputation in France as a far less engaging person than François Couperin, but an even greater composer. Surprisingly little is know of his life. Except in music, he appears to have been a poor student. He was nearly forty—quite a late age in those times—before making a name for himself in Paris. Like Couperin, he wrote volumes of harpsichord music, but also chamber works and some thirty theater pieces, including ballets and operas, and hybrid forms of each.

His music is more complex than Couperin's, and his contemporaries tended to find it demanding and difficult. Nevertheless, he commanded respect for his mastery of orchestration and his bold experiments in harmony. Only recently have his masterpieces begun to be heard with pleasure outside France, thanks to scholars and musicians who have restored his scores and who play his music with style and vigor.

Harpsichord Music

Currently the best—and very generous—selection is provided by Christophe Rouuset on his digital double-disc set, fabulously played. If you would like a more abbreviated introduction, a little Rameau helps make up Trevor Pinnock's highly enjoyable single-disc recital, "The Harmonious Blacksmith."

Rousset. L'Oiseau-Lyre 425886 (2) [DDD]
Pinnock. "The Harmonious Blacksmith," DG Archiv 413591 [DDD] + Bach: *Italian Concerto,* short pieces by Handel, Couperin, Scarlatti and others

Orchestral Music

Several recordings have been made of orchestral selections, mostly from Rameau's theater music, but one in particular does yeoman duty in presenting a balanced program of representative selections with expert performers for this repertoire.

Herreweghe, Chapelle Royale Orchestra; Christie, Les Arts florissants. Harmonia Mundi 290808

Domenico Scarlatti (1685-1757)

Scarlatti was born, you will note, in the same miraculous year as Bach and Handel, and one might be forgiven for considering this a lucky omen. His father, Alessandro, though now largely forgotten, was once the world's most famous composer of oratorio and opera, and a major influence on Handel. Naturally, he was his son's teacher, and went far beyond that in vigorously promoting Domenico's career; in this he did his job too well, for the fame of the younger Scarlatti all but wiped out the elder's memory.

Scarlatti met Handel while the latter was working in Italy. They became good friends, and it is said that years later, whenever Handel's name was mentioned, Scarlatti crossed himself reverently (we do not know what the good Lutheran Handel thought of that).

About 1720, Scarlatti became music master to a Portuguese princess who later became queen of Spain, taking her beloved teacher with her. Scarlatti spent the second half of his life at the Spanish court, virtually disappearing from public view, though we know he married twice and had nine children. We are also told he became addicted to gambling and was repeatedly saved from ruin by his devoted royal patroness.

Obviously, he did not spend all his time in lovemaking and dicing. In addition to operas, oratorios, cantatas, serenades, and assorted other works, he composed the 555 sonatas (or as he called them, "essercizi") for the harpsichord for which he is particularly remembered.

Sonatas for Harpsichord

These short pieces—full of Latin dance rhythms, harmonically unpredictable, dramatic and poetic by turn—were aptly called by that peripatetic music-maven of the eighteenth century, Dr. Charles Burney, "original and happy Freaks." Even in faraway England they had become wildly popular well before the composer's death, to the point that critics spoke of a "Scarlatti sect."

The modern standard for authentic harpsichord performance is set by Trevor Pinnock on a single, well-selected all-Scarlatti disc; a more modest sample comprises part of his valuable recital entitled "The Harmonious Blacksmith." On piano, Andras Schiff offers fifteen very well-played sonatas on a starter disc. The famous Horowitz record is now available as a single CD; it is great playing, but at its age there is scant excuse for charging full price.

Pinnock. DG Archiv 419632 [DDD]
A. Schiff. London 421422 [DDD]
Horowitz. Sony 53460 [ADD]

Georg Philipp Telemann (1681-1767)

In his day, Telemann was one of the most famous composers in Europe, and possibly the most prolific of all time. He wrote an estimated two thousand works—more than Bach and Handel put together—including some forty operas, forty-four passions, six hundred overtures, seven hundred songs, and stacks of chamber music.

He was a man of letters, founding the first German music magazine, and authoring three somewhat contradictory autobiographies. He had a university education in languages and science. At almost sixty years of age he discovered, like Handel, a love of botany, developing an "avarice for ranunculi, and particularly, anemones." Handel thereafter often sent plant speciments to Telemann from England.

Telemann incorporated both French and Italian principles in his compositions, and even wrote works based on Polish folk dances. He lived to the ripe age of eighty-six and achieved universal adoration in his own time, his music being performed even more widely than Bach's. He was forgotten in the nineteenth century, then revived under questionable auspices in the twentieth as a "pioneer of the classical style."

It is sad that such a fine musician has been both egregiously under- and overrated. Let us admit that he falls short of the sublimities of Bach and Handel, and is in fact perhaps the least of the composers in this chapter. But there is little in his recorded output that is less than pleasant to hear, and the lover of the Baroque is sure to find countless gems in Telemann's treasure chest of music.

One of my own favorites is a children's opera called *Der Schulmeister,* in which an incompetent pedagogue attempts to teach scales to an unruly boys' choir; at the end they all good-naturedly admit defeat and bray like jackasses. Natures less innocent than mine might prefer his suite, *The Prostitute,* which contains the song "Come up and see me sometime."

I would like to say that Telemann's range was unique in music, but it was not. Mozart, as everyone now knows, wrote scatological songs in between his sublime masterpieces, and Brahms played the piano in a whorehouse. May I add to these examples that of the Czech-American composer Paul Reif, author of distinguished music for wind ensemble and string quartets, a song cycle on poems of T. S. Eliot, and so on, who while on duty in Africa during World War II managed to eclipse his intellectual accomplishments with the popular soldiers' song "Dirty Gertie from Bizerte."

Suite in A Minor for Recorder and Strings

This is the one piece among Telemann's thousands that has come closest to becoming a chestnut. It is very representative and has had quite a few recordings. That on Naxos is a budget-priced digital bargain, well done and accompanied by other enjoyable concerti. The performance and sound on Michala Petri's disc are even better, but be prepared to pay at least twice as much.

Stivin, Edlinger, Capella Istropolitana. Naxos 8.550156 [DDD] (budget)
Petri, Brown, Academy of St. Martin-in-the-Fields. Philips 410041 [DDD]

Antonio Vivaldi (1678-1741)

Vivaldi had a life colorful enough to match his vivid red hair. Though trained early as a musician, his first career was as a Catholic priest. Before the first year of his pastorate was out, however, he developed a mysterious chest ailment which frequently prevented him from finishing the saying of Mass. Just as mysteriously, the malady seemed to disappear when he was conducting an orchestra or playing the violin.

At this same time he became music director for a Venetian school for orphaned girls and unwed mothers. Many of Vivaldi's more than four hundred instrumental concertos apparently were written for, and first performed by, this prococious and highly competent "all-girls orchestra." History records no scandal involving the "red priest" and his presumably vulnerable charges; that was to come years later when he took up with Anna Giraud, a soprano who was to star in many of his operas, and her sister, who became his traveling companions during the height of his international fame.

After about 1730, Vivaldi's popularity began to fade. Although he had once performed for the Pope himself, his operas were banned by the Church in 1737 because of his inattention to priestly duties and his association with the two women. The next year the Foundling School refused to renew his contract. Four years later, desperately seeking work in Vienna, he died, and was buried there in a pauper's grave.

His surviving works number about 750. This is picayune compared with Bach or Telemann, but impressive in the level of general high quality. He was acknowledged as the master of the concerto, a form to which he apparently first brought the concept of one instrumental virtuoso engaging in dramatic conflict with an orchestra. One of Vivaldi's most ardent admirers was J.S. Bach, who transcribed and arranged many of his concerti, or incorporated parts of them in his own works.

Aside from *The Four Seasons,* the rest of the four hundred concerti are often difficult to differentiate one from the other. This is not because, as the tired taunt goes, "Vivaldi wrote the same concerto four hundred times," but because they are all about equally good. He composed thirty-seven concerti just for the bassoon, more than anyone else in history; and there are dozens more for cello, flute, guitar, horn, mandolin, oboe, piccolo, recorder, trumpet, viola d'amore, and violin, plus combinations of these, as well as "concerti for orchestra," and "concerti for diverse instruments." The astonishing thing is that there are none for harpsichord, nor any solo pieces for that ubiquitous instrument of the Baroque. Perhaps he shared the disdain of Sir Thomas Beecham, who said that to him the harpsichord sounded "like two skeletons copulating on a tin roof in a hailstorm."

Vivaldi's music remained largely forgotten by the public from his death until about 1960, when it experienced a veritable explosion of renewed popularity. That happened in part, no doubt, because much of it can be listened to with one ear as a kind of elegant dinner music. But this is the listener's fault, not Vivaldi's; there is plenty in his output to satisfy the most discriminating audience.

The Four Seasons

In one sense, these are nothing more than four of those four hundred concerti (here featuring the violin as soloist), taken out of context and highlighted with a programmatic title. The context is a set of twelve violin concerti, op. 8, bearing the collective label "The Contest between Harmony and Invention." These demonstrate Vivaldi's characteristic sense of the dramatic in contrasting traditional rules of composition with wilder flights of imagination.

In *The Four Seasons* the composer contrives, by purely musical means, to suggest singing birds, raging thunderstorms, barking dogs, squawking bagpipes, buzzing flies, hunters' gunshots, and the cracking of ice on frozen ponds. Who could resist? (Well, there are some; perhaps no classical music is so reviled by self-appointed sophisticates and esthetes. Or is it aesthetes?)

A quick check of a recent *Schwann Opus* catalog showed eighty-one recordings of *The Four Seasons* in print. On period instruments, the very cream of these are probably those conducted by Pinnock, Hogwood, and Sparf. On modern instruments the standard choices are Marriner and Accardo. Many of the other seventy-six versions are at least adequate, but these are the most musically elegant (Accardo even uses a different Stradivarius for each of the four concerti).

Standage, Pinnock, The English Concert. DG Archiv 400045 [ADD]
Hogwood, Academy of Ancient Music. L'Oiseau-Lyre 410126 [DDD]
Sparf, Drottningholm Baroque Ensemble. BIS 275 [DDD]
Loveday, Marriner, Academy of St. Martin-in-the-Fields. Argo 414486 [ADD]
Accardo, International Festival of Naples Soloists. Philips 422065 [ADD]
+ two concerti for 3 and 4 violins

Gloria in D. Rv.589

The most famous of Vivaldi's choral works, and justly so. The celebrated opening bars are among the most joyfully triumphant in Baroque music. If the *Gloria* doesn't make you feel good, you are suffering too much.

Versions conducted by Neville Marriner, Simon Preston and Trevor Pinnock have dominated the ratings for several years, but Richard Hickox has recently been admitted into their august company.

Marriner, Academy of St. Martin-in-the-Fields, King's College Choir, Cambridge. London Jubilee 421146 [ADD] + Haydn: *Lord Nelson* Mass (mid-price)
Preston, Academy of Ancient Music, Christ Church Cathedral Choir. L'Oiseau-Lyre 414678 [ADD] + Bach: *Magnificat*
Pinnock, The English Concert and Choir. DG Archiv 423386 [DDD] + A. Scarlatti: *Dixit Dominus*
Hickox, Collegium Musicum 90. Chandos 0518 [DDD] + Bach: *Magnificat*

The Classical Period
(1750-ca. 1820)

In the generation following the death of J.S. Bach, several influences came together to create what Goethe was to denominate the Classical period in music. The tremendous popularity of Italian opera was reflected, in every form of composition, in an emphasis on dramatic expression and a simpler, broader melodic style. Harmonies were simplified, counterpoint was abandoned, and polyphony replaced by broken-chord accompaniment. A new structural principle, sonata form, established itself as the basis for most instrumental composition. A new orchestral form, the symphony, began to replace the Baroque orchestral suite and concerto grosso. Regional and national differences in style began to melt away as French, Italian, and German techniques became widely diffused and tended to merge with each other.

Not all of the new characteristics came solely from within the musical establishment. Rationalist philosophy, as exhibited in the writings of Rousseau, Kant, and Voltaire, was favored among the educated and cultured classes. The old system of court patronage for the arts was breaking down in the wake of the democratic movement, which in turn was to contribute to the American and French Revolutions. Composers were swept up in the ideals of the age, which stressed the importance of the individual and his feelings.

Meanwhile, the beginnings of modern technology were forcing changes in musical style by making available new possibilities, through improvements to existing instruments and the introduction of entirely new ones. Most notable was the advent of the piano, which during the classical period gradually supplanted the harpsichord. Not only did the piano have greater sonority, but gradations of expression were possible by varying the pressure on the keys. Mechanical changes of this type left their mark on how composers viewed their materials, and what they decided to give their audiences.

Carl Philipp Emanuel Bach (1714-1788)

Carl was J.S. Bach's second oldest son, and in every opinion is the greatest of the four Bach progeny who themselves became composers. He is also the perfect transitional figure between the Baroque and Classical periods. As a Bach, he obviously was heir to the greatest glories of the Baroque, but he was not content to merely copy his father. He had a lively intellect of his own and struck out in bold new directions.

For twenty-seven years he worked in the Baroque manner as a court musician (for Frederick the Great of Prussia). In 1767 he took over the position in Hamburg of his just-deceased godfather, Georg Philipp Telemann, and in the speech accepting his appointment he uttered these prophetic words: "It seems to me that music must, above all, touch the heart." For the rest of his life he strove to find ways to base musical compositions upon poetic ideas. Although C.P.E. Bach was partial to the clavichord and harpsichord to the last, his skill and innovation in developing personal expression had a profound impact on both Haydn and Beethoven.

Perhaps this is the place to point out that C.P.E.'s youngest brother, Johann Christian, influenced in a similar way the music of Mozart. After studying opera in Italy, J.C. Bach moved to London, where the eight-year-old Mozart met him during his tour as a child prodigy. In later years, Mozart was to acknowledge the lessons he learned from the "London Bach." Thus we see that, contrary to the conventional opinion that Johann Sebastian Bach's art stagnated and died with him, his legacy lived on through his children, and later was transmuted into the masterpieces of Haydn, Mozart, and Beethoven.

Concerto in A for Cello and Orchestra, W.172

This has been one of the most widely admired of the composer's numerous concerti. Our preferred recording offers it and two companion concerti in persuasive and authentic performances, brightly recorded.

> **Bylsma, Leonhardt, Orchestra of the Age of Enlightenment.** Virgin Classics 59541

"Hamburg" Symphonies (6), W.182

These are C.P.E. Bach's finest orchestral works, along with the equally good but lesser known set of four, W.183. There have been several admirable versions, including those conducted by Pinnock, Hogwood, and Haenchen.

> **Pinnock, The English Concert.** DG Archiv 415300 [ADD]
> **Hogwood, Academy of Ancient Music.** L'Oiseau-Lyre 417124
> **Haenchen, C.P.E. Bach Chamber Orchestra.** Capriccio 10106

Ludwig van Beethoven (1770-1827)

Like C.P.E. Bach, Beethoven was a transitional figure, but between different eras—the Classical and the Romantic. We place him here only because the tendency in recent years has been to stress his roots with Haydn (with whom he studied, however intractably) and his affinities with Mozart, not to mention (as we did in the previous chapter) his worship of Handel. This view is, I think, to the good; but it does not compel us to abandon the view that Beethoven was also the first great Romantic composer.

Born in Bonn, then only a small provincial town, Beethoven removed to Vienna when in his early twenties. There he became famous as a piano virtuoso and composer, and hobnobbed with those members of the aristocracy who were to support him financially for years to come, despite his unwillingness to show them the customary deference. Indeed, no composer was more devoted to the ideals of rationalism and revolution. Many of his greatest works have at their core the themes of democracy and brotherhood, e.g. *Egmont*, Symphony No. 9, and *Fidelio*.

Beethoven's career as a pianist fell victim to increasing deafness, a condition which was total by 1818. Always brusque and impatient by nature, be became positively antisocial after this time. His refusal, however, to give up music, his determination to continue composing ever greater works in the face of despair, his well-publicized policy of staring down the Fates and shaking his shaggy mane at the gods, all contributed to the romantic image we now all know as the "suffering artist." More than any composer before him, he insisted on his prerogatives as a creative genius. When reminded of his obligations to royalty, he countered by describing himself as a "prince of Art."

Shy and introspective, Beethoven never married, though he loved several women. He often sat for hours plunged in thought, so unaware of his surroundings that his rooms degenerated into rank squalor. "Never," said his admirer Goethe, "have I seen an artist with more concentration, more energy, more inwardness." (Apparently the great poet had not seen his apartment.)

Critics of Beethoven's day often found his works impossibly wayward and incomprehensible. He returned their scorn, often filling his next work with the very qualities they had condemned in his last. To this day there are people who believe the elliptical arguments of his late string quartets are not the musings of genius, but the ravings of madness. By the end of his life Beethoven had covered more ground, from his first simple pieces for mandolin to the cosmic cries of the Ninth or "Choral" Symphony, than any composer who had lived until then.

Within a few years of his death, he was widely considered the founding father and greatest genius of the Romantic movement in music. Though he is still probably the most popular of the great composers, there has been a reaction in recent years by those who resent his role, by extension, as greatest composer of all. Heretical detractors have pointed to his lack of ease in composing, his struggle to think up great melodies, his difficulty with vocal writing, his reliance on melodramatic contrasts and military rhythms to make an effect.

But to others—most others—he is, and no doubt always will be, in his sense of inevitability, poetic depth, dramatic cogency, and force of expression, the musical corollary of Shakespeare in literature, and of Michelangelo in art. Whatever the opinion, one thing seems certain: even if Bach or Mozart before him was greater, no one has surpassed him since. Two centuries later, there is no composer who has even a remote chance of achieving consensus as Beethoven's equal.

Concerti (5) for Piano and Orchestra

Written by Beethoven between ages twenty-five and thirty-nine, before deafness finally ended his love affair with the piano, these concerti have no earlier rivals than Mozart's, and few later ones except for Brahms's. The first two, indeed, have several affinities with Mozart, though even here we can frequently discern the young lion roaring. The third is more characteristic, but still conservative. By No. 4, Beethoven has become the more familiar iconoclast: traditional rules are broken, drama is heightened, poetic ideas are developed with grandeur and eloquence. And the fifth is so majestic, so symphonic in breadth, that it has earned the nickname "Emperor."

No. 5 in E-flat, Op. 73 "Emperor"

Every recording listed is outstanding and I would not hesitate to recommend any of them; nevertheless I have tried to arrange them in something like descending order of desirability based on a combination of factors including price, age of recording, quality of pianism, couplings, etc. Your preference should prevail, if you have one ready-made.

Perahia, Haitink, Concertgebouw Orchestra. CBS 42330 [DDD]

Bishop-Kovacevich, C. Davis, London Symphony Orchestra. Philips 422482 [ADD] + Piano Sonata No. 30 (mid-price)

Brendel, Haitink, London Philharmonic Orchestra. Philips 434148 [ADD] + Fantasia in C Minor (mid-price)

R. Serkin, Bernstein, New York Philharmonic Orchestra. Sony 47520 [ADD] + Piano Concerto No. 3 (mid-price)

Arrau, C. Davis, Dresden Philharmonic Orchestra. Philips 416215 [DDD]

Fleisher, Szell, Cleveland Orchestra. CBS Essential Classics 46549 [ADD] + Triple Concerto (budget)

Ashkenazy (pianist and conductor) **Cleveland Orchestra.** London 421718 [ADD] + Choral Fantasy, Op. 80

Complete sets:

Fleisher, Szell, Cleveland Orchestra. CBS Essential Classics 48397 (3) [ADD] + Triple Concerto (budget)

Perahia, Haitink, Concertgebouw Orchestra. CBS 44575 (3) [DDD]

Brendel, Levine, Chicago Symphony Orchestra. Philips 411189 (3) [DDD]

Ashkenazy, Solti, Chicago Symphony Orchestra. London 425582 (3) [ADD] + Bagatelles (mid-price)

Lubin (fortepiano), **Hogwood, Academy of Ancient Music.** L'Oiseau-Lyre 421408 (3) [DDD]

Concerto in D for Violin, Op. 61

Now regarded by many as the crown of violin concerti, this work was proclaimed "tedious and repetitious" by its first reviewer. Beethoven wrote it with uncharacteristic speed and apparently the soloist at the 1806 premiere, Franz Clement, sight-read the score. It was mid-century before the piece really caught on.

Although the listed recordings featuring Yehudi Menuhin and Jascha Heifetz may be a bit old for some listeners (1953 and 1958, respectively), they are so famous and great that it would be totally remiss to leave them out just to satisfy those who demand a "DDD pedigree" before all else. The Menuhin in particular is a fine transfer, and the Heifetz has a unique coupling of two basic violin concerti.

There have been many other fine performances on disc (my personal favorite is by Arthur Grumiaux with Alceo Galliera conducting the Philharmonia Orchestra, available on Philips 426064), but truth to tell, among the more recent efforts Itzhak Perlman has been clearly dominant. His 1981 version with Giulini conducting (still available as Angel 47002 [DDD]) was the most often recommended digital disc—until he recorded it again with Barenboim conducting in 1986. Most critics agreed he had outdone himself, the sound was that much newer, and there were two additional pieces included where the earlier disc had none.

Menuhin, Furtwängler, Philharmonia Orchestra. Angel 69799 (mono) [ADD] (mid-price)
Heifetz, Munch, Boston Symphony Orchestra. RCA 5402 [ADD] + Brahms: Violin Concerto
Perlman, Barenboim, Berlin Philharmonic Orchestra. Angel 49567 [DDD] + 2 Romances for Violin and Orchestra

Concerto in C Minor for Violin, Cello, Piano and Orchestra, Op. 56

This "triple concerto" reminds us how little removed in time Beethoven was from the Baroque. It is less dramatic, more chamber-like, than most of his concerti, and it takes a while to really get going. But it has an appeal all its own, and should win you over by the end.

Oistrakh, Rostropovich, Richter, Karajan, Berlin Philharmonic Orchestra. EMI 64744 + Brahms: Double Concerto (mid-price)
Stern, Rose, Istomin, Ormandy, Philadelphia Orchestra. Sony Essential Classics 46549 [ADD] + Piano Concerto No. 5 (budget)

Overtures

Beethoven wrote several overtures for ballets, plays, or operas. One or two are not known to have been written for any event in particular. He wrote four different overtures, all still in the repertoire, for his only opera; the *Fidelio* overture is good, but the one called *Leonore* No. 3 (reflecting his original choice of title) is the most famous, and is often heard separately as a concert piece. It and the overture to *Egmont* (a patriotic play by Goethe) are among Beethoven's most stirringly dramatic works.

The recordings listed contain several overtures. Often you will pick up one or more of the standard overtures by default as fillers on recordings of the Beethoven symphonies, as you will see in the symphony listings farther on.

> **C. Davis, Bavarian Radio Symphony Orchestra.** (Omits *Leonore* Overture No. 2) CBS 44790 [DDD] (mid-price)
> **Karajan, Berlin Philharmonic Orchestra.** DG Galleria 427256 (2) [ADD] (mid-price)

Quartets for Strings

The sixteen string quartets are among the greatest chamber works ever written, and provide an interesting chronological picture of Beethoven's evolution as a composer. They are traditionally divided into three groups referred to as Early, Middle, and Late, corresponding to distinct phases in his stylistic development. You can begin sampling with single discs that contain a couple of the more famous quartets, or perhaps get a box set of the Middle Quartets, which are meatier than the Early Quartets but easier to digest than the Late ones.

The Alban Berg Quartet have a beautifully played and recorded box of the Middle Quartets, otherwise known as nos. 7-11, while the Lindsay Quartet offer splendid performances of nos. 8 and 9 on a single disc. No. 9 is paired with one of the Late Quartets, no. 14 (Beethoven's own favorite of all his quartets), on a value-filled disc from the Talich Quartet.

> **Alban Berg Quartet.** Middle Quartets (nos. 7-11), Angel 47130 (3) [DDD]
> **Lindsay Quartet.** Nos. 8, 9, ASV 554 [DDD]
> **Talich Quartet.** Nos. 9, 14, Calliope 9638

Sonatas (32) for Piano

These are core works for understanding Beethoven. Their composition spanned his entire life, and they reveal virtually every facet of his imagination and experimentation with his favorite instrument. It is an enormous amount of music, and the beginner will usually want to start with the three most beloved sonatas: No. 8 in c, Op. 13, "Pathétique;" No. 14 in c#, Op. 27, No. 2, "Moonlight;" and No. 23 in f, Op. 57, "Appassionata." Although dozens of fine pianists have recorded the sonatas, the most famous version with just these three all together, with Rudolf Serkin playing, is available on a mid-priced CD. Why pay more?

R. Serkin. CBS 37219 [ADD] (mid-price)

Sonatas for Violin and Piano No. 5 in F, Op. 24, "Spring;" No. 9 in A, Op. 47, "Kreutzer"

Of the ten sonatas for violin and piano, these two are the best known, and the beginning collector will surely want to start with them, especially the "Kreutzer" (named for the violinist who was to have played it, but never did), with its combination of brilliance and profundity, which first took the violin sonata out of the parlor and into the concert auditorium.

Besides complete sets of the ten sonatas, there have been any number of single discs containing these two together. In either format, the combination of Itzhak Perlman and Vladimir Ashkenazy makes an easy first choice for performance and sound.

Perlman, Ashkenazy. London 410554 [ADD]

Symphonies

As a body, these are the most famous and beloved symphonies ever written, and for many people they are the first and most essential classical works to which they are exposed. For many later Romantic composers, they were the summit of musical art and the object of almost religious veneration, a phenomenon which had an unfortunate inhibiting effect (Brahms, for instance, dithered over his great first symphony for more than twenty years, troubled by "hearing Beethoven's footsteps" close behind him).

This exaggerated adulation is what many of today's Beethoven detractors are reacting against. Perhaps we should clear our minds of preconceptions and received opinion and just enjoy the symphonies for the exciting, dramatic paeans to Beethoven's revolutionary ideals that they are.

Many people like to buy all nine symphonies in one convenient set. There have been many such compendia (and they often contain bonuses of miscellaneous fillers, such as the overtures) which offer a savings over buying them all separately. But be aware that no set has ever had total consensus from the critics, which is to be expected since it is asking too much for any one conductor to produce the best performances of all nine symphonies.

The most nearly successful has probably been Herbert von Karajan, who recorded no fewer than three complete sets, issued in 1963, 1977, and 1985. Happily, the earliest set is the best musically, and costs far less than the other two.

Close competition at a similar price-per-disc is offered by the Otto Klemperer set, but it takes seven discs instead of Karajan's five. Of course, you get more with it, including the famous overtures, the *Grosse Fuge*, and the incidental music to *Egmont*.

If you are looking for a combination of artistic merit and state-of-the-art sound, try Günter Wand's digital set. Also digital are Nikolaus Harnoncourt and Roger Norrington; just be aware that they use period instruments and the symphonies may sound shockingly different from what you are used to if you are not familiar with this type of performance.

The classic George Szell and Bruno Walter performances are steals at budget prices. The Toscanini set is legendary, and you might want to have it just as an icon of recording history; but at mid-price instead of budget, and with the worst sound of all versions, I have placed it last.

Karajan, Berlin Philharmonic Orchestra. DG 429036 (5) [ADD] (mid-price)

Klemperer, Philharmonia Orchestra. EMI 68057 (7) [ADD] (mid-price)

Wand, North German Radio Symphony Orchestra. RCA 60090 (6) [DDD]

Harnoncourt, Chamber Orchestra of Europe. Teldec 46452 (5) [DDD]

Norrington, London Classical Players. EMI 49852 (6) [DDD] + 3 overtures

Szell, Cleveland Orchestra. Sony Essential Classics 48396 (5) [ADD] + 3 overtures (budget)

B. Walter, Columbia Symphony Orchestra. Sony 48099 (6) [ADD] + 2 overtures (budget)

Toscanini, NBC Symphony Orchestra. RCA 60324 (5) [ADD] (mid-price)

The really dedicated Beethoven symphony fan, especially one on a less restricted budget, will want to collect these works individually, as follows:

No. 1 in C, Op. 21; No. 2 in D, Op. 36

Although less remote from Mozart than the later symphonies, these first two are still unquestionably by Beethoven. Nevertheless, they stand apart from the others, and since they fit perfectly together on one disc that is how you will usually find them. Listed are good versions for every purse.

Hogwood, Academy of Ancient Music (period instruments). L'Oiseau-Lyre 414338 [DDD]

Tilson Thomas, English Chamber Orchestra. Sony 44905 [DDD] (mid-price)

Ferencsik, Hungarian State Orchestra. Hungaroton White Label 110 [ADD] (budget)

No. 3 in E-flat, Op. 55, "Eroica"

No doubt the story will never stop being told that Beethoven wrote this symphony to honor Napoleon, then crossed out the dedication when that supposed champion of democracy proclaimed himself emperor. It is a beloved, even believable story, but there is not a shred of evidence that it is true, and the music is quite dramatic enough without it. In fact, what is significant is that the "Eroica" truly represents a revolution—not in politics, but in music: a vast expansion of symphonic thought, contained within a highly intellectual and logical design. This symphony is usually taken as the real beginning of the Romantic era, much as Wagner's *Tristan und Isolde* represents for many the beginning of the Modern period.

The 1961 Klemperer stereo recording is the classic of the catalog, but is currently available only in the seven-disc complete set listed above. Günther Wand is a favorite in digital sound on modern instruments, and Christopher Hogwood on period instruments. Also famous for the *Eroica* is Leonard Bernstein.

Wand, North German Radio Symphony Orchestra. RCA 60755 [DDD] + overtures

Hogwood, Academy of Ancient Music. L'Oiseau-Lyre 417235 [DDD] + overtures

Bernstein, Vienna Philharmonic Orchestra. DG 431024 [ADD] + overtures (mid-price)

No. 4 in B-flat, Op. 60

Dismissed by many critics, especially in the nineteenth century, as a lightweight, this symphony abounds in wild alterations of rhythm and mood. There is no "program," no nickname, no explanation, no pat way to characterize what is going on, so the Fourth remains one of Beethoven's least known and discussed works. Yet the second movement contains one of Beethoven's most beautiful melodies: Berlioz likened it to the Archangel Michael singing at the gates of heaven.

Herbert von Karajan is good with this symphony, and on one (digital) disc it is conveniently coupled with the best of his four versions of the Symphony No. 7. Another fine digital version comes from Sir Georg Solti, paired with Symphony No. 5; Christopher Hogwood has the same combination, also digital, but on period instruments. Great low-priced versions include George Szell (coupled with Symphony No. 7) and Bruno Walter (with Symphony No. 8).

Karajan, Berlin Philharmonic Orchestra. DG 415121 [DDD] + Symphony No. 7

Solti, Chicago Symphony Orchestra. London 421580 [DDD] + Symphony No. 5

Hogwood, Academy of Ancient Music. L'Oiseau-Lyre 417615 [DDD] + Symphony No. 5

Szell, Cleveland Orchestra. Sony Essential Classics 48158 [ADD] +
Symphony No. 7 (budget)
B. Walter, Columbia Symphony Orchestra. CBS 37773 [ADD] +
Symphony No. 8 (mid-price)

No. 5 in C Minor, Op. 67

Amazingly, the most famous of all symphonies has never acquired a nickname. It is just "Beethoven's Fifth." Indeed, many people know what you mean if you just refer to "The Fifth" without mentioning the composer. Everybody agrees that this exceptionally dramatic, and in the end, joyful symphony "means" something special, that it implies some kind of "program." But what that might be, most listeners seem to prefer to imagine for themselves. Perhaps that is why this tends to be one of the works that people most treasure as a personal possession. Beethoven himself gave a clue when he pointed to the famous four opening notes and said, "Thus Fate knocks at the door!"

Of course, this bestseller has had hundreds of recordings. Still, a handful can be described as having superlative qualities. A favorite of many critics continues to be the urgent, electrifying reading by Carlos Kleiber; a drawback is the absence of any coupling, making it possibly the shortest full-price disc in existence, and if you want digital, it isn't. Karajan gives better value with a coupling of Symphony No. 8, in an analog performance that some think is very nearly as good as Kleiber's. "Karajan's Fifth" in its digital incarnation makes an appearance on another disc coupled with his best version of Symphony No. 6. Another strong challenger, with digital sound and a bonus of Symphony No. 8, is the recording by Günter Wand.

Solti and Hogwood were mentioned above under Symphony No. 4 as coupled with No. 5, offering modern and period instruments respectively, both digital.

Now, if you are not concerned about digital or even stereo, but just want to hear Beethoven's Fifth played to the nines by the kind of conductor of yesteryear who makes most of today's jet-setters sound like they have just sucked helium, please purchase Wilhelm Furtwängler's 1952 recording, coupled with Symphony No. 7, and learn why this disc is in a series called Great Recordings of the Century.

C. Kleiber, Vienna Philharmonic Orchestra. DG 415861 [ADD]
Karajan, Berlin Philharmonic Orchestra. DG 419051 [ADD] +
Symphony No. 8, *Fidelio* Overture
Karajan, Berlin Philharmonic Orchestra. DG 413932 [DDD] +
Symphony No. 6
Wand, North German Radio Symphony Orchestra. RCA 60092 [DDD] +
Symphony No. 8
Solti, Chicago Symphony Orchestra. London 421580 [DDD] + Symphony
No. 4

Hogwood, Academy of Ancient Music. L'Oiseau-Lyre 417615 [DDD] + Symphony No. 4

Furtwängler, Vienna Philharmonic Orchestra. Angel 69803 [ADD] (mono) + Symphony No. 7 (mid-price)

No. 6 in F, Op. 68, "Pastorale"

The antisocial Beethoven is reported to have once said "I love a tree more than a man." He put his money where his mouth was in this symphony, for which he provided an explicit program. The movements are marked "Awakening of happy feelings upon reaching the countryside," "Scene at the brook," "Cheerful gathering of country folk," "Thunderstorm," and finally, "Shepherd's song: Happy, grateful feelings after the storm." Here, for once, those stern musicologists who are always warning us against reading pictorial meanings into music maintain a red-faced silence.

The early 1960s recording by Bruno Walter has taken on legendary status, and has been digitally remastered for a welcome low-priced reissue. The digital Karajan and Wand editions have already been recommended above. Also noted for this symphony and recorded digitally are Vladimir Ashkenazy (coupled with the *Egmont* and *Leonore* No. 3 overtures) and Klaus Tennstedt (coupled with Symphony No. 8).

B. Walter, Columbia Symphony Orchestra. CBS 36720 [ADD] + *Leonore* Overture No. 2 (mid-price)

Karajan, Berlin Philharmonic Orchestra. DG 413932 [DDD] + Symphony No. 5

Wand, North German Radio Symphony Orchestra. RCA 60094 [DDD]

Ashkenazy, Philharmonia Orchestra. London 430721 [DDD] + *Egmont, Leonore* No. 3 overtures (mid-price)

Tennstedt, London Philharmonic Orchestra. EMI 63891 [DDD] + Symphony No. 8 (mid-price)

No. 7 in A, Op. 92

Beethoven here indulges himself in rhythmic experimentation to create an abandoned outpouring of pure kinetic energy. Wagner called this symphony "the apotheosis of the dance." Beethoven himself called it "one of my best works." But it has remained problematical for some listeners who miss the nobility or thoughtfulness they find in the other symphonies. Some contemporary critics thought the feverish final movement was proof Beethoven was going insane. The late conductor Sir Thomas Beecham hated the Seventh: "It sounds," he said, "like a bunch of yaks jumping about." Certainly Beethoven was in high spirits when he wrote it!

Carlos Kleiber is not so universally admired here as on his recording of No. 5, but still he is a top contender for driving excitement. Karajan is at least a runner-up with his best No. 7, paired with a previously recommended No. 4. The best sound comes from the version by Claudio Abbado, the best entry in his Beethoven cycle, coupled with No. 8. George Szell wins the budget trials with a disc already recommended under Symphony No. 4, and Wilhelm Furtwängler represents the "legendary" category with his version, already listed above under Symphony No. 5.

> **Kleiber, Vienna Philharmonic Orchestra.** DG 415862 [ADD]
> **Karajan, Berlin Philharmonic Orchestra.** DG 415121 [DDD] + Symphony No. 4
> **Abbado, Vienna Philharmonic Orchestra.** DG 423364 [DDD] + Symphony No. 8
> **Szell, Cleveland Orchestra.** Sony Essential Classics 48158 [ADD] + Symphony No. 4, overtures (budget)
> **Furtwängler, Vienna Philharmonic Orchestra.** Angel 69803 [ADD] (mono) + Symphony No. 5 (mid-price)

No. 8 in F, Op. 93

Beethoven wrote this symphony at the same time as No. 7, and it has been seen as a more relaxed exercise in rhythmic devices. Sir George Grove suggested the nickname "Humorous" for No. 8, and certainly there are plenty of outlandish moments that one might take for Beethovenian "raspberries"; the second movement, for example, would seem to make comic reference to the recently invented metronome, concluding with a mechanical breakdown.

Karajan was especially known for this symphony, having recorded it on three separate occasions. A great value is the one coupled with a fine Symphony No. 5 and the *Fidelio* Overture. Abbado's and Tennstedt's digital versions have already been listed under Symphonies Nos. 7 and 6, respectively, and Bruno Walter with No. 4 is our choice in the budget category.

> **Karajan, Berlin Philharmonic Orchestra.** DG 419051 [ADD] + Symphony No. 5
> **Abbado, Vienna Philharmonic Orchestra.** DG 423364 [DDD] + Symphony No. 7
> **Tennstedt, London Philharmonic Orchestra.** EMI 63891 [DDD] + Symphony No. 6 (mid-price)
> **B. Walter, Columbia Symphony Orchestra.** CBS 37773 [ADD] + Symphony No. 4 (mid-price)

No. 9 in d, Op. 125, "Choral"

Beethoven's final symphony was also his largest in scale, and, until the colossi of Bruckner and Mahler, the longest. More than thirty years before he finished the Ninth, Beethoven had confided to a friend that he wanted to set Friedrich Schiller's Ode "To Joy" to music. He decided to incorporate it as the last movement of his last symphony, only after much soul-searching. Early audiences found it puzzling or embarrassing. Beethoven's fellow composer Ludwig Spohr, usually an admirer, called it "tasteless and monstrous;" and a modern critic, Norman Suckling, has referred to it as "Beethoven's celebrated misfire."

This is not to denigrate the creative imagination and iron control which produced this mighty work, but to indicate how unnecessary it is to bow meekly before masterpieces as if they were gods. We ought to approach them as friends; none, perhaps, without fault, but all with something to love, though never demanding our worship. Beethoven, an apostle of democracy, a man who denounced Napoleon when he turned tyrant, would not stand for such an attitude.

It is fair to question whether words are needed to drive home a message that might have been more subtly conveyed by musical means alone—especially when the words are so fulsome as Schiller's (least favorite line: "Wollust ward dem Wurm gegeben," or "Even to a worm ecstasy is granted"). But Beethoven apparently wanted to be sure no one missed the poem's message of universal brotherhood, and the surging rapture of the last movement seldom fails to enthrall an audience. One is hard-pressed not to be moved at the line "Seid umschlungen, Millionen": it is difficult not to believe that the bitter, lonely Beethoven is writing, as he once said, "From the heart, to the heart," when the chorus cries "O you millions, let me embrace you."

Herbert von Karajan shines again in the Ninth, and the second of his three versions—widely considered the best even though it is analog—makes a superlative value at mid-price. A close contender is Sir Georg Solti's analog version, also at mid-price; it is particularly famous for its slow movement. At least the equal of Solti artistically, with the same orchestra but older sound, is the Fritz Reiner mid-price reissue.

Leonard Bernstein has the distinction of getting two separate versions on the list: his 1979 analog studio performance of goose-pimpling intensity, and his thrilling 1989 live digital recording celebrating the destruction of the Berlin Wall. Finally, Carlo Maria Giulini wins the budget sweepstakes for overall sound and performance.

Karajan, Berlin Philharmonic Orchestra. DG Galleria 415832 [ADD] (mid-price)
Solti, Chicago Symphony Orchestra. London Jubilee 430438 [ADD] (mid-price)
Reiner, Chicago Symphony Orchestra. RCA Gold Seal 6532 [ADD] (mid-price)
Bernstein, Vienna Philharmonic Orchestra. DG 410859 [ADD]
Bernstein, members of various famous orchestras. DG 429861 [DDD]
Giulini, London Symphony Orchestra. EMI Encore 67763 (budget)

Trio in Bb, Op. 97, "Archduke"

The clear champion among Beethoven's eleven trios for piano, violin and cello, the "Archduke" is named for one of the composer's most generous patrons. It is distinguished by melodic beauty and wide-ranging vision, qualities which are thoroughly mined by Vladimir Ashkenazy, Itzhak Perlman, and Lynn Harrell on their superlative recording.

Perlman, Harrell, Ashkenazy. EMI 47010 [DDD] + Trio No. 10

Luigi Boccherini (1743-1805)

Boccherini wrote about five hundred works, but is remembered today mainly for one cello concerto and a famous minuet so tiny we cannot give it space here. Boccherini's admirers are growing in number, however, and his stock continues to rise. One of his earliest fans was, in fact, Franz Joseph Haydn, who called him "a genius." Their styles were so interrelated that a contemporary musician in a famous phrase called Boccherini "the wife of Haydn."

At age thirteen he was already an accomplished cellist, and in his mid-twenties he settled in to a lucrative position at the Spanish court. Alas, after a few years of wealth and fame, he fell out with the new monarch, Charles IV, who prohibited not only the performance of Boccherini's music, but even the mention of his name. By 1803 he was living with his wife and five children in a single room where he eventually died, we are told, of sickness and starvation.

Boccherini has tremendous historical importance as the true inventor of the modern string trio, quartet, and quintet. His compositions, while they may fall short of Beethoven's and Mozart's in stature, are tuneful, graceful, suavely harmonized, inventive, and virtuosic. While not sublime, they are very far above the ordinary, and they make exceedingly pleasurable listening.

Concerto in B-flat for Cello and Orchestra

The most popular of Boccherini's twelve known cello concertos has in the twentieth century become one of the staples of the cello repertoire. It is idiomatically written for the instrument, so any competent cellist can do well with it.

You may wish to get a full-price superstar version, such as the recording with Yo-Yo Ma and Pinchas Zukerman, or pick up the budget Naxos recording with unknown artists that sounds very nearly as good.

Ma, Zukerman, St. Paul Chamber Orchestra. Sony 39964 + J.C. Bach: Sinfonia Concertante
Kanta, Breiner, Capella Istropolitana. Naxos 8.550059 [DDD] + Haydn: Cello Concerti Nos. 1 and 2 (budget)

Christoph Willibald von Gluck (1714-1787)

Almost exclusively an opera composer, in the course of it Gluck became one of the most significant figures in the history of the opera form. He composed some forty works for the lyric stage, of which only six comprise the "reform operas" for which he became famous, and of which only one, *Orfeo ed Euridice,* is still regularly performed. There are few composers who have been held in higher regard, yet have a smaller public.

He was born of German and Bohemian stock, his father being a huntsman and forest ranger to various aristocrats. Christoph, musically talented, grew up playing chamber music in noble households. He studied with Sammartini in Milan for three years, and then began producing his first operas in several cities, picking up along the way an eclectic view of style. Indeed, although he was of Teutonic blood, he wrote all his operas in Italian or French, and eventually was looked upon as an internationalist.

By the age of forty he had written about twenty operas, married a rich banker's daughter, and been engaged as musical director of the Imperial court in Vienna, where he fell in with a faction who wanted to modernize opera by getting rid of the castrati (male sopranos), making the drama more realistic and unified, and balancing the roles of music and words. (Up to this time opera was usually a rather stilted affair of mythological allegories with a heavy tilt towards vocal display.)

Gluck was more or less selected by the reform faction at court to implement their theories, which he first did in the opera *Alceste.* To it he affixed a famous written preface laying down the manifesto of the new movement. Despite this, Gluck was a true composer of his era, trained to compose on command, and he continued to write operas in the old style even after causing a sensation with his greatest "reform" opera, *Orfeo ed Euridice.*

In his last years, partially paralyzed by a stroke, Gluck was befriended by both Salieri and Mozart, and the latter honored him by improvising a set of variations on Gluck's comic opera, *La Rencontre imprévue.* Ironically, while the ideals of "reform opera" were much trumpeted later on by Wagner, they actually influenced mainly the French school, especially Berlioz. Today, the general public is familiar only with the haunting aria "Che faro" and the *Dance of the Blessed Spirits,* both from *Orfeo ed Euridice;* but an investigation into his other operas, especially *Alceste* and *Iphigénie en Tauride,* can be a revelation. This is often music of great beauty and nobility.

Orfeo ed Euridice

The most famous of Gluck's operas reworks the old Greek legend of the god of music who goes down to the Elysian Fields to retrieve his beloved wife from the land of death, but he invests it with the innovations of the reform faction at the Viennese court: the music outlines and underlines the words and the scenes are composed straight through. Everything is subservient to the dramatic conception, instead of being the slave of some artist or fashion.

The finest digital performance stars Dame Janet Baker and is conducted by Raymond Leppard. This is the original Italian version; the later French adaptation can be heard in a beautifully sung recording from 1957 with tenor Léopold Simoneau, conducted by Hans Rosbaud.

Leppard, London Philharmonic Orchestra, Baker. Erato 45864 (2) [DDD] (mid-price)
Rosbaud, Lamoureux Orchestra, Simoneau. Philips 434784 (2) [ADD] (mid-price)

Franz Joseph Haydn (1732-1809)

Haydn was born of a humble but musical rural Austrian family, and early revealed a beautiful singing voice. He was sent off as a lad to St. Stephen's Cathedral in the big city of Vienna, where he picked up the rudiments of theory, and got himself thrashed by the Empress herself when she caught him clambering about the church scaffolding.

"I never had real teachers," he confessed towards the end of his life. Thrown on his own resources at age sixteen, when his choirboy's voice broke, he taught himself the scores of C.P.E. Bach's sonatas on a broken-down old spinet in an unheated garret. He survived by playing evening serenades and giving lessons.

He was not a child prodigy in the manner of Mozart, who has for generations overshadowed him. He plodded away at his work sixteen to eighteen hours a day, and he was past forty when he wrote the works for which he is most admired today. In the course of a well-ordered, industrious life he became known as the "father" of the symphony and the string quartet. Although he did not actually invent these forms, he was the first to develop them to an eminence which would provide a standard for later composers.

When Haydn was forty-nine he first met the twenty-five-year-old Mozart and recognized in him a genius even greater than his own. Without a trace of jealousy, and never too smug to keep learning, Haydn studied the younger man's work and enriched his own compositions with its lessons. The two became dear friends, and Haydn was crushed by Mozart's death in 1791.

Haydn lived on for another eighteen years, to the age of seventy-seven, renowned for his wisdom, piety, patience, honesty, and modesty; yet there were those who said they had never seen him laugh, and that even when he was joking there was a certain sadness in his eyes.

He died full of honors during the French occupation of Vienna. It was not his countrymen alone who mourned him; Napoleon himself ordered a guard of honor to accompany the corpse. At the memorial service, Mozart's *Requiem* was sung.

Concerto in E-flat for Trumpet

This is the most famous of all trumpet concertos. Strangely, it dropped from view after Hadyn's death until 1928, when it was revived on a radio broadcast. Then it became a hit, and it has stayed at the top of the brass charts ever since.

The recordings featuring Wynton Marsalis and Gerard Schwarz are very good, but Håkan Hardenberger has the best orchestral accompaniment and offers the most value for the money, with three additional concerti on his disc. All three recordings are digital, and all include the Hummel, so, on points, Hardenberger seems the clear winner to me.

Hardenberger, Marriner, Academy of St. Martin-in-the-Fields. Philips 420203 [DDD] + Trumpet concerti by Hummel, Stamitz, Hertel

The Creation

This is the best known and most beloved oratorio after Handel's *Messiah*. Written near the end of the composer's long life, it is a moving testimony to his gentle faith. The most famous moments are the thrilling burst of sound at the words "And there was light" and the magnificent chorus "The heavens are telling the glory of God," which only Handel's "Hallelujah" chorus exceeds in popularity.

Conductor Herbert von Karajan recorded *The Creation* twice. While the 1982 digital version is excellent, it is surpassed in performance values by the 1969 stereo edition, which features six superb soloists, including baritone Dieterich Fischer-Dieskau and the late tenor Fritz Wunderlich. In addition to this classic performance, there are fine digital recordings of more recent vintage from Christopher Hogwood and James Levine. (The Karajan and Levine are sung in the original German; Hogwood's performance is sung in English.)

Karajan, Vienna Philharmonic Orchestra. DG Galleria 435077 (2) [ADD] (mid-price)
Hogwood, Academy of Ancient Music, Oxford New College Choir. L'Oiseau-Lyre 430397 (2) [DDD]
Levine, Berlin Philharmonic Orchestra, Stockholm Radio and Chamber Choirs. DG 427629 (2) [DDD]

Mass No.11 in D Minor, "Nelson"

If you are averse to liturgical music, fear not. Had Haydn lived two centuries longer this might have been his film score for *Raiders of the Lost Ark*. It was actually written just as Admiral Nelson had defeated Napoleon in the Battle of the Nile, and its Latin subtitle means "Mass in Time of Fear." Its rumbling of drums, pealing of trumpets, and choral pleadings and rejoicings would knock the shingles off a church.

Trevor Pinnock leads a bone-rattling version on period instruments. Leonard Bernstein's "modern" performance bristles with drama. Neville Marriner's now-classic recording is coupled with a recommended Vivaldi *Gloria* at mid-price.

Pinnock, The English Concert. DG Archiv 423097 [DDD] + Te Deum
Bernstein, New York Philharmonic Orchestra, Westminster Choir. Sony 47563 (2) [ADD] + Mass No. 10, Symphony No. 88 (mid-price)
Marriner, Academy of St. Martin-in-the-Fields, King's College Choir, Cambridge. London Jubilee 421146 [ADD] + Vivaldi: *Gloria* (mid-price)

Quartet in C, Op. 76, No. 3, "Emperor"

This is only the most familiar string quartet out of dozens by Haydn, scarcely a one of which fails to deliver for the aficionado of chamber music. The nickname comes from the second, or slow, movement, which is a set of four variations on an original (and noble) melody which has served as both the German and Austrian national anthems.

A wonderful recording by the Alban Berg Quartet, coupled with Mozart's Quartet No. 17, used to make a perfect introduction to two of the basic chamber works of these companionable composers, but it has disappeared from the catalog. I mention it in case it is reissued after this book is published. As of this writing, the best choices are probably the Tátrai, Takács, and Kodály Quartets—all from Hungary, where performance of Haydn quartets is a well-developed specialty. Since the Tátrai is a double set with only mediocre sound, I prefer to list here just the two single discs, one digital, one budget.

Takács Quartet. London 421360 [DDD] + Quartets Op. 76/1, 2
Kodály Quartet. Naxos 8.550129 [DDD] + Quartets Op. 76/1, 2 (budget)

Symphonies

Officially, Haydn wrote 104 symphonies, though we now know that one more is lost, and two others are disguised in his catalog as "divertimenti." There truly is not one that is not melodious, infectious, and well-built. We may sense that they are not on quite the same level as Mozart's and Beethoven's—we feel happiness and sadness rather than joy and tragedy—but no composer other than Haydn produced such a quantity of symphonic music at such a consistently high level. Perhaps the most amazing thing is that we are not talking about a fumbling search from primitive beginnings to later mastery, but a steady, confident progression from the first little masterwork right up the ladder to the top, scarcely ever missing a rung.

If there is any composer who made it to Heaven, it would have to be Haydn, who inscribed each of his scores "In the name of the Lord," and "Praise to God," who had no enemies, and committed no sins worth mentioning.

You can easily recognize which Haydn symphonies are the most popular, because virtually all of them have nicknames—given not by the composer, but by his grateful publishers and listeners. The earliest one that still appears frequently on orchestra programs is No. 45, the "Farewell" symphony, so named because Haydn wrote the last movement to allow groups of players to conclude their parts and leave the stage one after another until no one is left.

Other famous symphonic nicknames include "The Bear" (No. 82), "The Hen" (83), "Oxford" (92), "Surprise" (94), "Miracle" (96), "Military" (100), "Clock" (101), "Drum Roll" (103), and "London" (104). On top of that, Nos. 93 through 104 are known collectively as the "London" or "Salomon" Symphonies, and Nos. 82-87 as the "Paris" Symphonies. Perhaps we would do better to call Haydn the "Father of the Nickname" instead of "Father of the Symphony."

One of the great recording projects of the 1970s was Antal Dorati's readings of all the Haydn symphonies, including variants, in ten volumes of LPs for London. These have now happily been made available in eight sets of four CDs each; or, you can buy them as one thirty-two-disc set, on London 430100 [ADD] (mid-price).

The "Paris" Symphonies (82-87) are conveniently available in a two-disc set at mid-price in very good performances led by Sir Neville Marriner. Fine versions of the "London" Symphonies come in a mid-price box of four CDs conducted by Sir Colin Davis. A double set from George Szell presents Nos. 93-98 at mid-price as well.

The other recommendations given are various excellent single-disc performances of some of the more famous symphonies.

Dorati, Philharmonia Hungarica. Nos. 94, 96, 100, London 417718 [ADD] (mid-price)
Marriner, Academy of St. Martin-in-the-Fields. Nos. 82-87, Philips Duo 438727 (2) [ADD] (mid-price)
C. Davis, Concertgebouw Orchestra. Nos. 93-104, Philips Silver Line 432286 (4) [ADD] (mid-price)
Szell, Cleveland Orchestra. Nos. 93-98, Sony 45673 (2) [ADD] (mid-price)
Szell, Cleveland Orchestra. Nos. 92, 94, 96, Sony 46332 [ADD] (mid-price)
Bernstein, Vienna Philharmonic Orchestra. Nos. 88, 92, DG 413777 [DDD]
Hogwood, Academy of Ancient Music. Nos. 94, 96, L'Oiseau-Lyre 414330 [DDD]

Wolfgang Amadeus Mozart (1756-1791)

Mozart is the finest all-time example of a Wunderkind with staying power. There were other child prodigies who became composers: Mendelssohn, Bizet, Boccherini, Arriaga, and Lekeu come to mind—but you see how quickly the list fades into obscurity. Most infant geniuses burn out by their twenties. What kept Mozart's flame burning ever brighter, from his first compositions at age five, to his 626th masterpiece at age thirty-five? No one knows.

It is fashionable nowadays to sniff at the traditional epithet "Divine" applied to Mozart, to belittle or doubt his reported ability to compose great works in his head while playing billiards and to write them down at his later convenience, to emphasize his scatalogical language and love of roistering as if to prove he was scarcely different from you or I.

Well, it won't wash. There is too much evidence that his talents, perceptions and intuitions were light years beyond the ordinary. He seemed to know most of the basics of music by the age most of us are just learning to tell the big hand from the little hand. Melody, gorgeous melody, flowed from him like sparkling waters from an artesian well. At every turn in his works there are little subtleties and details about which critics have written whole books of analysis; if Mozart had taken time to ponder each of them he would have needed to live another thirty-five years—but he didn't. His music sounds effortless. With almost any other composer (Beethoven is a good example), composition is a result of long, deep thinking and numberless revisions, "art concealing art." With Mozart it is different. It *is* effortless!

No other composer is so resistant to being taken apart and exposed as a set of cogs and gears, his accomplishments shown to be nothing more than the result of preordained chemical reactions. I am not exaggerating when I say that there are pages of his music which to the experienced eye look clumsy, or impossible to play, but when heard sound smooth as silk. No one knows how Mozart's mind made the leap of intuition from page to stage. There are hours upon hours of pieces that sound "pretty" on the surface, but carry some nameless undercurrent that unsettles or moves the soul. No one is able to explain just what Mozart has done, musically, to produce this effect, which on paper looks identical to the genial, untroubled music of Haydn.

Perhaps we should simply let Haydn say what he thought: "If I could tell every music lover...what I feel about the inimitable works of Mozart, their depth of emotion and their unique musical quality, every nation would compete to possess such a great person within its boundaries." This from a composer twenty-five years older, far more famous and successful at the time, and considered the genius of his era. Haydn did not need to say this—he simply had no choice.

Though Mozart's life was short, it was full of incident, and we can only touch on the highlights here. He was born in Salzburg, Austria to a musical family. His proud and parsimonious father, Leopold, trotted him out as a sideshow wonder at the age of five, eager to burnish the family name and make a fortune. Dressed in lace jabeau and buckled shoes, little Wolfgang played the harpsichord before the Empress herself. By his late teens he had toured much of Europe, and along the way picked up the styles and techniques of many contemporary composers.

For several years he suffered employment in the oppressive music establishment of the Archbishop of Salzburg, being released in 1781 "with a kick," as he said, "on my ass." He was soon happier in Vienna, where he married, had children, and enjoyed his first public recognition. As time passed, however, he experienced increasing difficulties in health and finances. His brief moment in the sun clouded over, and he was reduced to contant borrowing to support his family.

One day an ominous stranger appeared at his door, offering to pay Mozart to write a Requiem Mass. The man was anonymously representing an eccentric nobleman who bought works from indigent talents and passed them off as his own, but the ailing Mozart imagined this visitor to have come from the Beyond, to warn him of his own death. And die he did, in the middle of the winter, with the great Requiem incomplete. His wife was too ill to attend the funeral. He was buried in an unmarked pauper's grave, whose exact location was soon forgotten.

It was only a few years before romantic fantasies began to embellish Mozart's image. One of the most macabre was that he had not died of natural causes but had been poisoned by a rival composer, Antonio Salieri. This theory inspired several fictional works, most notably in our time Peter Shaffer's play *Amadeus,* and the popular film based on it. Historians justly complain about distorting and fictionalizing a life that is already dramatic and unbelievable enough. But what can you expect? Mozart, like Alexander the Great or Charlemagne, was bigger than life. When people or events surpass our comprehension, we mythologize them. And thus have we done with the Divine Mozart, for whom we can find no parallel among our brethren.

Concerto in A for Clarinet, K.622

Mozart wrote this work of "greatness and transcendent beauty" (Alfred Einstein) for his good friend, the great clarinetist Anton Stadler. It is one of his very last works, and is one of those that speaks most poignantly of a sadness underlying the surface calm.

Antony Pay uses the "basset" clarinet, the historic instrument Stadler would have played. Mr. Pay's recording is coupled with the Oboe Concerto, K.314. On the modern clarinet, Jack Brymer's classic reading has been reissued on CD with the Bassoon Concerto, K.191; or for digital sound there is David Shifrin, heard also with the Clarinet Quintet, K.581. Marcellus/Szell and Prinz/Böhm are outstanding analog choices at mid-price.

Pay, Hogwood, Academy of Ancient Music. L'Oiseau-Lyre 414339 [DDD] + Oboe Concerto, K.314

Brymer, C. Davis, London Symphony Orchestra. Philips Silver Line 420710 [ADD] + Clarinet Quintet (mid-price)

Shifrin, Schwarz, Mostly Mozart Orchestra. Delos 3020 [DDD] + Clarinet Quintet

Marcellus, Szell, Cleveland Orchestra. CBS 37810 [AAD] + Sinfonia Concertante, K.364 (mid-price)

Prinz, Böhm, Vienna Philharmonic Orchestra. DG 429816 [ADD] + Oboe Concerto, K.314, Bassoon Concerto, K.191 (mid-price)

Concerti for Flute: No. 1 in G, K.313; No. 2 in D, K.314

Mozart claimed to hate the flute. After hearing these sparkling works, one might wonder: with an enemy like this, who needs friends? They were commissioned by a wealthy Dutch sea captain who was an amateur flutist on the side. Weird, but true.

The best-known artists who have recorded these are James Galway and Jean-Pierre Rampal, but some critics have extravagant praise for Susan Milan or William Bennett as well. Both concerti are generally paired on one recording.

> **Galway (flutist and conductor), Chamber Orchestra of Europe.** RCA 7861 (2) [DDD] + other Mozart selections
>
> **Rampal, Mehta, Israel Philharmonic Orchestra.** CBS 44919 [DDD] + other Mozart selections
>
> **Milan, Leppard, English Chamber Orchestra.** Chandos 8613 [DDD] + other Mozart selections
>
> **Bennett, Malcolm, English Chamber Orchestra.** London Weekend Classics 421630 + Cimarosa: Double Flute Concerto (budget)

Concerti (4) for Horn, K.412, 417, 447, 495

Like the Clarinet Concerto, the French Horn Concerti were written for a close friend—this time, horn player Joseph Leutgeb, "ass, ox, and fool" as Mozart described him, à la Don Rickles. This quartet of genial pieces remains at the pinnacle of French horn literature.

Dennis Brain's legendary 1953 mono recording, with Karajan conducting, has been reissued in clear sound on CD. Brain's closest rivals in more recent times have been Barry Tuckwell and Alan Civil, who have each produced three or four separate recordings of these concerti. Hermann Baumann is equally fine on his recording with Harnoncourt conducting, using a period instrument. I should stress, however, that in the case of the "natural," or valveless horn, there is no difference in sound whatsoever from the modern keyed horn, if played properly. It is just much harder to control, so playing it well amounts to little more than showing off, or merely satisfying those period instrument enthusiasts who have gone a bit over the top.

> **Brain, Karajan, Philharmonia Orchestra.** Angel 61013 (mono) (mid-price)
>
> **Tuckwell, Marriner, Academy of St. Martin-in-the-Fields.** EMI 69569 + other Mozart selections (mid-price)
>
> **Civil, Marriner, Academy of St. Martin-in-the-Fields.** Philips Silver Line 420709 [ADD] + Rondo, K.371 (mid-price)
>
> **Baumann, Harnoncourt, Vienna Concentus Musicus.** Teldec Das Alte Werk 42757

Concerti for Piano and Orchestra (27)

Mozart was the first great composer to prefer the piano over the harpsichord, and his enthusiasm shows. These represent the largest body of great concerted piano music by any composer, and Mozart's highest overall achievement in instrumental music.

The first eight have their youthful charms, but it is with No. 9, written when Mozart was twenty-one, that he hits his stride. It is perhaps a bit unusual that the most famous of the set is No. 20, rather than the seven which come after it.

Regardless of individual merits, all the piano concerti are significant and one might well wish to opt for a complete boxed set. If so, the top choice is Murray Perahia, notwithstanding Alfred Brendel's and Mitsuko Uchida's considerable achievements on other labels.

As for individual concerti, I have tried to condense the hundreds of available recordings to a dozen representative famous ones, listed in ascending numerical order by the first concerto on the disc so as to give some variety of couplings.

Complete sets:

Perahia (pianist and conductor), English Chamber Orchestra. Sony 46441 (12) [ADD, DDD] (mid-price)

Brendel, Marriner, Academy of St. Martin-in-the-Fields. Complete Mozart Edition, Vol. 7, Philips 422507 (12) [ADD] (mid-price)

Uchida, Tate, English Chamber Orchestra. Philips 438207 (9) [DDD] (discounted)

Single discs:

Perahia, English Chamber Orchestra. Nos. 9, 21, Sony 34562 [ADD]

Brendel, Marriner, Academy of St. Martin-in-the-Fields. Nos. 15, 21, Philips 400018 [DDD]

R. Serkin, Szell, Cleveland Orchestra. Nos. 19, 20, CBS 37236 [ADD] (mid-price)

De Larrocha, Segal, Vienna Symphony Orchestra. Nos. 19, 22, London 410140 [DDD]

Perahia, English Chamber Orchestra. Nos. 19, 23, CBS 39064 [DDD]

Bilson (fortepiano), **Gardiner, English Baroque Soloists.** Nos., 20, 21, DG Archiv 419609 [DDD]

Brendel, Marriner, Academy of St. Martin-in-the-Fields. Nos. 20, 24, Philips Concert Classics 420867 [ADD] + additional pieces (mid-price)

Kempff, Klee, Bavarian Radio Symphony Orchestra. Nos. 21, 22, DG Musikfest 415920 (budget)

Casadesus, Szell, Cleveland Orchestra. Nos. 21, 24, CBS 38523 [AAD] (mid-price)
Moravec, Vlach, Czech Philharmonic Orchestra. Nos. 23, 25, Supraphon 11-0271 [AAD]
Ashkenazy (pianist and conductor), Philharmonia Orchestra. Nos. 25, 26, London 411810 [DDD]
Uchida, Tate, English Chamber Orchestra. Nos. 26, 27, Philips 420951 [DDD]

Concerto No. 5 in A for Violin, K.219

Mozart wrote just five violin concerti, all as a youth of nineteen. The last three are much the best, and the fifth is the most popular for its final movement in "Turkish" style.

Itzhak Perlman and Cho-Liang Lin both have outstanding digital recordings of this concerto paired with No. 3. An older budget disc has even more music (Concerti Nos. 1, 3, and 5) played by the great Yehudi Menuhin.

Perlman, Levine, Vienna Philharmonic Orchestra. DG 410020 [DDD] + Violin Concerto No. 3
Lin, Leppard, English Chamber Orchestra. CBS 42364 [DDD] + Violin Concerto No. 3
Menuhin (violinist and conductor), **Bath Festival Orchestra.** EMI Encore 67779 + Violin Concerti 1, 3 (budget)

Don Giovanni, K.527

This is the greatest opera ever written. At least that is the opinion of a large number of critics and just plain opera lovers. It may not be the most popular, or the most historically significant, but there is something about it that makes it seem somehow, well, greater. Maybe it is the ambiguous tone, neither really comic nor tragic, combined with the wonderful melodies, and the excellent text by the greatest of all opera librettists, Lorenzo da Ponte.

One evening long ago, little Charles Gounod, the composer-to-be of another great opera, *Faust,* was taken by his mother to the Paris Opera to see *Don Giovanni.* When the solemn trombones intoned the theme of the Commendatore in the overture, the wide-eyed lad scrunched down in his seat. "Mama," he whispered, "this is real music!" That is all you need to know. No musicology, no terminology.

Carlo Maria Giulini set the standard for great recordings in the early 1960s, and his remains first choice for most listeners. Not far behind—and even ahead in the dramatic final scene—is a true stereo 1955 performance led by Josef Krips, a fine conductor little remembered by today's audiences, most attractive at mid-price. Among digital recordings, Nikolaus Harnoncourt conducts a vivid period instrument version, and Sir Neville Marriner wins by a modest margin in the modern instrument category.

Giulini, Philharmonia Orchestra and Chorus. Angel 47260 (3) [ADD]
Krips, Vienna Philharmonic Orchestra and State Opera Chorus. London 411626 (3) [ADD] (mid-price)
Harnoncourt, Concertgebouw Orchestra. Teldec 44184 (3) [DDD]
Marriner, Academy of St. Martin-in-the-Fields, Ambrosian Opera Chorus. Philips 432129 (3) [DDD]

Exsultate, Jubilate, K.165

This short motet (under fifteen minutes) might serve as an introduction to Mozart's sacred choral music, which includes other motets (e.g. the lovely *Ave, Verum Corpus*, K.618); two settings of the vespers, or evening, service; four litanies; eighteen masses, of which the best known are those nicknamed "Credo," "Coronation," and "The Great" and the famous *Requiem*, listed separately below. The *Exsultate, Jubilate* is, as you might guess even if you have no Latin, a joyful effusion, and concludes with a coloratura "Alleluia" which has long been the joy of sopranos.

The standard recorded favorite for some time has been that featuring soprano Kiri Te Kanawa, with Colin Davis conducting. A newer version, highly praised, offers soprano Emma Kirkby, with Christopher Hogwood conducting—but be aware that this is a slightly different edition of the score.

Te Kanawa, C. Davis, London Symphony Orchestra and Chorus. Philips 412873 [ADD] + other short choral works
Kirkby, Hogwood, Academy of Ancient Music, Westminster Cathedral Boys' Choir. L'Oiseau-Lyre 411832 [DDD] + other short choral works

The Magic Flute (Die Zauberflöte), K.620

"Magic" is indeed the word to describe this funny, joyful, moving, fantastic opera from the end of Mozart's life, a children's adventure on one level and an adult allegory on another. This is the opera to try on opera-haters; if they don't catch on, they are hopeless. From the glorious overture to the final chorus, there is hardly a page of this score that does not enchant the ear and the imagination.

Sadly, there has never been a recording that has won universal admiration. The definitive *Magic Flute* is yet to come; but maybe that is part of the magic. For now, all of the following stand high in the recording roster, with the early 1960s Klemperer a standout for great cast, radiant orchestral playing, and reasonable price.

Klemperer, Philharmonia Orchestra and Chorus. Angel Studio 69971 (2) [ADD] (mid-price)

Marriner, Academy of St. Martin-in-the-Fields, Ambrosian Opera Chorus. Philips 426276 (2) [DDD]

Haitink, Bavarian Radio Symphony Orchestra and Chorus. Angel 47951 (3) [DDD]

Solti, Vienna Philharmonic Orchestra and State Opera Chorus. London 433210 (2) [DDD]

The Marriage of Figaro (Le Nozze di Figaro), K.492

This is Mozart's greatest comedy, and one of the masterpieces of all comic opera. The unsophisticated listener is swept along by the delightful story and the endless profusion of beautiful melodies, while the more experienced hand is amazed by the complexity and unerring skill of the architecture and orchestration, and the perfectly balanced blend of farce and warm humanity. It is a work that demands both affection and reverence.

Carlo Maria Giulini's recording from the early 1960s is such a classic that it still commands top spot in our listings; the cast is exceptional, and the conducting seems genuinely inspired. Sir Georg Solti's "early digital" (1981) version is a common first choice in modern sound, along with John Eliot Gardiner's period instrument performance.

Giulini, Philharmonia Orchestra and Chorus. Angel Studio 63266 (2) [ADD] (mid-price)

Solti, London Philharmonic Orchestra. London 410150 (3) [DDD] (mid-price)

Gardiner, Monteverdi Choir, English Baroque Soloists. DG Archiv 439871 (3) [DDD]

Overtures

Mozart was one of the very greatest opera composers, and even if you are not an opera fan you will still enjoy the brilliant, tuneful overtures to his vocal works. Even some of the obscure operas have preludes equal to those from the more famous ones.

Sir Neville Marriner's digital anthology is a standard, with Bruno Walter revered at mid-price. A recent entry is from the budget Naxos label, with eighteen overtures digitally recorded by little-known but excellent artists.

Marriner, Academy of St. Martin-in-the-Fields. Angel 47014 [DDD]
B. Walter, Columbia Symphony Orchestra. CBS 37774 + *Eine Kleine Nachtmusik, Masonic Funeral Music* (mid-price)
Wordsworth, Capella Istropolitana. Naxos 8.550185 [DDD] (budget)

Quartets Nos. 14-19, "Haydn Quartets"

Mozart wrote twenty-three string quartets in all, but this integrated set of six probably represents the summit of his writing in the chamber music category. It was inspired by the quartets of his teacher and friend, Franz Joseph Haydn, but goes beyond anything the older master composed, a fact which Haydn ackowledged with respect and affection. In turn, Mozart dedicated the set to Haydn in a famous letter.

The complete Mozart quartets have been recorded with poetic imagination by the Quartetto Italiano, but are not currently available; you might watch for reissues. Meanwhile, the Chilingirian Quartet has produced a fine set of the six "Haydn" Quartets. No. 17 "Hunt" and No. 19 "Dissonant" are the two best-known Mozart quartets, and they are available on a single disc from both the Melos and the Alban Berg Quartets.

Chilingirian Quartet. "Haydn" Quartets (6), CRD 3362, 3363, 3364 [DDD]
Melos Quartet. Nos. 17, 19, DG 429818 [ADD] (mid-price)
Alban Berg Quartet. Nos. 17, 19, Teldec 43055

Quintet in A for Clarinet and Strings, K.581

Like the Clarinet Concerto (see above), this smaller-scaled work was written for Mozart's friend Anton Stadler. The composer's love for the clarinet—his favorite wind instrument—is obvious here in the warm, expressive writing.

Daniel Shifrin is superb in first-rate digital sound and offers the best possible coupling in Mozart's Clarinet Concerto. The same coupling pertains to Jack Brymer's classic account, now at mid-price. Also a bargain is Harold Wright's Marlboro Festival perfor-mance from the 1960s, paired with a fine reading of Schubert's Trout Quintet.

Shifrin, Chamber Music Northwest. Delos 3020 [DDD] + Clarinet Concerto
Brymer, Allegri String Quartet. Philips Silver Line 420710 [ADD] + Clarinet Concerto (mid-price)
Wright, Marlboro Ensemble. Sony 46252 [ADD] + Schubert: Trout Quintet (mid-price)

Requiem, K.626

The well-known story of how this work came to be written is told above in the biography of Mozart. Since he died before its completion, his wife authorized one of his students, Franz Süssmayr, to finish it using Mozart's sketches. This version has prevailed until recent years, when some scholars began trying to reconstruct Mozart's intentions. I regret to report that so far no PhD professors have managed to fool me into thinking they were Mozart (and by the way, Bach and Beethoven didn't go to college either).

Cheap recordings of such a masterpiece do it a disservice. Go full-price digital on this one: John Eliot Gardiner for period instruments, Peter Schreier for modern.

Gardiner, English Baroque Soloists. Philips 420197 [DDD] + Kyrie in D Minor, K.341
Schreier, Dresden State Orchestra. Philips 411420 [DDD]

Serenade in G, K.525, "Eine Kleine Nachtmusik"

Mozart wrote a dozen or more serenades on commission from various nobles as a kind of background music for elegant soirées. Most of them have five movements. It would seem one movement is missing from the most famous of them, the "Little Night Music." Nevertheless, what is left is the most enchanting of all Mozart's lighter orchestral works, which include also the Divertimenti and Cassations, along with assorted marches and country dances.

In a very crowded field, Sir Charles Mackerras shines in digital with a coupling of one of Mozart's other best serenades, No. 9 "Posthorn." If you prefer a pairing with No. 6 "Notturno," as well as period instruments, Christopher Hogwood awaits you. Bruno Walter is unbeatable at mid-price, offering also four Mozart overtures and the Masonic Funeral Music. A perfectly good—if not out of the ordinary—version by Richard Stamp is greatly enhanced by its outstanding couplings of a great *Peter and the Wolf* with Sir John Gielgud narrating, and *Carnival of the Animals*, and brilliant digital sound.

Mackerras, Prague Chamber Orchestra. Telarc 80108 [DDD] + Serenade No. 9 "Posthorn"
Hogwood, Academy of Ancient Music. L'Oiseau-Lyre 411720 [DDD] + Serenade No. 6 "Serenata Notturno"
B. Walter, Columbia Symphony Orchestra. CBS 37774 [ADD] + four overtures, Masonic Funeral Music (mid-price)
Stamp, Academy of London. Virgin Classics 59533 [DDD] + Prokofiev: *Peter and the Wolf*; Saint-Saens: *Carnival of the Animals*

Sinfonia Concertante in E-flat for Violin and Viola, K.364

This is the greater of two works bearing this description, which means "a symphony in the nature of a concerto." It is an eighteenth century form, giving two or more instrumentalists the chance to show off, which has pretty much become extinct nowadays. This Mozart work is considered by all critics the best such piece ever written.

There is a rather startling number of superb recordings of this work. Perlman/Zukerman and Lin/Laredo are neck-and-neck for full-price digital honors, making the tie even harder to break by having the same coupling, the Concertone, K.190. Brown/Suk are a real bargain at mid-price, in a digital performance about as good as the preceding, but coupled with Violin Concerti Nos. 2 and 4. Druian/Skernick at mid-price give one of the great Mozart performances on record, coupled with the Clarinet Concerto, but the 1963 sound is only fair. Another mid-price recording from England showcases less well-known artists, Brainin/Schidlof, and has the oddest coupling, Symphony No. 39, but it is quite good and luminously recorded.

Perlman/Zukerman, Mehta, Israel Philharmonic Orchestra. DG 415486 [DDD] + Concertone, K.190

Lin/Laredo, Leppard, English Chamber Orchestra. Sony 47693 [DDD] + Concertone, K.190

Brown/Suk, Academy of St. Martin-in-the-Fields. London Jubilee 433171 [DDD] + Violin Concerti Nos. 2, 4 (mid-price)

Druian/Skernick, Szell, Cleveland Orchestra. CBS 37810 [AAD] + Clarinet Concerto (mid-price)

Brainin/Schidlof, Gibson, Scottish National Orchestra. Chandos 6506 [DDD] + Symphony No. 39 (mid-price)

Sonata No. 11 in A for Piano, K.331

Mozart wrote seventeen sonatas for solo piano. They have not been as popular with audiences as Beethoven's sonatas, or indeed as Mozart's piano concerti. They are splendid works nonetheless, and if you are doubtful, start with this one, whose final infectious movement is often heard separately as the "Rondo alla Turca."

Mitsuko Uchida's digital single disc with this sonata and two other works makes a splendid introduction to her six-CD box of the complete sonatas, volume seventeen from the Complete Mozart Edition (Philips 422115). An excellent budget version by Walter Klien offers six additional Mozart piano pieces.

Uchida. Philips 412123 [DDD] + Sonata No. 12, Fantasia in D Minor, K.397

Klien. Vox/Turnabout 7194 [ADD] + Sonata No. 8, five other pieces (budget)

Symphonies (41)

Mozart wrote his first symphony at the age of eight, probably with at least a little help from his father. It is no masterpiece, but it is surprisingly effective, and some of its tunes linger on in the memory. Not bad for eight. Still, the next twenty-three symphonies exhibit more talent than genius. By No. 25 the sleeping giant is rousing himself, and Nos. 28 and 29 reach a high level of sophistication. However, the last six symphonies are what define Mozart's true maturity as a composer. In many ways they surpass Haydn's achievement, and they equal at least part of Beethoven's. They will always be on the short list of the greatest symphonies every written.

A footnote: there is no longer a Symphony No. 37 by Mozart! And actually, there never was. The former No. 37 in G, K.444, long attributed to Mozart, was eventually discovered to be in reality the Symphony No. 26 by Michael Haydn, younger brother of Franz Joseph. But by then, nobody wanted to re-number Mozart's greatest symphonies, and so things stand.

What Dorati did for Haydn, so Christopher Hogwood and Sir Neville Marriner did for Mozart. Hogwood recorded the complete symphonies and all variants on period instruments in seven volumes of two- and three-CD sets, with fascinating scholarly notes besides. This is probably not, however, the place to start your collection, but to end it.

Marriner's complete set is in two boxes of six CDs each, even less convenient to buy—but an easy recommendation is his two-CD mid-priced set of "The Last Five Symphonies."

Those plus one more fill another two-CD mid-priced set by Bruno Walter, including possibly the greatest recorded performance of No. 41 "Jupiter," but with fairly old sound. Similar in sonics, but offering even more of a sampling (eleven) of Mozart's greatest symphonies is the mid-priced four-CD Otto Klemperer box.

The remainder of the listings are representative famous single discs of the major symphonies.

Marriner, Academy of St. Martin-in-the-Fields. The Last Five Symphonies, Philips Duo 438332 (2) [ADD] (mid-price)

B. Walter, Columbia Symphony Orchestra. Nos. 35-36, 38-41, Sony 45676 (2) (mid-price)

Klemperer, Philharmonia Orchestra. Nos. 25, 29, 31, 33-36, 38-41, Angel 63272 (4) [ADD] (mid-price)

Mackerras, Prague Chamber Orchestra. Nos. 36, 38, Telarc 80148 [DDD]

Mackerras, Prague Chamber Orchestra. Nos. 25, 28, 29, Telarc 80165 [DDD]

Szell, Cleveland Orchestra. Nos. 35, 40, 41, Sony Essential Classics 46333 [ADD] (budget)

Szell, Cleveland Orchestra. Nos. 35, 39, CBS 38472 [ADD] (mid-price)

Bernstein, Vienna Philharmonic Orchestra. Nos. 40, 41, DG 431040 [DDD] (mid-price)

Gibson, Scottish National Orchestra. No. 39, Chandos 6506 [DDD] + Sinfonia Concertante, K.364 (mid-price)

A final word on Mozart recordings: the most monumental CD project yet is the Complete Mozart Edition from Philips, comprising virtually everything the composer ever wrote: over 220 hours of music on 180 digital discs in forty-five boxed sets. The list price is $2,336.

The Early Romantics
(ca. 1820-1850)

Individualism and emotional expression were not characteristics that suddenly appeared in the Romantic era—we have noted previously that they already had taken root in the Classical period of music history—but by about 1820, they had evolved from being important elements to becoming the dominant aspects of musical esthetics.

The Germans led the Romantic charge in literature as well as in music. Just as Beethoven's *Eroica* Symphony is generally taken as a marker for the beginning of musical Romanticism, Goethe's *The Sorrows of Young Werther* can be considered the cornerstone of Romantic fiction. The rest of the Western world fell into line in short order. Soon, each of the fine arts was feeding Romantic ideals and techniques to the others: Schopenhauer and Nietzsche in philosophy; Byron, Poe, and Lamartine in literature; Manet and Whistler in art. All of them succumbed to Romantic principles, then served as models and inspirations for each other.

The Romantic idea of personal expression was reinforced by an increasing nationalism and competition between cultures, which in turn were fostered by the Industrial Revolution, the rapid development of science and invention, and the bitter rivalries of wars, from those of Napoleon to the Franco-Prussian conflict of 1870. (This is, of course, a grossly simplified scenario, but it is not false.)

In music, an emphasis on subjectivity resulted in a cult of instrumental virtuosity, a warmer and more rhapsodic type of melody, a search for colorful and dramatic effects, an expansion of musical forms, and a frequent reliance on fanciful or even grotesque subject matter for programmatic works. These goals were achieved with the aid of several technical innovations, including an increase in the use of chromatic harmonies, a gradual obscuring of the rules of tonality and modulation, the virtual abandonment of counterpoint, and the introduction of entirely new musical instruments or mechanical improvements to the old ones.

The important composers of the early Romantic period, generally acknowledged as extending from about 1820 to about 1850, share a general feeling of fresh, youthful lightness and spontaneity. There is no mistaking the refreshing breeze that blows through Schumann's *Spring* Symphony, or the "fairy music" of Mendelssohn. The pulse of impetuous youth is irresistibly apparent in the primary colors of Rossini's surging crescendos, or the *Roman Carnival* and *Fantastic* Symphony of Berlioz. The easygoing Romanticism of this early period could sometimes devolve into mere parlor sweetness or bourgeois sentimentality; we can sense things veering perilously in this direction occasionally in the music of Chopin and Schubert, though their superior genius almost always saves them from the crudities of their lesser contemporaries.

Perhaps another way of defining the "early Romantics" is to specify what they were not. They were not the cool, objective formalists of the Classical period, nor were they the fierce nationalists or ponderous philosophizers of the later nineteenth century. Their forms were loose: analysts often refer politely to Schubert's as "discursive," and those of Berlioz usually defy definition altogether. Their melodies floated in the airy realms of *Scenes from Childhood,* or an *Invitation to the Dance.* Their themes were as evanescent as a scherzo of Queen Mab, a trout tumbling down a country brook, or an enchanting dream of a mid-summer night.

Vincenzo Bellini (1801-1835)

Bellini was the flashing meteor among Italian opera composers. Showing talent at an early age, he was successful with a lyrical stage work while still a student at the Naples Conservatory. Shortly after, his second opera was hailed by his generous older contemporary, Gaetano Donizetti, with "our Bellini—bella! bella! bella!"

And "Bellini" ("little beautiful one") he was, in both his exquisite long-breathed melodies (the joy and inspiration of Chopin), and in his angelic countenance (the joy and inspiration of numerous women). He never married, preferring liaisons such as the one he had with a Milanese woman who had a rich and accommodating husband. Bellini expressed his thanks to her for "protecting me from marriage."

Bellini never became much of an orchestrator, but he was no facile tune-spinner either. His melodies had integrity as well as beauty. Bellini shunned the pyrotechnics of Rossini, and was the first opera composer to insist that his works actually be performed as written. This dismayed many a singer of this day, but set the standard for his later compatriot, Giuseppe Verdi.

After his initial successes in Italy, Bellini found himself the toast first of London, and then of Paris, where he became the intimate of Chopin, Rossini, and other luminaries—including, much to his detriment, the poet Heinrich Heine. Bellini, not only angelic but positively childlike, was much attracted by magic and superstition. Heine, who once described Bellini as "a sigh in ballroom slippers," loved to tease him. One evening at a seance at the home of the Princess Belgioioso, the poet said that since Bellini was a genius, he should expect to die young, like Mozart. A few days later, at the tender age of thirty-four, he succumbed to a stomach infection.

Norma

The supreme masterpiece among Bellini's ten operas contains the aria "Casta Diva," a moonlit invocation of a Druid priestess, and one of the sublimely beautiful creations for the human voice.

The most famous singer to record the opera complete was soprano Maria Callas. A recent record catalog showed no fewer than six complete recordings starring "La Divina," all with different supporting casts. Of these, four are "pirates," and two are (legal) commercial releases. Of the latter two, the earlier (with Stignani, Filippeschi, Rossi-Lemeni, and Serafin conducting) is to be preferred as displaying the diva in her best voice. Be careful— four of the six recordings are conducted by Serafin, and some of the listed singers show up on the other recordings; but only our recommended version will have the exact combination of soloists listed here.

Serafin, La Scala Orchestra and Chorus, Callas, Stignani, Filippeschi, Rossi-Lemeni. Angel 47303 (3) (mono)

Hector Berlioz (1803-1869)

With his tousled hair and avant-garde ideas, Berlioz was the wild man of the early Romantics. His father, a cultured country doctor, instilled in him a love of the classics, especially Virgil. He failed, however, to convince Hector to become a physician like himself. Cut off from parental support, young Berlioz lived the bohemian life for several years.

In 1827 he attended his first performance of Shakespeare. Although he knew virtually no English, he fell passionately in love with both Hamlet and Harriet Smithson, the actress who played Ophelia. He pursued her for several years, idolized her in his programmatic *Symphonie fantastique,* and in 1833 actually married her. Reality, alas, did not measure up to the Romantic ideal; after a while, they drifted apart.

More than any composer up to his time, he was interested in creating a synthesis of music and literature. He looked to Shakespeare (*Romeo and Juliet*), Byron (*Harold in Italy*), Goethe (*The Damnation of Faust*), Scott (*Rob Roy, Waverley*), and even the American James Fenimore Cooper (*Le corsaire*), for his subjects. His early exposure to Virgil led to what many consider his masterpiece, the gigantic epic opera *The Trojans.*

He became a master of orchestration, enlarging the orchestra to unheard-of dimensions in order to depict his vast conceptions. He paid little attention to the conventional rules of form. His structures were dictated by the literary or poetic exigencies of his imagination instead of rules from some handbook of composition. He ended up writing his own text on orchestration, and the first theoretical work on the art of conducting.

He was better known as a conductor, in fact, than he was as a composer. In his day, his music was considered "ear-splitting." And most of his income was actually derived from his journalistic career, as a critic writing about the music of other composers. In later years he had some success abroad, but at home in France he was always considered something of an amusing eccentric. He became progressively more embittered and spent his last years obsessed with thoughts of death.

Berlioz was to become for many later composers, especially Wagner, the archetype of the Romantic in music. His stubborn commitment to his artistic ideals and his passionate self-absorption inspired even those who did not agree with him on every detail. Critical opinion varied widely on the intrinsic worth of his music, and the argument is by no means settled today. Until the conductor Colin Davis began championing his works in the 1960s, I believe a majority of musicologists still wrote Berlioz off as a composer who was historically important but whose music one needed not actually hear.

Berlioz assuredly had his weaknesses. Among all the great composers, he seemed to have the most trouble coming up with memorable melodies, and those that work often seem too short, or after a promising beginning trail off into the ether. His stentorian gestures sometimes degenerate into bombast. Listeners who love to follow musical logic had better leave him alone; the great critic Tovey, while acknowledging his genius, once irritably complained that he simply did not have time to follow "the butterfly vagaries" of Berlioz's mind.

In the last generation or so, however, there has been a considerable explosion of interest in this music. Perhaps it is no accident that the works of an iconoclastic, free-thinking, opium-smoking, bohemian radical caught on in the 1960s; but don't expect to hear rock 'n' roll! What we can wallow in today is the colorful—almost cinematic—unfolding of musical images so vivid that they seem to tell a story without the aid of words. Berlioz was indeed the creator of program music as we think of it, and his best works are brilliant records of a fevered and fertile imagination.

The Damnation of Faust, Op. 24 (selections)

This "dramatic legend," sometimes performed as an opera, is really a loosely connected series of scenes from the Faust story, some with vocal parts, some without. Three purely orchestral selections are often heard separately at concerts.

The complete score was recorded superbly by the herald of the Berlioz revival, Sir Colin Davis. A more recent digital recording was made by Sir Georg Solti. But for the new student of Berlioz I would recommend a single digital disc containing the famous highlights of this work (*Minuet of the Will-o'-the-Wisps, Dance of the Sylphs,* and the exciting *Rákoczy March*), along with basic selections from other famous Berlioz works, conducted by David Zinman.

Zinman, Baltimore Symphony Orchestra. Telarc 80164 [DDD] + selections from *Roméo et Juliette* and *Les Troyens,* two overtures, *Hymne des Marseillais*

Harold in Italy, for Viola and Orchestra, Op. 16

The great violin virtuoso Paganini asked Berlioz to write him a concerto to show off his new instrument, a Stradivarius viola. Not surprisingly, Berlioz found himself unable to write a conventional, three-movement concerto. Instead he created a four-movement symphony with pictorial associations based on a drama by Byron, and featuring the viola as a rather reticent commentator. Also not surprisingly, the flashy Paganini begged off playing the piece, complaining that the viola part had "too many rests." It has become far more popular nowadays, being considered one of the composer's more lyrically poetic tone-pictures.

Berlioz expert Sir Colin Davis conducted this work twice on records: the older version was with Yehudi Menuhin playing the viola, the newer with Nobuko Imai; both are outstanding, but only the latter is currently available. Pinchas Zukerman solos under the baton of Charles Dutoit on a beautifully recorded digital version.

Imai, C. Davis, London Symphony Orchestra. Philips 416431 [ADD] + *Tristia,* Prelude to Act II of *Les Troyens*
Zukerman, Dutoit, Montreal Symphony Orchestra. London 421193 [DDD]

Roméo et Juliette, Op. 17

Another Berlioz hybrid form, this "dramatic symphony" is neither a symphony nor an opera, but a series of twelve numbers grouped in three sections, depicting episodes in Shakespeare's play. The composer himself considered the love music in Part II to be his greatest inspiration; also famous are the diaphanous "Queen Mab Scherzo," and the final scene in the tomb.

A good introduction to the highlights is provided by the Zinman disc already recommended under *The Damnation of Faust,* above.

Zinman, Baltimore Symphony Orchestra. Telarc 80164 [DDD] + selections from *The Damnation of Faust* and *Les Troyens,* two overtures, *Hymne des Marseillais*

Symphonie fantastique, Op. 14

By far the best known work of Berlioz, the "Fantastic Symphony" was inspired by his passion for Harriet Smithson (see biography). Naturally, being by Berlioz, it departs somewhat from convention. It has five movements instead of four, and each bears a programmatic title: "Visions and Passions," "The Ball," "Scenes in the Country," "March to the Gallows," and "Dream of a Witches' Sabbath." The work's pictorial associations had a profound influence on Franz Liszt, and later Richard Strauss, both of whom carried forward the development of the "tone poem." The striking and innovative orchestration was also influential; and Wagner's use of the Leitmotif can be traced, at least in part, to the introduction here of a recurrent theme—the *idée fixe*—as a unifying device.

As one of the most brilliant orchestral "showpieces," the *Symphonie fantastique* has enjoyed numerous fine recordings. Certainly the three versions led by Sir Colin Davis take pride of place as irreplaceable legacies of the most honored Berlioz interpreter, with the second (1974) being the accepted standard. But the truly magical 1957 reading by Sir

Thomas Beecham, though monophonic, still gives pleasure, while Charles Dutoit has perhaps the finest digital version. Roger Norrington is also digital, but employs period instruments; if you are interested in the fine points of historicity, this is a fascinating performance.

C. Davis, Concergebouw Orchestra. Philips 411425 [ADD]

Beecham, French National Radio Orchestra. EMI 64032 (mono) + *Le Corsaire* Overture, *Royal Hunt* and *Storm* from *Les Troyens* (mid-price)

Dutoit, Montreal Symphony Orchestra. London 414203 [DDD]

Norrington, London Classical Players. Angel 49541 [DDD]

Frédéric Chopin (1810-1849)

For a century and a half, Chopin has been generally accepted by both critics and people (there is a distinction) as the greatest composer of music for the piano. Despite his fame and familiarity, however, there is scarcely another composer whose image has been more distorted by the media, then and now.

Chopin's father was a Frenchman who emigrated to Poland, married a Polish woman, and became an ardent Polish patriot. He had lived in his adopted land more than twenty years by the time Fryderyk—to give his un-Frenchified name—was born. The child swiftly developed as a piano prodigy and in short order was performing before the rich and the royal.

Poland was under one of its many foreign dominations at the time, and the expanding ranks of nationalists and revolutionaries turned to the young pianist as one of their symbols of hope for independence. He was not to disappoint them, even though he moved more or less permanently to Paris at age twenty-one in search of wider recognition and greater fortune. He stayed in close touch with Polish expatriates in Paris, and generously supported Polish artists and musicians.

This he could well afford, since he was one of the earliest composers to get rich through his music. The Parisian nobility fawned over him as giddily as had the Polish—especially aristrocratic ladies, who found the gaunt, dreamy-eyed Chopin the paragon of Romantic idealism. He, in turn, charged them enormous fees for private lessons.

Despite the availability of countless countesses, Chopin chose for his one passionate love an older woman who dressed like a man, smoked cigars, and professed socialism. Aurore Dudevant—known to literature and posterity as George Sand—was a novelist of dumpy figure and limber mind. In addition to a husband, she was known to have several lovers besides Chopin, including Prosper Merimée (who wrote the novelette *Carmen*), the poet Alfred de Musset (whose texts several French composers set to music), and probably Franz Liszt. Not surprisingly, one of the principal themes of her novels was a disdain for the institution of marriage.

The peculiar affair lasted for nine years, until constant bickering, much of it involving wrangles with "George's" two adult children, drove them apart. Meanwhile, Chopin had ruined his always delicate health; what was intended for a romantic idyll on Majorca in the winter of 1838-39 turned into a miserable ordeal of damp weather that dangerously weakened his lungs. He was not yet forty when he died of tuberculosis. He was buried in France, but accompanying his body was a silver urn containing Polish soil which Chopin had brought with him from his native land two decades before.

The incidents of his life have proved irresistible to novelists and filmmakers of sentimental tendencies. Through them much of the public has received an image of the dainty, swooning pianist of the glittering salon, succumbing to the Freudian lure of an androgynous woman, and paying for his neurotic obsession by dying a tragic early death, clutching a couple of crumpled polonaises in one withered hand. This is an exaggerated picture. His body was indeed frail, and his pianism delicately refined, but he had a hard business head, as his publishers learned to their dismay. He may have seemed effeminate, but he had no homosexual liaisons, and before taking up with the mannish but man-eating George Sand he had had several physical relations with attractive young women. And though he was sincerely patriotic, he did not hesitate to take up residence in Paris for half of his life in order to live in luxury.

But the most significant distortion that needs correcting is that Chopin's music is insubstantial. A few decades ago it was fashionable on Tin Pan Alley to arrange Chopin's most striking melodies into syrupy popular songs or backgrounds for tearjerker movies. True, Chopin wrote dozens of suave melodies, strongly influenced by early Italian opera, which he loved. But he also loved Bach, and underpinning these gorgeous tunes there is a solid and sophisticated harmonic and rhythmic structure that almost never fails to save them from triviality. The "pop" versions, stripped of the composer's rich textures, give a falsely cloying impression of the music. But even in Chopin's day, many did not see beneath the deceptive prettiness of his work's surface. It took another great composer, Robert Schumann, to characterize it perfectly: "Cannon—buried in flowers."

Concerto No. 1 in E Minor for Piano, Op. 11
Concerto No. 2 in F Minor for Piano, Op. 21

As a genius in smaller forms, Chopin struggled with these larger structures and soon abandoned the effort. They are not very well orchestrated, but they have survived because the solo piano parts are so attractive. The Concerto "No. 2" is actually the earlier, more compact, and fresher of the pair.

Both concertos can be had on one recording by Chopin's most famous twentieth-century interpreter, Artur Rubinstein, who recorded them multiple times. Most critics prefer the third (1961) version with Skrowaczewski conducting No. 1, and Wallenstein No. 2. In newer analog sound, Krystian Zimerman is highly regarded, and Murray Perahia is the standard for these couplings in digital.

Rubinstein, Skrowaczewski (in No. 1), **Wallenstein** (in No. 2), **New Symphony Orchestra of London.** RCA 5612 [ADD]

Zimerman, Giulini, Los Angeles Philharmonic Orchestra. DG 415970 [ADD]
Perahia, Mehta, Israel Philharmonic Orchestra. Sony 44922 [DDD]

Piano Anthologies

Rubinstein's classic recordings of the solo pieces have been reissued on CD in various assortments of favorite pieces, titled "The Chopin I Love," "The World's Favorite Chopin," and "Selections from the Chopin Collection." In newer sound, Vladimir Ashkenazy has recorded the complete works of Chopin, and then has compiled over a dozen greatest hits for his "Favorite Chopin" CD. Happily, both recordings are reasonably priced.

Rubinstein. "Selections from the Chopin Collection," RCA 7725 [ADD] (mid-price)
Ashkenazy. London Jubilee 417798 [DDD] (mid-price)

Sonata No. 2 in B-flat Minor for Piano, Op. 35

Best known of the three sonatas, No. 2 displays the greatest unity: its theme is Death, highlighted by the famous Funeral March in the third movement. No other piece of music has become so identified with the Grim Reaper; Chopin is reported to have composed it while dressed in a shroud and clutching a real skeleton in one arm.

Artur Rubinstein is again the classic for a recording, with Vladimir Ashkenazy offering the same coupling in better sound.

Rubinstein. RCA 5616 [ADD] + Sonata No. 3, Fantaisie in F Minor, Op. 49
Ashkenazy. London 417475 [ADD] + Sonata No. 3, Fantaisie in F Minor, Op. 49

Gaetano Donizetti (1797-1848)

Donizetti was born in Bergamo, Italy, of humble parentage, in a cellar apartment where "no ray of light," as he later wrote, "ever penetrated." The best job his father ever had was janitor in a pawnshop. Little Gaetano showed musical talent at an early age, enrolling in the local music school at nine. When he was only thirteen his music teacher wrote a miniature opera for his students and cast Gaetano in the title role of "The Little Composer." One of his prophetic lines was: "I have a vast mind, swift talent, ready fantasy—and I'm a thunderbolt at composing."

In a career spanning only thirty years Donizetti wrote some seventy operas, sometimes as many as four in a single year. Unlike most Italian opera composers he wrote hundreds of other works as well, including sixteen symphonies, nineteen string quartets, twenty-eight cantatas, and three oratorios. Such prodigality was accompanied, unfortunately, by considerable unevenness of quality, and it undermined his health.

As early as 1829 he was showing symptoms of the syphilis that was to kill him almost twenty years later, after spending his last year and a half in excruciating suffering in a madhouse. "While his melodies," wrote Heinrich Heine, "ravish the world with their happy accents and are sung and trilled everywhere, he himself sits, a frightening image of insanity, in a sanatorium not far from Paris...he recognizes no one. Such is the fortune of poor mankind."

He wrote his first opera at the age of nineteen, but was twenty-five before he had a significant success—with what was already his ninth stage work. He had to wait for Rossini's retirement before being crowned king of Italian opera with *Anna Bolena* in 1830. (A dubious but wonderful story has someone asking Donizetti if he believed the reports that Rossini wrote *The Barber of Seville* in only thirteen days, with the younger composer snapping back: "Why not? He's so lazy!") One triumph then followed another, peaking with *Lucia di Lammermoor* in 1835. He was named director of the prestigious Naples Conservatory in 1837, but after a short tenure became disgusted with various irritations and moved to France, where he composed some of his best works, including *La Fille du Régiment* and a comic opera, *Don Pasquale*, which is perhaps surpassed only by Rossini's *Barber of Seville*.

Lucia di Lammermoor

"Bel canto," literally "beautiful singing," was a specific style of Italian opera that flourished in the early nineteenth century. As one might readily deduce, its focus was not on logical plots or philosophical profundity, but on providing opportunities for vocal display. *Lucia* is easily the most representative of bel canto operas, with its florid mad scene and its stupendous sextet. It became a cultural icon in its own time; Tolstoy in *Anna Karenina* and Flaubert in *Madame Bovary* both used it almost as a character, as a symbol of the Romantic sensibility.

I have been an opera fan for more than forty years, and I must say that if there is any recording more exciting than the Sextet from *Lucia* as sung by Maria Callas, Giuseppe di Stefano, Rolando Panerai, and three other singers, then I have missed it. A recent catalog lists *nine* complete recordings of *Lucia* with Maria Callas on various labels with suspiciously similar-looking casts. These are indeed each slightly different "takes" from around the same period, but be careful to buy only the exact performance listed below, Angel 63631, from 1955, conducted by Herbert von Karajan.

For years this was a bestseller as an illegal pirate recording, until Angel got smart and decided to keep the money for themselves. If it's too exciting for your blood pressure, and you want another great performance in newer sound, try one of Joan Sutherland's two recordings: she is in better voice in 1959, but has a better supporting cast, including Luciano Pavarotti, and of course better sound, in 1971.

Karajan, RIAS Symphony Orchestra, Callas, etc. Angel 63631 (2) [ADD]
(mid-price)
Pritchard, Santa Cecilia Academy Orchestra, Sutherland, Cioni, etc.
London 411622 (2) [ADD] (mid-price)
Bonynge, Royal Opera House Orchestra, Sutherland, Pavarotti, etc.
London 410193 (3) [ADD] (mid-price)

Mikhail Glinka (1804-1857)

Glinka is the acknowledged founder of the nationalist school of Russian composition, although his historical position is perhaps more significant than the works themselves. Not one of music history's more prepossessing characters, Glinka was a spoiled rich kid and a mama's boy. Though admittedly of a delicate constitution, he exaggerated his health problems as an excuse to take vacations in Spain. His requirements in women were that they be extremely young and extremely stupid. Eventually he married one of these bimbos, then proceeded to be constantly unfaithful to her. She, in turn, despised music, and complained that he spent too much money on staff paper.

Glinka came along at a time when musical culture in Russia was barely discernible. He was largely self-taught, and his influences came more from Bellini and Donizetti than from Beethoven or Mozart. And yet, years later, Tchaikovsky dared to equate Glinka with Mozart, whom he worshipped above all other composers.

Few of Glinka's works are regularly heard today except in Russia. They sound pleasant enough, but there is certainly nothing greatly remarkable, let alone revolutionary, about them. Glinka's good fortune was to decide, in the mid-1830s, to write a Russian opera starring the peasants instead of the nobility, spiced with beloved native folk songs. In a country that did not even have a music conservatory until 1850, *A Life for the Tsar* (later renamed *Ivan Susanin* by the Bolsheviks) seemed like a burst of creative genius. He gave Russian composers a hero to look up to, and a new respect in greater Europe. Glinka's influence is obvious in the masterpieces of Tchaikovsky, Rimsky-Korsakov, and Mussorgsky, all of whom surpassed him in quality, but might never have existed without him.

Russlan and Ludmila: Overture

This was the first truly Russian opera. Although the whole work is seldom heard outside Russia, the whirling, stamping overture remains Glinka's top hit.

Any number of fine conductors include the overture on recordings of light music, but Sir Georg Solti's has a reputation as the most exciting. For the closest digital equivalent, try Leonard Slatkin's disc. Both have excellent couplings of other Russian Romantic "essentials."

Solti, London Symphony Orchestra. London Weekend Classics 417689 [ADD]+ Borodin: Overture and *Polovtsian Dances* from *Prince Igor;* Mussorgsky: *Night on Bald Mountain,* Prelude to *Khovanshchina* (budget)
Slatkin, St. Louis Symphony Orchestra. Telarc 80072 [DDD] + Borodin: *In the Steppes of Central Asia;* Rimsky-Korsakov: *Russian Easter* Overture; Tchaikovsky: *Marche Slave*

Felix Mendelssohn (1809-1847)

Unlike Glinka, Mendelssohn is one of the most attractive figures in the history of music. Handsome and hard-working, gentle and genteel, he impressed men at the chessboard and women on the dance floor. Born into a wealthy, cultured family, he wore his inheritance so lightly that it aroused little resentment. He had a touchingly close relationship with his sister Fanny, herself a talented musician and composer, and a happy marriage that produced five children (one of the latter-day descendants was George Mendelssohn, founder and president for many years of Vox Records).

After Mozart, with whom he has been favorably compared by Schumann and many others since, Mendelssohn was perhaps the most astonishing child prodigy of music, not so much because of his young age, but for the high quality of what he wrote. No teenager—perhaps not even Mozart—ever wrote pieces more melodically memorable, stylish and energetic, refined and finished than the Octet in E-flat, or the overture to *A Midsummer Night's Dream.* It is true that many of his later works seemed to decline in freshness and spontaneity, but the common impression that Mendelssohn "burned out" at an early age is exaggerated.

In his day, Mendelssohn was as important a scholar and conductor as he was a composer. Almost singlehandedly (and at the age of twenty!) he revived the long-neglected music of Bach by leading a performance of the *St. Matthew Passion* from a manuscript copy. He founded the Leipzig Conservatory of Music, and conducted its orchestra, which is still alive and prominent today. He raised the standards of orchestral playing in Europe and offered generous assistance to struggling young composers. Although extremely popular in his native Germany, he achieved even more success in England, which he visited numerous times as the favorite composer of Queen Victoria.

Unquestionably overrated in its time, Mendelssohn's music came in for compensatory contempt in the mid-twentieth century. Many treated it as facile, lightweight, and overly sentimental. Nowadays a better balance has been struck. Most critics and historians, while admitting that the music plumbs no great depths, rightly point out that it does not intend to do so, and that to despise its fresh lyricism, poise, and youthful poetry is to take a very cheap shot indeed.

Concerto in E Minor for Violin, Op. 64

This is probably the most popular of all violin concertos. A recent record catalog showed nearly fifty performances in print. The reason is obvious: it overflows with enchantingly beautiful melodies, never letting down for a moment, and while eschewing profundity, it manages to delight the novice and the connoisseur at once.

Cho-Liang Lin is the most often praised artist for recent digital recordings of this work, coupled with the Bruch Violin Concerto No. 1. Close runners-up are Kyung-Wha Chung and Takako Nishizaki (the latter on a budget label), paired with the Tchaikovsky Violin Concerto, which some purchasers will find more desirable. A "legendary" recording features Yehudi Menuhin with Wilhelm Furtwängler conducting, from the early 1950s, coupled with the Beethoven Violin Concerto; I only include such mono recordings when they are of very superior quality.

> **Lin, Tilson Thomas, Philharmonia Orchestra.** CBS 44902 [DDD] + Bruch: Violin Concerto No. 1
> **Chung, Dutoit, Montreal Symphony Orchestra.** London 410011 [DDD] + Tchaikovsky: Violin Concerto
> **Nishizaki, Jean, Slovak Philharmonic Orchestra.** Naxos 8.550153 [DDD] + Tchaikovsky: Violin Concerto (budget)
> **Menuhin, Furtwängler, Berlin Philharmonic Orchestra.** Angel 69799 [ADD] (mono) + Beethoven: Violin Concerto (mid-price)

A Midsummer Night's Dream: Incidental Music, Op. 21, 61

The magical overture was written when Mendelssohn was seventeen, a feat not equalled in quality even by Mozart. Many years later he was commissioned to write additional music illustrating Shakespeare's comedy and he produced thirteen more numbers, of which the best known are the *Nocturne*, the *Scherzo*, and the famous *Wedding March*, which in an organ transcription has sent millions of newlyweds out the church door.

James Levine's highlights with the Chicago Symphony, aptly coupled with Schubert's incidental music for *Rosamunde*, made an ideal starter record in digital, but it has frustratingly disappeared from the catalog; watch for a possible reissue. That leaves three great recordings, all analogs but at mid-price, and a good if not great digital recording also at mid-price, and with very good couplings. Each disc contains highlights from the complete incidental music.

> **Szell, Cleveland Orchestra.** Sony Essential Classics 48264 [ADD] + Smetana: *The Moldau;* Bizet: Symphony in C (with Stokowski conducting National Philharmonic) (budget)

Szell, Cleveland Orchestra. CBS 37760 [ADD] + Symphony No. 4 (mid-price)

C. Davis, Boston Symphony Orchestra. Philips Silver Line 420653 [ADD] + Symphony No. 4 (mid-price)

Dutoit, Montreal Symphony Orchestra. London 430722 [DDD] + Symphony No. 4 (with Dohnanyi, Vienna Philharmonic), *Hebrides* Overture (mid-price)

Overtures

Aside from the wonderful overture to *A Midsummer Night's Dream*, Mendelssohn wrote several others, most famous of which is the lovely landscape painting called the *Hebrides*, or *Fingal's Cave*, Overture. It was inspired by a visit to the Scottish Highlands. Consciously or not, Richard Wagner seems to have adapted its opening theme as his *leitmotif* for the three Rhinemaidens in *The Ring of the Nibelung*.

Other Mendelssohn overtures include *Calm Sea and Prosperous Voyage, Ruy Blas, The Fair Melusina*, and *Athalia*. Claudio Abbado had a fine disc of most of these, which now seems to be in limbo. But a new young conductor, Claus Peter Flor, has come up with a similar program in even better sound.

Flor, Bamberg Symphony Orchestra. RCA 7905 [DDD]

Octet in E-flat Major for Strings, Op. 20

Mendelssohn was even younger (sixteen) when he wrote this miraculously beautiful and delicate chamber piece than when he composed the *Midsummer Night's Dream* Overture. But then, he had been writing chamber works since he was eleven, so he had plenty of practice. Most famous is the fleet Scherzo movement, the very distillation in tones of innocent youth.

The most frequently recommended recording is by the Academy of St. Martin-in-the-Fields Chamber Ensemble.

ASMF Chamber Ensemble. Philips 420400 + String Quintet No. 2

Symphony No. 4 in A Major, Op. 90 "Italian"

Only the last movement of the most popular of Mendelssohn's five symphonies offers anything identifiably "Italian," but we can say that the entire work is gloriously sunny. It is a bundle of happy memories of the composer's trip to Italy at age twenty-one when, already a famous composer, and rich and handsome to boot, he was mobbed by enamored ladies at the Roman Carnival, who pelted him with sugar candies. Sweet! And so is this delicious symphony.

Giuseppe Sinopoli conducts the best of the recent digital recordings, with a coupling of Schubert's Unfinished Symphony. Claudio Abbado and Christoph von Dohnányi both lead slightly older digital recordings with other basic Mendelssohn works as couplings. Two classic analog recordings, led by Sir Colin Davis and by George Szell, both including *A Midsummer Night's Dream* selections, are now available at mid-price.

Sinopoli, Philharmonia Orchestra. DG 410862 [DDD] + Schubert: Symphony No. 8

Abbado, London Symphony Orchestra. DG 427810 [DDD] + Symphony No. 3

Dohnányi, Vienna Philharmonic Orchestra. London 430722 [DDD] + *A Midsummer Night's Dream* sel. (with Dutoit, Montreal Symphony Orchestra), *Hebrides* Overture (mid-price)

C. Davis, Boston Symphony Orchestra. Philips Silver Line 420653 [ADD] + *A Midsummer Night's Dream* sel. (mid-price)

Szell, Cleveland Orchestra. CBS 37760 [ADD] + *A Midsummer Night's Dream* sel. (mid-price)

Niccolò Paganini (1782-1840)

Paganini is remembered principally as the all-time wizard of the violin. That's "wizard," not "genius." Before he was born, it is said, his mother had a dream that her son would become the world's greatest violinist. Papa Paganini took the prophecy seriously and drove the boy to practice day and night. By age eleven, Niccolò was a master virtuoso. By his mid-teens, he was wealthy, and he had already begun the endless round of gambling, drinking, and womanizing which was to mark his lifestyle to the end.

Paganini revolutionized violin-playing. He added one astounding new technique after another, until his performances were so amazing that many believed the rumor that he had signed over his soul to the Devil. This, of course, only made the audiences larger and more fanatical. The artist, capitalizing on his cadaverous frame and sunken cheeks, did nothing to discourage the idea.

The bulk of his compositions were for the violin (although he also wrote for the viola and guitar), and were designed for his personal use. Many of them he carried only in his head so that no other violinist could try to outdo him, and they are now lost to us. Of his six surviving violin concerti, the manuscripts of four came to light only in recent years. Also noteworthy is the set of twenty-four *Caprices,* one of which has held a curious fascination for a number of later composers; Rachmaninoff, for instance, used it as the basis for his great *Rhapsody on a Theme of Paganini.*

In the hands of a master violinist, Paganini's works provide hours of kinetic thrills. Lightning bolts flash, sparks fly, hearts leap into throats; this was how people entertained themselves before the roller coaster was invented. Of course, there is not a single bar of his music which touches the soul. Perhaps Paganini *was* in league with the Devil, after all.

Concerto No. 1 in D Major for Violin, Op. 6

Paganini deliberately withheld many of his works from publication in order to monopolize the virtuoso circuit. No. 1, whose publication he allowed, remains by far the most popular to this day. It has been recorded both in the full-length original version, and in tightened-up editions by both Fritz Kreisler and August Wilhelmj.

Itzhak Perlman has been the standard for some years, coupled with the Carmen Fantasy by Pablo de Sarasate, but young Gil Shaham has made a fair bid to match him, in newer sound, and with a more basic coupling for the beginning collector.

Shaham, Sinopoli, New York Philharmonic Orchestra. DG 429786 [DDD] + Saint-Saëns: Violin Concerto No. 3
Perlman, Foster, Royal Philharmonic Orchestra. EMI 47101

Gioacchino Rossini (1792-1868)

Rossini was the first opera composer to become a wealthy international superstar, a feat he accomplished partly by piling one thrilling effect upon another. For example, his technique of ending an overture or a scene with an exciting buildup of repeated runs on the strings was virtually patented; to this day it is known as the "Rossini crescendo," and no one would dare to copy it. To this extent he paralleled Paganini—but in truth, he was a far better composer. Paganini wrote slick, superficially brilliant scores to cover up his deficiencies; Rossini deliberately suppressed his grounding in Haydn and Mozart to play to the galleries, and thus make more money.

At first glance this seems reprehensible, but reading Rossini's life and becoming familiar with his magnificent sense of humor almost forces one to wink at his artistic peccadilloes. He was prodigally gifted; sunny, robust Italianate melody seemed to gush from him as from a Roman fountain. He was also blessed—or cursed—with a prodigal appetite, and by middle age he had become an enormous mass of mirthful flesh. He claimed to have wept only three times in his life: when his mother died, when his first opera failed, and when once, on a cruise, he accidentally dropped a truffled turkey overboard.

Rossini wrote about three dozen operas, both serious and comic, but only one, *The Barber of Seville,* got the formula exactly right. So right, in fact, that hardly anyone would dispute to this day that it is the most perfect comic opera ever written.

Suddenly, at the age of thirty-seven, at the height of his fame, Rossini virtually stopped composing. Although he lived almost forty more years, the once prolific genius wrote nothing beyond a *Stabat Mater* and some short songs and piano pieces, a situation unique in the history of music. Reams of theory have been written about this "great renunciation," but no one explanation seems totally satisfactory. It is clear that Rossini suffered for the first twenty-five years of his retirement from some kind of mental or emotional problem; he could not sleep, he could not digest, he experienced panic attacks, he fell into long depressions.

It is pleasant to report, however, that by 1855 his symptoms seemed to abate, and he was able to spend his last thirteen years in good spirits, living the good life in Paris, entertaining lavishly, delighting one and all with his mordant wit—to wit: when Rossini's great operatic rival, Meyerbeer, died, an aspiring young musician approached Rossini with a projected elegy for the funeral. The aged maestro listened uncomfortably as the youth hammered out his lugubrious and uninspired opus at the keyboard. At length the budding composer concluded and looked up hopefully. "Not bad," Rossini coughed, "not bad. But, don't you think it would have been better if you had died, and Meyerbeer had written the music…?"

The Barber of Seville

The premiere, in 1816, of the greatest comic opera ever written was almost as comical as the opera itself. An anti-Rossini clique came to boo, a cat ran across the stage, one of the main characters tripped and fell flat on his face. As the mishaps piled up, the audience grew more and more derisive. One observer said it seemed that all the whistlers in Italy had rendezvoused at the theater. But later that night, when Rossini's friends stopped by to console him, they found him sleeping like a baby. His confidence was vindicated: by the second performance, *The Barber of Seville* was a hit.

The best modern recording features a fine ensemble cast led by Sir Neville Marriner. Also a good choice in digital is Patané's version with an early appearance by the now-famous Cecilia Bartoli. The classic of an earlier era is the Callas-Gobbi performance conducted by Galliera.

Marriner, Academy of St. Martin-in-the-Fields, Baltsa, Allen, etc. Philips 411058 (3) [DDD] (mid-price)
Patané, Bologna Teatro Comunale, Bartoli, etc. London 425520 (3) [DDD]
Galliera, Philharmonia Orchestra, Callas, Gobbi, Alva, etc. Angel 47634 [ADD]

Overtures

Except for *The Barber of Seville*, Rossini's operas are known today principally through their sprightly overtures. The most famous of them are *William Tell, Semiramide, La gazza ladra, La Cenerentola, L'Italiana in Algeri, La scala di seta*, and, of course, *The Barber*. Every one of the recommended recordings contains the *William Tell* Overture, and most, if not all, of the others.

Reiner, Chicago Symphony Orchestra. RCA Gold Seal 60387 [ADD] (mid-price)
Levi, Atlanta Symphony Orchestra. Telarc 80334 [DDD]

Abbado, London Symphony Orchestra. "Basic 100, Vol. 13," RCA 61554
+ Verdi overtures (mid-price)
Giulini, Philharmonia Orchestra. Angel Studio 69042 (mid-price)
Norrington, London Classical Players (on period instruments). EMI
54091 [DDD]

Franz Schubert (1797-1828)

Schubert was surely the greatest of the early Romantics. In nearly a thousand compositions, completed in his brief thirty-one years (a life even shorter, you will note, than Mozart's), he frequently touches the most ineffable depths of human emotion. Yet except to a close circle of devoted friends, Schubert remained virtually unknown until years after his tragic death. His brief life, spent entirely in Vienna, was remarkably uneventful. His father, though no Leopold Mozart, was a schoolmaster and musician, and gave young Franz his first lessons. The boy showed considerable precocity. By age twenty-one he had already written hundreds of songs, and most of his symphonies. He followed in his father's footsteps for a while, but soon tired of schoolteaching and attempted to make his way as a composer— that is, he became a habitué of beer gardens and late-night parties.

Many were the evenings he spent among his Bohemian friends, quaffing tankards and accompanying vocalists in his songs. Apparently, even though he was short, pudgy, and unkempt, he was the center of these events, for even then they were known affectionately as "Schubertiades." These carefree days, alas, were numbered. By his mid-twenties Schubert had contracted syphilis, and soon afterwards his circle of companions began to break apart. He suffered gradually increasing bouts of depression, yet in his final precious few years he wrote some of the most lyrical and lovable chamber, symphonic, and vocal music in the history of music.

In May of 1827 Schubert visited the dying Beethoven, and in a few days was serving as a torchbearer in the funeral procession. The next year, he himself was dead, but was mourned only by a handful of family and friends. The world quickly forgot him, and his music gathered dust for some forty years. But long before the inevitable revival, the poet Grillparzer had contributed these lines to Schubert's tombstone, as wrenching as any of the composer's melodies: "Music has here entombed a rich treasure—but still fairer hopes."

Moments Musicaux, Op. 94 (D.780)

These six little pieces, with their passing shadows and glints of sunshine, are characteristic examples of a genre that has been called "bourgeois classicism." They also charmingly display Schubert's winning manner. There is a lovably bumpkinish quality even about the original title page, which reads, in peddler's French, "Moments Musicals." No. 3 in F minor is the best known, with its staccato notes in the left hand and its delicious quasi-Russian melody in the right.

There is no first-rate mid-price or budget version available at this writing. There should be minimal reluctance to spend a little more for a great Alfred Brendel record, coupled with a great Schubert sonata.

Brendel. Philips 422076 [DDD] + Piano Sonata in C Minor, D.958

Quartet No. 14 in D minor, D.810 "Death and the Maiden"

"Each night, on going to bed, I hope I may not wake up again, and each morning only recalls yesterday's grief." So wrote Schubert in 1823, when he had begun to realize that his health would never again be robust. Several works from this and his few succeeding years are unabashedly morbid in tone, none more so than this famous string quartet whose slow movement is based on the theme from an earlier song about Death coming for a young person. As if to underscore the point, Schubert quotes another of his songs about death, "The Erl-King," in the last movement.

The Quartetto Italiano have long been associated with this work, but their recording is unaccountably missing from the catalog at this time. Another great version features pianist Clifford Curzon with a Vienna quartet, coupled very intelligently with the "Trout Quintet"; the only drawback is somethat pallid stereo sound. The Alban Berg Quartet play beautifully, if occasionally somewhat coldly, at full price; the Prague Quartet are not quite in the same league artistically but offer digital sound at mid-price (both the Alban Berg and Prague versions have Schubert's Quartet No. 13 for a coupling).

Curzon, Vienna Philharmonic String Quartet. London 417459 [ADD] +
Trout Quintet (mid-price)
Alban Berg Quartet. Angel 47333 + Quartet No. 13
Prague Quartet. Denon 8005 + Quartet No. 13 (mid-price)

Quintet in A, D.667 "Trout"

Once again Schubert uses one of his songs ("Die Forelle"—"The Trout") as a theme for a chamber composition, this time in the fourth movement. The work is structurally odd in two respects: it has five movements instead of four, and replaces one of the standard two violins of the ensemble with a viola. The profuse lyricism which flows from the pages of this score has assured its place as the most beloved chamber work by Schubert.

Curzon's recording, recommended under the Quartet No. 14 above, remains an esthetic triumph, but Andras Schiff and the Hagen Quartet come very close in far better sound (they offer no coupling, however). At mid-price, another possibility is the fine 1967 Marlboro Festival recording, especially if you prefer the coupling of Mozart's Clarinet Quintet.

Curzon, Vienna Octet members. London 417459 [ADD] + Quartet No. 14 (mid-price)
A. Schiff, Hagen Quartet. London 411975 [DDD]
R. Serkin, J. Laredo, Naegele, Parnas, J. Levine. Sony 46252 [ADD] + Mozart: Clarinet Quintet (mid-price)

Rosamunde: Incidental Music, Op. 26 (D.797)

Rosamunde was a play by a dotty middle-aged lady named Wilhelmina (or Helmine) von Chezy. By being simultaneously rich, dowdy, and supremely self-confident, she had managed to draw around her a circle of devoted dilettantes. Mme. von Chezy was able to force several of her abominable stage works upon desperate and impecunious composers— such as Schubert, who wrote about an hour's worth of music to accompany *Rosamunde*. The play had exactly one performance, on December 20, 1823. Generally, the critics praised the score, or what they could hear of it, for the restless audience chattered loudly throughout. The author thundered that her play had been ruined by insufficient rehearsal, by a poor prompter, and so on. But to her everlasting credit, she did not dare to blame Schubert's music; it was, she stoutly insisted, "magnificent." As far as is known, this was the only correct artistic judgment she ever made.

With the disappearance of James Levine's CD containing the standard highlights from both *Rosamunde* and Mendelssohn's *A Midsummer Night's Dream,* an invaluable introduction to these works has been lost; one may hope a reissue occurs during the life of this book. Meanwhile, Claudio Abbado's recording of the complete incidental music to *Rosamunde* can be confidently recommended.

Abbado, Chamber Orchestra of Europe. DG 431655 [DDD]

Sonata in B-flat Major for Piano, Op. Posth. (D.960)

This last of Schubert's twenty-two piano sonatas, of which some are incomplete, is generally agreed to be his best. One may understandably wonder what even greater heights he might have reached had he lived beyond his thirty-one years. Some critics fault Schubert for not following the rules of sonata form as perfected by Beethoven (Schubert often favors his melodies at the expense of working them out in development sections). This may horrify Prussian musicologists, but many will prefer the view that Schubert was an avant-gardist among the early Romantics, creating a synthesis of classical form with the Romantic spirit. Both elements, incidentally, are admirably balanced in this sonata.

Both Artur Rubinstein and Alfred Brendel have outstanding performances of this work on CD, and both offer couplings of the basic *Wanderer Fantasy.*

Rubinstein. RCA 6257 [ADD] + 2 Impromptus, *Wanderer Fantasy*
Brendel. Philips 422062 [DDD] + *Wanderer Fantasy*

Songs (Lieder)

Schubert is acknowledged as the greatest of all classical song composers, period. He wrote some six hundred songs in his three decades, and even the very first ones, written in his teens, sound like the polished works of a master of the medium. There was something in a poem that inspired Schubert to recreate it melodically and harmonically in a way that almost always made a bad poem seem good, and a good poem even better.

Although they may occasionally indulge in both, most classical singers specialize in opera, while others concentrate on what is called in the trade "art song"—that is, short solo vocal works set to a poem and composed with all the accoutrements of classical music, as opposed to folk or popular songs. This is one of the genres most difficult to introduce to people with no classical music background, partly because most of it is in non-English languages, partly because the idiom is so unfamiliar and formal in comparison to pop music. It helps to take Lieder in short doses at the beginning and invest in a little study, including making the effort to follow along with a translation when listening. If an art song is good, its words will be crucial to enjoying it.

The singer most associated with Schubert's songs in recent decades has been the German baritone Dietrich Fischer-Dieskau. He has actually recorded all six hundred of them in three box sets comprising twenty-one CDs, but there is an inexpensive single disc anthology which captures him in his prime and singing twenty-one of the best-loved songs. If you would prefer a female voice, an excellent recommendation is the Lieder specialist Elly Ameling offering thirteen songs on one disc at mid-price. Both artists have superlative accompanists (Gerald Moore and Dalton Baldwin, respectively).

Fischer-Dieskau, Moore. Angel Studio 69503 [ADD] (mid-price)
Ameling, Baldwin. Philips Silver Line 420870 [ADD] (mid-price)

Symphony No. 5 in B-flat Major, D.485

Schubert was only nineteen when he wrote this enchanting, rather Mozartian symphony of chamber-orchestra proportions (sorry, no trumpets, no drums). All four movements have graceful, dancelike qualities—and, of course, lovely melodies.

Two digital recordings dominate the recommendations here, both coupled with the Unfinished Symphony. Sir Georg Solti offers one of his very best performances, which is saying a great deal, and Leonard Bernstein is dramatic and thoughtful by turn.

I'm not really satisfied with any of the available lower priced discs for this repertoire.

Solti, Vienna Philharmonic Orchestra. London 414371 [DDD] +
Symphony No. 8
Bernstein, Concertgebouw Orchestra. DG 427645 [DDD] + Symphony No. 8

Symphony No. 8 in B Minor, D.759 "Unfinished"

There are other famous unfinished symphonies (Bruckner's No. 9 and Mahler's No.
10, for example), left incomplete at their composers' deaths. But it was not death that
caused Schubert to stop after writing only two movements (and a few bars of a third) of his
most famous symphony, which is also one of the most beloved symphonies ever written by
anybody. No one knows why he laid this score aside, going on later to compose the much
longer (and complete) Symphony No. 9.

It seems clear that he had no intention of proceeding beyond the second movement,
for several months after writing it he sent the half-torso score to a music society as a gift for
electing him a member. The most satisfying theory is that, following these two incomparably sad and mysterious movements, Schubert just could not think of a way to top them;
rather than write an anticlimax, he simply let the tantalizing question mark stand. Our
astonishment is only increased by learning that this strange, towering work lay for forty-three
years in a drawer of one of Schubert's friends before having its first public performance.

Giuseppe Sinopoli has walked away with the digital trophy for recording this work,
and his instantly classic performance is available with two different couplings, at (inexplicably) two different prices. With highlights from Mendelssohn's *A Midsummer Night's Dream*
one pays full price, with Schumann's Symphony No. 3 the tab falls to mid-price. Situations
like this are the cause of the ancient adage: "It's useless to try to explain the record business."

If this makes you throw up your hands, you can still fall back on Sir Georg Solti or
Leonard Bernstein, as recommended above under Symphony No. 5.

Sinopoli, Philharmonia Orchestra. DG 410862 [DDD] + Mendelssohn: *A
Midsummer Night's Dream*
Sinopoli, Philharmonia Orchestra. DG 427818 [DDD] + Schumann:
Symphony No. 3 (mid-price)
Solti, Vienna Philharmonic Orchestra. London 414371 [DDD] +
Symphony No. 5
Bernstein, Concertgebouw Orchestra. DG 427645 [DDD] + Symphony No. 5

Symphony No. 9 in C, D.944 "The Great"

Schubert's last symphony had a slightly better fate than his Unfinished; at least there
was an attempt to have it performed before he died. But the Vienna Philharmonic decided
it was too difficult. Eleven years after the composer's death, the same orchestra did put the

first two movements on a program—but with an aria from Donizetti's *Lucia di Lammermoor* inserted between them to keep the audience awake! Both Schumann and Mendelssohn championed the work, to little avail. Mendelssohn tried to include it in an 1844 concert he conducted, but had to withdraw it after his players kept cracking up over passages they found ridiculous.

Today, audiences are at a loss to decide what is more wonderful, this symphony's beautiful melodies, its magical harmonic transitions, or its magnificent structural development, concluding with one of the most joyful outbursts of sunshine in all music. "In originality of harmony and modulation, and in his gift of orchestral coloring," wrote Antonin Dvořák in 1894, "Schubert has had no superior…I do not hesitate to place him next to Beethoven, far above Mendelssohn, as well as above Schumann." Take that!

As in Symphonies Nos. 5 and 8, Sir Georg Solti proves himself a preeminent Schubertian in No. 9, where conductor and orchestra seem to find perfect harmony. As good as any, but in older sound, is Bruno Walter. Both discs are bargains; this offsets the situation with Symphony No. 5 above.

> **Solti, Vienna Philharmonic Orchestra.** London 430747 [DDD] (mid-price)
> **B. Walter, Columbia Symphony Orchestra.** CBS Odyssey 44828 [ADD] (budget)

Trio No. 1 in B-flat Major, Op. 99 (D.898)

This wonderful chamber piece gives us Schubert in his most untrammeled happy mood; little in music can be more pleasing. A feeling of bliss prevails virtually from the first bar to the last, even in the nocturnal slow movement.

The Beaux Arts Trio are a standard at mid-price on a double set. The trio of David Golub, Mark Kaplan, and Colin Carr are superb in digital, but also on a two-CD set. Both of these are paired with the Trio No. 2 and one or two smaller pieces. For a single disc with just the more famous Trio No. 1, and an interesting coupling of Dvořák's best trio, No. 4 "Dumky," the London Mozart Trio offer an excellent digital performance.

> **Beaux Arts Trio.** Philips 412620 (2) [ADD] + Trio No. 2, *Notturno* in E-flat
> **Golub, Kaplan, Carr.** Arabesque 6580 (2) [DDD] + Trio No. 2, *Notturno* in E-flat, Sonata Movement in B-flat, D.28
> **London Mozart Trio.** IMP PCD 1006 [DDD] + Dvorak: Trio No. 4 "Dumky"

"Wanderer" Fantasy for Piano in C Major, Op. 15 (D.760)

The title is not a wry comment on Schubert's reputation for desultory writing, but yet another reference to a song which provides thematic material ("Der Wanderer"). This piece looks forward, structurally, to the rhapsodic view of sonata form embraced by Franz Liszt. It is one of Schubert's most dramatic keyboard works.

Artur Rubinstein's 1965 recording is still the classic of the catalog, coupled with two Impromptus. Among digital versions, Murray Perahia with the Schumann Fantasia in C, and Alfred Brendel with Schubert's Piano Sonata in B-flat, D.960, are prime picks.

Rubinstein. RCA 6257 [ADD] + 2 Impromptus, Sonata in B-flat, D.960
Perahia. Sony 42124 [DDD] + Schumann: *Fantasia* in C
Brendel. Philips 422062 [DDD] + Sonata in B-flat, D.960

Winterreise, Op. 89 (D.911)

This cycle of twenty-four songs could be considered the diametric opposite of the Trio No. 1, as there is scarcely a cheerful moment in it. It is a powerfully eloquent, heartrending diary of the Winter Journey of a rejected lover, whose unquenchable pain leads him to quiet madness and a longing for death.

The effect is akin to seeing a series of snapshots of a person gradually disintegrating over time. The piano accompaniment is often vividly wrenching, suggesting falling leaves, growling dogs rattling their chains, or the ominous beating of the wings of a crow, yet Schubert's pure harmonies keep the music well away from the edge of melodramatic hysteria. There are few works of vocal music more convincing in their tragedy.

As with the individual songs discussed earlier, Dietrich Fischer-Dieskau has been the par excellence artist in the song cycles for decades. Gerald Moore was his inimitable accompanist, and served another great singer, bass-baritone Hans Hotter, equally well years earlier in a memorable recording preserved at mid-price.

Fischer-Dieskau, Moore. DG 415187 [ADD]
Hotter, Moore. Angel 61002 (m) (mid-price)

Robert Schumann (1810-1856)

Schumann was nothing if not methodical. With a self-discipline unique among composers, he confined himself first to piano pieces, then moved on to songs, orchestral works, and chamber music. Despite this—or possibly because of it—he died in a madhouse, the tragic victim of an utterly disordered brain.

Ironic no doubt, but then Schumann was no stranger to paradox. He expounded the most fantastic and fanciful aspects of the Romantic credo, yet in his private life was considered to be conservative and dull. He spoke and wrote constantly about the "music of the future," but had minimal appreciation for his two contemporaries, Liszt and Wagner, who were its embodiments.

Even his fabled love affair with Clara Wieck seems far less ideal, upon close scrutiny, than legend would have it. True, their long courtship in defiance of her father's wishes did result in lifelong marriage and several children, but before the courtship Schumann contracted syphilis; during it he was briefly engaged to another woman; and after it the relationship suffered from both Robert's jealous resentment of Clara's own considerable musical talents and her driving him to the point of exhaustion in a quest for greater financial reward, insisting that he write the large symphonic works for which he was ill-suited by temperament.

It was in the smaller forms, the piano pieces and songs, that Schumann seemed most comfortable. Indeed, his successful longer works, such as *Carnaval*, are frequently really a series of short pieces strung together. The chamber works, though graced with lovely ideas, are sometimes clumsily structured; and the fresh poetry of the four symphonies is hobbled here and there by awkward orchestration.

Yet there may have been no composer better than Schumann in overcoming technical deficiencies by sheer force of inspiration. His innate sensitivity to the portrayal of shifting moods almost never fails him, and in his best works one is struck over and over by the impression that each scene or emotion is colored in just the right way.

Schumann had literary aspirations, but it was in his music that he created true poetry. He was the favorite composer of another miniaturist, the Venezuelan composer Reynaldo Hahn (1875-1947), who once wrote of Schumann: "There is no emotion that he has not experienced; all the phenomena of nature are familiar to him—moonlight, bright or hazy, sunrise and sunset, confused shadows, dull weather, radiant weather, fresh scents, the majesty of evening, swirling mists, powdery snow—he has known them all and can impart to us the thousand and one emotions associated with them."

Carnaval, Op. 9

Of all the early Romantics, Schumann was the most effective at injecting playful wit into his music, and there is no more delightful display of it than in this kaleidoscopic keyboard picture of carnival characters. Among the numerous portraits are two that reveal Schumann's "split personality": "Eusebius" represents his poetic, dreamy side, while "Florestan" indicates the fiery crusader within him. Schumann continued to use these pseudonyms when writing reviews and articles about music, so he seems to have been aware of his paradoxical nature.

Artur Rubinstein's 1962 recording has never been surpassed, and offers generous bonuses of the *Waldscenen* and *Fantasiestücke*. An outstanding digital version is by Howard Shelley, coupled with the *Kinderscenen* and Toccata in C.

Rubinstein. RCA 5067 [ADD] + *Waldscenen, Fantasiestücke*
Shelley. Chandos 8814 [DDD] + *Kinderscenen,* Toccata in C

Concerto in A minor for Piano, Op. 54

Now one of the most beloved Romantic piano concertos, this work was unsuccessful at its premiere in 1845 and for many years thereafter. The starched-shirt critics of those days were mightily offended by its rhapsodic, free nature, not to mention its lack of virtuoso display. Both traditional sonata form and showiness were inimical to Schumann's spirit; once, years before he actually wrote the Piano Concerto, he predicted it would be "a compromise between a symphony, a concerto and a huge sonata." It is. And it is (mostly) ravishingly tender rather than thunderous or brilliant.

Stephen Bishop-Kovacevich has had wide recognition since 1972 as the master of this work in stereo. More recent competition comes from the 1988 digital version by Murray Perahia. It must mean something that the two best recordings in sixteen years have the same conductor, Sir Colin Davis. They also have the same coupling, the Grieg Piano Concerto, but that means nothing more than it is the traditional coupling.

Bishop-Kovacevich, C. Davis, BBC Symphony Orchestra. Philips 412923
[ADD] + Grieg: Piano Concerto
Perahia, C. Davis, Bavarian Radio Symphony Orchestra. CBS 44899
[DDD] + Grieg: Piano Concerto

Dichterliebe, Op. 48

Schumann is second only to Schubert in the realm of art songs—in number (about 140 compared with Schubert's six hundred), and in familiarity, if not in inspiration. At least in variety of style and expression, Schumann may be Schubert's superior. While the vast majority of Schubert's songs are lyrical romances, Schumann ranges freely from those all the way to such unexpected things as the terrifying ballad "Die beiden Grenadiere" ("The Two Grenadiers"). Perhaps the best known of all Schumann songs is "Ich grolle nicht" ("I'll not complain"), a song with a penetrating idea, an unforgettable melody, and a highly original declamatory structure. "Ich grolle nicht" is, however, only one of sixteen marvellous songs making up the cycle *Dichterliebe*—"Poet's Love."

Dietrich Fischer-Dieskau, the King of Lieder, is first choice in digital accompanied by Alfred Brendel, Prince of Pianists, with a bonus of another Schumann song cycle, *Liederkreis,* Op. 39. At mid-price, try Fritz Wunderlich's version from the 1960s leavened by some Beethoven and Schubert songs thrown in; Wunderlich, who died in an auto accident not long after this release, had not yet reached the depth of interpretation of a Fischer-Dieskau, but his singing is young and fresh, and the voice incomparably beautiful.

Fischer-Dieskau, Brendel. Philips 416352 [DDD] + *Liederkreis,* Op. 39
Wunderlich, Giesen. DG Dokumente 429933 [ADD] + Songs by Schubert and Beethoven (mid-price)

Kinderscenen, Op. 15

This baker's dozen of short pieces are Schumann's touching and amusing recollections of childhood. Although he intended them for adults to play, there actually were some children who could play them (before the invention of television). People who have never heard, or perhaps even wanted to hear "classical music" are often startled to find they can hum the tunes from "Scenes of Childhood," so pervasive have they become in our culture, turning up everywhere from elevators to Laurel and Hardy movies.

Howard Shelley's sumptuous recording recommended earlier under *Carnaval* is a prime medium for these pieces, especially with the extra coupling of the exciting Toccata in C.

Shelley. Chandos 8814 [DDD] + *Carnaval,* Toccata in C

Symphony No. 1 in B-flat Major, Op. 38 "Spring"

The "Spring" Symphony, in which Clara professed to hear clearly "the buds, the scent of violets, the fresh green leaves, the birds in the air," was written in the dead of winter, 1840-41. The "Spring" in it was not meant to be the season of the year so much as the beginning of Robert's career, and his honeymoon with Clara. There are no literal nature-paintings in it, but if it doesn't lighten your step, you may need your hearing or your heart re-tuned.

Christoph von Dohnányi has one of the best digital versions recorded, and it is conveniently coupled with Symphony No. 2. At mid-price, George Szell leads a great performance paired with Symphony No. 4. Interestingly, both recommended recordings are played by the Cleveland Orchestra, about twenty years apart.

Dohnányi, Cleveland Orchestra. London 421439 [DDD] + Symphony No. 2
Szell, Cleveland Orchestra. CBS 38468 [ADD] + Symphony No. 4 (mid-price)

Symphony No. 2 in C Major, Op. 61

This is the least known of Schumann's symphonies, but it has many beauties often overlooked. The second movement, a Scherzo, is as exhilarating an orchestral romp as anyone has written.

Dohnányi is recommended above under Symphony No. 1, or for a coupling with Symphony No. 3 try the recording conducted by James Levine.

Dohnányi, Cleveland Orchestra. London 421439 [DDD] + Symphony No. 1
Levine, Berlin Philharmonic Orchestra. DG 423625 [DDD] + Symphony No. 3

Symphony No. 3 in E-flat Major, Op. 97 "Rhenish"

Inspired by scenes of life along the Rhine river, the "Rhenish" is both the most original and most popular of Schumann's symphonies. Two of the five movements were inspired by the then-unfinished Cathedral of Cologne, where Schumann witnessed the majestic enthronement of an archbishop. Other parts of the symphony suggest peasant dances, morning sunrises, and so on.

Dohnányi rounds out his Schumann symphonies here with Nos. 3 and 4 on one disc, while Levine includes No. 2, recommended above.

Dohnányi, Cleveland Orchestra. London 421643 [DDD] + Symphony No. 4
Levine, Berlin Philharmonic Orchestra. DG 423625 [DDD] + Symphony No. 2

Symphony No. 4 in D Minor, Op. 120

This was originally Schumann's Symphony No. 2, written shortly after the "Spring" Symphony. Its premiere was not well-received, and even the composer had second thoughts. He laid the score aside for ten years, then revised it extensively and brought it out as Symphony No. 4, which it has remained. The four movements are continuous—that is, distinct from each other but linked by bridge materials, without full stops between them. The work could almost be described as a tone poem constructed on symphonic principles.

We already have Dohnányi from his esteemed No. 3 above, and we can add George Szell at mid-price, as recommended earlier for No. 1. Isn't that tidy?

Dohnányi, Cleveland Orchestra. London 421643 [DDD] + Symphony No. 3
Szell, Cleveland Orchestra. CBS 38468 [ADD] + Symphony No. 1 (mid-price)

Carl Maria von Weber (1786-1826)

The earliest of the early Romantics, Weber deserves much credit for establishing and popularizing the whole Romantic movement in music. Sadly, he has fallen on hard times in our century; his works are the least played and known of all his contemporaries, and several attempts to start revivals have fallen flat. This is partly because of his short career (he died at age thirty-nine), partly because his music is so thoroughly—almost provincially— German that it doesn't "travel" well. But mostly it is because his style was soon subsumed under that of his spiritual descendant, Richard Wagner, whose works were longer, louder, and better marketed. They quite drowned out poor Weber.

Weber was the most talented member of a musical family with ambition. A grandfather added the honorific "von" to the family name; his father was a small-town

Kapellmeister, his mother a talented singer; and his two cousins, Aloysia and Constanze, were both involved with Mozart: the former was his great love, the latter became his wife.

As a child, despite being crippled by a hip deformity, Carl Maria was dragged around Europe as a child prodigy by his father, who wanted him to be seen as another Mozart. The boy was able to study with Haydn's younger brother Michael (who was Mozart's friend), and published his first compositions at age eleven. He became a concert pianist at twelve, had his first opera produced at fourteen, and by fifteen had won the post of Kapellmeister at Breslau. A frail constitution and a grinding schedule wore him down, and he died while in London, where he was buried. Eighteen years later, his remains were returned to Germany. In the harbor, ships of many nations dipped their flags in homage, and at the re-interment the graveside eulogy was delivered by the one man who owed the most to Weber: Richard Wagner.

Invitation to the Dance, Op. 65

Originally written for piano solo, this piece is most familiar in a brilliant orchestral transcription by Berlioz. Another Weber innovation, it is the first symphonic waltz, the direct ancestor of all those wonderful waltzes by the Strauss family, and every bit their equal. (The recommended recording is cited below, under "Overtures.")

Overtures

Most of Weber's operas no longer hold the stage, but their dramatic and melodious overtures survive.

A fine introduction to all of the above comes from a period instrument orchestra, the Hanover Band, conducted by Roy Goodman. *The Invitation to the Dance* is joined by six sparkling overtures, including those to *Der Freischütz, Oberon,* and *Euryanthe.*

Goodman, Hanover Band. Nimbus 5154 [DDD]

The Mainstream Romantics
(ca. 1850-1890)

The Early Romantics were given dates of about 1820 to 1850. Mainstream Romanticism, however, is not so much defined by dates as by a state of mind. The composers whom we think of as the "central" composers of the Romantic era in music definitely did not do their work in the first half of the nineteenth century, but some of them overlapped with those we can distinguish as Late Romantics towards the end of that era.

We can often identify the Mainstreamers by their strong tendency to emphasize ethnicity and nationality; by the greater weight and seriousness of their vision as compared to the Early Romantics; and most of all, by the full-blooded rhapsodic manner of their expression, which obliterated all traces of those ties to the Classical Period that we can always hear in the works of Mendelssohn, Schubert, or even Rossini.

Until about 1960 they were, with the exception of Beethoven, the composers who heavily dominated orchestral concert programs. For the better part of a century it was Brahms and Tchaikovsky who were played most often, with Mozart thrown in occasionally, almost as a sop to historians, and Haydn was a distinct oddity on a program.

The same situation prevailed in opera. Mozart's masterpieces were heard only sporadically, and all but a handful of the once wildly popular operas of Bellini, Donizetti, and Rossini vanished from the stage. The lyrical theater scene belonged to Verdi and Wagner.

Although the most famous of the Mainstream Romantics are still doing perfectly well at the box office, they have had to learn to share with earlier and later composers. The great revival of interest in Baroque music, especially in the 1960s, threatened for a while to block them out, and renewed respect and love for Haydn and Mozart further diluted their hegemony, creating a growing suspicion that their vast heavings and stentorian pronouncements were perhaps more hot air than true profundities. And the assault continued from the other side, from a growing appreciation of the modern composers for whom the Mainstream Romantic approach so often seemed to be anathema.

The Mainstreamers were thus squeezed for a generation or more between the simpler, clearer lines of earlier music and the nonsentimental esthetic of the modernists. But by the 1990s it was clear that the Mainstream Romantics were being rapidly rehabilitated. Not only was Tchaikovsky chic again, there was even a deluge of recordings of works by totally forgotten Mainstreamers such as Joachim Raff, Anton Rubinstein, and Alexis de Castillon.

The secret of this renaissance was simple: once listeners stopped believing Mainstream Romantic music was sacred writ and purged its dogmatisms from their systems, they could take it again to their hearts on a new basis. One no longer had to worship at the shrine of

Wagner, or brood darkly on his half-baked theories on Man and His Destiny; as soon as one realized Wagner was a magnificent entertainer who misread himself as a prophet, his music became available again as a source of delight. But from that point on, it would be understood as more sensuous than intellectual.

Georges Bizet (1838-1875)

Bizet must turn in his grave every day, frustrated that although he was nearly as great a child prodigy as Mozart or Meldelssohn, and that his opera *Carmen* is the most-performed opera in the world, beloved of audiences and critics alike, he is never mentioned as one of the five or even ten greatest composers, let alone as the greatest opera composer. Many music lovers know about this paradox; few, however, are aware that Bizet was a virtuoso pianist, called by Liszt one of the three best in Europe, though he chose not to follow a keyboard career.

He was an only child in a musical family, entered the Paris Conservatory at the early age of nine, and wrote his ever-fresh Symphony in C at age seventeen. A student of Gounod, and later his good friend, he won the Prix de Rome in 1857 and immediately embarked on his chosen career as an opera composer. Though praised by Berlioz, among others, Bizet suffered one artistic disaster after another, and was often reduced to turning out hack dance music to stay alive.

He persisted, carried along by his modesty, common sense, and faith in his abilities. Though he was no great innovator, and founded no school, he was a master of orchestration, and one of the finest of all French melodists. His ability to make his characters come alive, to portray their conflicts with intenstiy and convincing realism, enabled him to practically finish off the old French Grand Opera.

He worked rapidly. Like Mozart, he composed most of his works in his head before writing them down. He felt, in fact, a strong affinity with Mozart as a similarly "natural" and "balanced" musician. The two men died at nearly the same ages, but, of course, the sounds they produced were very different: Bizet, though he liked to say his heart was really German or Italian, and who set every one of his operas in countries other than France, was French to the bone. Not, however, the French of Debussy, of moonlit waves and medieval forests, but of the sunlit Mediterranean and the passionate tempers of modern men and women.

Carmen

One of the few operas to appeal equally to audiences and critics, *Carmen* features a compelling story of the tragic love of a Spanish officer for a gypsy cigarette girl, set to music that is constantly ablaze with inner or outer passion. It teems with memorable melodies and moves right along to the suspenseful and shocking ending. It was more or less a flop at its premiere in 1875, however, and Bizet did not live to see it become one of the most popular operas ever written.

A famous mid-50s recording starring Risë Stevens and conducted by Fritz Reiner may be old, but it still sizzles, and though mono, at mid-price it is still a steal. Just a few years newer, the version starring Victoria de los Angeles as a Carmen with dignity, and idiomatically conducted by Sir Thomas Beecham, is in stereo and still desirable, though Angel refuses to drop the price. Herbert von Karajan is well-known for his versions of Carmen: both the RCA edition starring Leontyne Price and the DG recording with Agnes Baltsa are highly recommendable and have reduced price tags.

Reiner, RCA Victor Orchestra. RCA 7981 (3) (mono) (mid-price)

Beecham, French National Orchestra and Chorus. Angel 49240 (3) [ADD]

Karajan, Vienna Philharmonic Orchestra and State Opera Chorus (Price). RCA Gold Seal 6199 (3) [ADD] (mid-price)

Karajan, Berlin Philharmonic Orchestra (Baltsa). DG 410088 (3) (mid-price)

L'Arlésienne Suites; Carmen Suites

Three years before *Carmen,* Bizet accepted a commission to write incidental music for Alphonse Daudet's play about rustic love in Provence called *L'Arlésienne* ("The Maid from Arles"). Best known in two suites for concert performance, the most famous piece is the breathless Farandole from Suite No. 2. Bizet also arranged two suites from Carmen for concert hall use.

These suites happen to fit conveniently on one disc and make the most natural possible pairing, so there is little reason not to purchase them so, especially when there are several fine versions to choose from. One of the most atmospheric is Leopold Stokowski's 1977 recording at mid-price; for digital, the obvious choice is Charles Dutoit.

Stokowski, National Philharmonic Orchestra. CBS 37260 [ADD] (mid-price)

Dutoit, Montreal Symphony Orchestra. London 417839 [DDD]

Symphony No. 1 in C

Bizet was but a stripling of seventeen when he wrote this symphony as a test piece for the Paris Conservatory. It was never played in his lifetime, and was forgotten until the 1920s. Even then it waited another decade for its premiere—no one was prepared to believe it could be very good. They were wrong. It is extremely well written, and there is hardly another symphony that breathes more naturally the fresh air of youth.

Stokowski is a great choice again, this time at an even lower price, coupled with great George Szell performances of Mendelssohn's *Midsummer Night's Dream* music and Smetana's *The Moldau.* It doesn't hurt one's enjoyment to be aware that the indomitable

Stokowski was ninety-five when he recorded this resilient reading of a youthful master-piece. In digital, the conductorless Orpheus Chamber Orchestra has won plaudits for verve and realistic sound; this choice too has apt couplings.

Stokowski, National Philharmonic Orchestra. Sony Essential Classics 48264 [ADD] + Mendelssohn: *A Midsummer Night's Dream* (sel.); Smetana: *The Moldau* (with Szell, Cleveland Orchestra) (budget)
Orpheus Chamber Orchestra. DG 423624 [DDD] + Prokofiev: Symphony No. 1; Britten: Simple Symphony

Alexander Borodin (1833-1887)

Borodin was one of the most appealing characters among the composers. Beginning life with a severe handicap as the illegitimate son of a Russian nobleman who farmed the child out to one of his serfs, Borodin nevertheless showed talent in both music and science at an early age and managed to secure an excellent education.

He spent his entire professional life as a chemist, teacher, and administrator of the St. Petersburg Medico-Surgical Academy, where he took a leading role in establishing medical education for Russian women, and wrote such yawners as *The Solidification of Aldehydes* and *Researches on the Fluoride of Benzol*. His beloved hobby of composing was relegated to his few spare hours, mostly during vacations, and even then he was subject to endless inter-ruptions from family and friends (and sometimes from his pet cats as they walked across the keys of his piano).

Despite these obstacles he was recognized early on as a major talent and was readily included in the group later known as the "Mighty Five." These were the great Russian nationalist composers, including Mussorgsky, Cui, Balakirev, and Rimsky-Korsakov. Many of Borodin's works remained incomplete, or needed orchestration, which was usually con-tributed by Rimsky-Korsakov or Alexander Glazunov. Yet of all these professional com-posers, Borodin wrote the best integrated forms, had the strongest grasp of symphonic development, and showed the most consistent employment of thematic material. And his strikingly beautiful melodies, though fewer in number, are as distinctive as Tchaikovsky's.

Plagued by numerous health problems, including cholera and several heart attacks, Borodin was only fifty-four when he died at a masquerade ball. He was wearing a red peas-ant shirt and boots, laughing and joking, we are told, when just at the stroke of midnight he collapsed and was gone—fulfilling the desirable end envisioned by Keats:

To cease upon the midnight,
With no pain.

Prince Igor: Overture; Polovtsian Dances

Borodin's opera *Prince Igor* is one of the most colorful in the Russian repertoire, and it is a wonder it is not heard more often in the West, especially since a number of its great melodies have long since become familiar through the American musical *Kismet*. The overture was actually sewn together by Glinka and Rimsky-Korsakov after Borodin's death, based on remembrances of his playing them on the piano. The spectacular Polovtsian Dances occur as part of Khan Konchak's victory celebration in Act II, and contain choral parts often omitted in concert performance.

Sir Georg Solti's great analog recording of Russian favorites is a steal at budget price. Enrique Bátiz leads an excellent digital disc coupled with the Symphony No. 2 at mid-price, but on a British label that not every store carries. Easier to find is Robert Shaw's brilliant-sounding digital performance coupled with Stravinsky's *Firebird* Suite. Sir Thomas Beecham offers superlative readings of this music and Rimsky-Korsakov's similarly exotic *Scheherazade,* but one chokes at a 1957 recording, no matter how well transferred, being offered at full price. Antal Dorati's glittering remaster is well worth having if the couplings please, although he is best in the Rimsky works, and the disc omits the *Prince Igor* Overture.

Solti, London Symphony Orchestra. London Weekend Classics 417689 [ADD] + Glinka: *Russlan and Ludmila* Overture; Mussorgsky: Prelude to *Khovanshchina, Night on Bald Mountain* (budget)

Bátiz, Mexico State Symphony Orchestra. ASV Quicksilva 6018 [DDD] + Symphony No. 2 (mid-price)

Shaw, Atlanta Symphony Orchestra and Chorus. Telarc 80039 [DDD] + Stravinsky: *Firebird* Suite

Beecham, Royal Philharmonic Orchestra. EMI 47717 [ADD] + Rimsky-Korsakov: *Scheherazade*

Dorati, London Symphony Orchestra. Mercury 434308 [ADD] + Rimsky-Korsakov: *Capriccio espagnol, Le Coq d'or* Suite, *Russian Easter* Overture (mid-price)

Quartet No. 2 in D

One of the few works Borodin actually completed, the Quartet No. 2, like *Prince Igor,* contains themes that found a wider audience in the musical *Kismet*. It was dedicated to the composer's wife, probably as a twentieth anniversary gift, and sustains a happy mood throughout.

The fortuitously named Borodin Quartet play this work and the earlier quartet as if they were written for them.

Borodin Quartet. EMI 47795 [DDD] + Quartet No. 1

Symphony No. 2 in B Minor

This symphony is so ultra-Russian it makes Tchaikovsky sound Danish. In fact, it is probably the best Russian Romantic symphony outside of Tchaikovsky's. And when was the last time you heard it on your orchestra's program?

Enrique Bátiz's version was already recommended under the *Prince Igor* selections above; a marvelous bargain disc conducted by Stephen Gunzenhauser offers all three symphonies in digital sound.

Bátiz, Mexico State Symphony Orchestra. ASV Quicksilva 6018 [DDD] + *Prince Igor:* Overture and *Polovtsian Dances* (mid-price)
Gunzenhauser, CSR Symphony Orchestra (Bratislava). Naxos 8.550238 [DDD] + Symphonies 1, 3 (budget)

Johannes Brahms (1833-1897)

If Brahms did not have a "split personality," he certainly had a double nature. Born into humble circumstances, he grew up in a cramped three-room apartment and earned money as a youth by playing the paino in taverns and brothels. We may not be surprised, then, to discover that he developed a lifelong obsession for settled, respectable, bourgeois comfort—but this was in constant conflict with the demands of genius.

Although he became immensely successful both artistically and financially, he continued all his life to live in a modest house, wear rumpled old clothes, and eat in the cheapest restaurants. He was parsimonious in acquiring money, but prodigal in giving it away. He was preoccupied with trying to secure a permanent conducting post, yet turned down most offers he received; and when he did get a position, he soon found an excuse to give it up.

He fell in love many times, most famously with Robert Schumann's wife Clara. He never married, and was never able to tell Clara his feelings, even long after Robert had died. Always shy by nature, he became morose and even rude in later years. The story was that when Brahms left a gathering, he was apt to say, "If there is anyone here whom I have forgotten to insult, I beg his forgiveness." Yet there was no one more likely to rush to the aid of a needy friend, nor to make gifts and loans of money without fanfare and without demand for repayment.

He was a native of Hamburg, but spent his most productive years in Vienna, where his shaggy beard and mane of hair, fuming cigar, and ill-fitting suit hugging his portly frame became legendary fixtures of the local scene. With his prickly temperament, perhaps it was not entirely coincidental that one of his favorite taverns was named The Red Hedgehog.

Brahms's musical career began in the shadow of his heroes: Schubert, Schumann, and especially Beethoven. Although he appreciated the fantasy elements of some of the early Romantics, he was repulsed by the free and rhapsodic constructions of contemporaries such as Liszt; nor did he have any aptitude for opera or dramatic music as did Wagner. Much was made of the rivalry between Brahms and Wagner, and indeed they were living symbols of antithetical artistic ideals, but the controversy was more accurately between their followers, not between the men themselves.

Brahms stayed true to the last to the traditional formal bounds of composition, developing an antiquarian interest in later life which led him to collect—and sometimes edit—works of innumerable Renaissance and Baroque composers. He was a scholarly intellectual who collected not only old music manuscripts, but books on religion, philosophy, history, and poetry.

In his own music he kept his personality in the background, emphasizing structure and rich harmony. There is a gentle but dark solemnity about much of his output which has led inevitably to the adjective "autumnal" being applied to it. Not for Brahms the sparkling cascades of Saint-Saëns, the lightning brilliance of Liszt, or the blinding colors of Wagner. His was a serious and austere art, and in its magnificent execution it brought to a full cadence, just as Bach had done long before, the entire tendency of an age. As his biographer Karl Geiringer wrote, "The musical output of five hundred years is summarized in Brahms's works."

Academic Festival Overture, Op. 80

The title perfectly mirrors the union here of the scholarly and the festive, a trick known to few other than Brahms. It was written in thanks to the University of Breslau for conferring on him a Doctorate of Philosophy in 1880. Four traditional student songs are woven into the brilliant textures, culminating in a joyful outburst of the Latin song *Gaudeamus igitur* ("Therefore let us rejoice").

The overture is easily obtainable as "filler" on any number of Brahms discs of larger works, of which the following may be mentioned as recommendable under the major titles.

Abbado, Berlin Philharmonic Orchestra. DG 423617 [DDD] + Violin Concerto

Bernstein, Vienna Philharmonic Orchestra. DG 410082 [DDD] + Symphony No. 2

Szell, Cleveland Orchestra. Sony Essential Classics 46330 [ADD] + Symphony No. 4, *Tragic* Overture (budget)

Szell, Cleveland Orchestra. Sony Essential Classics 48398 (3) [ADD] + Symphonies 1-4, *Hungarian Dances*, *Tragic* Overture, *Haydn Variations* (budget)

Concerto No. 1 in D Minor for Piano, Op. 15

This was Brahms's first major orchestral work, written when he was in his early twenties. It is one of the longest concerti ever written, partly because it evolved from a projected symphony which Brahms abandoned after sketching it out in a two-piano version. The whole concerto can be interpreted as a struggle between the majestic opening theme of the first movement and other materials, with the original theme triumphant at the end.

Russian pianist Emil Gilels has long had special recognition for his recordings of both concerti under conductor Eugen Jochum, but they are available only as a two-CD set. For a single disc, Brendel is recommendable, or Rudolf Serkin at mid-price.

Gilels, Jochum, Berlin Philharmonic Orchestra. DG 419158 (2) [ADD] +
Concerto No. 2, *Fantasias,* Op. 116
Brendel, Abbado, Berlin Philharmonic Orchestra. Philips 420071 [DDD]
R. Serkin, Szell, Cleveland Orchestra. Sony 37803 [ADD] (mid-price)

Concerto No. 2 in B-flat for Piano, Op. 83

A frequent candidate for greatest piano concerto ever written, this work is unusual in its four-movement form, massive scale, and relatively subdued role for the solo instrument. The Viennese critic Eduard Hanslick called it "a symphony with piano obbligato." Brahms impishly referred to it as "a tiny, tiny piano concerto, with a tiny, tiny wisp of a scherzo."

Gilels is first again (see under Concerto No. 1, above), the Vladimir Ashkenazy for a single digital disc (in especially clear sound), or Rudolf Serkin at mid-price.

Gilels, Jochum, Berlin Philharmonic Orchestra. DG 419158 (2) [ADD] +
Concerto No. 1, *Fantasias,* Op. 116
Ashkenazy, Haitink, Vienna Philharmonic Orchestra. London 410199
[DDD]
R. Serkin, Szell, Cleveland Orchestra. Sony 37258 [ADD]

Concerto in D for Violin, Op. 77

Like the two piano concerti, Brahms's single violin concerto is symphonic in scope and style. It was written for, and dedicated to, the composer's friend Joseph Joachim, one of the great violinists of that era. It was premiered on New Year's Day, 1879, to a reception as chilly as the weather. One reviewer called it "a concerto against the violin." In time, nevertheless, it became the chief rival of Beethoven's violin concerto in eminence.

Sorting through all the fine recordings of this work was heavy weather, but at this time I would put it this way: Arthur Grumiaux is the best value at mid-price, in excellent analog sound. Sholom Mintz approaches the great soloists in very superior sound and with a basic coupling, but at full price. Itzhak Perlman's 1976 recording is a bellwether, but it is full price with no coupling. Jascha Heifetz is at legendary status, but the sound is below average at full price, although the coupling of the Beethoven Violin Concerto almost makes up for it (and has much better sound). Nearly as good as Mintz and in digital is the little-known Hideko Udagawa, with a different coupling, and on a label a bit harder to find than the others. (No, I didn't forget Anne-Sophie Mutter, but that famous recording is out of the catalog as I write this. There's always something!)

Grumiaux, C. Davis, Philharmonia Orchestra. Philips Silver Line 420703 [ADD] + Bruch: Violin Concerto No. 1 (mid-price)

Mintz, Abbado, Berlin Philharmonic Orchestra. DG 423617 [DDD] + *Academic Festival* Overture

Perlman, Giulini, Chicago Symphony Orchestra. EMI 47166 [ADD]

Heifetz, Reiner, Chicago Symphony Orchestra. RCA 5402 [ADD] + Beethoven: Violin Concerto

Udagawa, Mackerras, London Symphony Orchestra. Chandos 8974 [DDD] + Bruch: Violin Concerto No. 1

Concerto in A for Violin and Cello, Op. 102

This too was written for Joachim, but also for the cellist Robert Hausmann. And like the violin concerto, it had a dismal premiere, being denounced as "unplayable," "joyless," and "autumnal." Autumnal it surely is; the composer's final orchestral work, it is resigned and reflective in tone throughout. Most modern audiences, however, find it poignantly beautiful rather than joyless.

Violinist David Oistrakh and cellist Mstislav Rostropovich are pretty much untouchable in this work, and the reissued mid-price disc offers a generous coupling of Beethoven's Triple Concerto. If you must have digital, Mutter and Meneses are fine, but there is no coupling even at full price. Francescatti and Fournier are recommendable at mid-price if you can't find the Oistrakh/Rostropovich, but in older sound and with a more meager coupling; still, a classic performance.

Oistrakh, Rostropovich, Szell, Cleveland Orchestra. EMI 64744 [ADD] + Beethoven: Triple Concerto (plus Sviatoslav Richter, with Karajan conducting) (mid-price)

Mutter, Meneses, Karajan, Berlin Philharmonic Orchestra. [DDD]

Francescatti, Fournier, B. Walter, Columbia Symphony Orchestra. CBS 37237 [ADD] + *Tragic* Overture (mid-price)

German Requiem, Op. 45 (Ein Deutsches Requiem)

Inspired, if that is the word, by the death of his mother, this unique choral work established Brahms's fame at age thirty-five. Unlike all other Requiems, this one is a prayer for the living instead of the dead. It eschews the traditional Latin Catholic text for sections of the Luther Bible, chosen by Brahms himself; faith and consolation are the keynotes.

André Previn's traditional approach in digital sound is at mid-price, and may be a bit safer starting place than John Eliot Gardiner's unique period-instrument version—but if that doesn't worry you, dive in—it has gotten nothing but rave reviews. The old classic is the Klemperer reading; great, but still full price for a 1961 recording?

Previn, Royal Philharmonic Orchestra. Teldec 75862 [DDD] (mid-price)
Gardiner, Orchestra Révolutionnaire et Romantique, Monteverdi Choir. Philips 432140 [DDD]
Klemperer, Philharmonia Orchestra and Chorus. EMI 47238 [ADD]

Hungarian Dances (orchestral versions)

Originally written for piano four-hands (i.e., piano duet, two pianists sitting at one instrument), these have become among the most familiar short works by Brahms in their orchestral transcriptions—sometimes by the composer, sometimes by others. They are perhaps not ideal for continuous listening, but they are essential to have around the house; play two or three every so often to get yourself going.

Kurt Masur brings real gypsy paprika to his digital version; István Bogár is extremely good on a budget digital disc, although Naxos has the listings mixed up on the back cover; and Szell is magnificent on an early stereo budget three-CD set with other Brahms works.

Masur, Leipzig Gewandhaus Orchestra. Philips 411426 [DDD]
Bogár, Budapest Symphony Orchestra. Naxos 8.550110 [DDD] (budget)
Szell, Cleveland Orchestra. Sony Essential Classics 48398 (3) [ADD] + Symphonies 1-4, *Academic Festival* Overture, *Tragic* Overture, *Haydn Variations* (budget)

Quintet in B Minor for Clarinet and Strings, Op. 115

Among Brahms's last works are four inspired by his acquaintance with the clarinetist Mühlfeld. This quintet is among the composer's most sonorous and satisfying chamber works; the ecstatically trance-like slow movement is quintessentially "autumnal" Brahms.

Great clarinet tone and svelte sound come together with Daniel Shifrin's digital recording, paired with another fine Brahms chamber work.

Shifrin, Chamber Music Northwest. Delos 3066 [DDD] + String Quintet in G, Op. 111

Symphonies (4)

Nowhere is Brahms more successful than in his four famous symphonies in achieving his ideal of uniting nineteenth-century Romantic ideals with eighteenth-century Classical form. His speech is clearly post-Beethoven, yet his orchestration is far more restrained than Bruckner or Mahler, or even, much earlier, Berlioz. There are no Romantic "programs" in the Brahms symphonies, only "absolute" music. They rely on grand architecture, rich harmonization, dramatic force, and poetic melodies to achieve the synthesis that makes them the most admired of all Mainstream Romantic symphonies.

If you are looking to collect all the Brahms symphonies in a set, you could scarcely do better than to get Günter Wand's splendid versions in a three-CD mid-price box, and digital besides. The Szell recordings are many years older, but they were standards of the 60s and come now in an even cheaper box with loads of fine couplings; not a bad way to get acquainted with the bulk of Brahms's orchestral music.

Wand, North German Radio Symphony Orchestra. RCA Gold Seal 60085 (3) [DDD] (mid-price)

Szell, Cleveland Orchestra. Sony Essential Classics 48398 (3) [ADD] + *Academic Festival* Overture, *Hungarian Dances, Tragic* Overture, *Haydn Variations* (budget)

Symphony No. 1 in C Minor, Op. 68

Haunted by the imaginary tread of Beethoven behind him, Brahms was forty-three when he got brave enough to try out a first symphony. To those who tried to hurry him, he snapped: "A symphony is no joke." His fears were validated when the 1876 premiere was tepid. Critics harped on the similarity of the main theme of the last movement to that of the finale of Beethoven's Ninth. "Any fool," glowered Brahms, "can see that." Obviously, he intended the resemblance as a symbolic launching point. Today its grandeur and nobility make it the most popular of his symphonies.

Günter Wand's No. 1 is a first choice for many critics, but it is available only in the three-CD set detailed above under the complete symphonies discussion. The comparable single digital disc is from Claudio Abbado with a non-basic coupling. Bruno Walter is classic on a budget disc.

Abbado, Berlin Philharmonic Orchestra. DG 431790 [DDD] + *Gesang des Parzen*

B. Walter, Columbia Symphony Orchestra. CBS Odyssey 44827 [ADD] (budget)

Symphony No. 2 in D, Op. 73

Unusually genial for Brahms, the second symphony followed closely upon the long-delayed first, written just a year later at a holiday resort where, presumably, the sun-drenched waters contributed to its warm inspiration. Its premiere, unlike that of Symphony No. 1, was a complete success.

Claudio Abbado has recorded all the Brahms symphonies on four individual discs, and pretty much now heads critics' lists for digital recordings, aside from Günter Wand; he especially shines in Nos. 2 and 3. Wand (unlike the situation with No. 1) is available singly, and more cheaply. Karajan is also excellent in digital, with a bonus of the *Haydn Variations,* and Leonard Bernstein's live 1983 performance has a special cachet, with a coupling of the *Academic Festival* Overture.

> **Abbado, Berlin Philharmonic Orchestra.** DG 427643 [DDD] + *Alto Rhapsody*
> **Wand, North German Radio Symphony Orchestra.** RCA Gold Seal 60087 [DDD] (mid-price)
> **Karajan, Berlin Philharmonic Orchestra.** DG 423142 [DDD] + *Haydn Variations*
> **Bernstein, Vienna Philharmonic Orchestra.** DG 410082 [DDD] + *Academic Festival* Overture

Symphony No. 3 in F, Op. 90

Several years passed before Brahms resumed his symphonic activity. He was now fifty, and even commentators not given to reading things into music have suggested that its subject is the struggle between youth and age. The premiere in 1883 was tumultuous, far beyond the reception of the previous two symphonies, despite attempts by a Wagner clique to disrupt the performance. The mostly stormy final movement is unusual in its ending of a peaceful rainbow of sound.

Günter Wand is so good in No. 3 he outshines even Abbado, especially at a lower price and with No. 4 thrown in on the single digital disc. Abbado, however, zooms up next on the list, and you may want to have all four of the Abbado performances anyway. Karajan offers good value for his fans on a mid-price disc, also coupled with No. 4; he has a good digital version, but I would go with Wand.

> **Wand, North German Radio Symphony Orchestra.** RCA Gold Seal 60088 [DDD] + Symphony No. 4 (mid-price)
> **Abbado, Berlin Philharmonic Orchestra.** DG 429765 [DDD] + *Tragic* Overture, *Song of Destiny*

Karajan, Berlin Philharmonic Orchestra. DG Galleria 437645 [ADD] + Symphony No. 4 (mid-price)

Symphony No. 4 in E Minor, Op. 98

The final Brahms symphony is his most austere and Classical, often melancholy in mood, but never tragic. The last movement, a set of thirty variations with a magnificent conclusion, is a deliberate slap in the face of some of Brahms's more loosely Romantic fellow composers. Brahms himself conducted the first performance in 1885.

A little more variety of choice here, as Abbado, Wand, and Karajan, by now inevitable, are joined for honors by Leonard Bernstein with the best of his Brahms cycle; Carlos Kleiber with a memorable digital version; and George Szell offering unbeatable value at a budget price.

C. Kleiber, Vienna Philharmonic Orchestra. DG 400037 [DDD]
Bernstein, Vienna Philharmonic Orchestra. DG 410082 [DDD] + *Tragic* Overture
Abbado, Berlin Philharmonic Orchestra. DG 435349 [DDD] + *Haydn Variations, Nänie*
Wand, North German Radio Symphony Orchestra. RCA Gold Seal 60088 [DDD] + Symphony No. 3 (mid-price)
Karajan, Berlin Philharmonic Orchestra. DG Galleria 437645 [ADD] + Symphony No. 3 (mid-price)
Szell, Cleveland Orchestra. Sony Essential Classics 46330 [ADD] + *Academic Festival* Overture, *Tragic* Overture (budget)

Tragic Overture, Op. 81

Which tragedy? Oh, none in particular. Who else but morose old Brahms would think to write a generically tragic overture just for the fun of it? Actually, it was conceived as a more serious companion piece to the ebullient *Academic Festival* Overture, which Brahms may have worried was altogether too jocular for a man of his reputation.

This work is available on recordings already recommended under other Brahms titles, as follows:

Abbado, Berlin Philharmonic Orchestra. DG 429765 [DDD] + Symphony No. 3
Bernstein, Vienna Philharmonic Orchestra. DG 410082 [DDD] + Symphony No. 4

Szell, Cleveland Orchestra. Sony Essential Classics 46330 [ADD] + *Academic Festival* Overture, Symphony No. 4 (budget)

Szell, Cleveland Orchestra. Sony Essential Classics 48398 (3) [ADD] + Symphonies 1-4, *Academic Festival* Overture, *Hungarian Dances, Haydn Variations* (budget)

B. Walter, Columbia Symphony Orchestra. Sony 37237 [ADD] + Double Concerto (mid-price)

Trio in E-flat for Horn, Violin, and Piano, Op. 40

One of Brahms's most expressive chamber works, this unusual trio relies on the intrinsic nature of the French horn to create the desired atmosphere of Romantic nature-painting, tinted with gentle melancholy.

The classic recording features hornist Barry Tuckwell, with violinist Itzhak Perlman and pianist Vladimir Ashkenazy, with Tuckwell dropping out for the coupling of Franck's Violin Sonata. This is about as star-studded as a chamber recording can get. For a digital version, the less glittery names of Thompson, Dubinsky, and Edlina do just fine, coupled with the Clarinet Trio.

Tuckwell, Perlman, Ashkenazy. London 414128 [ADD] + Franck: Violin Sonata

Thompson, Dubinsky, Edlina. Chandos 8606 [DDD] + Clarinet Trio

Variations on a Theme by Haydn, Op. 56a

This brilliant orchestral tour de force is far more entertaining than its dustily academic title portends. The theme, as modern muckrakers have discovered, isn't even by Haydn anyway, so forget about scholarship and just listen while Brahms takes this attractive (anonymous) melody and tosses it up and down and around the orchestra until it finally bounces joyfully into the blue.

Finally, this work shows up on discs recommended above under other titles, and there is no need no look further, at least not first time around.

Karajan, Berlin Philharmonic Orchestra. DG 423142 [DDD] + Symphony No. 2

Abbado, Berlin Philharmonic Orchestra. DG 435349 [DDD] + Symphony No. 4, *Nänie*

Szell, Cleveland Orchestra. Sony Essential Classics 48398 [ADD] + Symphonies 1-4, *Academic Festival* Overture, *Hungarian Dances, Tragic* Overture (budget)

Max Bruch (1838-1920)

Bruch seems, on paper, about as stuffy and conservative as a nineteenth-century German composer could get. Writing once about a new opera by his contemporary, Hans Pfitzner—not exactly a liberal himself—Bruch called it "unspeakably despicable...the sad product of...a sick brain...of a super-aesthetic," adding that it was nothing more than "dismaying fantastic nonsense."

We might expect the music of such a backward-looking composer to be plodding and dull, yet he wrote two of the sprightliest works in the violin repertoire, and took an abiding interest in the national music of several cultures and incorporated elements of them into his own works. Not bad for a fuddy-duddy.

Bruch had a career as both conductor and conservatory teacher, but composing was his meat. In his long life of eighty-two years he wrote operas, symphonies, choral and chamber works, and piano pieces. His best works are enlivened by a warmly ingratiating melodic style. He was also a skillful illusionist: those who hear his snappy *Scottish Fantasy* or his deeply soulful *Kol Nidrei* for the first time are equally surprised to learn that he was neither Scottish nor Jewish.

Concerto No. 1 in G Minor for Violin, Op. 26

Neither profound nor tightly organized, this beloved concerto gets by on enormous charm and surface beauty. If you stick up your nose at this sort of thing, stranger, pass by.

Cho-Liang Lin is the runaway winner on this piece, radiant playing coupled with the Mendelssohn Violin Concerto and a couple of encores, in digital at mid-price. Hard to beat, but it's still worth throwing in Arthur Grumiaux's version which, though analog, is mid-price and has a different coupling—one of the great recordings of the Brahms Violin Concerto which some may prefer; also, Hideko Udagawa's previously recommended version of the Brahms gives you a fine digital disc.

Lin, Slatkin, Chicago Symphony Orchestra. CBS 44902 [DDD] + Mendelssohn: Violin Concerto (with Michael Tilson Thomas conducting the Philharmonia Orchestra); encores by Sarasate and Kreisler (mid-price)
Grumiaux, C. Davis, Philharmonia Orchestra. Philips Silver Line 420703 [ADD] + Brahms: Violin Concerto (mid-price)
Udagawa, Mackerras, London Symphony Orchestra. Chandos 8974 [DDD] + Brahms: Violin Concerto

Anton Bruckner (1824-1896)

Bruckner was one of those people who make others cough, fidget, and leave the room when they enter. Possibly today we would label him an idiot savant. He barged around Vienna in rumpled clothes and mismatched socks, a shapeless figure with a shaved head, speaking in a rough rustic dialect.

He either did not know how to act or simply never grew up. His manners were atrocious. He frequently proposed marriage to teenage girls, sometimes immediately after meeting them. When he met his hero, Richard Wagner, he fell on his knees before him and kissed his hand. When he was pleased with the rehearsal of one of his symphonies, he tipped the conductor a dollar. And when the Austrian Emperor asked if he could do anything for him, Bruckner nervously suggested that perhaps he could "take care of" the critic Hanslick, who made such merciless fun of his music.

Occasionally one of these inappropriate actions or remarks transcended itself, as when after the rehearsal of another of his symphonies, Bruckner ran up excitedly to the bored conductor and asked how he had liked it. The maestro coughed and fidgeted. "Very nice Anton, very nice...but don't you think it's a little too long?" The composer's face turned livid. "No!" he shot back, "my symphony is not too long. You are too short!"

Bruckner came from the countryside in Upper Austria. His father, a schoolmaster and organist, died when Anton was twelve. The boy was educated at a nearby monastery. He was a slow but determined learner, especially in music. When assigned to write an exercise in counterpoint, he would stay up all night and turn in sheets full of examples the next day.

Eventually he moved to Vienna, where he was able to secure a professorship at the Conservatory. He spent the rest of his life teaching, and trying, with limited success, to get his music performed. He wrote a few fine choral works, but his focus was on the symphony. He wrote eleven of those altogether (the last incomplete at his death), although they have such clear family resemblances that one of Bruckner's more withering critics claimed he had actually written only one symphony—nine times. (He said "nine" because that is how many are officially numbered. There were two very early works which Bruckner never meant to publish; they have been retrieved, revived, and renumbered as the "Student" Symphony and Symphony No. "0.")

Once considered clumsily and ineptly written, the symphonies are more often now seen as uniquely original. Audiences and critics, as ploddingly slow as Bruckner himself, have gradually come to find in them a noble, even mystical, beauty. Those whose visual imaginations are stimulated by music generally interpret Bruckner's symphonic world as one of dark forests and mysteriously murmuring streams, which are now and then bathed in bursts of overwhelming radiance. Whether this is the light of the morning sun striking the peaks of Bruckner's beloved Alps, or the glory of the Catholic God in whom he so simply and devoutly believed, it is hard to say. Perhaps it is both.

Symphony No. 4 in E-flat, "Romantic"

Surely the nickname is redundant, but this is the shortest and most immediately accessible of Bruckner's symphonies; its sonorities are radiant, its structure compact, its mood joyful.

[First, a few words about the Bruckner recording situation in general. There are several conductors who are especially noted for their Bruckner. In recent years, Klaus Tennstedt, Sir Georg Solti, Günter Wand, Bernard Haitink, Karl Böhm, Eugen Jochum, and Herbert von Karajan have all had outstanding recordings of various of the symphonies. Farther back, Bruno Walter, and especially Wilhelm Furtwängler, set standards for all time.

There is a problem, however, in that very often the best versions by these conductors are not the ones currently in print. Günter Wand is a good example: he has recorded some of the symphonies multiple times, and although he is one of the great Brucknerians and you will see his discs listed in the catalogs, these are not the particular recordings he is famous for. Picking around in what is currently available did not leave many choices for really prime readings, and it is to be hoped that the future will bring reissues of some versions now sorely missed.]

As to Symphony No. 4, the first choice would have been Karl Böhm's great reading, a standard of the catalog for many seasons, but now lamentably deleted. Thankfully, we have a fine digital version from Claudio Abbado, and an excellent mid-price analog from Eugen Jochum to keep us going.

Abbado, Vienna Philharmonic Orchestra. DG 431719 [DDD]
Jochum, Berlin Philharmonic Orchestra. DG 427200 [ADD] (mid-price)

Symphony No. 7 in E

Bruckner spent two years writing this symphony, the first composition by anyone to use a quartet of "Wagner tubas" outside of Wagner's own stage works. Well over an hour long, it is structurally complex, but easy to listen to based on its beautiful melodic material. Bruckner claimed the principal theme was whistled to him in a dream by his friend Ignaz Dorn; he immediately woke up, lit a candle, and wrote it down.

Claudio Abbado and Daniel Barenboim both have recent digital recordings that make vivid cases for this symphony, but just a bit older is Herbert von Karajan's digital version, which has special interest in being his very last recording for DG before his death. There is also a fine double-CD budget recording from Bruno Walter, with an extra symphony under a different conductor.

Abbado, Vienna Philharmonic Orchestra. DG 437518 [DDD]
Barenboim, Berlin Philharmonic Orchestra. Teldec 77118 [DDD]
Karajan, Vienna Philharmonic Orchestra. DG 429226 [DDD]
B. Walter, Columbia Symphony Orchestra. CBS Odyssey 45669 (2) [ADD] + Symphony No. 5 (conducted by Eugene Ormandy) (budget)

Symphony No. 8 in C Minor

The composer took not two, but six years to work on this, his own choice for his greatest symphony. In its first revised version, both audience and critics greeted warmly the premiere performance on December 18, 1892. His fellow composer Hugo Wolf wrote that "this symphony is the creation of a giant." Even longer than No. 7, it concludes with one of the truly overpowering symphonic finales—a gradual and ever more splendiferous sunrise over the Alps. Or so it is in *my* dreams.

Herbert von Karajan holds the lead here in a very famous recording, the best of his three readings of this symphony. The only recording to hold a candle to it is by the great Furtwängler; it is mono and very old, but if you become a real Bruckner fan and want to hear the master at work, add it to your mix.

Karajan, Vienna Philharmonic Orchestra. DG 427611 (2) [DDD]
Furtwängler, Berlin Philharmonic Orchestra. Music and Arts 624 [AAD]
(mono)

Symphony No. 9 in D Minor

Bruckner died before completing this mystical, sometimes harsh and terrifying symphony, so that it concludes with an adagio movement. Its tonal structure is Bruckner's most forward-looking. Its premiere took place in 1903, several years after the composer's death, and even then it was considered necessary to revise the orchestration to make it more palatable. Today it is usually played unvarnished, in all its craggy grandeur.

Carlo Maria Giulini boasts the best digital recording available, and Bruno Walter outdoes himself on a very desirable budget recording from 1959, the sound exceptional for its time.

Giulini, Vienna Philharmonic Orchestra. DG 427 345 [DDD]
B. Walter, Columbia Symphony Orchestra. CBS Odyssey 44825 [ADD]
(budget)

Emmanuel Chabrier (1841-1894)

In his day, Chabrier was considered a talented amateur. He was, indeed, a civil servant (an employee of the Ministry of the Interior in Paris), but music was his true love, and at the age of thirty-eight, after seeing a performance of Wagner's *Tristan und Isolde,* he quit his job and devoted himself to composing and to playing the piano—if "playing" is not too weak a word. Alfred Cortot called him "demolisher of pianos." Performing "à la Chabrier" came to mean indulging in what Vincent d'Indy described as "contrasting accents: pianissimi that became inaudible, then sudden explosions in the midst of the most exquisite softness.'

After a Chabrier recital, the corners of the keys were likely to be broken, and the lid scratched and gashed. "In his native town," Cortot reminisced, "they still remember his last visit, after which all the local pianos had to be repaired."

Enormously fat, Chabrier was equally expansive in wit and drollery. He was once accosted by Benjamin Godard, a composer of little talent whose sentimental pieces had some currency at the time. Said Godard, "What a pity, my dear Emmanuel, that you took to music so late." Replied Chabrier, "It is much more annoying, my dear Benjamin, that you took to it so early."

Chabrier's piano music was harmonically in advance of its time. Erik Satie and the members of *Les Six* acknowledged their debt to Chabrier; Ravel vastly admired him, and Poulenc called him "my spiritual grandfather." It is ironic, but perhaps not surprising, that Chabrier is most remembered today for one of his few orchestral works, *España*.

España

About a year after a stimulating trip to Spain, Chabrier concocted this brew of *jotas* and *malagueñas* which has become a mainstay of the light orchestral repertoire. British composer Constant Lambert went so far as to call *España* "the most perfectly orchestrated composition of the last century." Such a judgment is even more amazing when one knows that Chabrier had to teach himself orchestration by copying out Wagner's *Tannhäuser!*

In digital sound, Yan-Pascal Tortelier has a lovely disc from Ireland with an additional Chabrier piece, the *Suite Pastorale*, and two by Dukas, *La Péri* and *The Sorcerer's Apprentice*. (The Irish and the French have always got along well.) At mid-price, Paul Paray's marvellous analog recording has been reissued with five other Chabrier pieces and the Suite in F by Albert Roussel, an excellent piece not covered in this book, but very worthwhile.

Tortelier, Ulster Orchestra. Chandos 8852 [DDD] + *Suite Pastorale;* Dukas: *La Péri, Sorcerer's Apprentice*
Paray, Detroit Symphony Orchestra. Mercury 434303 [ADD] + other Chabrier pieces; Roussel: Suite in F (mid-price)

Ernest Chausson (1855-1899)

Ernest was the son of a wealthy construction contractor named (appropriately, perhaps) Prosper Chausson, who was prominent in the remodelling and reconstruction of Paris as advocated by Mayor Haussman in the mid-nineteenth century. Ernest's two brothers died young and he was doted on, being educated at home by private tutors and introduced into the most fashionable salons by age fifteen.

He quickly developed a taste for all the fine arts. At first he divided his attention among music, painting, and literature, but by age twenty-four he entered the Paris Conservatory and settled on a career as a composer. He studied with Massenet, and attended lectures given by Franck. But it was the then-new and exciting music of Wagner that gripped his imagination. Chausson's few surviving compositions bear the marks of all these influences, and yet have a distinctive sound of their own.

He was just beginning to hit his stride when an accident took his life. He was riding a bicycle down a hill when he lost control and hit a brick wall. He was only forty-four years old. Many years later, in 1936, his widow auctioned off some of his collection of paintings. There were major works by Gauguin, Manet, Degas, Corot, and Delacroix, which today would sell for many millions of dollars. This composer's life was tragically short, but at least he did not suffer like so many others the shame and agony of poverty.

Poème for Violin and Orchestra, Op. 25

Inspired by his teacher Franck's theories of cyclical form, the haunting *Poème* is Chausson's best-known work and has been danced as a ballet.

Itzhak Perlman's recording swamps the field here, abetted by several fine couplings, including two from the "basic" list of this book.

Perlman, Mehta, New York Philharmonic Orchestra. DG 423063 [DDD]
+ Saint-Saëns: *Havanaise, Introduction* and *Rondo Capriccioso;* Ravel: *Tzigane;*
Sarasate: *Carmen Fantasy*

Symphony in B-flat, Op. 20

While picking up where Franck's only symphony leaves off, Chausson's only symphony is spiced with Wagnerisms, yet highly individual. One could not guess by my brevity how much I love it.

A very fine digital reading by Jean Fournet may be a bit difficult to find; it is coupled with Fauré's *Pelléas and Mélisande* Suite. Michel Plasson is great at mid-price with two additional tone poems by Chausson.

Fournet, Netherlands Symphony Orchestra. Denon 73675 [DDD] +
Fauré: *Pelléas et Mélisande*
Plasson, Toulouse Capitole Orchestra. EMI 64686 + 2 tone poems (mid-price)

Léo Delibes (1836-1891)

Delibes was a star pupil at the Paris Conservatory, winning a first prize at the age of fourteen. At seventeen he secured the first of several appointments as church organist which supported him, along with accompanying on the piano at the Théatre Lyrique opera house, until 1871, when he was at last able to live off the revenues of his compositions.

His first breakthrough was the ballet *Coppélia* (1870). Another few years brought success with the ballet *Sylvia,* and the opera *Lakmé.* His charming music plumbs no depths, but shows a talent beyond the routine as well as a masterly grasp of orchestration, albeit conventional. His ballets had an enormous influence on Tchaikovsky, who in fact expressed a preference for the music of Delibes over that of Brahms; and years later, that other great Russian ballet composer, Igor Stravinsky, rated Delibes higher than Beethoven on a list of great melodists! (Nowadays it is a struggle to get a music critic to rate Delibes over Gounod.)

Coppélia Suite; Sylvia Suite

Coppélia and *Sylvia* are very high peaks in the nineteenth-century range of ballets, with ravishing melodies ravishingly scored. Suites from either or both of them make a concentrated case for their beauties.

One of Herbert von Karajan's most admired recordings out of hundreds was of the *Coppélia* Suite, with Offenbach's *Gaité Parisienne* ballet and *Les Sylphides,* a concoction made up from orchestrations of Chopin piano pieces. This is now available at mid-price. Also very desirable is Eugene Ormandy's budget disc with both suites and Tchaikovsky's *Nutcracker* Suite. This is as basic as ballet recordings get, and Ormandy was in his métier here. Either recording is a winner.

Karajan, Berlin Philharmonic Orchestra. DG Galleria 429163 [ADD] + Offenbach: *Gaité Parisienne;* Chopin: *Les Sylphides* (mid-price)
Ormandy, Philadelphia Orchestra. Sony 46550 [ADD] + Tchaikovsky: *Nutcracker* Suite (budget)

Antonin Dvořák (1841-1904)

Antonin was the eldest of eight children born to the innkeeper and sausage-maker František Dvořák and his wife Anna, a former serving maid in a lord's castle, in the picturesque town of Nelahozeves, thirty miles north of Prague. His family was socially humble, but intelligent, loving, and hardworking—qualities the musically talented Antonin inherited and never lost.

"I would gladly give all my symphonies," he once said, "had I been able to invent the locomotive!" He was a railroad buff, a pigeon breeder, a nature lover, a card player, a connoisseur of sausages, and a devoted family man. He almost *did* give away his symphonies, but not for a train; he was so absent-minded he misplaced and forgot about his first four symphonies. They were rediscovered one by one, beginning as late as 1923, and until very recent years even the enormously popular "New World" Symphony, now known as No. 9, was listed as No. 5.

Dvořák began playing the fiddle as a small boy, and sang in the church choir. Soon he was picking up the viola, piano, and organ, too. His doting father hoped against hope that Antonin would become a butcher, and by age fifteen he had indeed advanced from apprentice to journeyman in that trade; but at last, prodded by the boy's admiring teacher, František conceded that music was his son's true calling, and let him go off to the capital to study.

Slowly Antonin made his methodical way up the musical ladder, playing in orchestras throughout his twenties, and trying his hand at composing. Many of these early works ended up in the fireplace—or like those first four symphonies, in the closet. By his thirties he had won the admiration of several influential musicians, most notably Johannes Brahms, who remained a lifelong friend and supporter. Until recent years Dvořák was often characterized as a kind of "peasant Brahms," as if he were forever condemned to be second-rate. Brahms himself never thought any such thing. "I'd be delighted," he said to a Dvořák detractor, "to think up a main theme as good as those that Dvořák has discarded."

Dvořák's essentially gentle life was marred now and then by tragedy. The worst year was 1876, when his first three children all died of various diseases within a few months of each other. Stunned by grief, Dvořák worked through his feelings in a moving setting of the *Stabat Mater,* the medieval poem in which Mary contemplates the sacrifice of her son on the cross. The work is a testimony to the composer's emotional stability and deep faith.

He was fifty years old before he was fully recognized even in his native Bohemia, and he had had to pave the way in the previous decade with six trips to England, where his warm personality and rich melodic gift were more readily appreciated. Better known to Americans are the three years he spent in the U.S., beginning in 1892, as director of the (now defunct) New York National Conservatory of Music.

His summer vacations were spent in the hamlet of Spillville, Iowa, where a band of immigrants had created a charming slice of Bohemia in America. The town is still on the map, and a day's side trip to visit the Dvořák museum and other quaint attractions is well worth a music lover's time. After fifteen years, I still fondly remember consuming corn fritters served on red-and-white-checked oilcloth-covered tables at the Czech Inn, while outside in the town square a uniformed band played in the gazebo.

I felt Dvořák's spirit very much alive in the New World.

Carnival Overture, Op. 92

Although programmatic music was not Dvořák's forte, he attempted a few overtures with story lines. The only one that has won wide popularity is *Carnival,* an irresistibly boisterous picture of a Slavic fair.

Happily, the definitive recording of this work is on a budget disc with other very basic selections; there is really no need to start anywhere else for this music.

Szell, Cleveland Orchestra. CBS 36716 + Smetana: Dances from *The Bartered Bride, The Moldau* (budget)

Concerto in B Minor for Cello, Op. 104

Had he written nothing else, Dvořák would be considered a genius for this greatest of all cello concerti. Brahms is said to have given up an idea to write a similar work after hearing this one. Not only is its melodic material exquisite, but at every turn Dvořák has ingeniously sidestepped or conquered the inherent problem of hearing the solo cello over a full orchestra.

The great Russian cellist Mstislav Rostropovich has recorded this work half a dozen times; I list the one usually considered the best. It is not digital, however, and you may wish to try Yo-Yo Ma for that. There is also an excellent budget version with French cellist Pierre Fournier with very nice couplings.

Rostropovich, Karajan, Berlin Philharmonic Orchestra. DG 413819 [ADD] + Tchaikovsky: *Rococo Variations*
Ma, Maazel, Berlin Philharmonic Orchestra. CBS 42206 [DDD] + *Rondo Capriccioso, Silent Woods*
P. Fournier, Szell, Berlin Philharmonic Orchestra. DG Musikfest 429155 [ADD] + Bloch: *Schelomo;* Bruch: *Kol Nidrei* (budget)

Quartet No. 12 in F, Op. 96, "American"

It took Dvořák only two weeks to write the most popular of his fourteen string quartets, during one of his summers in Spillville. He is said to have taken great interest in the music of a band of American Indians visiting the town, and may have incorporated some features into this and others of his works written in the U.S., although one is hard-pressed to make much distinction between Indian folk scales or rhythms and those of Bohemia, or anywhere else. Only direct quotations of specific melodies would prove the case, and these Dvořák did not provide.

Lamenting briefly the disappearance (temporary, I hope) of the more or less perfect recording by the Quartetto Italiano, we move on to outstanding versions by the Emerson Quartet (digital) and the Guarneri Quartet (analog, mid-price).

Emerson Quartet. DG 429723 [DDD] + Smetana: Quartet No. 1
Guarneri Quartet. RCA Gold Seal 6263 [ADD] + Piano Quintet in A, Op. 81 (with Artur Rubinstein) (mid-price)

Slavonic Dances, Opp. 46, 72

Dvořák's two sets of *Slavonic Dances,* written first for piano duet and then orchestrated, were directly inspired by the similar *Hungarian Dances* of Brahms. Success of the first set was directly responsible for establishing Dvořák's fame outside of Bohemia. Eight years passed before he got around to satisfying his salivating publisher with the second group.

Superior sonics grace an idiomatic reading from Christoph von Dohnányi, and George Szell conducts a beautifully remastered budget version with the same orchestra, years earlier.

Dohnányi, Cleveland Orchestra. London 430171 [DDD]
Szell, Cleveland Orchestra. CBS Essential Classics 48161 [ADD] (budget)

Symphony No. 7 in D Minor, Op. 70

This is the first of Dvořák's nine symphonies to achieve unquestioned parity with the great masters, and many critics still consider it his best, although Nos. 8 and 9 are more popular with the public. Dvořák was consciously working here to be serious and to employ strict symphonic logic; what the less intellectual listener misses is the customary profusion of Bohemian folk-like melody.

István Kertész made famous and near-definitive recordings of all the Dvořák symphonies in the 1960s, and his versions of the last three are alive and well on budget reissues. Nos. 7 and 8 come together on one disc. If this is not readily available and you have a couple of extra dollars, you won't go wrong with the same coupling from Sir Colin Davis at mid-price. If digital is your goal, André Previn probably gets the nod, but the disc offers only No. 7, with a coupling of the overture *My Home.*

Kertész, London Symphony Orchestra. London Weekend Classics 433091 [ADD] + Symphony No. 8 (budget)
C. Davis, Concertgebouw Orchestra. Philips 420890 [ADD] + Symphony No. 8 (mid-price)
Previn, Los Angeles Philharmonic Orchestra. Telarc 80173 [DDD] + *My Home* overture

Symphony No. 8 in G, Op. 88

After the critical success of No. 7, Dvořák seems to relax and write a more folksy symphony for his own enjoyment. Infused throughout with Bohemian rustic idioms, No. 8 is the sunniest and most lovable of them all.

Kertész is first choice, followed by Sir Colin Davis, as listed above under No. 7, while Vaclav Neumann is the leader on digital for this symphony.

Kertész, London Symphony Orchestra. London Weekend Classics 433091 [ADD] + Symphony No. 7 (budget)

C. Davis, Concertgebouw Orchestra. Philips 420890 [ADD] + Symphony No. 7 (mid-price)

Neumann, Czech Philharmonic Orchestra. Supraphon 7703 [DDD]

Symphony No. 9 in E Minor, Op. 95, "From the New World"

Musicologists have shouted themselves hoarse reminding us that the only thing truly New Worldish about Dvořák's best-known symphony is its title, and the fact that it was written in Spillville, Iowa. Dvořák himself warned an early note-writer: "Leave out all that nonsense about my having made use of original American melodies. I have only composed in the spirit of such melodies."

None of this has stopped American audiences from feeling strongly that there is something uniquely native about this music, and uncountable listeners still believe the haunting theme of the second movement is an authentic Negro spiritual called "Goin' Home," although it was first published as such eighteen years after Dvořák's death!

There have probably been hundreds of recordings of this popular symphony, yet it is easy to snap two out of the pile for basic library choices; both are great performances, one budget analog, one digital.

Kertész, Vienna Philharmonic Orchestra. London Weekend Classics 417678 [AAD] + Smetana: *The Moldau* (budget)

Neumann, Czech Philharmonic Orchestra. Supraphon 7702 [DDD]

In addition to all the above, there is a very fine two-CD set of Dvořák's last three symphonies all together with Christoph von Dohnányi conducting, if you would like the convenience.

Dohnányi, Cleveland Orchestra. London 421082 (2) [DDD]

César Franck (1822-1890)

As the spelling of his surname hints, Franck was a Walloon—a French-speaking Belgian, an ethnic group traditionally mocked, if not despised, by pedigreed French. Nevertheless, Franck made his career in Paris playing the organ, teaching, and composing. Condescendingly tolerated by the musical establishment as a naively pious "pater seraphicus," he exerted an almost mystical hold over a small but significant band of devotees including d'Indy, Chausson, and Duparc.

The unpleasant French habit of lampooning Belgians was actually abetted by Franck's serene imperviousness to criticism, and resulted in an unusually large number of spiteful remarks being directed at this gentle soul. His fellow composer Charles Gounod pronounced Franck's Symphony in D Minor to be "the affirmation of impotence pushed to dogma." Another rival, Saint-Saëns, sniped of his Prelude, Chorale and Fugue that "the chorale is not a chorale, and the fugue not a fugue." Disregarding all this, Franck calmly went about his work, following his own muse, and saying nothing derogatory about anybody, including his detractors.

He was born in Liège (now in Belgium, then in the Netherlands) and showed musical talent early, especially on the piano. His father pushed him to become a virtuoso, but his studies at the Paris Conservatory led him to a lifelong love of the organ. This instrument thereafter dominated his life; he loved nothing more than sitting in the loft, dreaming over the keys, or quietly discussing it with, or teaching it to, his students. His composing was limited to spare moments, and even his orchestral works, like Bruckner's, often betray the influence of his devotion to organ technique.

He was a bit like Bruckner in other ways as well: his clothes were ill-fitting, he grimaced to himself as he hurried nervously down the street, he was absent-minded and sometimes embarrassingly childlike. If no one showed up for his classes at the Conservatory, he might stop by Massenet's classroom, pop his head in the door and plaintively ask, "Isn't there anyone for me?" All of this only made him more lovable to his clique of followers. Known as *la bande à Franck,* they believed in him as a musical prophet, based primarily on his development of "cyclic form," and thought of him as a saintly father.

Philip Hale once wrote of Franck that he "went through this life as a dreamer, seeing little or nothing of that which passed about him, thinking only of his art, and living only for it." Perhaps this contributed to his death, for one April day in 1890, Franck was struck by a bus while he was scurrying to the house of a student to give a lesson. He picked himself up and went on with the lesson, but his health began to deteriorate, and several months later he died of complications from the accident. In his last days, with his devoted students around him, the ever-solicitous "angelic father" murmured "My children! My poor children!"

Sonata in A for Violin and Piano

In his time, Franck was best known for his organ music, and his compositions for organ are ranked next to those of Bach. All the stranger, then, that his lone sonata for violin and piano should outshadow in fame everything but his notorious symphony. Written in 1886, it is always melodically memorable, often rhythmically exciting, and occasionally structurally innovative.

No digital version is currently available that can seriously challenge our two splendid analog performances, so why bother? This isn't *The Planets,* after all. Itzhak Perlman and Vladimir Ashkenazy are paired with the basic Brahms Horn Trio and two additional short pieces by other composers. The only disadvantage is full price; if this is a problem, turn to the equally good performance at mid-price by Kyung-Wha Chung and Radu Lupu. The couplings are just not as basic.

Perlman, Ashkenazy. London 414128 [ADD] + Brahms: Horn Trio, short works by Saint-Saëns and Schumann

Chung, Lupu. London 421154 [ADD] + pieces by Debussy and Ravel (mid-price)

Symphony in D Minor

Few beloved symphonies have been more maligned than this one. Beginning with the premiere in 1889, critics have carped that the opening theme is a ripoff of either Beethoven's String Quartet No. 16 or (!) Liszt's *Les Préludes;* that the themes are too chromatic (too many sharps and flats); that the spaces between the notes in the themes are too close together; that the themes are too similar to each other; that there are only three movements instead of the usual four; that the cyclical structure is awkward and artificial; that the orchestration is too thick and unimaginative; and, worst of all for those at the first performance, that an English horn is used in the second movement! Such an unthinkable thing had never been done. The critics shouted during the music, the audience booed—even the players in the orchestra booed! Leaving the concert hall, Franck (who was nothing if not placid) commented only: "It sounded just as I thought it would."

In the papers the next day, the symphony was variously described as dismal, morose, graceless, and even immoral. Critics still make fun of it, but audiences have come to love it for reasons critics are constitutionally incapable of understanding: most people listen to what the composer is saying, not the mechanics of how he is saying it. Once audiences got the point—that it is a symphony analogous to a bud which slowly but inexorably unfolds until it blossoms into a sun-drenched rose—they found it beautiful. So will you, if you don't study it too much.

Pierre Monteux's 1961 recording has been the standard for over thirty years, and no one is yet prepared to say it has been superseded, especially at the price and with its desirable couplings. If digital is a must, there is a fine alternative in Charles Dutoit, also with d'Indy's basic symphony.

Monteux, Chicago Symphony Orchestra. RCA Gold Seal 6805 [ADD] + d'Indy: *Symphony on a French Mountain Air;* Berlioz: Overture to *Béatrice et Bénédict* (mid-price)

Dutoit, Montreal Symphony Orchestra. London 430278 [DDD] + d'Indy: *Symphony on a French Mountain Air*

Edvard Grieg (1843-1907)

Grieg is the most famous Norwegian nationalist composer. Ironically, he was of half-Scottish descent, found his principal musical inspiration in Denmark, and employed only a handful of genuine folk tunes in the hundreds of pieces that audiences assume are ethnically authentic. It was Grieg's genius to create a musical fingerprint that signified the Norwegian spirit—minus jingoism—to all the world, while remaining almost wholly original.

His mother, an accomplished pianist, began training him from the age of six, and he wrote his first piece at age nine. Later he studied at the Leipzig Conservatory, where Arthur Sullivan, who would go on to collaborate with Gilbert, was a classmate. After a few years going back and forth to Denmark, where Copenhagen's leading composer, Niels Gade, encouraged him, he settled down once and for all in Norway.

He was all of twenty-three years old when he founded the Norwegian Academy of Music. Only two years later, with thirty-nine years of life ahead of him, he wrote his masterpiece, the Piano Concerto in A Minor. Subsequently, he largely restricted himself to the smaller forms, principally songs and short piano pieces, which gained him his permanent, if not entirely accurate, reputation as a miniaturist, as well as the even less appropriate nickname of "the Chopin of the North."

Although his incidental music for Ibsen's play *Peer Gynt* is his other best-known work, connoisseurs would point to his exquisitely crafted, poetically expressive Norwegian songs as perhaps his most significant achievement. Unfortunately, these have little currency outside of Norway.

Despite frail health he made frequent tours abroad to promote Norwegian music, including that of other composers. A man of principle and courage, he was the only famous musician to speak out publicly in defense of Alfred Dreyfus when that military officer was being railroaded by French anti-Semites. A letter of support from Grieg was printed in newspapers across Europe, and he himself became an object of ugly prejudice; one piece of hate mail arrived marked "To the Composer of Jewish music, Edvard Grieg."

He also suffered from critical barbs. In his time, and even to this day, a large portion of the critical establishment gave Grieg's music short shrift. George Bernard Shaw dismissed *Peer Gynt* as "two or three catchpenny phrases served up with plenty of orchestral sugar." Claude Debussy said Grieg's music had the taste of "a pink bonbon filled with snow." But if his works sometimes lent themselves to sentimental exploitation, it was not the composer's intention. "It is surely no fault of mine," Grieg once snapped, "that my music is heard in third-rate restaurants, and from schoolgirls."

For the most part however, Grieg lived a quiet and uneventful life with his beloved wife Nina, a talented singer for whom most of his songs were written, at their idyllic home, Troldhaugen ("Hill of the Trolls") a few miles from Bergen, until his death at age sixty-four. By then he had written a large body of quintessentially Romantic pieces in a warmly lyrical style, accumulated countless awards and honors, and won the love of both his countrymen and the world. His was a life devoid of grandiose theatrics, exhibiting instead an even temper, a becoming modesty, and a noble humanity.

Concerto in A Minor for Piano, Op. 16

Grieg was only twenty-five when he wrote his only piano concerto, and it shows. Its structure is partly cribbed from Schumann's concerto (in the same key), the various sections are awkwardly joined together, repeats and restatements are repeated verbatim without even minimal alterations to increase interest. But nobody cares about such academic concerns (except, of course, academics); what people hear are the fresh melodies and the enchantment of their poetry. It has become the very prototype of the Romantic Piano Concerto, and Sergei Rachmaninoff, for one, considered it the greatest ever written.

The many fine recordings easily boil down to two top choices: Stephen Bishop-Kovacevich, long the tasteful choice in analog, and Murray Perahia in digital. Both performances—remarkably—are conducted by Sir Colin Davis, and both are coupled with the Schumann Piano Concerto.

> **Bishop-Kovacevich, C. Davis, BBC Symphony Orchestra.** Philips 412923
> [ADD] + Schumann: Piano Concerto
> **Perahia, C. Davis, Bavarian Radio Symphony Orchestra.** CBS 44899
> [DDD] + Schumann: Piano Concerto

Peer Gynt Suites Nos. 1, 2, Opp. 46, 55

Henrik Ibsen himself invited Grieg, then aged thirty-one, to write the incidental music for his folk drama, *Peer Gynt*. Intimidated at first, Grieg gradually warmed to the commission, producing twenty-two musical numbers. Most people become familiar with the score through the two suites Grieg made for concert hall use. Although "Solvejg's Song" and "Åse's Death" were the composer's favorite excerpts, the public has chosen "Morning" and "In the Hall of the Mountain King."

Plenty of good choices here: Neeme Järvi has admirably recorded the complete incidental music, but for the beginning collector the single disc with the two *Peer Gynt* Suites and two other characteristic orchestral suites by Grieg makes an outstanding introduction (and at mid-price besides). Herbert von Karajan and Sir Thomas Beecham are both classics, also at mid-price, and there is even a well-filled digital budget disc with excellent performances.

> **Järvi, Göthenburg Symphony Orchestra.** DG 427807 [DDD] + *Sigurd Jorsalfar* Suite, *Lyric* Suite (mid-price)
> **Karajan, Berlin Philharmonic Orchestra.** DG 419474 [DDD] + *Holberg* Suite, *Sigurd Jorsalfar* Suite (mid-price)
> **Beecham, Royal Philharmonic Orchestra.** Angel 64751 + Symphonic Dance No. 2, Overture "In Autumn" (mid-price)
> **Gunzenhauser, CSSR State Philharmonic Orchestra of Košice.** Naxos 8.550140 [DDD] + two Lyric Pieces: *Sigurd Jorsalfar* Suite, *Wedding Day at Troldhaugen* (budget)

Franz Liszt (1811-1886)

Liszt was about seven or eight people rolled into one: piano virtuoso, composer, conductor, music teacher, author, man of the cloth, notorious lover, and all-around unforgettable character. No one else in the history of classical music was more rabidly Romantic, more outrageous, more controversial, more energetic, more downright amazing. Asked late in life if he had written his memoirs, Liszt replied, "It is enough to have lived such a life as mine."

He invented the "tone poem," a short orchestral form of loose construction meant to picture or apostrophize a poetic, literary, or historical subject. He originated a type of composition based on "transformation of themes" which went against the established dogmas and influenced dozens of composers after him. He was the first to give solo piano recitals (in fact, the term "recital" probably was his coinage), and the first to perform at the piano in "profile position."

Despite his many notorious liaisons with high-titled women (accompanied by duels, attempted poisonings, and grotesque adventures outlandish enough to fill a dozen purple novels), Liszt's significance to history is principally as a pianist. He was said by everyone who heard him—and that was half of Europe—to be the greatest pianist who ever lived, and although there are no recordings to document that claim, most scholars are still convinced of it. With his long hair and demonic good looks, he had women swooning at his concerts, but despite an excess of showmanship, there was real substance to his musical style. He was apparently able to sight-read almost anything, playing it on a read-through with a mixture of spontaneity and depth, chatting all the while with ladies right and left of the piano.

Cosmopolite and sybarite he was; born in Hungary of German parents but French in taste and upbringing, Liszt was a man of the world, yet with yearnings toward spirituality. He was a fantastic pastiche of colorful contradictions, in whose music we find the wildness of the gypsy, the solemnity of the abbé, and sometimes an astonishing avant-gardism that points far down the road of musical evolution.

One of his most admirable traits was a genuine interest in encouraging young musical talent. He gave unstintingly of money and moral support to a host of other developing musicians, most famously Richard Wagner, who was to become his son-in-law by marrying his daughter Cosima (after stealing her from her rightful husband, but that is another story).

More than a hundred years after his death, Liszt has yet to take an unassailable place in the pantheon of composers. Much of his music—that, unfortunately, which is best known—is marred by bombast, yet there are pages of the most refined delicacy which are far less often heard. Looking back, there still seem to be several Franz Liszts, and few are prepared even now to say which one, if any, is the one whom a more distant posterity will honor.

Concerti (2) for Piano and Orchestra

Although the Piano Concerto No. 1 in E-flat is dramatic in tone, and No. 2 in A is moody and reflective, both of them have so many other features in common that they are often spoken of almost as twins. Each is cast in a single continuous movement and is developed through Liszt's principle of the "transformation of themes." Both were sketched in the 1830s, but not finished and premiered until 1855 and 1857, respectively, Liszt soloing in the first, then conducting in the second. Although they were frankly designed to show off Liszt's virtuosity, they contain poetry as well, if the performer and listener will both pay attention.

The classic recording of the concerti together is Sviatoslav Richter from 1961, now at mid-price. Just to be nice the manufacturer has thrown in Beethoven's Cello Sonata No. 2 to fill out the disc. Weird, but wonderful. The best digital version is by Krystian Zimerman, coupled with Liszt's *Totentanz.*

Richter, Kondrashin, London Symphony Orchestra. Philips Insignia 434163 [ADD] + Beethoven: Cello Sonata No. 2 (mid-price)

Zimerman, Ozawa, Boston Symphony Orchestra. DG 423571 [DDD] + *Totentanz*

Hungarian Rhapsodies (orchestral versions) (6)

After making a serious study of Hungarian folk music for several years, Liszt undertook to write nineteen piano rhapsodies based on his understanding of gypsy idioms, characteristically alternating between the poles of *lassan* (slow, voluptuous music) and *friskan* (fast voluptuous music). Subsequently he (and Franz Doppler) orchestrated six of these; just beware, the numbers attached to the orchestral versions are not the same as the piano versions. By far the most famous is (orchestral) No. 2, a masterpiece of fiery abandon.

The choice Willi Boskovsky disc is no more, but Antal Dorati makes a great showing at mid-price with the addition of Enesco's basic *Rumanian Rhapsody* No. 1

Dorati, London Symphony Orchestra. Mercury 432015 [ADD] + Enesco: *Rumanian Rhapsody* No. 1 (mid-price)

Les Préludes (Symphonic Poem No. 3)

Far and away the most famous of Liszt's thirteen tone poems, *Les Préludes* was inspired by a bit of tortured poetry by Alphonse de Lamartine characterizing life as a series of preludes to the afterlife. The spirit of the piece, then, is man's struggle to the stars. In many minds, however, its association is with the Lone Ranger, since parts of it were used as bridge music on the classic radio and television show. Few people are aware of this, however, believing it all to be part of Rossini's *William Tell* Overture and getting frustrated when they can't find it there.

Herbert von Karajan practically owned this piece during his lifetime, and one of his best versions is still available at mid-price, along with three other all-basic Romantic-era couplings. It would be hard to do better.

Karajan, Berlin Philharmonic Orchestra. DG Galleria 427222 [ADD] + Sibelius: *Finlandia;* Tchaikovsky: *Overture 1812, Capriccio italien* (mid-price)

Sonata in B Minor for Piano

If the pieces described above are a bit tawdry and crass in places, no such catering to the galleries will be found in Liszt's great piano sonata, surprisingly the only one he wrote. Although it is written in accord with his usual theories, it is altogether more tasteful and noble; it even contains a fugue. At the same time, it has plenty of drama.

Alfred Brendel is the standard for digital versions, and adds some short encores. Van Cliburn is featured on a mid-price edition with several short works by other composers.

Brendel. Philips 434078 [DDD] + encores
Cliburn. RCA Gold Seal 60414 [ADD] + encores (mid-price)

Modest Mussorgsky (1839-1881)

Mussorgsky was at once among the most original and least polished of all the great composers. His ideal was not Beauty, but Truth, and in the course of his idealistic quest he created a sound and style so distinctive that hardly anyone has dared to follow it for fear of being accused of plagiarism. He is the great primitive of classical music, who like Grandma Moses in painting managed to overwhelm the senses (and ultimately the critics) by sheer force of personality and inspiration.

He was born to wealth, growing up carefree on a large estate. He showed an early propensity for music, and was able to perform a large piano concerto by age eleven. Although his father loved music and encouraged the boy, he thought music was no more than a pastime and packed him off to military school. The director there was puzzled by the youth's studious demeanor. He tried to get him to drink wine and chase women like any proper officer (Tailhook, we see, is nothing new), but he preferred to study German philosophy and read classical literature.

After graduation, he became a fixture in St. Petersburg salons, playing inconsequential piano ditties in his uniform for adoring society ladies, and affecting aristocratic manners. Soon, however, he became a student of Mily Balakirev, founder of the Russian nationalist movement which culminated in the group, of which Mussorgsky was a member, called "The Five," or "The Mighty Handful."

Within two years he had decided to forsake military service for music, traveling the countryside and imbuing himself with Russian folk influences so immoderately that he suffered a temporary breakdown. A tendency to dabble in drugs and drink was exacerbated by his impoverishment in 1861, when the family fortune was lost in the abolishment of serfdom, and by the death of his beloved mother in 1865. His health steadily deteriorated, but his creative powers only increased. He shed his artistic inhibitions and let his natural idealism flower wherever and however it might, leaving many of his works incomplete as his restless mind turned from one project to another. All the while he was forced to support himself with a miserable clerical job in the Ministry of Transport, which left only the odd hour for his real vocation.

The death of a close friend in 1873, the scorn he suffered from "professional" composers, and the drudgery and loneliness of his daily life led irrevocably to spiraling dissolution. By the time of the unforgettable, unforgiving portrait by Repin, he dressed in rags, had sold his furniture to pay for liquor, and was often homeless. He died a week after his forty-second birthday, pleading pitifully for a bottle of cognac.

Only gradually over the decades has his music taken its rightful place—at first, usually in orchestrations or revisions by other composers, later in the original versions when their rough power was finally understood to need no fussy fixing to be valid. In his last stupefied days, no one would have been more amazed than Mussorgsky to foresee that *Boris Godunov* would one day by considered one of the handful of greatest operas ever written, *Pictures at an Exhibition* would be one of the handful of most performed and recorded orchestral works of all time, and *A Night on Bald Mountain* would be immortalized by Walt Disney. Patronized by his colleagues, it was Mussorgsky who, ironically, was to justify more than any of the others the epithet of "Mighty Handful."

Boris Godunov

I will pass over here the complicated story of the various versions of this great and unique opera; suffice it to say that there are basically two—Mussorgsky's original, and Rimsky-Korsakov's revision (although there are variants of these, and revisions by other parties altogether, including Shostakovich). Until recent years, the Rimsky-Korsakov orchestration was the only one allowed on stage; but gradually it became clear that Mussorgsky's original, once thought to be technically crude, had a power and integrity of its own which made Rimsky's well-meaning wax job look altogether too slick.

Whichever edition you prefer (and each has its points), you will find a work unexampled for dramatic integrity and seriousness of purpose, in which the musical line is so perfectly fitted to the text that they seem truly an organic whole. There are two protagonists in the story: the Tsar Boris (a real historical figure), and the Russian people (symbolized by the chorus). Pushkin's great drama, sometimes called the Russian *Macbeth*, is played out on two levels, the private and the public, and each enriches and explicates the other.

The music is dark and brooding, and not conventionally melodic; yet it is powerfully suggestive at almost every moment. In contrast to most operas, the heroes (flawed as they are) are basses, and the villains are tenors. There is a pair of lovers, but their romance is utterly cynical. The variety of incident is extraordinary, from the blazing splendor of the

Coronation Scene, to the hallucination of the Tsar when he sees the child he has murdered in the face of a clock, to the cockeyed song of the Simpleton as he watches Moscow go up in flames.

That the supposedly amateurish and untutored Mussorgsky could create one of the towering masterpieces of opera is astonishing, but no more so than that a small-town commoner with apparently only a village school education could write *Hamlet* and *King Lear*. Perhaps a couple of centuries from now someone will "prove" that Mussorgsky's works were actually written by someone else (Rimsky-Korsakov, perhaps?).

The classic recording of the Rimsky edition is a mono issue from 1952 conducted by Issay Dobrowen and starring bass Boris Christoff, one of the two most famous singers in this role since it was written. It is still eminently enjoyable, but is out of print as I write this. I have been informed, however, that it will soon be reissued; you will just have to figure out the catalog number yourself. Meanwhile, there is an excellent recording of Mussorgsky's original score conducted by Vladimir Fedoseyev, with Alexander Vedernikov in the title role and an excellent all-Russian supporting cast.

Fedoseyev, USSR Radio and Television Orchestra and Chorus. Philips 412281 (3) [ADD]

A Night on Bald Mountain

Originally written for *Salammbô,* an uncompleted opera, and later incorporated into another opera, *The Fair at Sorochinsk,* this musical picture of a witches' sabbath finally became famous as an independent tone poem, and served for one of the most memorable episodes in Walt Disney's animated film *Fantasia.*

There are two excellent digital versions that spring to mind, conducted by Lorin Maazel and Giuseppe Sinopoli; also, Sir George Solti's superb budget version already discussed under Glinka, and a Leonard Bernstein mid-price classic from 1958.

Maazel, Cleveland Orchestra. Telarc 80042 [DDD] + *Pictures at an Exhibition*

Sinopoli, New York Philharmonic Orchestra. DG 429785 [DDD] + *Pictures at an Exhibition;* Ravel: *Valses nobles et sentimentales*

Solti, London Symphony Orchestra. London Weekend Classics 417689 [ADD] + Prelude to *Khovanshchina;* Glinka: *Russlan and Ludmila* Overture (budget)

Bernstein, New York Philharmonic Orchestra. CBS 36726 [ADD] + *Pictures at an Exhibition* (mid-price)

Pictures at an Exhibition (orch. Ravel)

Now one of the most universally loved "orchestral spectaculars," Mussorgsky's original is for piano solo. At least a dozen other musicians have arranged it for orchestra, but by far the most famous is that by Maurice Ravel, and the recommended recordings are all of that version.

The piece is a tribute to Mussorgsky's friend Victor Hartmann, a painter, who had recently died. Each of the twelve main sections is a musical impression of an actual painting, linked by a theme marked "Promenade," which represents Mussorgsky walking from one exhibit to another. There is not a weak "picture" in the entire gallery, and all are crowned by the overwhelmingly majestic finale "The Great Gate at Kiev," possibly the noblest loud music ever written.

The Maazel and Sinopoli versions discussed under *A Night on Bald Mountain* above are great digital choices, but so are versions by Claudio Abbado and Sir Georg Solti (available with two different couplings). Indeed, couplings may determine your choice here. There are also three splendid analog versions at mid-price to choose from.

> **Maazel, Cleveland Orchestra.** Telarc 80042 [DDD] + *A Night on Bald Mountain*
>
> **Sinopoli, New York Philharmonic Orchestra.** DG 429785 [DDD] + *A Night on Bald Mountain;* Ravel: *Valses nobles et sentimentales*
>
> **Abbado, London Symphony Orchestra.** DG 423901 [DDD] + Stravinsky: *Petrushka*
>
> **Solti, Chicago Symphony Orchestra.** London 430446 [DDD] + Tchaikovsky: *Overture 1812;* Prokofiev: Symphony No. 1
>
> **Solti, Chicago Symphony Orchestra.** London 417754 [DDD] + Bartók: Concerto for Orchestra
>
> **Karajan, Berlin Philharmonic Orchestra.** DG 429162 [ADD] + Stravinsky: *Rite of Spring* (mid-price)
>
> **Bernstein, New York Philharmonic Orchestra.** CBS 36726 [ADD] + *A Night on Bald Mountain* (mid-price)
>
> **Muti, Philadelphia Orchestra.** Angel 64516 + Stravinsky: *Rite of Spring* (mid-price)

Jacques Offenbach (1819-1880)

Born Isaac Juda Eberst, Offenbach was the son of a synagogue cantor who was also a bookbinder and music teacher. He later changed his name, using his native village of Offenbach for the latter half. Since Offenbach was near Cologne, he sometimes referred to himself also as "O. de Cologne."

Wit, sometimes of the rapier variety, was the most memorable feature of his persona, and it informed the dozens of satirical operettas he composed over a very successful theatrical career, including *La Périchole, La belle Hélène,* and *Orphée aux enfers* (Orpheus in the Underworld), a parody on Greek mythology, and source of the naughty but immortal Can-Can. "Offenbach's music," said George Bernard Shaw, "is wicked… Every accent is a snap of the fingers in the face of moral responsibility."

He was but a teenager when he moved to Paris and began his career as a cellist; he wrote several notable works for cello, but these continue to be overshadowed by his infectious stage works. Despite the light nature of his subject matter, Offenbach was a composer with finely honed skills and considerable grace, earning him Rossini's accolade as "the Mozart of the Champs-Elysées."

Offenbach's artistic side was overlooked by most of his contemporaries, friends or foes. He accepted an invitation to make an American tour in 1876, the centennial of the United States, to perform his own works. Many orchestras honored him by featuring his music on their programs, but the ultra-Teuton Theodore Thomas, leader of one of America's most prominent orchestras, pointedly refused to have anything to do with such Gallic frippery. A yellow journalist tried to egg Offenbach on by asking him what he thought of the shocking snub. "Tell Mr. Thomas," he calmly replied, "that I shall be delighted to conduct his compositions when he achieves the dignity of becoming a composer."

Despite the fortune he made from his comedies, Offenbach did have a burning need to write something "serious" that would assure him that same dignity for posterity. He succeeded, but just barely; he died four months before the premiere of *The Tales of Hoffmann,* an opera unique in its haunting blend of tragedy, comedy, and grotesquerie.

Gaité Parisienne (arr. Rosenthal)

Oddly enough, Offenbach's most famous work was written fifty-seven years after his death. In 1937, the great American impresario Sol Hurok was in need of a new ballet to launch the reorganized Ballet Russe de Monte Carlo, and commissioned Manuel Rosenthal to raid Offenbach's numerous operettas for their most delectable quadrilles and can-cans, waltzes and galops. The result is a perfect, pre-digested Offenbach "sampler."

André Previn is wittily insouciant in his digital recording, and Herbert von Karajan is attractive at mid-price in one of his best discs, with two other ballets (see Delibes entry for original discussion).

Previn, Pittsburgh Symphony Orchestra. Philips 411039 [DDD]
Karajan, Berlin Philharmonic Orchestra. DG Galleria 429163 [ADD] +
Delibes: *Coppélia* Suite; Chopin: *Les Sylphides* (mid-price)

Nikolai Rimsky-Korsakov (1844-1908)

Rimsky-Korsakov stands as a beacon for those who imagine they can never learn enough to comprehend classical music; he began his career as a naval officer and ended up being one of the greatest orhestrators of all time and the teacher of Igor Stravinsky, considered by many the greatest twentieth-century composer.

Despite planning throughout his youth to follow a family tradition in the navy, he showed considerable musical talent. His study was sporadic at best until he fell in with Mily Balakirev, father of the Russian nationalist school of composition later known as "The Five," or "The Mighty Handful." Balakirev saw in the young enthusiast for Russian folk songs, native opera, and Orthodox chant a ripe convert for his own theories, which were designed to establish a native musical culture second to none.

Rimsky had a public triumph with his first symphony at age twenty-one, receiving a standing ovation while dressed in his crisp naval uniform. Still essentially an amateur, he went from one success to another, barely keeping ahead of the game by studying harmony and theory on his own in the most slapdash way, often discovering basic principles of composition simply through trial-and-error. But his talent was so great that despite his shaky credentials, he was invited in 1871 to become a professor of composition and instrumentation at the prestigious St. Petersburg Conservatory. Always becomingly modest, he wrote in his delightful autobiography that "At the time I could not harmonize a chorale properly, had never written a single contrapuntal exercise in my life, and had only the haziest understanding of strict fugue. I didn't even know the names of the augmented and diminished intervals or the chords!"

Eventually, Rimsky became so obsessed with mastering the techniques of music that he partially alienated those of his early supporters who thought he was betraying their ideals of a music rooted in the Russian people. He mollified them by producing the most monumental collection of Russian folk songs ever compiled. But the "Mighty Handful" was breaking up; by 1887, Mussorgsky and Borodin were dead, and Balakirev and Cui had drifted into other interests. Rimsky became by default the leader of his own group of nationalist composers, including Glazunov (his favorite), Liadov, Arensky, Ippolitov-Ivanov, and Stravinsky, whose ballet *The Firebird* owes very much to his teacher's influence.

Rimsky himself then blossomed as a significant composer, creating his greatest works over a twenty-year period, interrupted only by a two-year depression. He gave generously to other composers in encouragement and in helping them with their work; he actually contributed the orchestrations for several works by Borodin and Mussorgsky. Towards the end of his life he was dismissed from the Conservatory for supporting the revolutionary activities of the students, but public outrage forced his reinstatement. By this time, he was a national icon.

Capriccio espagnol, Op. 34

Rimsky-Korsakov was brutally frank about his motive in writing this piece that glitters with dazzling orchestral color. The reason, he says in his autobiography, was to create a work that "glitters with dazzling orchestral color." And there we could leave it, to be chewed up again as by a mangy dog or music critic. But that would ignore the fact that under the guise of a warhorse or chestnut, Rimsky was here reviving the Baroque technique of concertante playing, featuring solos by different instruments or groups of instruments. And it would pass over his concept, brilliantly implemented here, that the melodies and rhythms and structures of a piece must relate organically to the inherent qualities of the instruments used, a concept which had a direct influence on Stravinsky and his followers. If you wish, however, you may simply accept the standard view that the *Capriccio espagnol* is nothing more than a hackneyed dray horse of the pops repertoire. It's your life!

Sir Charles Mackerras leads an opulent version in digital sound with a brilliant *Scheherazade*. Antal Dorati and Leonard Bernstein both conduct outstanding mid-price readings; Bernstein is a bit skimpy on filling the disc, but Dorati has plenty.

Mackerras, London Symphony Orchestra. Telarc 80208 [DDD] + *Scheherazade*
Dorati, London Symphony Orchestra. Mercury 434308 [ADD] + *Russian Easter* Overture, *Le Coq d'or* Suite; Borodin: *Polovtsian Dances* from *Prince Igor* (mid-price)
Bernstein, New York Philharmonic Orchestra. CBS 36728 [ADD] + Tchaikovsky: *Capriccio italien* (mid-price)

Russian Easter Overture, Op. 36

It's a long, long way from "Christ the Lord is Risen Today" to the feverish sustained crescendo that is the *Russian Easter* Overture. In my many years in classical broadcasting I loved nothing more than to play this work without introduction on Easter Sunday and have people call up to complain that the music was totally inappropriate. The piece seems to have a lot more to do with pagan spring festivals of Old Russia than the Christian holiday, but whatever it is, it's exciting!

Dorati is recommended above under *Capriccio espagnol,* and Leonard Slatkin has a meaty digital disc loaded with Russian favorites.

Dorati, London Symphony Orchestra. Mercury 434308 [ADD] + *Capriccio espagnol, Le Coq d'or Suite;* Borodin: *Polovtsian Dances* (mid-price)
Slatkin, St. Louis Symphony Orchestra. Telarc 80072 [DDD] + Glinka: *Russlan and Ludmila* Overture; Borodin: *In the Steppes of Central Asia;* Tchaikovsky: *Marche slave*

Scheherazade, Op. 35

Inspired by the Arabian Nights, this huge tone poem disguised as a four-movement symphony is among the most colorfully orchestrated works in the repertoire, outstripping even most other pieces by Rimsky-Korsakov. There is an entire strain of quasi-Oriental compositions in classical music, and this is the king of them all—or, shall we say, queen. For such Scheherazade becomes by mellowing her scimitar-happy husband with her fascinating stories.

For recent sound, Sir Charles Mackerras is full of ardor, and not without subtlety, on the disc already recommended above under *Capriccio espagnol.* Two older classic recordings, by Sir Thomas Beecham and Fritz Reiner, have been beautifully remastered and still give great pleasure.

Mackerras, London Symphony Orchestra. Telarc 80208 [DDD] + *Capriccio espagnol*
Beecham, Royal Philharmonic Orchestra. EMI 47717 [ADD] + Borodin: *Polovtsian Dances* from *Prince Igor*
Reiner, Chicago Symphony Orchestra. RCA Gold Seal 60875 [ADD] + Debussy: *La Mer* (mid-price)

Camille Saint-Saëns (1835-1921)

Saint-Saëns had relatively easy sailing as an all-around musician throughout his life, but he paid for it posthumously. He began as an incredible prodigy on the piano, composing his first piece at three and playing Beethoven chamber music before he was five. He was a star pupil at the Paris Conservatory and soon developed into one of the greatest piano and organ virtuosos in Europe, securing a twenty-year tenure as organist at the great Church of the Madeleine.

His enormous energy and almost dizzying intellect expressed themselves in wide-ranging interests. He was a talented amateur astronomer and archaeologist. He learned several languages, was an excellent caricaturist, wrote poetry and plays. He wrote articles and books on literature, painting, hypnotism and philosophy. He was one of the first important nineteenth-century scholars of Renaissance music, and composed the first important film score, for the 1908 silent picture *The Assassination of the Duc de Guise.*

He was, in fact, the most highly and widely cultured composer known to history; yet today, his music is often conversely considered among the least profound. During most of his lifetime he was adulated; statues of him were erected, streets named after him, and a museum of his memorabilia was even opened while he was still living. He made stacks of money and was regularly mentioned in the same breath with Mozart and Beethoven.

Then he did the worst possible thing: he died. Almost at once a reaction set in. Typed as "the greatest talent who was not a genius," he was redefined as one whose enormous intelligence was spread too thin to achieve true greatness. His works, it was said, were facile and slick rather than substantive. (He himself justified his work by saying "The artist who does not feel completely satisfied by elegant lines, by harmonious colors, and by a beautiful succession of chords does not understand the art of music.")

Despite the critical sniffing, a surprising number of his works continue to hold their place because of their melodic beauty and suave orchestration, political correctness be damned. Saint-Saëns followed his own muse without too much concern for fashions. His heart was never fully in the nineteenth century anyway; over and over in his works we hear echoes of the Baroque. What seemed in his time to be stiff formality can be heard today as a touching nostalgia for an earlier era. Perhaps we can appreciate his preference for absolute music without comparing it unfavorably with his confreres, by enjoying it on his terms rather than just ours—that is, by savoring its elegance, proportion, and good taste on its own merits.

Carnival of the Animals

Tossed off as a joke for a Mardi Gras concert, *Carnival of the Animals* was never intended for publication, and Saint-Saëns would be mortified to discover it is today better known than all his other works. That doesn't mean it is bad, however. It is actually a piece of enormous wit, charm, and verve—far better than its composer apparently realized.

The digital recording led by Richard Stamp is a perfect CD for your children, with ideal couplings—including Sir John Gielgud narrating *Peter and the Wolf;* in addition, the artists' royalties are all donated to a center for physically handicapped children. Dutoit's digital version is not remarkable, but it is appended to one of the best recordings of the *Organ* Symphony, so you get it anyway in that case. Also, there is a jam-packed Eugene Ormandy budget disc, and Leonard Bernstein's classic analog at mid-price.

> **Stamp, Academy of London.** Virgin Classics 59333 [DDD] + Prokofiev: *Peter and the Wolf;* Mozart: *Eine Kleine Nachtmusik*
> **Dutoit, Montreal Symphony Orchestra.** London 430720 [DDD] + Symphony No. 3
> **Ormandy, Philadelphia Orchestra.** Sony Essential Classics 47655 [ADD] + Symphony No. 3, *Danse Macabre, Bacchanale* from *Samson et Dalila,* French Military March from *Suite Algérienne* (budget)
> **Bernstein, New York Philharmonic Orchestra.** CBS 37765 + Prokofiev: *Peter and the Wolf* (mid-price)

Concerto No. 1 in A Minor for Cello, Op. 33

An ingratiating example of one of the most difficult types of concerto, the first cello concerto dates from 1872 and was a lifelong favorite of Pablo Casals, who played it at his debut in 1905. Ostensibly in one movement, it is actually in three sections with a charming neo-Baroque minuet in the center like a big cherry.

A Sony mid-price digital disc is a wonderful bargain, with Yo-Yo Ma the soloist and generous couplings of two other major Saint-Saëns basic works.

Ma, Maazel, French National Orchestra. Sony 46506 [DDD] + Piano Concerto No. 2, Violin Concerto No. 3 (mid-price)

Concerto No. 2 in G Minor for Piano, Op. 22

Anton Rubinstein gave the premiere of this, the most popular of the five Saint-Saëns piano concerti, in 1868. Years later it became a mainstay of the repertoire of Artur Rubinstein (no relation to Anton!). The first movement begins with a very Bach-like prelude. The second movement contains one of the composer's most famous and memorable melodies. The final movement is a sort of "perpetual motion" that sweeps to a conclusion more akin to Offenbach than to Bach (a witty observation often attributed to Oscar Levant, but actually originated by the pianist Sigismund Stojowski. As long as I'm at it, let me point out that the famous quip "I cried all the way to the bank" was not first said by Liberace, but by the great coloratura soprano Amelita Galli-Curci).

Cecile Licad is the pianist on the same disc recommended above under Cello Concerto No. 1. Excellent!

Licad, Previn, London Philharmonic Orchestra. Sony 46506 [DDD] + Cello Concerto No. 1, Violin Concerto No. 3 (mid-price)

Concerto No. 3 in B Minor for Violin, Op. 61

Saint-Saëns's last violin concerto was written in 1881 for the great virtuoso Pablo de Sarasate, who contributed suggestions that were incorporated into it. It is surprisingly dramatic and symphonic for a composer supposedly so cavalier and facile, which seems to have made it a little less popular than some of his other great concerti. (Why do I get the feeling that people listen avidly to the worst pieces by Saint-Saëns and then complain that they are inferior?)

Once again I can recommend the triple-dip disc in the previous two listings, with Cho-Liang Lin the violinist here, but this time I must add Gil Shaham's great performance, coupled with the Paganini first violin concerto.

Lin, Tilson Thomas, Philharmonia Orchestra. Sony 46506 [DDD] + Cello Concerto No. 1, Piano Concerto No. 2 (mid-price)
Shaham, Sinopoli, New York Philharmonic Orchestra. DG 429786 [DDD] + Paganini: Violin Concerto No. 1

Danse Macabre, Op. 40

Along with Mussorgsky's *A Night on Bald Mountain*, this is the best-known piece of "Hallowe'en music." It is the most successful of four tone poems by Saint-Saëns, famous for its rattling "bones" which the composer quoted humorously as "Fossils" in *Carnival of the Animals*. It is a wonderful piece, and you may play it for your children with impunity as it is only about as scary as *Abbott and Costello Meet the Wolfman*.

The Ormandy bargain disc recommended above under *Carnival of the Animals* will fill the bill here, or try Dutoit at mid-price with a different program of Saint-Saëns gems.

Ormandy, Philadelphia Orchestra. Sony Essential Classics 47655 [ADD] + *Carnival of the Animals*, Symphony No. 3, *Bacchanale* from *Samson et Dalila*, French Military March from *Suite Algérienne* (budget)

Dutoit, Philharmonia Orchestra. London Jubilee 425021 [ADD] + *Havanaise, Introduction and Rondo Capriccioso, Marche héroique*, three tone poems (mid-price)

Havanaise; Introduction and Rondo Capriccioso

These are two separate pieces, but they are almost inseparable on recordings. If you can find one without the other, please let me know (not that I will do anything about it). They need no explanation; they are scintillating vehicles for displaying violinistic virtuosity. The *Havanaise* has a Cuban flavor.

These works come on two discs, one digital, one mid-price analog, that have already been recommended in previous listings.

Perlman, Mehta, New York Philharmonic Orchestra. DG 423063 [DDD] + Chausson: *Poème;* Ravel: *Tzigane;* Sarasate: *Carmen Fantasy*

Chung, Dutoit, Royal Philharmonic Orchestra. London Jubilee 425021 [ADD] + *Danse Macabre, Marche héroique*, three tone poems (mid-price)

Symphony No. 3 in C Minor, Op. 78, "Organ"

The huge orchestra for which this symphony is scored is augmented further by an organ. Had it been practical, Saint-Saëns would have added a herd of trumpeting elephants. It has long been a favorite for demonstrating great recorded sound, especially now on digital compact discs. The stupendous organ chorale which launches the final section is based on the melody of an Ave Maria by the Flemish Renaissance composer Jacob Arcadelt (a fact which I believe I discovered, with apologies if I am mistaken; at least I can attest that I figured it out on my own without reading it anywhere, search as I might).

Charles Dutoit leads the best-known digital recording, although James Levine's version is in hot pursuit. Charles Munch's 1959 recording was the standard for many years, and is now available beautifully remastered at mid-price. The Ormandy budget disc listed above also applies here.

Dutoit, Montreal Symphony Orchestra. London 430720 [DDD] + *Carnival of the Animals*

Levine, Berlin Philharmonic Orchestra. DG 419617 [DDD] + Dukas: *Sorcerer's Apprentice*

Munch, Boston Symphony Orchestra. RCA Living Stereo 61500 [ADD] + Debussy: *La Mer;* Ibert: *Escales* (mid-price)

Ormandy, Philadelphia Orchestra. Sony Essential Classics 47655 [ADD] + *Carnival of the Animals, Danse Macabre, Bacchanale* from *Samson et Dalila,* French Military March from *Suite Algérienne* (budget)

Bedřich Smetana (1824-1884)

A splendid musician, Smetana had the misfortune to be only the second greatest Czech (or more precisely, Bohemian) composer. Had Antonin Dvořák not existed, his star would surely be higher; as it turns out, he has at least held onto world fame through his stirring tone poem *The Moldau,* though he wrote a great deal of excellent music that patiently awaits discovery by the international public.

Largely self-taught as a child, Smetana was playing Haydn quartets by age five and composing by eight. Later on he got some formal training, came to the attention of Franz Liszt, who became his friend, and at age twenty-four founded the first important music school in Prague. Overcoming the tragedies of the deaths of his four-year-old daughter and the childhood sweetheart who had become his wife, he remarried and redoubled his efforts to promote Czech musical culture, writing musical criticism and founding or directing theaters, orchestras, and schools. Ironically, this great patriot was in his mid-twenties before he even began to learn the Czech language; his first tongue was German, the official language of the country when he was born.

At age fifty, tragedy struck again when he became stone deaf. But he overcame this handicap too, writing the great cycle of six tone poems *Ma Vlast* ("My Fatherland"), which includes *The Moldau,* long after he could not hear a note of it. Worn down by care and work, and by disappointment at flagging public interest in his music, he gradually fell prey to depressions. He spent the last year of his life in a mental institution. Belatedly, his countryment hailed him as the father of Czech music, and after the creation of the free republic of Czechoslovakia in 1924, Paul Stefan euologized Smetana as "the standard bearer and symbol of the history and liberation of his people."

The Bartered Bride: Overture and Dances

Few "ethnic" operas find success outside their native lands, but this one does. You don't have to comprehend every nuance of rustic Bohemian folk customs to enjoy the open humor and vivacious spirits of *The Bartered Bride*. The Overture and three famous dances—Polka, Furiant, and Dance of the Comedians—give a fair preview of the work.

George Szell was the most brilliant conductor of these pieces, and his record is still unchallenged—as well as still available, and at mid-price.

Szell, Cleveland Orchestra. CBS 36716 [ADD] + *The Moldau;* Dvořák: *Carnival Overture* (mid-price)

The Moldau (Vltava)

Bohemia's principal river is the subject of this beloved tone poem, second of the six making up the cycle "My Fatherland" *(Ma Vlast)*. Delicately rippling strings represent the tiny stream where the river originates; the orchestra continues vividly to suggest the course of the river and sights along its banks, such as old castles; and finally, it roars over St. John's rapids as Prague, the "golden city," comes into view. If there is any piece with "sweep," this is it.

The aforementioned George Szell is a first choice; it is also available with alternate couplings (at two dollars less!). But the budget István Kertész disc is also a winner, appended to a great performance of Dvořák's *New World* Symphony. With competition like this, no digitals need apply.

Szell, Cleveland Orchestra. CBS 36716 [ADD] + Dances from *The Bartered Bride;* Dvořák: *Carnival Overture* (mid-price)
Szell, Cleveland Orchestra. Sony Essential Classics 48264 [ADD] + Mendelssohn: *A Midsummer Night's Dream* (sel.); Bizet: Symphony in C (conducted by Stokowski) (budget)
Kertész, Vienna Philharmonic Orchestra. London Weekend Classics 417678 [ADD] + Dvořák: Symphony No. 9 (budget)

Johann Strauss II (1825-1899)

Johann Strauss II will forever be known as the Waltz King for his more than four hundred irresistible Viennese waltzes, polkas, operettas, and so on, but he must also share honors with his father and two younger brothers, all of whom were part of the unique family that has become synonymous with concert dance music. Although Johann, Jr. was the greatest and most prolific of them, it is sometimes startling to realize that some marvelous piece one thought was surely his is actually by Johann, Sr., Josef, or Edouard.

Johann, Jr. took over his father's famous dance orchestra upon his death in 1849, and began a long series of tours all over Europe. By 1863 he was appointed director of the Imperial Court Balls, and in the next few years wrote most of his best works, including the world's greatest waltz, *The Blue Danube,* and the world's greatest operetta, *Die Fledermaus* ("The Bat"). Although his music was "light," Strauss's accomplishments are nothing to sneeze at. They were greatly admired by Johannes Brahms, who is said once to have autographed Mme. Strauss's fan by inscribing a few bars of *The Blue Danube* and adding "Unfortunately, not by me."

After a career of extraordinary vigor and success, Johann Strauss II died of pneumonia in 1899, bringing to a close a century and an era. His music, so full of optimism, charm, camaraderie, and rich sentiment, still stands as the symbol of nostalgia for a golden age of Viennese Romanticism that can never come again.

Waltzes, Polkas, Overtures

Willi Boskovsky was the past master of the Strauss style in recent years, and several of his wonderful LPs were reissued on a series of five CDs, which at this juncture have already disappeared; but a single budget disc remains to tantalize us. Another bargain is the mid-price Fritz Reiner collection. Both of these collections contain *The Blue Danube.*

Boskovsky, Vienna Philharmonic Orchestra. London Weekend Classics 417855 [AAD] (budget)

Reiner, Chicago Symphony Orchestra. RCA Gold Seal 60177 [ADD] (mid-price)

Peter Ilyich Tchaikovsky (1840-1893)

Tchaikovsky was to become for many the apotheosis of the Russian Romantic; wild as a Cossack, palpitating with larger-than-life emotion, dripping with hyperinflated sentimentality—yet his inmost thoughts were entirely opposite: "I am so much in love with the music of *Don Giovanni* that, even as I write to you, I could shed tears of agitation and emotion. In his chamber music, Mozart charms me by his purity and distinction of style and his exquisite handling of the parts. No one else has ever known as well how to interpret so exquisitely in music the sense of resigned and inconsolable sorrow. It is thanks to Mozart that I have devoted my life to music."

The quotation is from a letter written in 1878 to Tchaikovsky's platonic friend and patroness Nadezhda von Meck, who like most music lovers in that era thought Mozart to be very weak tea next to Beethoven or Wagner. It may surprise us to find the composer of such lushly Romantic works as the *Romeo and Juliet* Fantasy Overture and *The Nutcracker* ballet rhapsodizing over purity of style and exquisite interpretation, when critics have been telling us for decades that Tchaikovsky is unsubtle, unintellectual, even downright crude. At the same time, of course, the public has been gorging itself on his music.

Who is right? Maybe all of the above. Tchaikovsky had little patience with the classic German rules of composition, preferring loose and free forms as vehicles for his passionately colored inspirations. Under adademic analysis his music reveals countless "faults" for critics to pounce upon; but in the concert hall, or on records, the vitality of rhythm, the astounding range of orchestral color, and the ravishing beauty of melody sweep everything and everybody before them.

Neurotic from childhood, Tchaikovsky led a tortured emotional life. He suffered alternately from hallucinations, hypochondria, colitis, hysteria, and self-pity. Much has been written (and filmed) about his obsessions, his sex life, his morbidity, but none of that has anything to do with enjoying his art, except to make a little clearer the sources of his intensely poetic expression.

Tchaikovsky stood apart from the ultra-nationalist Russian school, typified by such composers as Rimsky-Korsakov and Mussorgsky. Like them, he did use a certain amount of native folk idioms in his works, but he preferred the cosmopolitan musical language of Western Europe, particularly France. It was this cross-fertilization, in large part, that gave his music its distinctive blend of elegance and earthy passion.

His artistic credo was founded on a deep sense of destiny, of a cruel and relentless Fate which one can never overcome, but can only accept with (as he had gleaned from Mozart) "a sense of resigned and inconsolable sorrow." Even his death seemed an inevitable consequence of his anguished lifestyle: drinking a glass of unboiled water (which some believe was a deliberate suicide), he quickly contracted cholera and perished in unspeakable agony.

Capriccio italien, Op. 45

Similar in vein to Rimsky-Korsakov's *Capriccio espagnol,* with an obvious geographical difference, the Tchaikovsky piece was written seven years earlier and is less sophisticated in construction. It makes a similarly brilliant effect, however, and truth to tell, I have never heard anyone cry out at a performance "Long live Rimsky-Korsakov's more complex structure!"

Vladimir Ashkenazy and Charles Dutoit both conduct brilliant digital versions. Adrian Leaper is nearly as good at a much lower price. Herbert von Karajan and Leonard Bernstein are classics at mid-price.

Ashkenazy, Royal Philharmonic Orchestra. London 421715 [DDD] + *Romeo and Juliet, Francesca da Rimini, Elegy*

Dutoit, Montreal Symphony Orchestra. London 417300 [DDD] + *Marche slave, Nutcracker* Suite, *Overture 1812*

Leaper, Royal Philharmonic Orchestra. Naxos 8.550500 [DDD] + *Overture 1812, Marche slave, Romeo and Juliet* (budget)

Karajan, Berlin Philharmonic Orchestra. DG Galleria 427222 [ADD] + *Overture 1812;* Liszt: *Les Préludes;* Sibelius: *Finlandia* (mid-price)

Bernstein, New York Philharmonic Orchestra. CBS 36728 [ADD] +
Rimsky-Korsakov: *Capriccio espagnol* (mid-price)

Concerto No. 1 in B-flat for Piano, Op. 23

"Utterly worthless...absolutely unplayable...bad, trivial, vulgar," said Nicholas
Rubinstein after hearing the first play-through of what was to become the most popular
piano concerto of all time. And he was the composer's friend! But Tchaikovsky fixed the
problem; he turned the piece over to a different pianist, who gave the premiere in Boston
in 1875. The audience went wild, and so it has been ever since.

Van Cliburn's legendary 1958 recording has not given an inch since then. It is the best-
selling classical record of all time, and with good reason. Obviously, he learned the piece in a
previous life, to play it so well as a mere lad. The coupling is the basic Rachmaninoff second
piano concerto. Martha Argerich has also been a standard in this work; her coupling is the
Prokofiev third concerto. One of the best recordings, with Emil Gilels, is now available as a
budget, coupled with an excellent performance of the violin concerto.

Cliburn, Kondrashin, RCA Symphony Orchestra. RCA 5912 [ADD] +
Rachmaninoff: Piano Concerto No. 2
Argerich, Dutoit, Royal Philharmonic Orchestra. DG 415062 [ADD] +
Prokofiev: Piano Concerto No. 3 (with Abbado conducting)
Gilels, Mehta, New York Philharmonic Orchestra. Sony Essential Classics
46339 [ADD] + Violin Concerto (budget)

Concerto in D for Violin, Op. 35

Technically one of the most demanding violin concerti (as well as one of the half-
dozen most loved), Tchaikovsky's is no mere flashy display piece. In fact, it is one of his
soberer works. Nevertheless, the critic Hanslick wrote that "the Andante begins pleasantly
but soon plunges into the atmosphere of a Russian feast, where everybody is drunk and the
faces of the people are brutal and revolting."

Some of the finest recordings are couplings with works already recommended, one just
above, and the others under Mendelssohn's Violin Concerto.

Chung, Dutoit, Montreal Symphony Orchestra. London 410011 [DDD]
+ Mendelssohn: Violin Concerto
Heifetz, Reiner, Chicago Symphony Orchestra. RCA 5933 [ADD] +
Mendelssohn: Violin Concerto (with Munch conducting), *Sérénade
Mélancolique*, Waltz from Serenade for Strings

Oistrakh, Ormandy, Philadelphia Orchestra. Sony Essential Classics 46339 [ADD] + Piano Concerto No. 1 (with Gilels and Mehta) (budget)
Nishizaki, Jean, Slovak Philharmonic Orchestra. Naxos 8.550153 [DDD] + Mendelssohn: Violin Concerto (budget)

Marche slave, Op. 31

The Serbs, with Russian support, were fighting the Muslims. Bosnia in the 1990s? No, Serbia vs. Turkey, 1876. Tchaikovsky wrote this orchestral march as part of a benefit for wounded Serbian soldiers. The opening funeral march is transformed into a victory hymn at the end.

Here too, previously recommended recordings supply one's needs, except that we need to add Mikhail Pletnev's rousing version coupled with a great Symphony No. 6.

Pletnev, Russian National Orchestra. Virgin Classics 59661 [DDD] + Symphony No. 6
Leaper, Royal Philharmonic Orchestra. Naxos 8.550500 [DDD] + *Capriccio italien, Overture 1812, Romeo and Juliet* (budget)
Dutoit, Montreal Symphony Orchestra. London 417300 [DDD] + *Capriccio italien, Nutcracker* Suite, *Overture 1812*
Slatkin, St. Louis Symphony Orchestra. Telarc 80072 [DDD] + Glinka: *Russlan and Ludmila* Overture; Rimsky-Korsakov: *Russian Easter* Overture; Borodin: *In the Steppes of Central Asia*

Nutcracker Suite, Op. 71a

Only a modest success at its premiere in 1892, *The Nutcracker* has gone on to become one of the handful of most familiar classical works around the world. In some ways it is inferior musically to *Swan Lake* and *Sleeping Beauty;* its wider fame can be attributed to the success of the suite the composer made for concert hall use, which was actually performed *before* the complete ballet. (It brought down the house.)

A mid-price disc of the suites from all three Tchaikovsky ballets, conducted by Mstislav Rostropovich, has been the recording of choice since 1978. Charles Dutoit's lovely digital version has already been listed above, and Ormandy's budget disc was listed under Delibes.

Rostropovich, Berlin Philharmonic Orchestra. DG Galleria 429097 [ADD] + *Swan Lake* Suite, *Sleeping Beauty* Suite (mid-price)
Dutoit, Montreal Symphony Orchestra. London 417300 [DDD] + *Capriccio italien, Marche slave, Overture 1812*

Ormandy, Philadelphia Orchestra. Sony Essential Classics 46550 [ADD] + Delibes: *Coppélia* and *Sylvia* Suites (budget)

Overture 1812, Op. 49

Like the *Marche slave,* the *Overture 1812* is an occasional piece, designed to be played in a public square to commemorate the defeat of Napoleon in Russia. Despite the unmistakable and dominating quotations of the Tsarist national anthem and the French *Marseillaise,* which trumpet forth every few seconds, American audiences cheer and applaud when the overture is played, as it so often is, for Independence Day fireworks displays. Inexplicably, when at one of these I once cried out "Long live the Tsar!" I was severely reprimanded.

Sir Georg Solti (at mid-price) and Charles Dutoit both present brilliant digital versions with highly desirable couplings, but Adrian Leaper at budget price is highly competitive, with cannon as scary as anybody's. A previously recommended Herbert von Karajan mid-price disc brings a great analog 1812 along with it.

Solti, Chicago Symphony Orchestra. London Jubilee 430446 [DDD] + Mussorgsky: *Pictures at an Exhibition;* Prokofiev: Symphony No. 1 (mid-price)
Dutoit, Montreal Symphony Orchestra. London 417300 [DDD] + *Capriccio italien, Marche slave, Nutcracker* Suite
Leaper, Royal Philharmonic Orchestra. Naxos 8.550500 [DDD] + *Capriccio italien, Marche slave, Romeo and Juliet* (budget)
Karajan, Berlin Philharmonic Orchestra. DG Galleria 427222 [ADD] + *Capriccio italien;* Liszt: *Les Préludes;* Sibelius: *Finlandia* (mid-price)

Romeo and Juliet Fantasy Overture

Tchaikovsky chose the unusual designation to indicate that he did not intend a conventional tone poem with a specific narrative program, but an open-ended form that would suggest elements of the immortal story, thoroughly Russianized as it is in the composer's hands. It contains some of Tchaikovsky's most heartrending melodies, and has perhaps his most hair-raising conclusion.

The choice digital recording is conducted by Vladimir Ashkenazy, with Adrian Leaper a strong contender at budget price, and Eugene Ormandy providing a mid-price version as accompaniment to a fine Symphony No. 6.

Ashkenazy, Royal Philharmonic Orchestra. London 421715 [DDD] + *Capriccio italien, Francesca da Rimini, Elegy*

Leaper, Royal Philharmonic Orchestra. Naxos 8.550500 [DDD] + *Capriccio italien, Marche slave, Overture 1812* (budget)

Ormandy, Philadelphia Orchestra. RCA Silver Seal 60908 [ADD] + Symphony No. 6 (mid-price)

Sleeping Beauty Suite, Op. 66a

Instead of being, like most ballets, a string of more or less independent pieces, *Sleeping Beauty* has an integrated symphonic structure. By any measure, it is one of Tchaikovsky's finest scores. (The composer gave much credit to Delibes, by the way, for inspiring him.)

The Rostropovich disc recommended under *The Nutcracker* Suite will answer here.

Rostropovich, Berlin Philharmonic Orchestra. DG Galleria 429097 (mid-price) [ADD] + *Nutcracker* Suite, *Swan Lake* Suite (mid-price)

Swan Lake Suite, Op. 20a

The first of Tchaikovsky's three great ballets was unsuccessful at first (1877) and was withdrawn. He intended to revise it, but never had time. After his death it was better received, and has long since become a staple of the repertory; it has actually had more performances than the other two. Its score was a favorite mine for early film scores; it even shows up as the title music for the 1931 *Dracula* with Bela Lugosi!

For a starter recording, ditto the Rostropovich, already recommended.

Rostropovich, Berlin Philharmonic Orchestra. DG Galleria 429097 [ADD] + *Nutcracker* Suite, *Sleeping Beauty* Suite (mid-price)

Symphonies (6)

The first three of Tchaikovsky's symphonies have value, but are not unquestioned masterpieces. The finales of Nos. 1 and 2 are among my favorite subjects for "conducting calisthenics" when I need a little arm-waving to get going on a groggy day; nevertheless, I will confine myself to detailed recommendations of just the three later symphonies. Get those under your belt and you can indulge in the earlier ones.

The three "great" symphonies are available in one steaming two-CD set from the baton of the great Russian conductor Yevgeny Mravinsky, a classic of the catalog since 1960. It's still at full price, but for once I can't blame them. Vladimir Ashkenazy's set is very competitive, however, and includes the *Manfred* Symphony; there are three discs, but at mid-price it comes out about the same as Mravinsky.

If you decide to go for all six symphonies, the digital set conducted by Mariss Jansons is all the rage, and is priced as five discs. It too includes the *Manfred* Symphony. If you don't mind analog, a four-CD mid-price set conducted by Herbert von Karajan offers an even better orchestra, and an especially good No. 6.

Mravinsky, Leningrad Philharmonic Orchestra. DG 419745 (2) [ADD]
Ashkenazy, Philharmonia Orchestra. London 425586 (3) [ADD] (mid-price)
Jansons, Oslo Philharmonic Orchestra. Chandos 8672/8 (7) [DDD]
Karajan, Berlin Philharmonic Orchestra. DG 429675 (4) [ADD] (mid-price)

Symphony No. 4 in F Minor, Op. 36

"Our symphony" is what Tchaikovsky called No. 4 in typical ambiguously suggestive correspondence with his arms-length patroness Madame von Meck, who proceeded to shell out even more rubles. Untypically, Tchaikovsky steadfastly maintained that this was his best symphony, even years later (normally, his favorite work was the one he had just written). The whole structure revolves around a "Destiny" motive introduced in the first movement on horns and trumpets.

The Mariss Jansons single disc is the outstanding digital version, with Leonard Bernstein providing a famously frenetic account at mid-price.

Jansons, Oslo Philharmonic Orchestra. Chandos 8361 [DDD]
Bernstein, New York Philharmonic Orchestra. CBS 37766 [ADD] (mid-price)

Symphony No. 5 in E Minor, Op. 64

The idea of the "Destiny" motive having worked so well in Symphony No. 4, Tchaikovsky turned to the gimmick again in No. 5, where it intrudes even more frequently. This annoys me so I have trouble enjoying even the beautiful melody in the slow movement, but most listeners don't seem to mind.

Mariss Jansons is good here, but equal weight can be given to Claudio Abbado; both are digital. I don't really have any comparable mid-price or budget recordings to suggest.

Abbado, Chicago Symphony Orchestra. CBS 42094 [DDD] + *The Voyevoda*
Jansons, Oslo Philharmonic Orchestra. Chandos 8351 [DDD]

Symphony No. 6 in B Minor, Op. 74, "Pathètique"

Tchaikovsky's most unconventional symphony is his most original and convincing. The nickname "pathetic" was given by the composer's brother after the first performance, where the audience was "a-pathetic." Traditionally symphonies end in triumph, or at least quiet affirmation, but this one concludes in heartrending despair.

Although Tchaikovsky attached no program to the work, it seems obvious that it means to suggest the journey of a soul. A mix of emotions in the first movement yields to a brief idyll of happiness in the second; the third movement begins as a jolly march-along, but evolves almost imperceptibly into a terrifying army whose boots crush all in their path, followed by the utter desolation of the final movement.

Not the least upsetting experience one can have in classical music is when uncomprehending audiences, as they regularly do, applaud vigorously at the end of the march; I can't help thinking these are the same kind of people who packed picnic lunches and spent their Sundays watching the guillotinings during the French Revolution.

Mariss Jansons maintains his reputation here, but Mikhail Pletnev has rocketed to the top of the list as well, and offers a bonus of the *Marche slave*. Eugene Ormandy's mid-price disc is very recommendable.

Jansons, Oslo Philharmonic Orchestra. Chandos 8446 [DDD]
Pletnev, Russian National Orchestra. Virgin Classics 59661 [DDD] + *Marche slave*
Ormandy, Philadelphia Orchestra. RCA Silver Seal 60908 [ADD] + *Romeo and Juliet* (mid-price)

Giuseppe Verdi (1813-1901)

Verdi is acknowledged as the greatest of all the Italian opera composers; with the possible exception of Monteverdi (no relation) centuries before, he is the greatest Italian composer, opera or no. He started inauspiciously enough, as the son of an innkeeper in an obscure village. In love with music from an early age, he tried to enter the Milan Conservatory at age nineteen but was rejected as too old, too uncouth, too untrained.

He continued to study privately, and by 1839 wrote his first opera, *Oberto*. It was a fair success, but shortly afterwards Verdi's young wife and a daughter both died, and his second opera, a comedy, was a fiasco. The feckless composer was understandably plunged into gloom, and for months secluded himself in an attic.

The director of the famed La Scala Opera House, Merelli, believed in Verdi's talent, however, and finally induced him to write a work based on the story of Nebuchadnezzar in the Bible. *Nabucco* was a triumph, and established Verdi as Italy's rising star of the lyric stage. Its moving chorus, "Va, pensiero, sull'ali dorate" ("Fly, my thoughts, on golden wings"), became almost a national anthem for those who sought freedom for Italy, then divided and under Austrian domination.

After this, Verdi began a steady progression to wealth and world fame with a string of some three dozen operas, with hardly a failure among them. He became so beloved that even his weak operas were quickly forgiven, and the public moved on with relief to his next masterpiece.

But Verdi never rested on his laurels, and there are few composers in whom one can trace such a clear development of steady improvement from the first work to the last. There is nothing more astonishing in music than Verdi's composition in his eightieth year of *Falstaff,* a comedy of Shakespearian scope, written with supreme effortless sophistication. Sixty years earlier, Verdi had been chugging out cheap marches for a provincial band. His very life was one long opera, with a glorious finale.

Aida

One of the most exotically colored operas in the repertoire, *Aida* is Verdi's most truly "grand" opera in the dictionary sense of the word. (The vernacular habit of calling all opera "grand" is sloppy at best; the term is properly limited to four- or five-act musical epics on heroic subjects, with elaborate scenery and plenty of spectacle.) Verdi here fills the bill, yet manages to invest this rather remote story of ancient Egyptian political maneuverings with some real characterization and human feeling.

It was commissioned by the Khedive of Egypt to help celebrate the planned opening of the Suez Canal in 1869. The Khedive, a generous sort, paid Verdi three times his normal fee. Nevertheless, the composer got behind schedule and the premiere took place two years late. Not long afterwards, Egypt went bankrupt and the Khedive was tossed out on his ear. The opera, however, is still raking it in at the box office.

A better cast may never be assembled than that used in the Jonel Perlea mono recording of the 1950s, and if you can live without digital, not to mention stereo, this budget set is the performance to beat; when the world's greatest bass does a walk-on in the first scene, you know this is the big time.

But on to sonics. Digitophiles should turn to James Levine's recording with Placido Domingo and Aprile Millo; Domingo also stars in an earlier analog recording conducted by Erich Leinsdorf, with a famous Aida in Leontyne Price, unfortunately still at full price; and at mid-price, Herbert von Karajan's 1979 analog reading with Mirella Freni and José Carreras is attractive.

> **Perlea, Rome Opera House Orchestra and Chorus.** RCA Victrola 6652 (3) [ADD] (mono) (budget)
> **Levine, Metropolitan Opera Orchestra and Chorus.** Sony 45973 (3) [DDD]
> **Leinsdorf, London Symphony Orchestra.** RCA 6198 (3) [ADD]
> **Karajan, Vienna Philharmonic Orchestra.** Angel Studio 69300 (3) [ADD] (mid-price)

Otello

Verdi was in his seventies and long retired when his young friend Arrigo Boito tempted him with a splendid adaptation of Shakespeare's play. He pretended indifference for a long time, but finally couldn't control himself; the libretto was too good, his love of the

Bard too deep to let the opportunity slip by. When the work premiered in 1887, after a fifteen-year hiatus in Verdi operas, the world was stunned to find the composer had been maturing in silence. His technique and authority were beyond anything that had gone before, and even more was to come a few years later in *Falstaff.* The newcomer to Verdi, however, will likely find *Otello* more immediately attractive.

James Levine's 1978 recording has a great cast, including Placido Domingo (probably the best Otello around), Renata Scotto, and Sherrill Milnes, and everybody is wound up. Tullio Serafin's fine performance of two decades earlier is a steal at mid-price, with Jon Vickers, the best Otello of his era, and the best of all Iagos in Tito Gobbi. Digital should not be an issue here.

Levine, National Philharmonic Orchestra (London), Ambrosian Opera Chorus. RCA 2951 (2) [ADD]
Serafin, Rome Opera House Orchestra and Chorus. RCA 1969 (2) (mid-price)

Requiem

Despite the enduring greatness of his operas, there are many who would say Verdi's best monument is his magnificent *Requiem,* written to commemorate the death of the Italian patriot Alessandro Manzoni. Written on a breathtakingly vast musical canvass, it is not so much a liturgical work as "Verdi's greatest opera." The depiction of the Day of Judgment, with menacing brass seeming to gradually approach from first one corner of the cosmos, then another, is one of the most unforgettably vivid moments in all Romantic music.

Robert Shaw's 1987 digital recording is as thrilling as they get, and has won every prize in the book. The only better performance musically is the classic Carlo Maria Giulini analog recording from the early 1960s; although it is still available, the sound quality is really not up to par, and at full price I can't see recommending it any more. Besides, if you ever needed digital, this is the time; the end of the world just doesn't make it in analog.

Shaw, Atlanta Symphony Orchestra and Chorus. Telarc 80152 (2) [DDD]
+ Verdi opera choruses

Rigoletto

The story concerns a vicious humpback whose obsession to protect his beautiful daughter backfires. The original play was by Victor Hugo, who until people miraculously came to their senses just a few years ago was widely considered to be a Great Author. With his customary skill, Verdi does make it a great opera, and it was the first one to bring him international fame. The most famous aria in all his operas, "La donna è mobile," comes from Act I.

The great *Rigoletto* recording comes from the mid-fifties, and like the great *Aida* above, is in mono; but you are not going to find a better Rigoletto than Tito Gobbi, nor a more stellar "supporting cast" than Maria Callas and Giuseppe di Stefano, all expertly coached and conducted by Tullio Serafin. In digital, conductor Giuseppe Sinopoli is exciting, and a good mid-price version comes from Sir Georg Solti with Robert Merrill in the title role.

Serafin, La Scala Orchestra and Chorus. Angel 47469 (2) (mono)

Sinopoli, Santa Cecilia Academy Orchestra and Chorus. Philips 412592 (2) [DDD]

Solti, RCA Italiana Opera Orchestra and Chorus. RCA Gold Seal 6506 (2) [ADD] (mid-price)

La Traviata

Alexander Dumas, Jr.'s once-popular play *The Lady of the Camellias* was the source for Verdi's ever-popular opera. It is the classic treatment of the "fallen woman" theme. On paper it all looks hopelessly hokey, but such is Verdi's commitment that the opera is deeply convincing and moving. It has been made into a commercially successful film, a singular feat for an opera.

No one has ever recorded a version of *La Traviata* that has satisfied even a majority of critics, let alone all, so with all quibbles aside we can boil it down to two that are the best of an imperfect lot: Richard Bonynge's digital recording stars Joan Sutherland and Luciano Pavarotti (neither at their peak), while Carlos Kleiber's analog has Ileana Cotrubas and Placido Domingo as the lovers. Frankly, the main thing critics gripe about in the Kleiber recording is that the soprano breathes too hard; I'm not sure why this is so bad, particularly under the circumstances. Both recordings are mid-price.

Bonynge, National Philharmonic Orchestra (London), London Opera Chorus. London 430491 (2) [DDD] (mid-price)

C. Kleiber, Bavarian Radio Symphony Orchestra and Chorus. DG 415132 (2) [ADD] (mid-price)

Richard Wagner (1813-1883)

Wagner became not just a composer, but a phenomenon. One of the great self-promoters of history, he was the barker, ringmaster, and center attraction of his own one-man circus. By sheer force of personality, if not character, he dominated the musical headlines in the late nineteenth century and beyond. He was a driven man who could not stand to not get his way.

People didn't like his operas? He would rename them "music dramas" and write books denouncing his detractors. Theaters wouldn't put them on? He would build his own theater and orchestra and create a cult of musicians performing his works. He literally established a religion with himself as the savior of music; it was called Wagnerism, and his devotees were known as Wagnerites. People wouldn't join the religion? They must be evil Jews.

The parallels with a vicious Austrian paperhanger were obvious to the architects of the Third Reich, who adopted Wagner as their composer laureate, further complicating history's assessment of an already complex issue. The music of Wagner was not heard in Israel until great Jewish musicians such as Leonard Bernstein and Daniel Barenboim pleaded for it, holding that the music itself should not be condemned for the sins of the man who wrote it.

In all fairness, Wagner's notorious anti-Semitism was nothing near the doctrinaire system espoused by the Nazis, and he was as likely to forget all about it if someone he needed to play or conduct his music was Jewish. Everything in his life had to be subservient to his artistic goals, and if anti-Semitism got in the way, it went out the window like anything else. Ironically, it has been fairly well established that Wagner was not the son of his putative father Carl Wagner, but the natural child of his mother's lover and later second husband, a Jewish actor named Ludwig Geyer.

In his early school days in Dresden, Wagner showed far more aptitude for literature than for music. Partly under the influence of a scholarly uncle, he imbibed the ancient classics, Shakespeare, and Goethe. Not until the relatively late age (for a musician) of fourteen did he decide, after hearing a Beethoven symphony for the first time, that he would devote himself to music. With the energy typical of a fanatic he plunged into a study of music theory, and was soon composing. Amazingly, the man who would for a time be proclaimed a greater composer than Bach, Mozart, or Beethoven was largely self-taught or tutored.

At first he concentrated on symphonic music, but by the end of his university days at Leipzig he had turned to opera, and took the job of director of a small company in Magdeburg. He married one of the singers there, Minna Planer, and with her was soon migrating all over Europe, pursued by creditors. Wagner's appetites were enormous, not least for clothes and luxuries, and he considered being asked to pay for them an affront to his artistic divinity.

The Wagners were near starvation when his opera *Rienzi* was finally a success. From then on it was a fairly steady climb upwards, assisted by the patronage of King Ludwig II of Bavaria (who turned his fairy-tale castle Neuschwanstein into a Wagner theme park) and the growing army of Wagnerites who fanned out across Europe to promote the theories and works of their Master (and so they called him). There were interruptions, as when Wagner had to flee for his life after supporting the Revolution of 1848, and another exile after he stole the wife of one of his closest friends, the conductor Hans von Bülow (further complicated by the fact that the woman was Franz Liszt's daughter Cosima—Liszt also had been a Wagner supporter).

Never one to think small, Wagner had in mind for years a magnum opus that would be based on the old German sagas and Norse eddas. The result, after many years of sporadic work, was *The Ring of the Nibelung,* a continuous epic which required four evenings to perform and led Wagner to build his own theater, the Bayreuth Festspielhaus, to stage it.

Like the man himself, his greatest work was bigger than life.

Wagner's theories of opera as a synthesis of all the arts; his method of composition, involving liberal use of the thematic device which he called the Leitmotif and a through-composed style of "endless melody" without set pieces and arias; and his vision of a "music of the future," which was little more than an expanded reliance on chromaticism (more sharps and flats!), created about him a cachet of almost supernatural authority. Not everyone fell for it, however, and there was always a vigorous anti-Wagner faction, with Johannes Brahms elevated somewhat reluctantly to its symbolic head.

Today, when Wagner has receded to the status of an enormously talented, if rather unpleasant, human, most people can listen to his music without bowing under its pseudo-philosophical baggage. It is music of stupendous force, color, and drama. Its harmonic innovations made possible a new direction in music, from Bruckner and Debussy to the present. It stirred up the world of the arts and made people think more than they ever had about the role of music and the musician in life. Isn't that enough?

Orchestral Selections

Most Wagnerites are first seduced by orchestral arrangements, minus the singing, of large sections (commonly called "bleeding chunks") of the operas. Almost all of these have had to have some surgery to extricate them from the original contexts. There are some overtures and preludes, and truncations with identifying labels such as "Forest Murmurs," "Ride of the Valkyries," and "Siegfried's Rhine Journey." Many people have heard only these Reader's Digest versions and are positively shocked to find out that there are words that go with them. Nevertheless, they are a legitimate way to enter Wagner's world, so let us hack away.

George Szell's famous excerpts from the 1960s have been unbelievably well-remastered and then reissued at budget price, making this one of the best bargains in the catalog. His disc specifically of *Ring* highlights is at mid-price for no discernible reason. There are a couple of great Fritz Reiner programs also, one at mid-price, one full; and two collections from Sir Georg Solti, partly or completely digital. Herbert von Karajan is represented by a mid-price collection from 1975, and Mariss Jansons has a recommendable general collection, a good choice for those whose destination is digital.

Szell, Cleveland Orchestra. Sony 48175 [ADD] (budget)
Szell, Cleveland Orchestra. *Ring* hlts, CBS 36715 [ADD] (mid-price)
Reiner, Chicago Symphony Orchestra, RCA Victor Orchestra. RCA Gold Seal 61792 [ADD] + Humperdinck: *Dream Pantomime* from *Hansel und Gretel* (mid-price)
Reiner, Chicago Symphony Orchestra. RCA 4738 [ADD]
Solti, Vienna Philharmonic Orchestra. London 440107 [ADD/DDD] (mid-price)

Solti, Vienna Philharmonic Orchestra. *Ring* hlts., London 410137 [DDD]
Karajan, Berlin Philharmonic Orchestra. EMI Studio Plus 64334 (mid-price)
Jansons, Oslo Philharmonic Orchestra. EMI 54583 [DDD]

The Flying Dutchman (Der fliegende Holländer)

This is Wagner's earliest opera to still hold the boards, and one of the easiest to slide into if you are ready to try the Whole Thing. He wrote it originally in one continuous long act; being a living god, he had of course forgotten that mortals need to go the restroom, and eventually under pressure he divided it up into three acts.

It is a mildly horrific Gothic tale of a ghostly sea captain who sails the oceans eternally with a spectral crew, seeking release from his curse through the pure love of a maid. The music positively reeks of the salt spray and the howling wind in the topsail, with more chain-rattling and bone-clanking than in *Spook Chasers* with the Bowery Boys. (Quite cinematic, come to think of it.)

Buyers are lucky on this one; the original one-act version with star singers and plenteous sound effects, conducted by Antal Dorati, has been reissued at mid-price, as has Herbert von Karajan's three-act version starring José van Dam—either is a bargain. But on top of that, Naxos has come out with a widely-praised performance at budget price in digital sound; the singers are not "names," but they do very well, and the conductor, Pinchas Steinberg, will probably be graduating soon to the high-price labels.

Dorati, Royal Opera House (Covent Garden) Orchestra and Chorus. London 417319 (2) [ADD] (mid-price)
Karajan, Berlin Philharmonic Orchestra. EMI 64650 (2) (mid-price)
P. Steinberg, Vienna ORF Symphony Orchestra, Budapest Radio Choir. Naxos 8.660025/26 (2) [DDD] (budget)

Der Ring des Nibelungen

The Ring, as it is familiarly called, is to a normal-sized opera (let's say *Rigoletto*) as the Pyramid of Cheops is to a summer cabin; very impressive, much bigger, but not necessarily better. I say that with all love, because the *Ring* is one of the great experiences a person can have in music. You can't very well ignore it. You can waste time walking around it, but it would be better just to climb up and explore it.

Wagner certainly had a sense of the epic, and he wisely chose the myths of his own culture on which to build his greatest monument. It took twenty-eight years of work, from the first sketches in 1848 to the premiere in 1876 at the theater Wagner had to have built to accomodate it. Although some aspects of the story are of limited interest to non-Teutons, most of it has universal resonance, and Wagner has poured into it the best of his considerable talent.

Once you have succumbed to the various bleeding chunks offered on highlights albums, there is a good possibility you will want to have the whole *Ring;* just remember you will have to set aside some fifteen or sixteen hours of listening time, and don't spread it too thin or you may forget the story and have to start over, despite the numerous recaps Wagner thoughtfully works into the text as it goes along. (Some listeners hate these as holding up the action.)

No serious Wagner collection can afford to be without Sir Georg Solti's historic *Ring* recording, made over the period 1959-1967. It is one of the capstones of recording history, with a unique magic of its own. The dramatic studio production, great singing, and blazing conducting add up to a whole that no other recording can quite match, and the sound— far ahead of its time— is highly competitive still.

Solti, Vienna Philharmonic Orchestra, Flagstad, Nilsson, Fischer-Dieskau, Hotter, Frick, etc. London 414100 (15) [ADD] (mid-price)

Tristan und Isolde

No one but Wagner would have written this stupendous five-hour drama as a diversion when he needed a break from the *Ring!*

It stands apart from his other compositions as an experiment in structure and especially harmony, and is often considered the seminal work which made twentieth-century music possible. Its roots, like the *Ring's,* are mythical, but in its treatment it explores depths of psychology which were never dreamed of in opera before Wagner's time. Whole books have been written on its significance, but if you can master the *Ring,* you should be able to toss this one off on a Friday night.

Wilhelm Furtwängler's 1952 recording occupies the same sanctified place in history as Solti's *Ring.* There were two great Isoldes in this century; one of them, Kirsten Flagstad, stars in Furtwängler's set (which, though mono, sounds fabulous); the other, Birgit Nilsson, headlines Karl Böhm's 1966 live performance, which has newer sound, one less disc, and a lower price.

Furtwängler, Philharmonia Orchestra, Covent Garden Chorus. EMI 47321 (4) (mono)
Böhm, Bayreuth Festival Orchestra and Chorus. DG 419889 (3) [ADD] (mid-price)

Die Walküre

"The Valkyrie" is the second of the four operas, or "evenings," as Wagner called them, that make up the *Ring,* and the one most often called on to stand alone. It does work quite well as a self-contained unit, and of the four probably offers the most for your money and time. If you aren't sure you want to invest in the complete *Ring,* you could start with *Die Walküre* and decide whether to pick up on the rest later.

You can choose the Solti, separated from its fifteen-disc box, or the vivid Karl Böhm performance recorded live in Wagner's Bayreuth Theater. Both are great, both are from the 1960s, both are analog, and both are at the exact same price, so it is essentially a tie, but Sir Georg goes first by protocol.

Solti, Vienna Philharmonic Orchestra. London 414105 (4) [ADD] (mid-price)
Böhm, Bayreuth Festival Orchestra and Chorus. Philips 412478 (4) [ADD] (mid-price)

The Late Romantics
(ca. 1890-1915)

The composers of this period, or sub-period if you will, were all born between 1845 and 1865. That places them chronologically, but they generally share more than dates. They share the fact that their most important work came after Liszt and Wagner, who with their rhapsodic forms and widening sense of tonality, had confused, if not revolutionized, the art of composition.

Many of these composers were not sure which way to turn. No one could go back to the pre-Wagnerian days, which were now considered a closed book at best, utterly passé at worst. But whither? No one was prepared to abandon everything overnight, although that is how many felt, standing in Wagner's intimidating shadow, hearing the Master's disciples tell them that all they had learned of music theory was superseded by the Music of the Future (whatever and wherever that was).

All of the Late Romantic composers chose to remain within the confines of the major-minor tonal system, even though some, like Debussy, stretched it to the limit. But they all sensed that the old system was somehow coming to an end. In Elgar and Delius we hear nostalgia for the long ago and far away; in Mahler the anxiety and angst of facing the unknown; in Richard Strauss and Humperdinck an attempt to keep the old Wagnerian juggernaut rolling along. Mascagni and Leoncavallo, and to a lesser extent Puccini, sought release from the old restraints through extremes of sensation. Fauré tried to stop the disintegration by binding modern tendencies with the glue of classicism. D'Indy called on his students to have faith in the midst of artistic crisis, to rise above despair through reason; and Dukas simply gave up and tore most of his music into shreds.

Whatever their response, all were seeking an answer to a nagging question: What future did Western music have after the old scaffolding was removed? None of them came up with a perfect solution, but most of them, each in his individual way, helped form a bridge to the future. It was a period of ferment and experimentation, alternating between hope and frustration, but no definite break with the past had yet come. That will be a story for the next chapter.

Claude Debussy (1862-1918)

Acknowledged today as one of the most original and seminal composers at the beginning of the twentieth century, Debussy was a popular success as well—a combination seldom to be noted. Here is a man who could turn harmony upside down and use it to write *Clair de lune,* a piece that has almost become Muzak. "A century of airplanes," he once said, "deserves its own music. As there are no precedents, I must create anew."

He was a talented child who entered the prestigious Paris Conservatory at only ten years of age. Except for four years of study in Italy, he remained in his beloved Paris all his life. His favorite description of himself was simply "musicien Française."

His artistic path was determined by exposure to the Symbolist poets, whose theories he wished to apply to music. Although he later repudiated Wagnerism, it was an early influence on him, and he took something away also from the Paris Exhibition of 1889, where he became fascinated by Javanese gamelan music. The result was a musical "school" known as Impressionism, of which Debussy became the chief (and frankly, almost only) composer. His goal was not, like his German contemporary Richard Strauss, to depict extramusical subjects in tones, but to suggest them.

He hit on a style which leaned heavily on the whole-tone scale, which has six notes instead of the conventional eight, with different intervals between them. With this device he was able to create unique melodies, chords, and harmonies that seemed earthy and sensual, yet at the same time exquisitely delicate and fragile. It was a fascinating sound, richly capable of evoking subtle sensations.

For its day, however, around the turn of the century, it was puzzling and upsetting to many listeners. Gone were the comfortable black and white rules and forms of musical composition, replaced by fleeting allusions, splashes of color, and hints of forbidden perfumes. It all smacked of subversiveness.

When Debussy's great opera was being rehearsed in 1902, the arch-conservative composer Camille Saint-Saëns was spotted in the street by a friend. "Maestro," he exclaimed, "I thought you were out of town." The old man glowered. "I have thtayed in Parith," he spat, in his notorious lisp, "to thpeak ill of *Pelléath et Mélithande!*" Debussy paid no attention to such criticism. Even as a student at the Conservatory he ignored the old rules. One of his professors, hearing him practicing bizarre chord progressions on the piano, barked at him "What rule do you follow?" Debussy quietly replied: "Mon plaisir."

Images pour orchestre

Written between 1908 and 1912 and later put together out of order, the three *Images* are "Gigues" (jigs), "Ibéria" (Spain), and "Rondes de printemps" (Spring round dance). "Ibéria," the longest section, is the most popular and is often heard separately. Manuel de Falla, the greatest composer of Spain, said Debussy had spent only a few hours in his country, but had caught its musical character more accurately than many native composers had done. "Ibéria" itself divides into three sections: "In the Streets and Byways," "Fragrances of the Night," and "Morning of a Festival Day."

As might be expected, Charles Dutoit turns in expert accounts of music for which he has such a natural feel. But if digital is not an issue, you can get magnificent analog performances of all Debussy's major orchestral work by Bernard Haitink in a two-CD set at half price.

Dutoit, Montreal Symphony Orchestra. London 425502 [DDD] + *Nocturnes*

Haitink, Concertgebouw Orchestra. Philips Duo 438742 (2) [ADD] + *Nocturnes, La Mer, Prelude to the Afternoon of a Faun, Jeux,* more (mid-price)

La Mer

Debussy loved the sea as much as any composer ever has: "She has shown me all her moods," he told his publisher. *La Mer* ("The Sea"), completed in 1905, is the composer's largest tone poem, and more than any other of his works fully represents what he meant by Impressionism. The three movements are marked "From Dawn till Noon on the Sea," "Play of the Waves," and "Dialog of the Wind and the Sea."

Dutoit is again the digital choice, while the Haitink set described immediately above is a marvelous value. And even beyond these, there are an embarrassing number of outstanding analog recordings available at mid-price which it would be unfair not to list, especially as various of them may have more or less appeal based on their couplings.

Dutoit, Montreal Symphony Orchestra. London 430240 [DDD] + *Prelude to the Afternoon of a Faun, Jeux, Martyrdom of St. Sebastian* (sel.)

Haitink, Concertgebouw Orchestra. Philips Duo 438742 (2) [ADD] + *Images pour orchestre, Nocturnes, Prelude to the Afternoon of a Faun, Jeux,* etc. (mid-price)

Munch, Boston Symphony Orchestra. RCA Living Stereo 61500 [ADD] + Saint-Saëns: Symphony No. 3; Ibert: *Escales* (mid-price)

Reiner, Chicago Symphony Orchestra. RCA Gold Seal 60875 [ADD] + Rimsky-Korsakov: *Scheherazade* (mid-price)

Karajan, Berlin Philharmonic Orchestra. DG 427250 [ADD] + *Prelude to the Afternoon of a Faun;* Ravel: *Boléro, Daphnis et Chloe* Suite No. 2 (mid-price)

Ansermet, Suisse Romande Orchestra. "Ansermet Edition, Vol. 1," London 433711 [ADD] + *Clair de lune* (orch. version), *Jeux, Petite Suite, Premiere Rapsodie* for Clarinet and Piano (mid-price)

Martinon, ORTF Orchestra. EMI 69587 [ADD] + *Nocturnes, Prelude to the Afternoon of a Faun* (mid-price)

Nocturnes

"The title 'Nocturnes,'" Debussy wrote, "is to be interpreted...in a decorative sense." It is meant to designate, he explained, "all the various impressions and the special effects of light that the word suggests." Again the work is in three sections: "Nuages" (clouds), "Fêtes" (festivals), and "Sirènes" (sirens, that is, of the feminine kind). Written 1897-99, the *Nocturnes* are heard much less often than they deserve due to the need for a female chorus in the last movement only.

Returning to a manageable list, helped by the legendary Claudio Abbado recording being unceremoniously kicked out of the catalogs, we revert to Charles Dutoit for a definitive digital version, and pick up Jean Martinon at mid-price from the previous recommendations.

Dutoit, Montreal Symphony Orchestra. London 425502 [DDD] + *Images pour orchestre*
Martinon, ORTF Orchestra. EMI 69587 [ADD] + *La Mer* (mid-price)

Piano Music

Debussy wrote a considerable body of significant music for one and two pianos, including two books of Preludes, but the one piece that everyone knows him by is *Clair de lune* ("Moonlight"), which is actually one movement of the *Suite Bergamasque*.

One of comedian Victor Borge's standard lines was pretending to misunderstand the title as "Clear the Saloon." That's good, but even better was a real-life incident when I once asked a very confused young music-seeker whether she liked Debussy, and with a perplexed expression she responded, "Fields?"

Hungarian pianist Zoltán Kocsis has a beautifully played digital album with the complete *Suite Bergamasque* and other Debussy piano works. A great analog performance of the complete Suite by Alexis Weissenberg is happily, if rather oddly, coupled with the Debussy and Ravel String Quartets on a mid-price issue. A well-selected anthology by Cristina Ortiz features just *Clair de lune*, along with other popular short piano pieces by Debussy, Ravel, and many more; the import label will not be carried in all stores, however.

Kocsis. Philips 412118 [DDD] + *Estampes, Pour le piano, Images oubliées*
Weissenberg. RCA Silver Seal 60909 [ADD] + Quartet in G Minor; Ravel: Quartet in F (mid-price)
Ortiz. IMP PCD 846 [DDD] + 2 *Arabesques, L'Isle joyeuse, Reflets dan l'eau, La Cathédrale engloutie, Golliwog's Cakewalk;* Satie: *Trois Gymnopédies;* works by Chabrier, Ibert, Milhaud, Poulenc, Ravel

Prélude à l'après-midi d'un faune

Inspired by a poem of the same name by the symbolist Stéphane Mallarmé, "Prelude to the Afternoon of a Faun" was Debussy's first hit. It describes a mythical faun drowsing in the afternoon sun, dreaming of two nymphs. In diaphonous music of magical haziness Debussy creates a perfect picture of dreamlike sensuality which has never been equalled.

Five different recordings already recommended above under *La Mer* contain this work:

Haitink, Concertgebouw Orchestra. Philips Duo 438742 (2) [ADD] + *Images pour orchestre, La Mer, Nocturnes, Jeux,* etc. (mid-price)

Dutoit, Montreal Symphony Orchestra. London 430240 [DDD] + *La Mer, Jeux, Martyrdom of St. Sebastian* (sel.)

Karajan, Berlin Philharmonic Orchestra. DG 427250 [ADD] + *La Mer;* Ravel: *Boléro, Daphnis et Chloe* No. 2 (mid-price)

Ansermet, Suisse Romande Orchestra. "Ansermet Edition, Vol. 1," London 433711 [ADD] + *La Mer, Clair de lune* (orch. version), *Jeux, Petite Suite, Premiere Rapsodie* for Clarinet and Piano (mid-price)

Martinon, ORTF Orchestra. EMI 69587 [ADD] + *Nocturnes, La Mer* (mid-price)

Quartet in G Minor, Op. 10

Debussy's only string quartet is actually one of his least characteristic works, having no program explicit or implied. It is experimental in form and style, but has become a standard of the chamber music repertoire nonetheless.

The Italian Quartet (Quartetto Italiano on some album covers) has long been a standard in the classic coupling of the Debussy and Ravel Quartets, and they are now available at mid-price. The Alban Berg Quartet is technically brilliant on digital, and the Guarneri Quartet is a fine alternate at mid-price, with a bonus of the *Suite Bergamasque* (including *Clair de lune*).

Italian Quartet. Philips Silver Line 420894 [ADD] + Ravel: Quartet in F (mid-price)

Alban Berg Quartet. EMI 47347 [DDD] + Ravel: Quartet in F

Guarneri Quartet. RCA Silver Seal 60909 [ADD] + *Suite Bergamasque* (with Alexis Weissenberg); Ravel: Quartet in F (mid-price)

Frederick Delius (1862-1934)

Delius is remembered mainly for a small number of small pieces, exquisitely serene tone poems with delicious titles such as *On Hearing the First Cuckoo in Spring, A Song Before Sunrise,* and *In a Summer Garden.* The opulent harmonies of these works lend themselves ideally to the subject matter, and are part and parcel of the Late Romantic style.

Sir Thomas Beecham, the conductor who more than anyone championed Delius and brought the music of this recluse to public attention, called him "the last great apostle in our time of romance, beauty and emotion in music." His sound is absolutely unique. Both rapturous and elegant, sensuous and refined, it is the sound of evanescent landscapes. The melodies are magically beautiful, but they are not the kind that are easy to remember and hum after you hear them; they evaporate into the twilight of the imagination, and the uncertain memory of them pulls you back to Delius with a desire to hear them again.

Delius was the son of a wealthy English wool merchant who did everything in his power to keep Frederick away from foolishness such as music; in fact, he refused to admit his son was a composer even after he was famous. The young Delius was packed off to Florida where he tried in vain for two years to manage some orange groves his father had bought as an investment. He spent most of his time studying theory with the organist of a church in Jacksonville and taking notes on the music of the freed slaves while the oranges rotted on the ground.

His father was finally willing to pay his way to the Leipzig Conservatory just to get rid of him. He studied there three years, then moved to Paris, where he married. The couple eventually decided to make their permanent home in the lovely small French town of Grez-sur-Loing outside of Fontainebleu; here they lived quietly for the remainder of his life, another thirty-seven years, and here Delius wrote most of the works for which he is remembered, becoming more and more withdrawn from the world.

In his final years he was incapacitated by blindness, but a young musician who was one of his admirers, Eric Fenby, made an offer unique in the history of composing: he would live with the couple and take dictation. Thus Delius "wrote" his last works, composing them in his head and then telling Fenby how to write them down, note by note, chord by chord.

Tone poems

As mentioned above, Sir Thomas Beecham, one of the greatest conductors on records, almost singlehandedly championed Delius right out of obscurity into the limelight. He once said of this music, "I found it as alluring as a wayward woman, and determined to tame it. And it wasn't done in a day!" His definitive (stereo) recordings, although they date back a few years, have been miraculously well remastered and sound virtually as good as new. If you are interested in Delius, you must have them. If you are not interested in Delius, you will be.

Beecham, Royal Philharmonic Orchestra. Angel 47509 (2) [ADD]

Paul Dukas (1865-1935)

Dukas is remembered almost exclusively for one tone poem, *L'Apprenti sorcier.* It is one of only a handful of works that survived his obsessive perfectionism, for he either abandoned or destroyed most of his compositions out of dissatisfaction.

Born in Paris of a mother who was an accomplished pianist, Dukas showed that early talent for music so common among composers. He later claimed that as a baby he had "given suck in 9/8 time." He entered the Paris Conservatory at age seventeen and stayed there for eight years, immersing himself in counterpoint and fugue.

His first public work, an overture, was successful in 1892, but it was the orchestral scherzo, *The Sorcerer's Apprentice,* which suddenly made him a sensation in 1897. Dukas was mortified, since he had only written the piece as an example to his students (he was now a professor at the Conservatory) of how *not* to write a scherzo!

The piece was indeed unrepresentative of its composer. Dukas was greatly influenced by Debussy, and his opera *Ariane et Barbe-bleue* is esteemed by connoisseurs as the greatest successor to *Pelléas et Mélisande*. What of Dukas's music that survives is distinguished by great delicacy of expression—not the rumbunctious cavortings of his greatest hit!

The Sorcerer's Apprentice (L'Apprenti sorcier)

Written long before Mickey Mouse was even thought of, the tone poem depicts the story precisely as Walt Disney told it. (It is the only music in *Fantasia* of which that can be said.) A young student of magic decides to try his hand when the master is away. He manages to get a broom to come to life and draw water for him, but he doesn't know how to undo the spell, and soon the house is flooded. Chopping the broom in half only creates two brooms to bring twice as much water. The apprentice's despairing cries bring the master back. He calms the waters, removes the spell, and gives the errant lad a kick in the pants.

James Levine and Yan-Pascal Tortelier have fine digital recordings already recommended under their couplings, and Leonard Bernstein's classic account is still available at mid-price.

Levine, Berlin Philharmonic Orchestra. DG 419617 [DDD] + Saint-Saëns: Symphony No. 3

Tortelier, Ulster Orchestra. Chandos 8852 [DDD] + *La Péri;* Chabrier: *España, Suite Pastorale*

Bernstein, New York Philharmonic Orchestra. CBS 37769 [AAD] + Saint-Saëns: *Danse Macabre, Bacchanale* from *Samson et Dalila;* Chabrier: *España;* Ravel: *Pavane for a Dead Princess;* Offenbach: Overture to *Orpheus in the Underworld* (mid-price)

Edward Elgar (1857-1934)

Dressed like any English squire in his vest and cravat, smiling benignly over a bushy mustachio, composing *Pomp and Circumstance* marches and a Coronation Ode for Edward VII, Elgar could easily have become a caricature of the establishment British composer-laureate. But there was another side to him, sensitive and intimate, which gives depth even to his "public" works, and which is all the more fascinating because he was so reluctant to show it.

The young Elgar learned music mostly from his father, an organist and piano tuner, and on his own. He had no university or professional training in music, but set himself up at age sixteen teaching piano and violin. He took what part he could in local musical life, but living in Worcester the best job he could get was conducting the orchestra at a mental hospital. He credited his experience arranging for wildly unlikely instrumental combinations at the "lunatic asylum" in helping him become a brilliant orchestrator later in life.

It was love that finally released his creative genius. In 1889 he married one of his piano students, Caroline Alice Roberts, nine years his senior. Thereafter, music poured from him and his fame increased, until he was knighted in 1904. No matter how public he became, however, he held his private life and thoughts as tenaciously secret as he could.

Recent biographers have tried to prove that some earlier love still lurked in his psyche, as hinted in the inscription to his Violin Concerto: "A qui esta encerrada el alma de...." ("Herein is enshrined the soul of...."), a quotation from LeSage's *Gil Blas*. But Elgar was ever fond of puzzles and mysteries, as evidenced by his famous *Enigma Variations,* and may have simply liked to tease.

Whatever other loves he may have had, the fact remains that his muse flourished until Caroline died in 1920, and from then until his death in 1934 Elgar wrote nothing, spending his time chopping wood or wandering the countryside.

Talking to a friend during his final illness, he suddenly began humming a tune from his last great masterpiece, the Cello Concerto. "If ever after I'm dead," he whispered, "you hear someone whistling this tune on the Malvern Hills, don't be alarmed. It's only me."

Concerto for Cello in E Minor, Op. 85

Elgar's more popular concerto (he wrote only two, the other for violin) was given its premiere in 1919 by Felix Salmond, for whom it was written, with the composer conducting. It is unusually intimate for Elgar, a kind of expression of sorrow from someone very shy. Its only major flaw is a tacked-on happy ending that nobody could possibly believe. Despite that, the work has taken its place beside the Dvořák as one of the great cello concerti.

A fine digital recording with cellist Julian Lloyd Webber, aptly coupled with the *Enigma Variations,* is unaccountably not available in the U.S. at this writing; you might watch for it as Philips 416354 in case things change.

In the meantime, young cellist Steven Isserlis turns in a fine digital performance with a coupling of the basic *Schelomo* by Ernest Bloch. Yo-Yo Ma's acclaimed 1985 version has been reissued at mid-price, coupled with the perhaps less "basic" cello concerto of William Walton.

Isserlis, Hickox, London Symphony Orchestra. Virgin Classics 59511 [DDD] + Bloch: *Schelomo*
Ma, Previn, London Symphony Orchestra. Sony 53333 [DDD] + Walton: Cello Concerto

Enigma Variations, Op. 36

A brilliant tour-de-force, this set of variations both humorous and mysterious is one of the best-orchestrated pieces anyone has written. It is also the apotheosis of Elgar's love for riddles. Each of the fourteen variations is a musical portrait of a friend, his wife, or himself.

Originally the persons were disguised under pseudonyms or initials, but they have all long since been identified.

There is a theme for the variations to be built on, but Elgar insisted there was another, unheard theme which is woven through the work. Many have striven since the premiere in 1899 to figure this riddle out, and every year or two someone claims to have the "proof" that explains it. The main clue Elgar gave was that it was so obvious he was amazed no one had guessed it. But he took the answer, if there is one, to his grave. As years passed he grew more and more irritable over the constant speculation. "There is nothing to be gained...by solving the enigma," he wrote; "the listener should hear the music as music."

My own belief is that there is no "enigma." I think it was a publicity stunt to call attention to the piece, or a private joke which got out of hand, and Elgar was too embarrassed or ashamed to admit it. Why else would he never reveal the answer and become so crotchety about being badgered? Or, he may have had an idea about an imaginary counterpoint that could be inferred but forgot later what it was! There are just as many possibilities in this direction as there are when assuming Elgar was serious. But, in this eternal puzzle, you may believe whatever you wish.

Two excellent digital recordings offer this work coupled with the *Pomp and Circumstance* Marches; André Previn at full price, and the less famous Alexander Gibson at mid-price. Musically speaking, Sir Adrian Boult's analog recording is unsurpassable, and is coupled with a famous reading of *The Planets* by Gustav Holst.

Previn, Royal Philharmonic Orchestra. Philips 416813 [DDD] + *Pomp and Circumstance* Marches

Gibson, Scottish National Orchestra. Chandos 6504 [DDD] + *Pomp and Circumstance* Marches (mid-price)

Boult, London Philharmonic Orchestra. EMI 64748 + Holst: *The Planets* (mid-price)

Pomp and Circumstance March in D, Op. 39, No. 1

There are five marches in the Op. 39 set, all of them grandiose in the way only the British can be, but No. 1 has always been the favorite. Its main theme, which the composer rightly pointed out "comes once in a lifetime," has become (with words added to it) virtually a second British national anthem. In America, it frequently serves more prosaically to accompany high school graduates down the aisle during their final ceremonies.

The Previn and Gibson recordings are recommended above under *Enigma Variations*.

Previn, Royal Philharmonic Orchestra. Philips 416813 [DDD] + *Enigma Variations*

Gibson, Scottish National Orchestra. Chandos 6504 [DDD] + *Enigma Variations* (mid-price)

Symphony No. 1 in A-flat, Op. 55

"The greatest symphony of modern times," said conductor Hans Richter, who led the premiere in 1908. Audiences agreed. They begged to hear it again, and within a year it had been given a hundred times around the world. This was the greatest success Elgar ever had. It has a beautiful slow theme which recurs throughout the symphony, marked *nobilmente e semplice* ("with nobility and simplicity"). It is so striking and characteristic that the word *nobilmente* has come to signify the essential spirit of Elgar's musical art.

André Previn's standard recording not currently appearing in the catalogs, I hand the digital palm to Leonard Slatkin, and the mid-price analog to Sir Adrian Boult. Each has a less well-known Elgar work as coupling.

Slatkin, London Philharmonic Orchestra. RCA 60380 [DDD] + *In the South*
Boult, London Philharmonic Orchestra. Angel 64013 + Serenade in E Minor (mid-price)

Gabriel Fauré (1845-1924)

Fauré was the least exhibitionistic, the most classical—to the point of being branded "Hellenistic"—of the Late Romantics. His response to the bankruptcy of Romanticism was to transcend it by looking both backward (to eighteenth-century ideals of form and restraint) and forward (not to overthrowing tradition, but to finding new ways to handle the tried and true materials). The art he developed was eminently civilized. Not everyone had patience with this gentle approach; one famous pianist slammed the lid down on Fauré's music, muttering that it was "too damned polite."

This apostle of restraint and gentility was the last of six children born to a father who was the last in several generations of butchers. He was "discovered" by an old blind woman of the village who heard the boy improvising over the keyboard in an old chapel and convinced his parents to send him, at the age of nine, to the then-new Niedermeyer School. Papa Fauré was worried about the expense, but when Louis Niedermeyer heard the boy play he waived all fees.

After Niedermeyer's death, Fauré came under the tutelage of Saint-Saëns. They were only ten years apart in age, and became lifelong friends. This was the beginning of a chain of connections between Fauré and most of the important French composers of his era: nearly forty years later, Fauré would become the teacher of Ravel.

Meanwhile, however, his career moved slowly but steadily. After fighting in the Franco-Prussian War he returned to the École Niedermeyer as a teacher. Over the years he worked frequently as a professional organist, working his way up to professor of composition at the Paris Conservatory, of which he became the Director in 1905.

No sooner, however, had he reached the pinnacle of respect and recognition than he began to grow deaf. Nevertheless, he produced many of his finest works in the last twenty years of his life, during which time his hearing diminished gradually to zero. During World War I he and his wife moved to a town in the Pyrenees, near his birthplace. There he lived out his last days, composing to the end as he gazed at the mist-covered mountains, hearing the music only in his private and isolated world of imagination.

Pelléas et Mélisande, Op. 80

A few years before Debussy wrote his opera on Maurice Maeterlinck's play, Fauré contributed incidental music for a London production starring one of the great actresses of that era, Mrs. Patrick Campbell. The suite has four sections, *Prelude, Fileuse* ("The Spinner"), *Sicilienne,* and *Death of Mélisande.* Pelléas gets short shrift in this mysteriously evocative music, the composer focusing almost exclusively on the heroine.

Charles Dutoit is head and shoulders above the competition here, coupled with the Requiem, except for Jean Fournet who has an excellent, if harder to find, version coupled with the Chausson Symphony, which would be the motivator in this case.

Dutoit, Montreal Symphony Orchestra. London 421440 [DDD] + Requiem, *Pavane*
Fournet, Netherlands Radio Symphony Orchestra. Denon 73675 [DDD] + Chausson: Symphony in B-flat

Requiem, Op. 48

Fauré's acknowledged masterpiece was written in bits and pieces over several years, but came together as a unified work in memory of his father, who died in 1885. It is one of the few Requiae which fulfill the promise of the implied command: Rest. Unfailingly tranquil, it presents Death as the Comforter, not a thing to be feared. Fauré drops the traditional *Dies irae* section describing the terrors of the Last Judgment, and ends uniquely with the *In Paradisum* ("May the angels receive thee in Paradise"), a musical setting which could serve as the dictionary definition of the word "exquisite."

Charles Dutoit, as noted under *Pelléas et Mélisande,* is the standard digital choice for most listeners; however, John Rutter has produced a great recording of the original chamber music instrumentation of this work on his Collegium label, joined with some other short choral works by Fauré. Another popular choice is Carlo Maria Giulini, who has the advantage of Kathleen Battle's radiant soprano, coupled less generously, but not less aptly, with Ravel's *Pavane for a Dead Princess.*

Dutoit, Montreal Symphony Orchestra and Chorus. London 421440
[DDD] + *Pelléas et Mélisande, Pavane*
Rutter, City of London Sinfonia, Cambridge Singers. Collegium 109
[DDD] + six short choral works
Giulini, Philharmonia Orchestra and Chorus. DG 419243 [DDD] +
Ravel: *Pavane for a Dead Princess*

Engelbert Humperdinck (1854-1921)

Humperdinck was not even remotely related to the Anglo-American pop singer allegedly of the same name. Arnold Dorsey, looking for a "stage name" that people would remember, apparently thought old Engelbert was so unknown that nobody would make the connection. Apparently, the gamble largely paid off: I once read a letter in an "Ask the Expert" newspaper column from one of the singer's fans inquiring as to whether Engelbert Humperdinck was his real name. "No," replied the Expert, "he just made it up."

The real Engelbert Humperdinck was a promising student of composition who became an assistant to Richard Wagner at Bayreuth, serving as stage manager at the premiere of *Parsifal.* Later he resumed his studies, becoming at last a professor, first in Spain, then in his native Germany.

Although he composed a number of operas and incidental music scores, his only enduring success was *Hansel und Gretel.* Ironically, he wrote the music with great reluctance at first, after being badgered by his sister to help with a children's play she had written based on the Grimm fairy tale. The score came to the attention of Richard Strauss, who immediately recognized it as a masterpiece and arranged for its production at Weimar in 1893. Since then it has become the closest thing there is to a perennial Christmas opera, especially, of course, in German-speaking countries.

Hansel und Gretel

The musical style of this enchanting children's classic is greatly under the influence of Wagner, and is surprisingly dense and heavy considering the subject matter. Nevertheless, the absence of any patronizing of its young listeners seems only to endear it to them the more. Children are, as their elders never remember, far more perceptive than they are normally credited to be.

A great classic of the catalog is Herbert von Karajan's 1953 mono recording, with two sublime singers, Elisabeth Schwarzkopf and Elisabeth Grümmer, as the children, and a reading that makes this modest work sound as glorious as *Die Meistersinger.* Despite the mono sound, this is treasurable at mid-price. If you must have digital, Jeffrey Tate comes closest to the Karajan ideal, with fine vocal contributions from Barbara Bonney and Anne Sofie von Otter.

Karajan, Philharmonia Orchestra. Angel 69293 (2) (mono)
Tate, Bavarian Radio Symphony Orchestra. Angel 54022 (2) [DDD]

Vincent d'Indy (1851-1931)

Vincent d'Indy was an aristocrat from the cradle to the grave. Able to trace his ancestry to King Henri IV, and entitled to be addressed as Vicomte d'Indy, he took his caste seriously, both personally and professionally. Fame and fortune were to be his, but were never his motivations. "An artist," he said in his speech inaugurating the Schola Cantorum, "knows that his mission is to serve." Very noble, but one might wonder how someone who went on to insist that the artist "must be touched by sublime charity" could at the same time be the most blatant anti-Semite of the composers, not excluding Wagner.

In fact, d'Indy was one of the most complex and contradictory men in music history. Extremes of behavior ran in his family. His mother died in childbirth, and he was reared for twenty-one years by a musical grandmother who alternated draconian music instruction with spontaneous bursts of doting affection. Young Vincent's childhood dream was not music, however, but the military; he was thrilled to lead a bayonet charge during the Franco-Prussian War in 1870, and to the end of his long life drove friends to despair by repeatedly restaging the Battle of Waterloo.

He also studied initially for the law, but gave it up and decided to concentrate on music, the love of which had been simmering inside him since he heard some Beethoven piano sonatas at the age of eight. He enrolled in the Paris Conservatory, but rebelled against its starchy atmosphere, and undertook private study with César Franck.

He became Franck's bulldog, championing his teacher's theories and music against all detractors throughout his career. He also became the most passionate French advocate of Wagnerism. Fed up by the Conservatory, he helped found a rival insitution, the Schola Cantorum, in 1894. He taught there until his death, though in 1912 he was reconciled with the Conservatory after some reforms were made, and he taught some classes there also.

Piously, devoutly Catholic, he scorned not only Jews, but democracy. Though a brilliant scholar, he was curiously indiscriminate about artistic talent; he professed to see no difference in quality between Beethoven and Meyerbeer, and thought neither Debussy nor Ravel had any future.

Yet he was scrupulously honest in his dealings, and unfailingly courteous, even to those he despised. Though widely disliked, he was just as universally respected. Despite his regimentation and dogmatism, he insisted that his students be exposed to all ideas and styles, no matter how much he might personally detest them.

In his day his music was generally regarded as cerebral and cacophonous. Although he espoused the Franckian system of cyclical form, he struck out in his own directions and cannot be said to have imitated anyone else; his style might be characterized as a hybrid of neo-Classicism and late Romanticism, with some intimations of Impressionism! His influence, however, was not through his works, but through his surprisingly open-minded molding of pupils as distinguished (and as different from their teacher) as Erik Satie, Arthur Honegger, Georges Auric, and Albert Roussel—and even, briefly, Cole Porter!

Symphony on a French Mountain Air, Op. 25

The one composition which has kept d'Indy's name unfailingly before the concertgoing public is truly a beautiful work; not really a symphony, but a piano concerto, it rings wonderful changes on a tune in the style of an Alpine shepherd song. It will make you shake your head to think that someone who could write so benevolently could be hateful, but geniuses are capable of anything, including paradox and evil.

The leading recordings are both coupled with the Franck Symphony, previously recommended.

Monteux, Chicago Symphony Orchestra. RCA Gold Seal 6805 [ADD] + Franck: Symphony in D Minor; Berlioz: Overture to *Béatrice et Bénédict* (mid-price)

Dutoit, Montreal Symphony Orchestra. London 430278 [DDD] + Franck: Symphony in D Minor

Ruggero Leoncavallo (1857-1919)

Leoncavallo had his fifteen minutes of fame, but it was set in the midst of many instances of poverty, disappointment, and defeat. His one surviving work, *Pagliacci* ("Clowns"), contains what is probably the most famous tenor aria ever written, *Vesti la giubba*. Ironically, its sentiments mirrored Leoncavallo's life: "On with the show! Put on your costume; the people pay, they want to laugh. So laugh, clown, and they will applaud; laugh at the sorrow that tears your heart." Perhaps it was personal experience that enabled the composer to make this one moment so searing and convincing.

Born in Naples, the son of a judge, he studied at the Bologna Conservatory. He entrusted his first opera and all his money to an alleged impresario who ran off with the funds, leaving the twenty-year-old destitute. He took to the streets, singing and playing the piano for pennies. Eventually he found a decent job as a pianist in Egypt, but a revolt against the British made life dangerous for foreigners and he had to disguise himself as an Arab to escape the country, riding a horse to Port Said for twenty-four solid hours.

His last money having been spent on ship fare, he found himself penniless again, but got by playing the piano in Parisian cabarets and writing popular songs. Desperate to claim the attention he felt his talent deserved, he remembered an incident of his youth when an actor, playing opposite his unfaithful wife in a drama, actually killed her on stage. He decided to write a one-act opera in the manner of Mascagni, whose mini-tragedy *Cavalleria Rusticana* had recently been a smash success.

Persistence won the day: Leoncavallo got the publisher Sonzogno to endorse him, and

Pagliacci had its premiere in 1892 under the baton of an up-and-coming conductor named Arturo Toscanini. Almost no one in that first audience had any idea who Leoncavallo was, but they shook the rafters at the end of the opera. The scene was described by all who were there as pandemonium.

Leoncavallo was headline material the next day, and became the toast of the opera world. Alas, with one partial exception, he never had another hit. Failure followed upon failure, and in the end he was more bitter than before, having lost all that he struggled so hard to win.

Leoncavallo's name is inextricably associated with that of Mascagni, since their two famous operas are almost always performed as a pair. But though they are the two icons of the so-called Verismo (realism) school of opera, they were far from identical. Leoncavallo was the better-trained artist, and he was subtler; all of his work is more refined and poetic than Mascagni's, and some who know his other works have claimed him as a better crafts-man even than Puccini. In fact, Leoncavallo wrote his own *La Bohème*, an opera based on the same book as Puccini's, but it came out a year later and was lost in the shuffle.

Pagliacci

In *Pagliacci*, one is gripped from the moment that the character Tonio appears before the curtain and sings the insinuating Prologue, warning the audience of the emotions to come, to the final wrenching shock, as Canio, the clown, having stabbed his wife in front of an initially uncomprehending audience, lets the bloody knife fall to the floor while quietly intoning one of the most famous lines in opera: "La commedia è finita." It could be the inscription on Leoncavallo's tomb.

Two recordings of yore—one more yore than the other—lead the field here, both recorded at the La Scala Opera House, Milan, where they know what they are doing with music like this. Carlo Bergonzi is the tenor with Herbert von Karajan (in the standard *Cav/Pag* coupling, plus more); Giuseppe di Stefano with Tullio Serafin (the latter throwing in Maria Callas and Tito Gobbi to keep the dramatic tension up there, on a single disc with no coupling, and still at full price).

Karajan, La Scala Orchestra and Chorus. DG 419257 (3) [ADD] + Mascagni: *Cavalleria Rusticana;* opera intermezzi (mid-price)
Serafin, La Scala Orchestra and Chorus. Angel 47981 (mono)

Gustav Mahler (1860-1911)

When asked as a child what he wanted to be when he grew up, Mahler replied, "A martyr." He became possibly the most driven of all the great composers. In his nine completed symphonies, an unfinished tenth, and the symphony-disguised-as-a-song-cycle, *Das Lied von der Erde,* he deliberately sought to stretch the definition of a symphony to the breaking point. Cast in unusual structures, Mahler's symphonies are vast in scope (No. 3 is the longest symphony in the repertory), employ sometimes gargantuan instrumental forces, often include vocal solos and choral parts, and flirt with various high-flown programmatic and philosophical concepts. The symphony, to Mahler, was "a world," a vehicle through which he sought to give voice to the "complete man."

His lifelong preoccupation with the themes of suffering and death, and the riddle of how to transcend them, seemed to take root early. His parents had an unhappy marriage, and many of his siblings died in childhood. Once when his father was brutalizing his mother, young Gustav fled the house, only to be enchanted by hearing a hurdy-gurdy playing "O, du lieber Augustin." Ever after he was fascinated by the fact that childlike innocence and inhuman cruelty can coexist so intimately; it was a subject he explored as the first composer to be treated by Sigmund Freud.

Mahler's musical training was enriched by studies in philosophy and the new discipline of psychology. Over time he became an ever-more impassioned and idealistic person, tormented by his embattled relations with musicians and orchestras. His career centered on conducting, not composing, his ascent was rapid, and he was eventually acknowledged as one of the greatest conductors in the world.

During his ten years as director of the Vienna Court Opera he appeared to perform miracles; the works he conducted seemed, his admirers said, "Herrlich wie am ersten Tag" ("Glorious as on the first day"). Nevertheless, he was vilified in the press, a victim of intrigues and anti-Semitism, hated by his enemies because of his unbending belief in himself, his arrogance with orchestra players, his perfectionism, and his sarcastic tongue.

In 1906 he suffered the death of a daughter, then shortly after was diagnosed with a terminal heart condition. Unable to take any more of Vienna, he came to New York City as conductor of both (!) the Metropolitan Opera and the New York Philharmonic Orchestra. Pressured to go easy on the musicians, lighten his programs, and hobnob with wealthy socialites, he found no peace. Under the strain of disappointment and an unrelenting concert schedule, he collapsed. Returned to Europe, he died in a nursing home, waving his finger like a baton and murmuring the name of his God: "Mozart."

Except for the premiere of his Eighth Symphony, Mahler had few successes in his lifetime as a composer. His huge symphonies, with their heaven-storming passages juxtaposed against music of childlike innocence, seemed grotesque to most listeners, a hodgepodge of bombast and naiveté. Hysteria and bathos are charged against him even today; but especially since being championed so convincingly by Leonard Bernstein in the 1960s, Mahler's music has become a major force in the concert halls of the world. Almost overnight the attitude towards his works among critics and audiences alike changed from ridicule to awe, and today most see (and hear) him as one of the most significant figures in the transition from Romanticism to Modernity, and the first great composer to voice both the anguish and hope of the twentieth century.

Das Lied von der Erde

"The Song of the Earth" was completed in 1909, the first major work since the doctor had given Mahler his death warrant. It is a symphony in all but name, with the addition of two solo vocal parts which are settings of Chinese poems about youth, beauty, loneliness, and leavetaking. The awareness of approaching death is contrasted with a poignant love of nature and life.

Carlo Maria Giulini is a first choice in digital, but Otto Klemperer's radiant 1960s recording with greater singers still sounds fresh. The legendary Bruno Walter recording from 1952 does not seem to be around at the moment, but keep an eye out—Walter led the world premiere, and his singers are even greater than Klemperer's. (I'll bet if they had had singers in the Jurassic period we would have the definitive versions of everything.)

Giulini, Berlin Philharmonic Orchestra. DG 413459 [DDD]
Klemperer, Philharmonia Orchestra and Chorus. EMI 47231

Symphony No. 1 in D

Mahler's first symphony began life as a giant symphonic poem, which he revised to fulfill a commission from the Budapest Philharmonic. As with many of his earlier works, he first provided a program, then later withdrew it as something that would only mislead listeners. It is still one of his more popular works, youthful and poetic, almost Schubertian in places, and highly personal. Much of its thematic material is borrowed from his earlier song cycle, *Lieder eines fahrenden Gesellen* ("Songs of a Wayfaring Lad"). The composer was twenty-nine when he conducted its premiere in 1889.

Leonard Bernstein's final recording before his death was a live performance of Mahler's First Symphony, and it is one of the best of his many recordings of the composer whom he, more than anyone, brought to the attention of modern audiences. Bruno Walter, Bernstein's mentor, was Mahler's friend, and conducted some of his premieres; his irreplaceable stereo recording has been reissued at mid-price. And even with such competition, Rafael Kubelik must be recommended at mid-price in a poetic reading very generously and aptly coupled with the "Wayfarer" Songs done by the King of Lieder, Dietrich Fischer-Dieskau.

Bernstein, Concertgebouw Orchestra. DG 427303 [DDD]
B. Walter, Columbia Symphony Orchestra. Sony 37235 [ADD] (mid-price)
Kubelik, Bavarian Radio Symphony Orchestra. DG Resonance 429157 [ADD] + *Lieder eines fahrenden Gesellen* (mid-price)

Symphony No. 2 in C Minor, "Resurrection"

Several years passed after the first symphony before Mahler completed his second, a work on an altogether larger scale. There are five movements, with vocal parts in the last two. The theme of the work is the impermanence of life and how faith can intervene to help mankind transcend sorrow. The final movement unites soprano, alto, and chorus in Klopstock's *Resurrection Ode* ("Rise again, my dust, after a short rest"), followed by Mahler's own words on faith in a future life. The symphony was first performed in 1895 with Richard Strauss conducting.

Simon Rattle's digital recording has won many awards and has two great soloists, Arlene Auger and Dame Janet Baker; Leonard Bernstein is represented by his great, if perhaps overheated, 1987 live performance.

Rattle, City of Birmingham Symphony Orchestra. Angel 47962 (2) [DDD]
Bernstein, New York Philharmonic Orchestra. DG 423395 (2) [DDD]

Symphony No. 4 in G

Mahler's most cheerful, and with the first, shortest symphony is the most popular of them all, a fact which is perhaps as well he does not know. It is laid out parallel with the four verses of the song "The Heavenly Life" from *Das Knaben Wunderhorn*, which Mahler set separately as a song cycle. The four-movement structure and the use of folk-like idioms make this symphony almost Haydnesque; at least in comparison to the others.

Lorin Maazel's glowing 1984 performance with soprano Kathleen Battle in the vocal parts has been the preferred recording of most critics since it was issued. George Szell provides an incomparable budget alternative from the 1960s, one of the great Mahler recordings, with soprano Judith Raskin, plus a fine performance of the "Wayfaring Lad" songs with Frederica von Stade and Andrew Davis conducting; there aren't many bargains this good. Sir Georg Solti's digital recording with soprano Kiri Te Kanawa would be a first choice were it not for the Maazel disc; you certainly will not go wrong to buy it if the others are not available.

Maazel, Vienna Philharmonic Orchestra. CBS 44908 [DDD]
Szell, Cleveland Orchestra. Sony Essential Classics 46535 [ADD] + *Lieder eines fahrenden Gesellen* (cond. A. Davis) (budget)
Solti, Chicago Symphony Orchestra. London 410188 [DDD]

Symphony No. 8 in E-flat, "Symphony of a Thousand"

The nickname comes from the number of performers. Mahler himself led the premiere just eight months before his death, though he had written the symphony four years earlier. The performance (1910) was a triumph, the one thousand performers joining the three thousand people in the audience in a thirty-minute ovation at the end.

The score calls for a children's choir, a large male choir, two large female choirs, a pipe organ, two pianos, a huge orchestra augmented by bells, an extra brass choir, and for good measure, a mandolin! Despite its length, the symphony is divided into just two parts, the first a setting of the medieval hymn *Veni, creator Spiritus* ("Come, creating Spirit"), the second the closing scene from Goethe's *Faust*. It is not the longest symphony (that was Mahler's Third), but it is the largest.

Two recordings are here at each other's throats, vying for first place. The Eighth is Sir Georg Solti's favorite Mahler symphony, and he is a great Mahler conductor; the soloists on his analog recording are all superstars, and the great orchestra quite outplays itself. One would think this could not be outdone, yet Klaus Tennstedt's digital recording has even better sound and there are those who think the reading is at least as good; the disc won first place in 1987's Gramophone competition. If you love this work you probably need to get both versions for comparing fine points; otherwise, considering the sonic needs of the work, perhaps the digital recording should come first.

Tennstedt, London Philharmonic Orchestra and Chorus. Angel 47625 [DDD]

Solti, Chicago Symphony Orchestra and Chorus. London 414493 [ADD]

Symphony No. 9 in D

Mahler's last completed symphony is his most despairing. It has the conventional four movements, but they are long, and the last is an adagio, as in Tchaikovsky's *Pathétique*. It is the composer's tormented valedictory to life; frequently quoted throughout the work is a little theme from Beethoven's *Les Adieux* ("Farewell") piano sonata.

Herbert von Karajan and Leonard Bernstein are the top contenders in digital this time around; their approaches are different—Karajan transcendent, Bernstein terrifying, as you will—though I believe Karajan has the critical edge. Bruno Walter is irreplaceable at mid-price in the first recording ever made (1938) of this symphony, and a powerful one (Mahler himself bequeathed the score to Walter in 1910). Despite the old mono sound, it is quite listenable and lives up to its billing as one of the Great Recordings of the Century. And, it fits on one disc.

Karajan, Berlin Philharmonic Orchestra. DG 410726 (2) [DDD]

Bernstein, Vienna Philharmonic Orchestra. DG 419208 (2) [DDD]

B. Walter, Vienna Philharmonic Orchestra. EMI 63029 [ADD] (mono) (mid-price)

Pietro Mascagni (1863-1945)

Mascagni led a life similar in many ways to Ruggero Leoncavallo, with whom his name will be ever entwined. He grew up in poverty and obscurity, had one huge success in opera, continued to compose but subsequently met mostly with failure, and spent his last days in bitterness and regret.

Showing musical talent as a youth, he was sent to the Milan Conservatory by a wealthy nobleman on whom his early compositions had made an impression. But Mascagni hated the school and dropped out to become conductor of a small traveling opera troupe. For several years he lived hand to mouth, teaching piano and tossing manuscripts of one-act operas in a drawer.

In 1889 the Sonzogno publishing house announced a competition for a one-act opera. Mascagni thought he had no chance, but his wife fished out the score of *Cavalleria Rusticana* and secretly dropped it in the mail. It won the first prize, and the promise of a performance in Rome in 1890.

The premiere was one of the great sensations in opera history. Mascagni had to take forty curtain calls. The cheering audience followed him out of the theater and set up camp in front of his apartment building. With the door blocked, the composer had to be pulled through a window to get inside. Parades were held in his honor, and he was invested with the royal Order of the Crown. *Cavalleria Rusticana* was staged with unprecedented rapidity in opera houses around the world.

Like Leoncavallo, Mascagni had high hopes of many more years of triumph, but out of fourteen more operas he had only sporadic, and relatively mild, successes. His last pitiful try for the spotlight was as virtual court composer for Mussolini. He wrote songs glorifying Fascism and enjoyed Il Duce's fulsome praise and patronage.

But after the Nazis were thrown out and Mussolini was hanged upside down, Mascagni's property was confiscated and his reputation ruined. Despised, he spent his last months in a cheap hotel, vainly trying to disavow his Fascist sympathies. Looking back on the glory days of his big hit with *Cavalleria,* the composer lamented: "I was crowned before I was king!"

Cavalleria Rusticana

Despite Mascagni's personal humiliation, his beloved opera never lost its hold on the public, and it is still a standard of the repertoire. The first opera of a movement that came to be called "Verismo" ("realism"), *Cavalleria Rusticana* moves swiftly with gut-wrenching vividness through its brief length to tell a tale of Sicilian passion, jealousy, and death. The most famous single passage is not an aria but the orchestral Intermezzo, which wordlessly sums up the poignant emotion of the story.

The famous Herbert von Karajan recording, starring Carlo Bergonzi and Fiorenza Cossotto, is already recommended above under the Leoncavallo entry. For a version without the *Pagliacci* coupling, the only one to have stars Jussi Björling, Zinka Milanov, and Robert Merrill, with Renato Cellini conducting, is at mid-price. This is superhuman singing.

Karajan, La Scala Orchestra and Chorus. DG 419257 (3) [ADD] + Leoncavallo: *Pagliacci*

Cellini, RCA Victor Orchestra, Robert Shaw Chorale. RCA Gold Seal 6510 [ADD] (mid-price)

Giacomo Puccini (1858-1924)

Puccini came from a long line of church musicians from Lucca, Italy. The first we know of, also named Giacomo, was born in 1712. Puccini's grandfather, Domenico, was a contemporary of Beethoven and composed a piano concerto which has been recorded. But church and pianos were not for the last and greatest of the line: "I was born many years ago," he wrote near the end of his life, "and the Almighty touched me with his little finger and said 'Write for the theater—mind, only for the theater!' And I have obeyed the supreme command."

He tried at first to follow the family tradition, but his irresponsible and impish nature fought against it. When playing organ improvisations in church he would interpolate opera arias, scandalizing the priests. As a teenager he walked thirteen miles to see the new opera by Verdi, *Aida,* and that was it. He stopped his foolishness and became a serious student at the Milan Conservatory.

For almost ten years after graduation he lived in dire poverty, living on beans, raw onions, and the pity of friends. In those days he was a close friend of Mascagni, from whom he absorbed the spirit of the Verismo movement, and whose success in 1890 with *Cavalleria Rusticana* inspired him. Then the triumph of *Manon Lescaut* in 1893 launched Puccini's meteoric career.

From then on he had almost uninterrupted success, bringing one hit after another to the world's stages. Somehow he found the key to continually touching listeners' hearts, which his friends Mascagni and Leoncavallo had been unable to do. Audiences proclaimed him the successor to Verdi. Some critics, however, carped at what they considered sentimentality, vulgarity, and bad taste. His music was described as unoriginal and shallow.

Puccini's defenders chalk a lot of that up to elitism: he may have targeted his audience, playing up to their love of passionate emotions and caressing melodies, but he was only doing his job, and doing it superlatively well. Indeed, despite much critical hesitation about Puccini over the years, his reputation as a good musician, skilled orchestrator, inspired melodist, and deft psychologist has been slowly but constantly rising.

He had an infallible instinct for the stage, despite raging inner doubts as to his worth and place in history. "Next to Wagner," he once said, "we are all mandolin players." His insecurity was mitigated by spending money. He took up the pose so often seen in his photographs: a dapper rake, elegantly suited, cigarette dangling from one hand, mustache trimmed, bowler hat atilt. He loved fine food and wine, fast women and cars.

Despite his profligacy and philandering, he lost neither his wife nor his public. When he succumbed to a heart attack following cancer surgery, a performance of *La Bohème* wa underway in Rome. The news arrived at the opera house, and the conductor stopped the orchestra. After a moment he lifted his baton again, and the musicians began playing the Funeral March of Chopin. The audience silently stood, weeping, and then quietly filed from the hall. Audiences ever since have been shedding tears for Puccini and for his heroines, and for the intensely poignant music he gave them.

La Bohème

A story about young bohemians in love with love, *La Bohème* is one of the handful of most popular operas ever written. Already long since a hit with classical music fans, it reached an even wider audience when a scene was featured in the film *Moonstruck*. This opera is the prototype of the so-called "soap" operas.

If there was ever a mono recording where you won't notice, Sir Thomas Beecham's incandescent 1956 reading of *La Bohème* is it, with luxurious singing from Victoria de los Angeles, Jussi Björling, and Robert Merrill. If you must have newer sound, I can only bring you up to 1972 with Mirella Freni and Luciano Pavarotti under Herbert von Karajan. After that, you're on your own.

Beecham, RCA Victor Symphony Orchestra and Chorus. EMI 47235 (2) (mono)
Karajan, Berlin Philharmonic Orchestra. London 421049 (2) [ADD] (mid-price)

Madama Butterfly

A fiasco at its premiere, *Madama Butterfly* was one of the few Puccini operas to flop. The composer made a few revisions, and within three months it was a hit like all his others. Puccini actually studied Japanese music to lend a tinge of authenticity to the score. The story concerns a typical Puccini heroine, a woman who kills herself rather than suffer shame at the hands of a faithless lover. This solution to infidelity seemed to please Puccini greatly, for he used it repeatedly.

Freni and Pavarotti teamed again, as in *La Bohème* above, are a standard choice in their primes under Karajan, and very reasonable. The fine 1958 Bergonzi/Tebaldi recording being missing from the catalog today, I can recommend the atmospheric Bergonzi/Scotto reissue with Sir John Barbirolli conducting at mid-price. There is a wonderful "sleeper" on an import label that not every store will have, starring the marvellous Hungarian soprano Veronica Kincses, who may be the creamiest and most convincing Butterfly ever, with Giuseppe Patané conducting superbly.

Karajan, Vienna Philharmonic Orchestra and Chorus. London 417577
(3) [ADD] (mid-price)
Barbirolli, Santa Cecilia Academy Orchestra and Chorus. Angel Studio
63411 (2) [ADD] (mid-price)
Patané, Hungarian State Opera Orchestra and Chorus. Hungaroton
12256/7 (2) [ADD]

Tosca

A woman flings herself from a tower in despair after her lover has been treacherously
executed by a brutal police chief whom she has stabbed to death after he tried to violate
her. A "shoddy little shocker" of a story, Joseph Kerman called it. It is the most "Verismo"
(verismatic?) of Puccini's operas, and second in popularity only to *La Bohème*. Although
musically inferior to several of his other works, it makes a strong impression in performance, thus demonstrating the composer's unerring sense of what works in the theater.

There is but one way to begin with this opera, especially if you don't want to take a
chance over being convinced. That is to buy and treasure one of Maria Callas's greatest
recorded moments in the title role—one which might have been written for her—perfectly
partnered by an ardent Giuseppe di Stefano and the evilest Scarpia that ever there was in
Tito Gobbi, the greatest actor among opera baritones. Oh, and the conducting of Victor
De Sabata is perfect, too. This has often been proclaimed "the perfect opera recording."
You won't believe it, especially since it's mono (sorry, there *was* great music before digital
recording).

De Sabata, La Scala Orchestra and Chorus. EMI 47174 (2) (mono)

Turandot

Considered by many Puccini's masterpiece, *Turandot* shows an advanced sophistication
in handling the orchestra. Its rather peculiar story set in a mythical China is framed by
music of great power, alternating with unusual poetry and delicacy—that is, as far as it
goes, for Puccini died before finishing it. The rather perfunctory conclusion we see today
was tacked on by another hand.

Zubin Mehta conducts the best all-around performance with Joan Sutherland,
Luciano Pavarotti, Montserrat Caballé and Nikolai Ghiaurov, and the early 1970s sound
still sounds marvelous. It pains me to leave out the 1960 Bjorling/Nilsson/Tebaldi recording, but perhaps I will reconsider if the price is lowered.

Mehta, London Philharmonic Orchestra, John Alldis Choir. London
414274 (2) [ADD]

Richard Strauss (1864-1949)

Richard Strauss once said he could describe a fork in music. That one quip, lightly tossed off, manages to sum up the whole esthetic and attitude of a composer who was both programmatic and pragmatic. "I am unable," he said, "to write without a program to guide me."

He knew better than anyone else how to imitate life and nature in music, but also how to stretch a dollar. Jokes were told about his tight-fisted ways. His son: "Papa, how much did you get for the rehearsal tonight?" Strauss, teary: "Now I know you are my boy!" Gustav Mahler's wife Alma once sat next to him at one of those rehearsals, and noted in her diary: "Strauss thought of nothing but money. The entire time he held a pencil and calculated the profits to the last pfennig."

He went through life sure of his talent and unperturbed by criticism. He wrote a giant tone poem, *Ein Heldenleben* ("A Hero's Life"), which he frankly admitted was about his own career. A few years later he composed the *Symphonia Domestica*, which is meant to portray himself, his wife, and infant son at home, giving baby a bath, making love, having a spat, and so on. When his self-absorption was challenged he replied that "I don't see why I shouldn't write a symphony about myself; I find myself quite as interesting as Napoleon or Alexander the Great."

Egomaniac he may have been, but his pragmatism let him stand curiously outside himself and reflect unsparingly on his own failings. At the end of his career he assessed himself more shrewdly than any critic: "I may not be a first-rate composer, but I am a first-rate second-rate composer." He did not argue with his musical nemesis, Claude Debussy, who admitted after hearing *Ein Heldenleben* that Strauss was "very nearly a genius." Strauss asked no more of life than that: just pay him his fee!

Richard Strauss (totally unrelated, by the way, to Johann Strauss and his brood) was the son of a famous French horn player, Franz Strauss, from whom he seems to have derived his utter self-assurance. Rehearsing a work with Wagner, the elder Strauss obstinately refused to change the way he played a passage. Flying into a rage, Wagner stormed off stage, leaving the orchestra in an embarrassed silence. Finally Franz Strauss rose, looked around serenely, and said "I have put him to flight!"

Young Richard studied music, especially conducting, under Hans von Bülow, and picked up influences from Berlioz and Brahms, but most of all Liszt and Wagner. He developed into one of the great conductors of the early twentieth century, and had his first compositional success in his early twenties with the tone poem *Don Juan*. A succession of further orchestral works, constructed like Liszt and orchestrated like Wagner, won him headline coverage as the natural heir to their legacies.

The Wagnerites, in particular, were thrilled to see the Master's theories vindicated in the brilliantly colorful works of this disciple. Some, in fact, dared to suggest Strauss was even greater, for he wrote orchestral works as well as operas. Just as with Wagner, a kind of cult grew up around Strauss in his lifetime. His flamboyant music, contrasted with his bourgeois persona, his sudden fame and enormous financial success, and the sometimes shocking subject matter of his music, such as the "decadent" opera *Salome,* made titillating newspaper copy, and he was regularly billed as the world's greatest composer.

He seems to have been utterly apolitical and amoral. He stayed in Germany during World War II and accepted the post of Reichsmusikkammer. He didn't seem to see anything much wrong with the Nazis, but he also defended his Jewish friends, much to the dismay of Hitler and Goebbels. He just didn't seem to get the point. His mind was elsewhere, reliving the past, contemplating more important issues, such as whether words or music should dominate in an opera. When the war was over he seemed bewildered by the defeat and destruction, and wrote another tone poem, *Metamorphosen,* to express his sorrow at all the damaged buildings.

As he grew old, his works became bigger and more densely orchestrated, but he had nothing new to say. In fact, he drew back from the forward-looking harmonies of *Salome* and *Elektra* to write music more acceptable to the masses, such as *Der Rosenkavalier,* with its neo-Johann Straussian waltzes.

Yet his style remains strikingly distinct and personal. No one can hear more than a few bars of his music and not know Strauss wrote it. With all their ostentation and pretension, their sometimes obscure symbolism, and a tendency towards excess in everything, Strauss's works continue to fascinate and entertain, if more by ingenuity and calculation than anything from the heart. Strauss was, after all, a truly great second-rate composer.

Also sprach Zarathustra, Op. 30

Intrigued and inspired by the "superman" theories of Nietzsche, this was one of Strauss's less famous tone poems until the opening measures created a sensation in the 1968 film *2001—A Space Odyssey* (which Arthur Schlesinger, Jr. characterized as "morally pretentious, intellectually obscure, and inordinately long," just the things that detractors say about much of Strauss). Many people still listen only to those few bars and then turn the player off. Too bad Stanley Kubrick didn't use the whole piece.

Herbert von Karajan was a master of this score, and his digital version coupled with *Don Juan* is a likely first choice; but nipping at its heels is the resplendent André Previn recording which offers *Don Juan* and *Death and Transfiguration* for the same price. The greatest performance of all, however, could be the 1954 (stereo!) classic led by Fritz Reiner (and at mid-price); with a bonus of the *Der Rosenkavalier* Waltzes and the incidental music to *Le Bourgeois gentilhomme,* it's worth the chance of suffering whiplash.

Karajan, Berlin Philharmonic Orchestra. DG 410959 [DDD] + *Don Juan*
Previn, Vienna Philharmonic Orchestra. Telarc 80167 [DDD] + *Don Juan,*
Death and Transfiguration
Reiner, Chicago Symphony Orchestra. RCA Gold Seal 60930 [ADD] +
Rosenkavalier Waltzes (arr. Reiner), *Le Bourgeois gentilhomme* (mid-price)

Death and Transfiguration (Tod und Verklärung), Op. 24

Strauss thought up his own scenario for this one: a dying artist lets his past play before his mind's eye, then senses an approaching redemptive joy. On his deathbed Strauss whispered to his daughter-in-law, "Alice, it's funny, but dying is just as I imagined it in *Tod und Verklärung!*"

Herbert Blomstedt has produced a wonderful digital version for Denon, with generous couplings, that can stand up even against the famous Karajan recordings (one of which is out of print, and the other has one less coupling). André Previn has already been recommended in the previous discussion. George Szell provides a very attractive mid-price recording, in performances of much grandeur.

Blomstedt, Dresden State Orchestra. Denon 73801 [DDD] + *Till Eulenspiegel, Metamorphosen*
Previn, Vienna Philharmonic Orchestra. Telarc 80167 [DDD] + *Also sprach Zarathustra, Don Juan*
Szell, Cleveland Orchestra. CBS 36721 + *Don Juan, Till Eulenspiegel* (mid-price)

Don Juan, Op. 20

Strauss's seminal success (no pun intended) was inspired by a poem on the legendary lover by Nikolaus Lenau, in which Don Juan is the type of a superhero brimming with the life force (an image dear to Nietzsche and other German philosophers of the time), who is undone only by excess. Strauss seemed not to heed the message.

Recordings already recommended above will satisfy all requirements for this work.

Karajan, Berlin Philharmonic Orchestra. DG 410959 [DDD] + *Also sprach Zarathustra*
Previn, Vienna Philharmonic Orchestra. Telarc 80167 [DDD] + *Also sprach Zarathustra, Death and Transfiguration*
Szell, Cleveland Orchestra. CBS 36721 + *Death and Transfiguration, Till Eulenspiegel* (mid-price)

Don Quixote, Op. 35

One of Strauss's most graphically illustrated tone poems, *Don Quixote* is nevertheless cast in the form of a mammoth set of variations on a cello theme. This tune represents the delightfully mad hero, who for Strauss symbolizes all who go through life chasing an illusion. By purely musical means, Strauss suggests the bleating of sheep, the battle with the windmills, and many other elements of the Cervantes story. It is one of the composer's most stunning bag of tricks, but one of his best-written and subtlest scores as well.

No digital recording can be said to have taken its place among the great versions, and the Karajan recording with Pierre Fournier has left the catalog for now. That still leaves two good choices from Leonard Bernstein or Fritz Reiner and their respective cellists, and both at mid-price. The Bernstein coupling is perhaps more basic to a starting collection.

Munroe, Bernstein, New York Philharmonic Orchestra. Sony 47625 [ADD] + *Dance of the Seven Veils* from *Salome*, Festival Prelude (mid-price)
Janigro, Reiner, Chicago Symphony Orchestra. RCA Gold Seal 61796 [ADD] + *Burleske* (with pianist Byron Janis) (mid-price)

Ein Heldenleben, Op. 40

Much as Wagner mocked his adversaries in *Die Meistersinger*, Strauss pilloried his in this depiction of himself standing up to his querulous and insipid critics, affirming life, love, and vigor, and at the end achieving illumination mixed with domestic bliss.

The concept may make one wince, but as music it is one of his most vital and well-structured compositions.

The standout performances are Herbert Blomstedt in digital, Fritz Reiner in analog.

Blomstedt, Dresden State Orchestra. Denon 7561 [DDD]
Reiner, Chicago Symphony Orchesta. RCA 5408 [ADD]

Der Rosenkavalier: Waltz Suite

"The Cavalier of the Rose," with text by Strauss's frequent collaborator Hugo von Hofmannsthal, is his best-loved opera, a deliberate throwback to the glittering days of the Waltzing Strausses, and an antidote to his harsh and shocking operas *Salome* and *Elektra*. For the composer, ever eager to show off, it was his way of demonstrating that he could successfully capture every mood and genre. The many waltz tunes strewn through the long score have been gathered into concert hall suites by various arrangers and by Strauss himself.

Fritz Reiner conducts his own arrangement in a great recording already recommended above under *Also sprach Zarathustra*.

Reiner, Chicago Symphony Orchestra. RCA Gold Seal 60930 [ADD] + *Also sprach Zarathustra, Le Bourgeois gentilhomme* (mid-price)

Salome: Dance of the Seven Veils

In the opera, Salome executes a sensual dance to win King Herod's acquiescence to her demand for the head of John the Baptist. This is one role generally off-limits to the more corpulent sopranos. The dance is a striking bit of pseudo-orientalia, though one may note that underlying the feverish hothouse sensuality is a...Viennese waltz!

Leonard Bernstein fills the bill here with a recording already recommended.

Bernstein, New York Philharmonic Orchestra. Sony 47625 [ADD] + *Don Quixote,* Festival Prelude (mid-price)

Till Eulenspiegel's Merry Pranks, Op. 28

For many people, even Strauss detractors, this is his most acceptable orchestral work. Late in his life, one of his quasi-acolytes asked him if he realized that in this work he had approached the metaphysical limits of humor. "Nothing of the kind," Strauss snorted, "I just wanted the people in the hall to have a good laugh for once." Even Strauss was tiring of the fakery and pseudo-intellectual gobbledy-gook with which his admirers tried to deify him.
Till Owl-Glass was a real person, a medieval rake who had a reputation for thumbing his nose at authority. In later legend he was credited with ever more outlandish feats of impudence, which are portrayed in Strauss's tone poem. At the end he is hanged for his rascality, but his ghost returns to give the judge the raspberries.

The Blomstedt and Szell recordings previously recommended take care of both digital and analog areas.

Blomstedt, Dresden State Orchestra. Denon 73801 [DDD] + *Death and Transfiguration, Metamorphosen*
Szell, Cleveland Orchestra. CBS 36721 + *Death and Transfiguration, Don Juan* (mid-price)

The Moderns
(ca. 1915-Present)

The term "modern" is self-defeating, since everything is modern to those who are contemporaneous with it. Once a definable period is past, it of course becomes the Ancient time, the Medieval time, and so on. If the Modern period in music is defined as the twentieth century, then it is about to conclude and be renamed. But as what? Not the "Atonal Period," or "Twelve-Tone Period," or "Neo-Classical Period," or any name derived from any of the many other -isms and -ologies that have made up the era, for no one of them has dominated.

Leonard Bernstein dubbed it the "Age of Anxiety," and perhaps that will do as well as any other. Although it is clear to every listener that music of the twentieth century differs from all that went before, at least in degree, it is difficult to find one thread that unites its disparate styles into a coherent pattern.

If there is one technical element that stands out, it is dissonance. There simply has been greater latitude for composers to use dissonance as an expressive tool ever since the loosening of tonal relations in Wagner's music, but of course that would apply to the Late Romantics as well. To get beyond them we must take into account the totality of several other changes, subtle and overt: a de-emphasis of melody, an increase in the angularity of rhythms, greater freedom of form.

Yet none of these quite enables us to add up to that thing we call the Modern style in classical music. The missing element in the equation is *angst,* that uniquely twentieth century pervasive feeling that somehow things are not quite right, that doom is possibly right around the corner. Angst is a twentieth-century term born of two World Wars, economic depressions, the discovery of the id, the invention of the Bomb, and all the other dreadful things we all know about only too well. Arnold Schoenberg actually subtitled his one-act monodrama *Erwartung* ("Expectation") as *Angsttraum*—"a dream of angst."

Certainly our lives have their happy and optimistic moments as well, but these tend not to be the things that inspire great art. And surely there was angst in previous ages; it is just that it was not a matter of public record. The bad things that happened long ago were interpreted in the arts as Tragedy, a somewhat remote and idealized form of suffering, reserved for those who were noble by birth or soul, forbidden to the vulgar. Even the composers who did not fill their works with angst can often be understood as reacting to it, as in the sardonic humor of Satie or Prokofiev, the retreat into mysticism of Holst, or the transcendentalism of Ives.

It is the very democratization of the Modern world that has permitted the development of a wide diversity of styles and forms of expression, in art and music as elsewhere, and made a pat definition of the age so hard to enunciate. There have been broad trends, such as Impressionism and Expressionism (and lately Minimalism), but no overarching umbrella to shelter them all.

Just as democratization legitimized a variety of "serious" art forms, it obviously did the same for the manifestations of popular culture. Ragtime, jazz, blues, popular song and their various offshoots could claim integrity and dignity right alongside the works of the "long-hair" composers; in fact, by the early 1960s the term "long-hair" had completely reversed itself and was applied to the Beatles and their kin instead of Franz Liszt and his.

One negative result of all this diffusion and fragmentation has been a widening gap between popular and "art" cultures, so that in the minds of many they have come to be enemies rather than neighbors. So-called classical (misnomer!) music has often been supported for the wrong reasons, as a symbol of affluence or aristocracy, a sign that its aficionados are a loftier breed of intellect and social position, a type of thinking I have always found repulsive (and which, quite rightly, repulses advocates of popular culture).

There have been art composers who have successfully incorporated popular styles in their works, e.g. Ravel, Milhaud, and Villa-Lobos, and composers like Gershwin and Grofé who came from the opposite direction, evolving their art out of popular song towards traditional "classical" forms, but none of these has bridged the gap between two cultures. The classical side often sees these pop elements as acceptable only if they are legitimized by classical composers; the pop side considers such re-creations to be prettified and eviscerated petrifactions of what ought to be a living art of the people.

Much of the art music of the twentieth century was born out of a sense of alienation—not only from popular culture, but also from the art culture of the past. It was this sensation that pushed Arnold Schoenberg over the edge, leading him to develop a music that was as unrelated as possible to either of them. His was the major single break with the past and it influenced many, though not all, of the later classical composers. (The fact that the other leading iconoclast, Igor Stravinsky, converted to the Schoenberg camp late in his career only increased the sense of alienation and betrayal for many younger composers.)

The "atonal" system developed by Schoenberg, and which he preferred to call, more accurately, "pantonal," avoids the traditional key system with its sense of tonal centers and with the dissonances always "resolving" into consonances. Each tone is now considered democratic, independent of the others, never subservient. This led naturally to Schoenberg's invention of the twelve-tone (or "serial") system, emphasizing the equality of all twelve notes of the chromatic scale (including all the sharps and flats), and using a predetermined sequence of all the notes (a "tone row") as the theme of every composition.

Although atonality and the tone-row system are not necessarily identical, they are popularly lumped together under the "atonal" designation. In this sense, we can say that atonalism is a prominent feature of the music of Schoenberg, Berg, and Webern, the leading members of the so-called Second Viennese School, and occurs occasionally in the works of many other later composers, especially Stravinsky in his last period. Much atonal music is also defined as Expressionistic, denoting the interpretation of inner feelings or psychological states.

Although Stravinsky began as a neo-Romantic, his significant "middle period" exemplified neo-Classicism, a style which few other composers directly imitated. Some of Hindemith's music fits this description, while other of it belongs to the category of *Gebrauchsmusik,* or "functional music."

Impressionism, a style that suggests rather than delineates, is derived from the works of Debussy in the previous period, and is noted mainly in the twentieth century in the works of Ravel and Respighi.

Nationalism, strongly influenced by folk music, was a stylistic theory carried over from the nineteenth century but updated for the twentieth with modernized techniques. Some composers who fall naturally in this category are Bartók, Bloch, Enesco, de Falla, Janáček, Khachaturian, Kodály, Nielsen, Sibelius, Vaughan Williams, and Villa-Lobos.

Neo-Romanticism was, of course, a carry-over as well, and is often applied to the major works of Barber, Hanson, and Rachmaninoff.

One branch of the French school emphasized polytonality, a system which keeps the old key system but has two or more frequently mixed together. Composers who belonged to this movement or derived from it include Milhaud, Honegger, Satie, and to a lesser extent, Poulenc. The American composer Virgil Thomson may be considered an offshoot of this style. Polytonality flourished in the 1920s, as did jazz and the American popular song, types which strongly influenced the music of Bernstein, Gershwin, Grofé, and Rodrigo.

Primitivism might be the category for Carl Orff and a number of lesser composers; it is also an occasionally accurate description for composers such as Bartók, Kodály, and Prokofiev.

In addition to all these, a number of eminent Modern composers do not fit snugly into any standard pigeonholes. Among these could be named Britten, Copland, Holst, Prokofiev, Shostakovich, and Walton, all of whom are reasonably Modern and not terribly conservative, but sometimes all or none of the above. All of them somehow managed to find distinctive musical personalities while not subscribing fully to any one school or style.

Having said all this, it must be added that in the democratic musical world of the twentieth century, hardly any of the composers named is exclusively identified with one style; almost all of them at least occasionally mix in something from a technique with which they are not normally associated. And just to confuse everything, there is Charles Ives, who was at one and the same time a proto-serialist, polytonalist, nationalist, Impressionist, primitivist, neo-Romantic!

Samuel Barber (1910-1981)

Barber was not so much a Romantic, as he was always billed, as an Emotionalist. His works vary in style. They may all sound "Romantic" to musicologists who listen to twelve-tone and aleatoric music all day (in fact, Barber used twelve-tone technique in several of his works), but they sound fairly modern to the average concertgoer.

Born in West Chester, Pennsylvania, Barber was a nephew of Louise Homer, a "golden age" contralto at the Metropolitan Opera, and he inherited a bit of voice himself; he not only took singing lessons, but made a record of his own—a setting of Matthew Arnold's poem *Dover Beach*.

His music study began early; at seven he was writing piano pieces, and at eight he was writing his mother: "To begin with, I was not meant to be an athelet [sic] I was meant to be a composer. And will be, I'm sure…Don't ask me to try to forget this…and go and play foot-ball. —Please— Sometimes I've been worrying about this so much that it makes me mad! (not very)."

This early penchant for whimsy stayed with him. He became a gourmand with a special interest in soups, and once expressed a wish to be buried "with a sprinkling of croutons over my coffin."

At age twelve he got a paying job as a church organist. Unfortunately, the choirmaster one day demanded little Sam hold a note longer than the score indicated. He refused, and was fired. Two years later he was admitted into the first class of the new Curtis Institute in Philadelphia. That city's great orchestra premiered his overture *The School for Scandal* when he was twenty-three.

In the 1930s he twice won the Pulitzer Prize for Music, and the American Prix de Rome, which allowed him to study in Italy.

One Italian who noticed him was Arturo Toscanini, who conducted the premieres of two of his orchestral works, including the *Adagio for Strings,* which Barber had arranged from a movement of his String Quartet No. 1.

Among Barber's other best-known works are his Violin Concerto, the ballet *Medea,* and the three Essays for Orchestra.

Adagio for Strings

This serene but dirge-like piece has a gently winding theme that fixes one's attention because it never goes where you think it will, and yet seems inevitable once it gets there. It first became nationally known when played on the radio at the announcement of President Franklin Roosevelt's death. It served the same function after the assassination of President Kennedy, and got renewed exposure as the theme of the film *Apocalypse Now.*

Leonard Slatkin's all-Barber digital disc is beautifully recorded and played, and makes a great introduction to this composer's music beyond the famed *Adagio for Strings.* Leonard Bernstein and Sir Neville Marriner are excellent choices at mid-price, the former coupled with his own works and Gershwin's *Rhapsody in Blue,* the latter with works of Copland and Thomson. An earlier Slatkin disc on another label couples the Barber piece differently, with "basic" works of Satie and Vaughan Williams, and a couple more.

Slatkin, St. Louis Symphony Orchestra. EMI 49463 [DDD] + Overture to *The School for Scandal,* Essays for Orchestra 1-3, *Meditation* and *Dance of Vengeance* from *Medea*

Bernstein, Los Angeles Philharmonic Orchestra. DG 427806 [DDD] + Bernstein: *Candide* Overture, *On the Town,* Symphonic Dances from *West Side Story* (mid-price)

Marriner, Los Angeles Chamber Orchestra. "American Miniatures," Angel Studio 64306 + Copland: *Fanfare for the Common Man,* three short pieces; Thomson: *Autumn, The Plow that Broke the Plains* (mid-price)
Slatkin, St. Louis Symphony Orchestra. Telarc 80059 [DDD] + Vaughan Williams: *Fantasia on a Theme by Thomas Tallis;* Fauré: *Pavane,* etc.

Béla Bartók (1881-1945)

Along with Mussorgsky, Bartók was the most original of all the "nationalist" composers. He was, as he called himself, "a son of the Hungarian plains," and virtually everything he wrote is suffused with the idiom and temperament of his country. Although he was an expert on Hungarian folk music, he seldom quoted an actual tune in his compositions; his object was to merge authentic folk elements with traditional compositional forms to create a new mode of expression. And this he accomplished.

He was found to have perfect pitch as a child, and his mother, a piano teacher, started him on the instrument when he was five. At age eleven he was giving recitals. He studied at the Budapest Academy of Music and composed some music much influenced by Franz Liszt and Richard Strauss.

In 1905 he and his friend Zoltán Kodály, who was to become the other most famous Hungarian composer of the twentieth century, took an Edison recording machine around the countryside and began studying and collecting folk songs. (His other hobby, by the way, was collecting insects.) From then on Bartók began to develop his distinctive style, terse and rugged, often dissonant, and sometimes savage.

People became alarmed at his music: when his *Bear Dance* was played in 1912, critic Philip Hale wrote that "the composer was regarded with a certain indulgence by the audience as, if not stark mad, certainly an eccentric person." There was some truth to that. Serious since childhood, Bartók had a morose streak all his life; he seemed to take pleasure in bad news and disbelieve the good.

His works received few performances in his own country, and in 1939, when his mother died and it looked as if the Nazis would be rolling through at any time, he moved to the United States. He was awarded an ethnomusicology position at Columbia University at a small salary. He and his wife had to live frugally, although not, as legend already has it, in dire poverty.

In the early 1940s he began to ail mysteriously. He had leukemia, although the doctors kept telling him they could make no diagnosis. Despite almost constant pain, weight loss, and fevers, Bartók composed some of his greatest works at this time, including one of his rare audience successes, the Concerto for Orchestra. He died in New York City, despairing that he had not done all he wanted to do. Ironically, his reputation began to soar shortly after his death, and within a few years he was universally recognized as one of the greatest composers of the Modern era.

Concerto for Orchestra

Bartók's most popular composition was commissioned by the Koussevitzky Foundation, following a suggestion made by both the conductor Fritz Reiner and the violinist Joseph Szigeti, both Hungarians. Composed in 1943, it was Bartók's last, and largest, orchestral work. It was a great success, and though seriously ill, the composer at last had the satisfaction of receiving an ovation.

Fritz Reiner's 1955 stereo (!) recording is considered one of the great performances on disc. Coupled with an equally wonderful version of Bartók's other orchestral masterpiece, in brilliantly reprocessed sound, this is still highly desirable at mid-price.

A wider selection of Bartók's music can be sampled on the half-price double set with various excellent artists on Philips, and Solti's digital recording at mid-price is a bargain, coupled with Mussorgsky's *Pictures at an Exhibition.*

Reiner, Chicago Symphony Orchestra. RCA Living Stereo 61504 [ADD] + Music for Strings, Percussion, and Celesta, *Hungarian Sketches* (mid-price)

Haitink, Concertgebouw Orchestra. Philips Duo 438812 [ADD] + Piano Concerti 1-3 (with Bishop-Kovacevich, C. Davis), Violin Concerto No. 2 (with Szeryng, C. Davis) (mid-price)

Solti, Chicago Symphony Orchestra. London 417754 [DDD] + Mussorgsky: *Pictures at an Exhibition* (mid-price)

Concerto No. 3 for Piano

Bartók knew he was dying and wrote this concerto as a parting gift to his wife Ditta Pásztory, who was a pianist also. He worked on it literally up to the minute he was taken to the hospital for the last time. The last seventeen bars were completed from sketches by Bartók's pupil, Tibor Serly. The middle Adagio movement is particularly famous for its moving nocturnal tranquillity.

All three Bartók piano concerti are given on one mid-price disc, intelligently performed by Stephen Bishop-Kovacevich with Sir Colin Davis conducting.

Bishop-Kovacevich, C. Davis, London Symphony Orchestra, BBC Symphony Orchestra. Philips Silver Line 426660 [ADD] + Piano Concerti, 1, 2 (mid-price)

Music for Strings, Percussion and Celesta

Uniquely constructed, imaginatively orchestrated, and memorably communicative, this work is a frequent candidate for the greatest single work of music written in the twentieth century. It really does have everything. A wide variety of materials, from folk rhythms to outer space sounds to a fugue of which Bach would be proud, are somehow tightly integrated into a seamless whole that manages to be both intellectual and emotional. Professors and peasants alike can appreciate it.

The Fritz Reiner recording recommended above under the Concerto for Orchestra is the preferred starter disc.

Reiner, Chicago Symphony Orchestra. RCA Living Stereo 61504 [ADD] + Concerto for Orchestra, *Hungarian Sketches* (mid-price)

Quartets (6)

Written over a span of thirty years, these greatest of modern quartets are an inseparable family group, providing a portrait of the composer in microcosm. You really must take them all, or not at all. Some, like No. 3, are very demanding of the listener; you might start with No. 2, one of Bartók's most beautiful (almost Romantic) works.

The fine Emerson Quartet is noted for their performances of Modern works and lead the digital field; though full price their version takes only two discs. The reissued Tokyo Quartet version is equally good at mid-price.

Emerson Quartet. DG 423657 (2) [DDD]
Tokyo Quartet. DG 445241 (3) [ADD] (mid-price)

Alban Berg (1885-1935)

Berg was the outstanding student of the originator of the twelve-tone, or "atonal" system of music. He was so good that many would say he outdistanced his master.

Berg was born into comfortable circumstances, the son of a merchant and the descendant of Bavarian court officials. His mother's side had some musical background, but Alban lagged behind his piano-playing sister and singing brother at first. At age fourteen he started taking a real interest, however, and by the next year was writing songs. At the same time, his father died and he had his first attack of what would be lifelong bronchial asthma. He failed his final exams at school, and tried to commit suicide after a love affair.

He recovered enough to take a civil service job, but gave it up in 1906 to devote himself to music after coming under the influence of Arnold Schoenberg, whose methods he adopted (this was, however, before the notorious twelve-tone system was completely formulated; Berg's first truly atonal work was the Lyric Suite,in 1926). He married in 1911. World War I interrupted his progress, but soon he was composing again and came to international attention with his Expressionist opera *Wozzeck* (1925).

The rise of the Nazis led to more problems after 1933, with both performances of his works and his income curtailed. He became so poor that he could not have his teeth fixed.

In the autumn of 1935 a bee stung him on the back. An abscess formed which was lanced, but it returned in a couple of months, probably exacerbated by Berg's run-down condition. Systemic blood poisoning developed, and despite operations and blood transfusions the composer died on Christmas eve in his wife's arms. He was fifty-one.

Concerto for Violin

Inspired by the tragic death of Manon Gropius, eighteen-year-old daughter of Gustav Mahler's widow by her second husband, this greatest of twentieth-century violin concerti was commissioned by violinist Louis Krasner, who later became a distinguished professor at Syracuse University, and whom I was privileged to know during three of those years.

Anne-Sophie Mutter is superb in her digital recording with James Levine conducting, but another German, Thomas Zehetmair, is not far behind under Heinz Holliger. Both recordings are highly recommendable with different couplings (none of which are "basic").
Earlier fine performances by Kyung-Wha Chung, Itzhak Perlman, and Arthur Grumiaux are out of print at this writing but are prime candidates for reissue; be on the lookout.

Mutter, Levine, Chicago Symphony Orchestra. DG 437093 [DDD] + Rihm: *"Time Chant"*
Zehetmair, Holliger, Philharmonia Orchestra. Teldec 46449 [DDD] + Janáček: Violin Concerto; Hartmann: *Concerto Funèbre*

Three Pieces for Orchestra, Op. 6

Prelude, Round Dance, and *March* make up this group of pieces written in 1915 and dedicated to Arnold Schoenberg on his fortieth birthday. The *Prelude* begins and ends with mysterious soft noises on the percussion, with the orchestra presenting a theme in between. The *Round Dance (Reigen)* is built on waltz rhythms and recalls Mahler's peasant dances. The *March* is a brutal affair with terrifying climaxes.

James Levine, music director of the Metropolitan Opera, may seem at first like an unlikely guide to this music, but actually it is one of his finest recordings, and the program provides a splendid way to meet all three leading lights of the Second Viennese School.

Levine, Berlin Philharmonic Orchestra. DG 419781 [DDD] + Schoenberg: Five Pieces for Orchestra, Op. 16; Webern: Six Pieces for Orchestra, Op. 6

Wozzeck

Despite his genius, Berg was a superstitious man. He was obsessed about the number twenty-three after his first asthma attack occurred on the twenty-third of July, 1900. One evening in Vienna he was fascinated by a performance of fragments of a drama by Georg Büchner, an Early Romantic playwright who died in 1837 at the age of—twenty-three. Berg decided he had to set this symbolic work to music.

Although the opera was attacked by many critics, it grew in public favor and had 166 performances in twenty-nine cities within a decade. Today it is one of the few Modern operas that can be said to have taken a regular place in the repertoire.

Christoph von Dohnányi provides a digital performance both more beautifully and more accurately played than any heretofore, the lead roles taken by Anja Silja and Eberhard Wächter, with a bonus of Schoenberg's one-act opera, *Erwartung* ("Expectation"), and at mid-price besides.

Dohnányi, Vienna Philharmonic Orchestra. London 417348 (2) [DDD] + Schoenberg: *Erwartung* (mid-price)

Leonard Bernstein (1918-1990)

Bernstein was a media phenomenon as well as a great musician. I say "musician" because it is still being argued whether he was a great composer. Certainly he was an enormously talented one, but his exact position in the pantheon is not yet universally accepted. But he *was* a star. From the fateful night when he substituted for ailing Bruno Walter as conductor of the New York Philharmonic in 1943, he was news. The dashing, flamboyant youth was in the papers the next day, and ever since.

Bernstein was born in Lawrence, Massachusetts. His father, Sam, a Russian Jewish immigrant, wanted his son to join him in the beauty supply business, but from age ten, when his aunt Clara gave the family an old upright piano, Lenny had ears only for music. He later studied at Harvard (with Walter Piston), the Curtis Institute (with Fritz Reiner), and at Tanglewood (with Serge Koussevitzky)—in other words, with three of the greatest musicians within a thousand miles.

From 1944, when he wrote the ballet (and later musical) *Fancy Free,* to 1957, the year of his triumph with *West Side Story,* Bernstein was most active on Broadway and in films (e.g., *On the Waterfront,* 1954).

After 1958, when he was appointed music director of the New York Philharmonic, his activities veered more towards the "serious" repertoire, both in composing and conducting. And what conducting! Leaping into the air, gyrating, he was the classical equivalent of Elvis Presley. Some critics rolled their eyes, but Bernstein said a good conductor should be an actor, and his often brilliant performances were his best defense.

His showmanship extended to a series of television programs in the 1960s, introducing classical music to the "masses," and resulting in both his well-known book *The Joy of Music,* which has had so many imitators, and in a series of Harvard lectures which were recorded in a huge box of LPs and sold right along with his numerous music recordings.

In the 1960s he also championed the music of Gustav Mahler to such an extent that it raised that composer's profile from a rather obscure sideshow to the forefront of discussion, interest, and orchestra programming around the world. Bernstein seemed to identify with Mahler's anguished questioning of the Meaning of Life, and he wrote his own tortured symphony with the subtitle "The Age of Anxiety."

Over the years he won Grammys and Emmys and Tonys, but never fully won the endorsement of the academic community. He had the image of a fast liver, a little on the wild side, very "New York," and he died of emphysema brought on by years of cigarette smoking. All the same, he could lead the Vienna Philharmonic in a Brahms symphony and bring down the house. He was America's Renaissance man of many musics, and it will be a while until we can evaluate him without the stardust in our eyes.

Candide: Overture

The musical had everything: a great story by Voltaire, a libretto hammered out by Dorothy Parker, John LaTouche, Lillian Hellman, and Richard Wilbur, music by Leonard Bernstein and a premiere in 1956 directed by Tyrone Guthrie. And still it flopped! Bernstein revised it in 1973, and again in 1982, and although its fortunes have improved, it's still the Overture that everybody knows, and the rest is still far down the track. That Overture, though, is as snappy and sassy as classical music gets.

Having the luxury of being a great conductor as well as a composer, Bernstein is always his own unimpeachable interpreter, sometimes multiple times. In this case, there are two outstanding recordings to choose from, one digital, one analog, and both at mid-price, with somewhat different couplings—which may be the deciding factor.

> **Bernstein, Los Angeles Philharmonic Orchestra.** DG 427806 [DDD] + *On the Town,* Symphonic Dances from *West Side Story;* Barber: *Adagio for Strings;* Gershwin: *Rhapsody in Blue* (mid-price)
> **Bernstein, New York Philharmonic Orchestra.** Sony 47529 [ADD] + Symphonic Dances from *West Side Story;* Gershwin: *Rhapsody in Blue, An American in Paris*

Chichester Psalms for Chorus and Orchestra

Both devotional and jazzy, this is easily the greatest choral work by an American composer. It was written in 1965 and continues to have a visceral impact on listeners.

Bernstein's own version, of course, has pride of place, and it is coupled with two other "basic" selections of twentieth century choral music. The only drawback is full price for an analog recording. Digital honors are swept by Robert Shaw's recording, coupled with a different Modern choral masterpiece.

Bernstein, New York Philharmonic Orchestra. CBS 44710 [ADD] +
Poulenc: *Gloria;* Stravinsky: *Symphony of Psalms*
Shaw, Atlanta Symphony Orchestra and Chorus. Telarc 80181 [DDD] +
Walton: *Belshazzar's Feast*

Dances from West Side Story

Bernstein's greatest musical dates from 1957 on Broadway, and was later made into a successful film. The suite of dances is popular as a concert piece.

Two versions conducted by the composer are already recommended above under the *Candide* Overture.

Bernstein, Los Angeles Philharmonic Orchestra. DG 427806 [DDD] +
Candide Overture, *On the Town;* Barber: *Adagio for Strings;* Gershwin: *Rhapsody in Blue* (mid-price)
Bernstein, New York Philharmonic Orchestra. Sony 47529 [ADD] + *Candide* Overture; Gershwin: *Rhapsody in Blue, An American in Paris* (mid-price)

Ernest Bloch (1880-1959)

Bloch both benefitted and suffered from being stereotyped as a "Hebraic composer." On one hand, it called attention to an important part of his heritage which he wanted to explore, share, and make universal, and on the other, it tended to limit his credibility when he wanted, especially in later life, to be known as well for his music with no apparent Jewish roots at all.

He was born to a clock merchant in Geneva, Switzerland and began his music study at age fourteen. In short order he was composing; by age sixteen he had completed an *Oriental Symphony.* He had little luck getting his works performed, however, and in his early twenties returned to help his father as a salesman and bookkeeper. In the evenings, however, he composed as assiduously as ever.

To his amazement, his first composition to be accepted for performance was not one of his short pieces or chamber works, but a full-length opera based on Shakespeare's *Macbeth,* which premiered at the famous Opéra-Comique in Paris in 1910. In the audience was the great critic (and I do not say that often!) Romain Rolland, who was so impressed that he traveled to Geneva to meet the composer. He was taken aback to find Bloch buried in ledger books and receipts. Encouraging him to strike out on his own, Rolland said, "I will answer for your becoming one of the masters of our time."

Bloch was fired now to create, and his first impulse was to write those works which expressed, as he said, "the complex, glowing, agitated soul that I feel vibrating through the Bible": *Schelomo* (Solomon), the *Israel Symphony,* the *Baal Shem* Suite, the *Trois Poèmes Juifs.*

In 1916, Bloch and his wife and children left for the U.S. for him to become a conductor for a touring dance program. Almost immediately his music came to the attention of well-placed musicians, and in just a few months an all-Bloch concert was being given at Carnegie Hall. He made the papers, always described as "the composer of Hebraic music."

But Bloch was ready for new challenges. In no way did he wish to repudiate his previous work or his spiritual heritage (although he suffered a crisis of faith during World War II), but he wanted to prove he was more than a provincial composer. Over the succeeding years he wrote both chamber and programmatic works with no overt Jewish connotations, winning a prize for his epic rhapsody *America,* a setting of Walt Whitman verses written to honor his adopted land.

In addition to composing, Bloch taught at the Mannes School of Music in New York City, became the first director of the Cleveland Institute of Music (1920-25), then the director of the San Francisco Conservatory, until he received an endowment in 1931 which made it possible for him to concentrate entirely on composing. He returned to Switzerland for a while, then moved to France and Italy until the anti-Semitic wave of the late 1930s swept him back to the U.S.

He settled in Agate Beach, Oregon, overlooking the Pacific, where he lived out his remaining twenty years of life, continually composing, continually developing, always learning and seeking new challenges. But it is still the "Hebraic" works of his young years—amounting only to about a quarter of his output—which listeners today remember most vividly, for their sensuous melodies and haunting harmonies seem to leap forth blazing from a richly passionate mind and soul.

Schelomo—Rhapsody for Cello and Orchestra

Far and away Bloch's most famous composition, *Schelomo* ("Solomon") is an evocation of the ancient king's court and personality, inspired largely by the Book of Ecclesiastes. There are suggestions of Solomon's power and pomp, the cries of slaves and warriors, dances of wives and courtiers; but woven throughout is the sad yearning of the king's reluctant wisdom: "I have seen all the works that are done under the sun, and behold, all is vanity…"

Three fine recordings are available with various enticements: Ofra Harnoy is intense as soloist on a mid-price digital disc, with a "non-basic" coupling. Steven Isserlis gives an outstanding performance with a more "basic" coupling but at higher price. Pierre Fournier's 1970 recording is at mid-price and has the most music of all, including the very "basic" Dvořák Cello Concerto.

Harnoy, Mackerras, London Philharmonic Orchestra. RCA Gold Seal 60757 [DDD] + Bruch: *Adagio on Celtic Themes,* etc. (mid-price)
Isserlis, Hickox, London Symphony Orchestra. Virgin Classics 59511 [DDD] + Elgar: Cello Concerto

P. Fournier, Wallenstein, Berlin Philharmonic Orchestra. DG Resonance 429155 [ADD] + Dvořák: Cello Concerto; Bruch: *Kol Nidrei* (mid-price)

Benjamin Britten (1913-1976)

Britten was the Golden Boy of twentieth-century English music—composer, pianist, conductor, founder of festivals, master of many styles, witty, prolific, darling of the critics, popular with the public, good or great at everything he tried and seldom stumbling.

The youngest of four children, he was a musical prodigy, composing a complete oratorio at the age of nine. At twelve he became a student of the composer Frank Bridge, honoring him a few years later with his first major work, the *Variations on a Theme of Frank Bridge.*

Studies at the Royal College of Music were followed by a stint writing incidental music for documentary films, which primed him for his later theatrical work and introduced him to the poet W. H. Auden, who had a major influence upon him. There followed a sojourn in the U.S. with the tenor Peter Pears, who was to become his lifelong companion and artistic collaborator. Here he wrote several important works, including the *Sinfonia da Requiem.*

He returned to England in 1942 with a commission in his pocket from the Koussevitzky Foundation to write an opera. *Peter Grimes* had its sensational premiere in 1945, being acclaimed the greatest English opera since Purcell's *Dido and Aeneas,* a judgment which still stands after fifty years. A demand for more operas followed, and in the ensuing years Britten produced a number of fine stage works, although none quite repeated the success of the first.

He and Pears founded the Aldeburgh Festival in 1948, and Britten acted as its director until his death. It was a venue for many important performances of his own and other compositions. Britten was also active as a pianist and conductor. In the latter capacity he made many distinguished recordings, some of his own works, of course, but also such things as one of the best sets ever made of Bach's *Brandenburg Concerti.*

Britten made a conscious effort to vary his style, ranging from the transparency of the *Simple Symphony* to complex experimental works such as *The Turn of the Screw* with its quasi-Schoenbergian harmonies. He seldom strayed far from what the public could readily absorb, yet retained just enough subtleties and academic touches to please the critics; this desire to please everybody does often give his music an unsettling air of calculation.

An unusual aspect of this composer was his emphasis on music for young people. Besides his famous *Guide to the Orchestra,* he wrote the song cycles *A Charm of Lullabies* and *Who Are These Children?,* the cantata *Saint Nicolas,* the "miracle play" *Noyes Fludde,* and an introduction to opera for children, *The Little Sweep.*

Serenade for Tenor, Horn, and Strings, Op. 31

The term "serenade" in this work implies not a lover's song to his beloved, but the older technical sense of "night music," when a serenade was a suite of instrumental pieces played at a person's house, preceded and followed by a march. The vocal part in Britten's composition comprises settings of six poems by Cotton, Tennyson, Blake, Ben Jonson, Keats, and Anonymous (fifteenth century).

A classic among classics, Britten's own conducting is joined by the singing of his alter ego Peter Pears, with effortless horn playing by the brilliant Barry Tuckwell and the addition of two Britten song cycles.

Pears, Tuckwell, Britten, London Symphony Orchestra. London 417153 [ADD] + *Les Illuminations, Nocturne*

Young Person's Guide to the Orchestra, Op. 34

In case anyone might think this title too flippant or popular, Britten judiciously gave it an alternate, *Variations and Fugue on a Theme of Henry Purcell,* which would be more acceptable to academics. It was originally written as the score for a documentary film on the instruments of the orchestra. The first concert performance was given in 1946.

There was a narrative written by Eric Crozier which is still sometimes used, but the work makes its points so clearly that many feel the addition of words is not only superfluous, but positively disruptive. I certainly don't care for it when things are just getting going and the music stops while an actor intones "Now this is the tuba, you little morons," or words to that effect.

The theme is taken from Purcell's incidental music to a play called *Abdelazar, or The Moor's Revenge.* It is an incredibly fertile tune, and its final statement on the brass is one of the exciting moments in orchestral music. Let 'er rip!

Britten's own version is again preferred, but for a digital recording, André Previn rivals the composer himself.

Britten, London Symphony Orchestra. London 417509 [ADD] + *Simple Symphony, Variations on a Theme of Frank Bridge*
Previn, Royal Philharmonic Orchestra. Telarc 80126 [DDD] + *Courtly Dances* from *Gloriana;* Prokofiev: *Peter and the Wolf*

Aaron Copland (1900-1990)

Copland became known as the Dean of American Composers at a surprisingly early stage in his long career. By the time he was twenty-five, two major American orchestras had performed his works; by thirty-five he was already an entry in every music history book; and by forty-five he was acclaimed as the greatest American composer.

This was an extraordinary ascent for one who was born in a drab neighborhood of Brooklyn without any real exposure to musical culture. Copland's attraction to art music was almost instinctive, and he was only sixteen when he determined to become a composer. His first lessons were uninspiring, and it was not until he was able to save enough to travel to Paris, where he came under the tutelage of Nadia Boulanger, that his talent found its proper direction.

Back in America he was noticed, and subsequently promoted, by Serge Koussevitzky, conductor of the Boston Symphony Orchestra and a vigorous champion of new music. A Guggenheim Fellowship freed Copland from drudge jobs so that he could concentrate on composing, and for a while he concentrated on complex works in an avant-garde idiom.

In the mid-1930s he reassessed his esthetic. "It seemed to me," he later wrote, "that we composers were in danger of working in a vacuum. Moreover, an entirely new public for music had grown up around the radio and phonograph. It made no sense to ignore them and to continue writing as if they did not exist. I felt that it was worth the effort to see if I couldn't say what I had to say in the simplest possible terms."

The results were those classics of Americana that have endeared Copland to a world-wide audience: the ballets *Appalachian Spring* (which won the Pulitzer Prize), *Rodeo*, and *Billy the Kid*; and the brief but unforgettable *Fanfare for the Common Man*, which has become a virtual calling card for the nation. In these works Copland managed, without sacrificing intellectual integrity, to create a sound-world that evokes unmistakably American poetic images: cowboys, the Wild West, farm life, the small town, and the hardy pioneers such as the Pennsylvania Shakers who possessed a wisdom that Aaron Copland took to heart and passed on:

> *'Tis a gift to be simple,*
> *'Tis a gift to be free.*

Appalachian Spring

Composed as a ballet for Martha Graham, this work had its premiere in the Library of Congress in 1944. It was originally entitled *Ballet for Martha*. The present title was taken from a poem by Hart Crane. The scenario concerns a young Pennsylvania Shaker couple celebrating their new farmhouse in springtime. The old Shaker hymn, "The Gift to Be Simple," was made world-famous through this ballet.

Leonard Bernstein's classic account of the Suite is available at mid-price, as is Leonard Slatkin's fine performance in newer sonics. The complete ballet (not much longer than the Suite) is heard in its original chamber instrumentation conducted by Dennis Russell Davies, or in the full orchestra version at mid-price with Antal Dorati. All are excellent, and the couplings may determine a choice.

Bernstein, New York Philharmonic Orchestra. Sony 37257 [ADD] + *Fanfare for the Common Man, El Salón México, Danza Cubano* (mid-price)
L. Slatkin, St. Louis Symphony Orchestra. EMI 64315 + *Billy the Kid, Rodeo, Dance Panels* (mid-price)

Davies, St. Paul Chamber Orchestra. Pro Arte 3429 [DDD] + Short
Symphony; Ives: Symphony No. 3
Dorati, Detroit Symphony Orchestra. London Jubilee 430705 [DDD] +
Rodeo, El Salón México (mid-price)

Billy the Kid

Although "Western" ballets have become rather common currency, they all descend
from *Billy the Kid,* first produced in 1938. The music employs authentic cowboy tunes, but
filtered through Copland's distinctive imagination. The concert suite from the complete
ballet was arranged by the composer.

Gerard Schwarz leads a brilliant-sounding digital version with generous couplings.
Leonard Bernstein's analog disc has less music, but it is a famous performance and the price
is reduced. Leonard Slatkin turns in a thrilling performance of the complete ballet at mid-
price, with the *Appalachian Spring* Suite. All three recordings include *Rodeo,* and Schwarz
adds Grofé's colorful *Grand Canyon* Suite.

Schwarz, Seattle Symphony Orchestra. "Out West," Delos 3104 [DDD] +
Rodeo; Grofé: *Grand Canyon* Suite
Bernstein, New York Philharmonic Orchestra. CBS 36727 [ADD] + *Rodeo*
(mid-price)
L. Slatkin, St. Louis Symphony Orchestra. EMI 64315 + *Appalachian
Spring, Rodeo* (mid-price)

Fanfare for the Common Man

At the beginning of World War II the conductor of the Cincinnati Symphony
Orchestra, Eugene Goossens, commissioned ten composers to write patriotic fanfares. Only
Copland's has thrived since, and the composer himself re-used it at the beginning of the
last movement of his Third Symphony.

Two discs previously recommended handily provide this short piece as an addendum.

Bernstein, New York Philharmonic Orchestra. Sony 37257 [ADD] +
Appalachian Spring, El Salón México, Danza Cubano (mid-price)
Marriner, Los Angeles Chamber Orchestra. "American Miniatures," Angel
64306 + three short pieces; Barber: *Adagio for Strings;* Thomson: *Autumn, The
Plow that Broke the Plains* (mid-price)

Rodeo

Copland's other "Western ballet" is altogether more cheerful than *Billy the Kid*, being a love story instead of the saga of a bloodthirsty killer. Its premiere took place in 1942 at the Metropolitan Opera House. The four sections are marked "Buckaroo Holiday," "Corral Nocturne," "Honky Tonk Interlude and Saturday Night Waltz," and (most famously) "Hoe-Down."

The three recordings recommended under *Billy the Kid* above apply here, plus the Dorati disc recommended under *Appalachian Spring*.

Schwarz, Seattle Symphony Orchestra. "Out West," Delos 3104 [DDD] + *Billy the Kid;* Grofé: *Grand Canyon* Suite
Bernstein, New York Philharmonic Orchestra. CBS 36727 [ADD] + *Billy the Kid* (mid-price)
Dorati, Detroit Symphony Orchestra. London Jubilee 430705 [DDD] + *Appalachian Spring, El Salón México* (mid-price)
L. Slatkin, St. Louis Symphony Orchestra. EMI 64325 + *Appalachian Spring, Billy the Kid* (mid-price)

Georges Enesco (1881-1955)

As he is immediately identifiable as the Greatest Composer of Romania, it would be easy to let Enesco stay in that easy-to-remember pigeonhole. But he keeps popping back out, reminding us that he was a composer of many styles, and Romantic nationalism was just one of them.

He was as precocious as any composer ever was, starting to teach himself the violin at age three. By age seven he had written several sonatas, and he gave his first public concert at eight. The director of the Vienna Conservatory not only accepted the boy before the normal age of admission, but let him live in his home, where he was the darling of all the famous musicians in town, including Brahms.

Enesco completed his studies in Paris under Fauré and Massenet, both of whom proclaimed him a genius, and it was there that he began using the French spelling of his Romanian name (originally "Enescu," and often listed that way—it's not a misprint). By 1910 he was widely recognized as a great composer, conductor, and violinist (I am listening to his recording of the Bach Sonatas and Partitas for Solo Violin as I write this), and he was the teacher of Yehudi Menuhin.

Enesco's early works are heavily influenced by Brahms and Wagner. Later he adopted a neo-Classical style, then began integrating Romanian folk idioms into his works, and finally experimented with several avant-garde techniques, including polytonality and microtonal music.

He was a fervent idealist and an apostle of hard work, encouraging musical culture in Romania and laboring to bring it to the attention of the wider world. His eclectic style made it difficult to place him precisely, and as Enesco ruefully realized, "People get annoyed when they can't really classify you." Nevertheless, he left a rich legacy of stimulating and often beautiful music which well repays investigation.

Romanian Rhapsody No. 1, Op. 11

World acclaim greeted Enesco with the joint premiere of his two *Romanian Rhapsodies* in Paris in 1908. The first rhapsody especially, with its slow buildup to whirlwind peasant dances, never fails to thrill. Although written for a quick buck, it's a great piece of its kind, and although hardly indicative of the composer's vast canvas, it will, hopefully, intrigue you enough to make you wonder about all the rest of his work.

Antal Dorati's classic recording of this piece with the six orchestral *Hungarian Rhapsodies* of Liszt is unbeatable at mid-price, in beautifully remastered sound.

Dorati, London Symphony Orchestra. Mercury 432015 [ADD] + Liszt: *Hungarian Rhapsodies* (6) (mid-price)

Manuel de Falla (1876-1946)

De Falla put Spain on the classical music map at last, after centuries of lassitude. Not since Tomás Luis de Victoria in the Renaissance had this important European country participated in serious music culture much beyond the zarzuela, or Spanish operetta (which, though delightful, isn't very serious).

Falla was born into a highly cultured family in Cadiz, starting piano study with his mother and later advancing to the Madrid Conservatory. There he studied in preparation for a career as a piano virtuoso, but another influence intervened. He came under the spell of his composition teacher, Felipe Pedrell, a fervent nationalist who encouraged study of Spanish folk song and dance and their integration into art music.

In 1905 Falla won first prize in a competition with his folk opera *La Vida Breve.* Two years later he left for Paris, where he became friends with Claude Debussy and hobnobbed generally with the leading lights of the intense musical activity going on there: Fauré, Ravel, Dukas, and others. Debussy's influence was as significant as Pedrell's to his compositional style, and indeed, Falla is sometimes counted among the Impressionists.

After seven years of absorbing everything musical which France had to offer, Falla returned to Spain and spent more years traveling his native land, studying its music and folklore. The first major product of the integration of all these elements was the ballet *El amor brujo,* the orchestral suite from which (including the inescapable *Ritual Fire Dance*) remains Falla's most popular work.

Subsequently, his position as Spain's major composer was solidified with the piano concerto *Nights in the Gardens of Spain,* and the ballet *The Three-Cornered Hat.* Although hardly a prolific composer, Falla maintained a high level of integrity and quality in all his work, which is characterized by vivid poetic feeling and intensely picturesque atmosphere.

Falla was a small, natty man, very dark of complexion (Debussy called him "le petit espagnol tout noir") and of melancholy disposition. His punctilious adherence to a strict personal schedule with each day's chores done at an exact predetermined time, including dinner at midnight, drove even his domestic help away. He had an aversion to wealth and honors, and for seventeen years lived in a modest house in Granada.

In addition, Falla was a superstitious hypochondriac who refused to see visitors during the full moon and was terrified of drafts. He was deeply religious, and at first supported Franco during the Spanish Civil War, believing the insurgents were a danger to the Church. But only a year after being appointed president of the Institute of Spain by the victorious Generalissimo, Falla became disillusioned and moved to Argentina, where he grew ever more frail and died in 1946.

El amor brujo

"Love, the Magician" is a gypsy ballet with a part for soprano. It first became a success in 1928 in Paris. The music is languorous and passionate, and includes the famous *Ritual Fire Dance.* The scenario concerns the legend of a dead lover's ghost which appears every time a new lover tries to replace him. The spell is broken by a magic kiss after the ghost has been distracted by a different girl.

Charles Dutoit, always adept at atmosphere and impressionism, does a star turn here in a digital version with all "basic" couplings at mid-price. Also at mid-price, Carlo Maria Giulini's classic early-60s recording is a fine alternative, with an all-Falla program and a greater singer.

Tourangeau, Dutoit, Montreal Symphony Orchestra. London 430703 [DDD] + *Nights in the Gardens of Spain;* Rodrigo: *Concierto de Aranjuez* (mid-price)

De Los Angeles, Giulini, Philharmonia Orchestra. EMI 64746 + *Three-Cornered Hat* (sel.), *Nights in the Gardens of Spain* (with Soriano, Frühbeck de Burgos) (mid-price)

Nights in the Gardens of Spain

The title is pretty much all the commentary that is needed. Not quite a piano concerto, but a set of impressionistic orchestral pieces with the piano wandering through the gardens of the imagination. Nights! Gardens! Spain! Get it?

The two recordings recommended above under *El amor brujo* are repeated here, with the addition of a fine-sounding digital version featuring pianist Carol Rosenberger. All have similar but slightly different couplings.

> **De Larrocha, Dutoit, Montreal Symphony Orchestra.** London 430703 [DDD] + *El amor brujo;* Rodrigo: *Concierto de Aranjuez* (mid-price)
> **Soriano, Frühbeck de Burgos, New Philharmonia Orchestra.** EMI 64746 + *El amor brujo, Three-Cornered Hat* (sel.) (with Giulini conducting) (mid-price)
> **Rosenberger, Schwarz, London Symphony Orchestra.** Delos 3060 [DDD] + *Three-Cornered Hat* (sel.)

The Three-Cornered Hat: Dances

Falla's other ballet is best known through excerpted dances. *El Sombrero de tres picos* was commissioned by the legendary impresario Serge Diaghilev and had an overwhelming success at its premiere in London in 1919. The story is adapted from a classic Spanish novel by Pedro del Alarcón.

Two recordings previously recommended will serve here to introduce this flavorful music.

> **Schwarz, London Symphony Orchestra.** Delos 3060 [DDD] + *Nights in the Gardens of Spain* (with Rosenberger)
> **Giulini, Philharmonia Orchestra.** EMI 64746 + *El amor brujo, Nights in the Gardens of Spain* (with Soriano, Frühbeck de Burgos) (mid-price)

George Gershwin (1898-1937)

Gershwin is almost unique in music history in showing that so-called popular idioms can be made as distinctive and durable as any art or "classical" music. He effectively blurred the lines that once demarcated these two supposedly separate worlds, bringing dignity to jazz and popular song and making the classical sphere less fearsome to the masses without trivializing it.

He had an unremarkable childhood in New York City, playing street hockey and rooting for the Giants. He even belonged to a gang, and thought boys who liked music were "Maggies." His father was a small-time businessman who variously ran a cigar store, pool hall, Turkish bath, and bookie operation.

One day, when he was ten and playing ball outside P.S. No. 25 on the Lower East Side, he was struck by the sounds of a violin coming from the school auditorium. A local prodigy (and later concert violinist), Max Rosen, was playing Dvořák's *Humoresque*. Young George was intrigued and soon made friends with Maxie, pumping him for information on music.

Before he knew it he was taking piano lessons and assiduously studying the Great Masters. Nevertheless, his teachers were alarmed by his continuing attachment to popular songs, ragtime, and jazz, and his irritable defense of them. Gershwin actually loved the classics, but he believed in the music of his milieu too, and was determined to prove it had value.

At age sixteen he became a publicist for the Tin Pan Alley publishing firm of Remick. In his spare time he often practiced Bach preludes and fugues. One day a fellow "plugger" asked if he was studying to be a concert pianist. "No," Gershwin replied seriously, "I'm practicing to become a popular-song composer."

Soon he got a job at thirty-five dollars a week writing songs for a rival publisher, Harms (with lyrics, as always, by his older brother Ira), and one of them, "Swanee," became a million-seller after being sung by Al Jolson in the show *Sinbad*. Gershwin was on his way. By age twenty-three he was the toast of Broadway—and even London, with songs that are now true classics of American popular culture pouring from him in profusion. A decade later, *Of Thee I Sing* became the first musical to win the Pulitzer Prize.

But the work that established Gershwin's international fame and made the serious music world take him, well, seriously, was *Rhapsody in Blue*, commissioned by bandleader Paul Whiteman in 1924 and orchestrated by Ferde Grofé. Suddenly jazz was respectable, and composers around the world were swept up in the new craze: Ravel, Milhaud, Kurt Weill and many others picked up the jazz bug and wrote concert works that included its idioms.

The tables of critical opinion had now turned upside down, and Gershwin's music was praised by Vaughan Williams and Bartók. Arnold Schoenberg became a regular tennis partner. Always looking to improve his technical skills, Gershwin asked for lessons, but the leader of the avant-garde refused: "I would only make you a bad Schoenberg, and you're such a good Gershwin already."

Going from one triumph to another on stage and screen, Gershwin became a real workaholic, often staying up all night composing, oblivious to everything around him except his beloved cigars. He never married because he was too busy to do so. At parties he would do nothing but play his own music on the piano. After one such marathon of monopoly, pianist Oscar Levant asked, "If you had to do it all over again, George, would you still fall in love with yourself?"

When at the height of his fame he began complaining of headaches, it was chalked up to overwork—even when he collapsed. But a second collapse led to the discovery of a brain tumor. He underwent surgery immediately, but died in the hospital. Since then, however, the world has not stopped being in love with George Gershwin's music.

An American in Paris

Gershwin explained: "My purpose here is to portray the impressions of an American visitor in Paris as he strolls about the city, listens to the various street noises, and absorbs the French atmosphere." The visitor was, of course, Gershwin himself, who traveled to France in 1928 hoping to pick up a few pointers on theory and orchestration. Mostly, however, he strolled around the city, listened to the various street noises, and...you get the picture. Speaking of pictures, *An American in Paris* was made into an Academy Award-winning film in 1951 starring Gene Kelly.

Leonard Bernstein has had almost a monopoly on this work for decades, and two of his recordings still make top choices, depending on couplings. Both are analog, however, and digitophiles should investigate Mitch Miller's outstanding recording on the Arabesque label, not as widely available in record stores as some discs.

Bernstein, New York Philharmonic Orchestra. Sony 47529 [ADD] + *Rhapsody in Blue;* Bernstein: *Candide* Overture (mid-price)

Bernstein, New York Philharmonic Orchestra. CBS 42264 [ADD] + *Rhapsody in Blue;* Grofé: *Grand Canyon* Suite

Miller, London Symphony Orchestra. Arabesque 6587 [DDD] + *Rhapsody in Blue,* Piano Concerto in F

Porgy and Bess

The original play was by DuBose Heyward. He and his wife Dorothy collaborated with Ira Gershwin to produce the libretto for this magnificent folk opera, which had its premiere in 1935. It is Gershwin's largest work, and probably his masterpiece. The composer had grown up in Harlem and absorbed a great deal from black musicians, including "Fats" Waller and Art Tatum. He lavished almost three years of work on his opera, but at first, critical opinion was divided. Acclaim was universal only years after Gershwin's death, *Porgy and Bess* becoming the first American opera ever presented at La Scala, Milan, the world's greatest opera house. It was also a hit in the Soviet Union.

Ironically, of the three available complete recordings, the English conductor Simon Rattle has received the best reviews, including a 1990 Grammy nomination, and his is the only digital version.

Rattle, London Philharmonic Orchestra. EMI 49568 (3) [DDD]

Rhapsody in Blue

Bandleader Paul Whiteman had enormous faith in Gershwin's ability to write in the larger forms, but the composer was reluctant to accept the invitation to write a symphonic work for a planned concert of experimental jazz at the Aeolian Hall in New York City. He only gave in after Whiteman announced in the papers that it was going to happen. Again, Gershwin's own evaluation of the piece: "I hear it as a sort of musical kaleidoscope of America—of our vast melting pot, of our incomparable national pep, our blues, our metropolitan madness."

Leonard Bernstein was even more famous for this work, as both piano soloist and conductor, than for *An American in Paris,* and I can here offer recommendations for two different readings in three assorted packagings. The Mitch Miller recording already recommended above features a fine pianist in David Golub, and André Previn must also be mentioned for his famous recording, preferred by some critics to all others; the full price is hard to justify, however.

Bernstein, New York Philharmonic Orchestra. Sony 47529 [ADD] + *An American in Paris;* Bernstein: *Candide* Overture, Symphonic Dances from *West Side Story* (mid-price)

Bernstein, New York Philharmonic Orchestra. CBS 42264 [ADD] + *An American in Paris,* Piano Concerto in F

Bernstein, Los Angeles Philharmonic Orchestra. DG 427806 [DDD] + Barber: *Adagio for Strings;* Bernstein: *Candide* Overture, *On the Town,* Symphonic Dances from *West Side Story* (mid-price)

Golub, Miller, London Symphony Orchestra. Arabesque 6587 [DDD] + *An American in Paris,* Piano Concerto in F

Previn, London Symphony Orchestra. Angel 47161 [ADD] + *An American in Paris,* Piano Concerto in F

Ferde Grofé (1892-1972)

As mentioned above under the Gershwin entry, Grofé orchestrated that composer's greatest hit, *Rhapsody in Blue*. He was another American who came up through the ranks of popular music, especially dancebands. One of his "serious" works, the *Grand Canyon* Suite, is also one of the most popular works ever written by an American, and his *Mississippi* Suite is hardly less appealing. But if you will ask any musicologist, academic, or critic to name the top ten American composers, I guarantee you will never hear him mentioned. Perhaps he should have stuck with his baptismal name, Ferdinand Rudolph von Grofé.

He was born in New York City. His father was a baritone and an actor, his mother a cellist. His maternal grandfather was principal cellist of the Los Angeles Symphony Orchestra for some twenty-five years, and before that played next to Victor Herbert in the Metropolitan Opera Orchestra. An uncle was a distinguished violinist.

The family moved to Los Angeles only a year after Ferdinand was born. His mother taught him to read music at age five, and soon he was accompanying her cello playing from the piano. His father died when Ferde was seven, and his mother moved to Leipzig, Germany for three years to submerge her grief in further music study.

After they returned to California, the young Grofé undertook a study of as many musical instruments as he could master, from the violin to the marimbaphone, and at seventeen he was paid for his first commercial work, a march commissioned for an Elks convention. Now Grofé was able to make a living with music, although at first he played a lot of dance halls and hotels, eventually working his way up to playing viola with the Los Angeles Symphony.

He did some Hollywood mood music work, during which he met the great bandleader

Paul Whiteman, who took Grofé on as a pianist and arranger in 1920. Their first hit, *Whispering*, sold a million and a half copies (I treasure my original 78 rpm copy!). Then came the opportunity to orchestrate Gershwin's masterpiece.

After the successful premiere of the *Grand Canyon* Suite in 1931, Grofé struck out on his own, leading his own orchestra, guesting, doing independent arranging, teaching orchestration at the Juilliard School, and writing a long series of orchestral suites such as the *Hudson River, Death Valley, World's Fair, Aviation,* and *Hollywood* Suites. There was even a *Rudy Vallee* Suite, provoking my friend, music librarian and polymath Rex Levang, to suggest that Grofé's range extended "from Death Valley to Rudy Vallee."

There is always a temptation to snicker at Grofé because of his unsophisticated concepts and his frank pandering to audience love of visual connotations tacked on to music. When the idea is executed so lovingly and skillfully, however, it seems ungenerous to deny listeners the melodic and harmonic pleasures of this kind of very literal program music. For those who would find fault, I direct their attention to the barking dogs in Vivaldi's *The Four Seasons,* the ticking clock in Haydn's Symphony No. 101, or (my favorite) the athletic amphibians in the great aria "Their land brought forth frogs" from Handel's oratorio *Israel in Egypt,* to name just a few of the composers who would have been proud to write the *Aviation* Suite (if only they had known what an airplane was).

Grand Canyon Suite

Grofé conceived his most famous suite, not surprisingly, while viewing the great natural wonder in 1922, but seven years later, when he began to write it, there were other images mixing themselves in his imagination: memories of a thunderstorm that frightened him as a boy *(Cloudburst)*, the rhythm of a piledriver outside his Chicago hotel *(On the Trail)*, looking at the sky on the ninth hole of a golf course in New Jersey *(Sunset)*. Presumably the other movements, *Sunrise* and *Painted Desert*, were inspired only by the Grand Canyon. At any rate, the suite was a complete success at its 1931 premiere; Grofé was anointed the "prime minister of jazz," and his diplomatic coup has since traveled the world.

Gerard Schwarz's disc has already been recommended under Aaron Copland. Erich Kunzel's version, also digital, is excellent too, and has a real thunderstorm tipped in for audiophiles, although the coupling is less "basic." Bernstein's classic 60s version must be included, but the full price is annoying at this late date.

Schwarz, Seattle Symphony Orchestra. "Out West," Delos 3104 [DDD] + Copland: *Billy the Kid, Rodeo*
Kunzel, Cincinnati Pops. Telarc 80086 [DDD] + Gershwin: *Catfish Row*
Bernstein, New York Philharmonic Orchestra. CBS 42264 [ADD] + Gershwin: *An American in Paris, Rhapsody in Blue*

Howard Hanson (1896-1981)

Hanson was born in Wahoo, Nebraska, the home town of two other eminent Americans: baseball legend Ty Cobb and Hollywood producer Darryl F. Zanuck. His parents were Swedish immigrants, and Hanson wrote his Symphony No. 1 "Nordic" in honor of his Scandinavian roots. His mother was his first teacher; later he received a degree from Northwestern University, and at age twenty was appointed professor of theory and composition at the College of the Pacific in San Jose, California. Only two years later he was named Dean of the Conservatory of Fine Arts.

In 1920 he became the first Fellow selected by the American Academy of Rome to study for three years in Italy. On his return he was immediately named director of the Eastman School of Music in Rochester, New York, where he continued until his retirement in 1964. He made the school one of the finest such institutions in the world, and for many years held an annual festival of American music there, to encourage and exhibit native composers.

He was a notable conductor, making several recordings of his own and other music. He won numerous awards, including the Pulitzer Prize for his Symphony No. 4 (1944). His style is neo-Romantic, and he has a better claim on that label than Samuel Barber, who so often wears it instead. His star is in temporary eclipse, but time will bring it around again some day.

Symphony No. 2, "Romantic," Op. 30

Hanson's most beloved work was written to celebrate the fiftieth season of the Boston Symphony Orchestra, who first played it in 1930 under Serge Koussevitzky. It is still regarded as one of the finest native symphonic works.

This symphony has always had good luck in recordings. Currently, Gerard Schwarz's digital version is one of his finest efforts, and the nominee and winner of several awards, including a highly unusual multi-Grammy nomination in 1990 for best classical album, best orchestral performance, and best-engineered classical recording. In addition, the composer's own definitive recording is available in superbly remastered sound at mid-price.

Schwarz, Seattle Symphony Orchestra. Delos 3073 [DDD] + Symphony No. 1, *Elegy in Memory of Koussevitzky*
Hanson, Eastman Rochester Symphony Orchestra. Mercury 432008 [ADD] + Symphony No. 1, *Song of Democracy* (mid-price)

Paul Hindemith (1895-1963)

Hindemith ran away from home as a youth when his parents would not hear of his making music his career. He earned a living playing in theater and cafe orchestras while attending the Frankfurt Conservatory, becoming one of the most rapidly developing students, and after a brief stint in the German army became concertmaster of the Frankfurt Opera Orchestra.

He founded the Amar String Quartet and attracted notice with some of his chamber works in the early 1920s. Few modern composers have devoted more of their energies to chamber music, both as composer and performer (Hindemith was an outstanding violist). From 1926 on, after the success of his opera *Cardillac,* Hindemith was acknowledged as a leading German composer (second only to Richard Strauss), and he became an esteemed teacher at the Berlin Hochschule.

At this time he began writing those works for which he coined the term *Gebrauchsmusik* ("functional music"), and which have haunted his reputation ever since. He did not, contrary to legend, stop writing works of high artistic inspiration, but supplemented them with pieces written frankly for mass comsumption and educational purposes. These works, limited in number and intended use, have been cited by many detractors over the years as proving that Hindemith was a workaday composer. "I felt," Hindemith wrote in *A Composer's World,* "like the sorcerer's apprentice who had become the victim of his own conjurations: the slogan *Gebrauchsmusik* hit me wherever I went; it had grown to be as abundant, useless, and disturbing as thousands of dandelions in a lawn."

Despite his fame, Hindemith ran afoul of the Nazis. He had married a Jew, he had Jewish friends, he made recordings with Jews, and although he was not Jewish, he staunchly refused to abandon any of them. Dr. Goebbels immediately discovered Hindemith's music to be both degenerate and obscene. Wasn't there an aria in one of his operas that was sung in a bathtub? Even worse, it was written in "the most atrocious dissonance of musical impotence."

Hindemith fled Germany in 1935, spending about a year in Turkey, then coming to the U.S. at the invitation of Elizabeth Sprague Coolidge, a great patron of the arts. He taught at Yale for several years and continued composing, producing some of his finest works. He took up residence in Zurich, Switzerland in 1953, but died back in Frankfurt in 1963, leaving nearly five hundred works in the catalog of his life's toil.

His reputation suffered greatly after the war, many composers of the younger generation seeing Hindemith as a musician who had abandoned his earlier progressive ideas and unfairly attacked the avant-garde movement. He was considered a fuddy-duddy who did not deserve the eminence and adulation he received in official quarters; he thus became a symbol of hypocrisy and reaction, and the label of *Gebrauchsmusik* was smeared unfairly over all his output.

Hindemith himself once said that eighty percent of his music was bad, but if it were not for that portion, the twenty percent that was good would never have been written. I rather like the estimation of Donald Francis Tovey (one of the few musicologists who is actually fun to read), who said of Hindemith: "As far as I can judge, his music does not bore many people, though it annoys some. He is never very long, he thumps no tubs, and he makes the best of modern life."

Mathis der Maler (Symphony)

Not really a symphony at all, this work is a suite of three sections excerpted from Hindemith's opera of the same name, which premiered in Switzerland in 1938. It is a dramatic allegory about the artist's dilemma in society, framed in the context of the historical defeat of German liberalism during the Peasants' Revolt of the early sixteenth century; these subjects did not endear the composer to the Nazi Party. The story is told through the life of the historical painter Matthias Grünewald, and each of the work's movements depicts a panel of the artist's altarpiece at the monastery church at Isenheim.

Herbert Blomstedt conducts a moving performance of this and Hindemith's other "hit" on a digital recording with "demonstration" sonics. At mid-price, Paul Kletzki is admirable with *Mathis der Maler,* joined by Claudio Abbado for the *Symphonic Metamorphosis.* Each disc has one additional coupling, the mid-price featuring Hindemith conducting his own Violin Concerto with David Oistrakh soloing—a stupefying bonus.

Blomstedt, San Francisco Symphony Orchestra. London 421523 [DDD]
+ *Symphonic Metamorphosis of Themes by Weber, Trauermusik*
Kletzki, Suisse Romande Orchestra. London Enterprise 433081 [ADD] +
Symphonic Metamorphosis on Themes by Weber (with Abbado conducting the London Symphony), Violin Concerto (with Oistrakh, violin, and Hindemith conducting) (mid-price)

Symphonic Metamorphosis of Themes by Weber

While teaching at Yale in 1943, Hindemith came across a volume of four-hand piano music by Carl Maria von Weber, and agreeing with your author that Weber is unjustly neglected, decided to make an orchestral work out of some of the themes. He did alter some of them a bit to suit his purposes, but they are very recognizable, and the piquant and brilliant orchestration of the resulting four-movement suite is quite in a class by itself.

The two recordings recommended just above remain the recommendations here.

Blomstedt, San Francisco Symphony Orchestra. London 421523 [DDD]
+ *Mathis der Maler* Symphony, *Trauermusik*
Abbado, London Symphony Orchestra. London Enterprise 433081 [ADD] + *Mathis der Maler* Symphony (with Kletzki and Suisse Romande Orchestra), Violin Concerto (with Oistrakh, violin, and Hindemith conducting) (mid-price)

Gustav Holst (1874-1934)

For much of his life, Holst was a frail, remote, mystical soul who, despite the enormous popularity of his suite *The Planets,* sought to avoid fame rather than curry it.

He came from a long line of musicians with Russian, German, and Swedish roots. His father was a piano teacher when Gustav was born in Cheltenham. At seventeen he began studies in London at the Royal College of Music, where he met and started a lifelong friendship with Ralph Vaughan Williams. Musically, he fell under the spell of Wagner, from which he was not to recover for a decade.

Neuritis forced him to give up a planned career as a pianist and he took up the trombone instead. He supported a wife and children for a while by playing in shows and bands, but in 1903 tried to make a go of it as a composer. His fees from published works were insufficient, however, and he turned to teaching, which occupied him the rest of his life except on weekends, when he tried to get in a little composing. Despite the burden teaching signified for him, he was often praised by his students as an enthusiastic and inspiring instructor.

Holst had abandoned Wagnerism by 1906 and took up study of his national roots— Henry Purcell, the madrigal composers of the English Renaissance, and folk song. Another deep interest was Hindu philosophy and literature, which reflected itself in such works as the opera *Savitri* and the *Hymns from the Rig Veda.* He went so far as to learn Sanskrit at the School of Oriental Languages so that he could translate the ancient texts himself.

His one notable public success was the introduction of *The Planets* in 1918, which dismayed him because he was afraid it would create expectations of more in the same vein, whereas Holst was always looking to do something new and different. A proper composer, he said, should "pray for failure." He never considered it anywhere near his best work, but much of his other music only bewildered audiences. (He refused the suggestion of one of the work's admirers that he follow up with a suite on the wives of King Henry VIII.)

Holst's health deteriorated after a fall in 1923, and he spent his last years more and more reclusively, sometimes withdrawing deeply into himself. He continued to compose, however, until the year before his death, and he also bequeathed to the world his brilliant daughter Imogen, an outstanding teacher and musician, and author of a fascinating biography of her father.

The Planets

The seven-movement suite has nothing to do with Greek mythology, but rather the symbolic astrological meanings of the planets. The associations are self-explanatory: "Mars, the Bringer of War," etc. Despite the obscurity of much of his other music, Holst's planetary suite has soared very near the top of the classical charts, and only grows in interest with the advance of recording technology, to which it responds brilliantly. The last planet, incidentally, is Neptune (the Mystic), since Pluto had not been discovered when the music was written.

Young British conductor James Judd has made quite a splash with his brilliant 1991 digital recording, extravagantly employing the great King's College Choir for the brief choral part. The Denon label is not carried in smaller stores (so go to a bigger one!). Probably easier to find, and otherwise superior to all other recordings in sonics, is the 1986 digital performance by Charles Dutoit.

If you can forego digital, then you will want the most famous musical interpretation by Sir Adrian Boult, who led the premiere in 1918 and received the tablets directly from the composer. His seventh (!) and last recording, made when Boult was a spry ninety, and generously coupled with Elgar's "basic" Enigma Variations, is a treasure at mid-price.

Judd, Royal Philharmonic Orchestra. Denon 75076 [DDD]

Dutoit, Montreal Symphony Orchestra. London 417553 [DDD]

Boult, London Philharmonic Orchestra. EMI Studio 64748 + Elgar: *Enigma Variations* (mid-price)

Arthur Honegger (1892-1955)

Honegger is today one of the most thoroughly neglected of the great composers, which ought, I think, to make him all the more interesting to explore. He is one of those who is difficult to pinpoint, which doesn't help his popular acceptance. You can't say he is conservative or avant-garde, and there is no one of his works that is universally known. He is a composer you need to hear a great deal of before you can decide whether or not he is for you.

He was born in France, but of Swiss parents, and he kept his Swiss citizenship all his life. He was groomed as a musician from childhood and received academic training both at the Zurich and Paris Conservatories. He started attracting notice for his compositions by 1916, and was soon made notorious by his apparent association with the Group of Six *(Les Six)*, consisting of composers who supposedly shared an inconoclastic viewpoint despising both the excessive rhetoric of Romanticism and the pallid intellectualism of the atonalists.

Honegger, religious and serious by nature, was an ill fit for this group if there ever was one, for it was really little more than a concept of the music critic Henri Collet. They had no meetings, they actually shared remarkably few viewpoints, and in any case they "disbanded" not long after they allegedly got together. By the 1930s Honegger specifically renounced any association with *Les Six;* nevertheless, we still read in music textbooks that he was a leading member of this group!

Between the two world wars Honegger created a body of music that defies easy categorization. His style smacks of neo-Classicism, but he liberally employs bitonality. There are hints of Impressionism in his work, a dab of the modern Russians here and there, sharp rhythms, lots of polyphony, and references to medieval chant and French folk song. It comes out not sounding terribly individual, but not particularly derivative, either.

One minute he was writing *Pacific 231,* which describes a railroad train, or *Rugby,* a picture of the sport (which actually had its premiere in a football stadium); the next he was composing *Le Roi David,* an atmospheric if occasionally turgid oratorio based on the Bible (which was once his biggest success, but seems to have faded greatly). Whether any of this is anything we should worry about is another matter.

Reading over what I have just written it sounds as if I have a fairly low opinion of Honegger, but that is not true. He is a favorite composer of mine, partly because he is so frustratingly eclectic and elusive. What holds his work together is spirituality and serious-ness of purpose. And there is something fascinating and touching in following his journey through the history of music, trying to find his own voice. I believe future generations will find his five symphonies to be his most lasting legacy, especially the moving Second, writ-ten during the occupation of Paris during World War II.

Pacific 231

"I have always loved railway engines passionately," Honegger once unguardedly told an interviewer. "For me they are living beings, and I love them in the same way as other men love women or horses." This came back to haunt him many a time. The name and number are taken from a type of locomotive engine, although the thought of connecting it to a train actually came after the fact, for the piece was originally written simply as an exer-cise in suggesting motion in general. But audiences loved it at once, and professed to be able to hear the gentle heaving of the engine at rest, the strain of picking up speed, and finally the sleek engine thundering through the night (not the day, mind you!).

A recently issued digital disc conducted by Mariss Jansons offers a vivid reading cou-pled with two great Honegger symphonies.

Jansons, Oslo Philharmonic Orchestra. EMI 55122 [DDD] + Symphonies 2, 3

Symphony No. 2

Although Honegger worked assiduously for the Resistance during World War II, the Nazis seem to have left him alone to compose without any special hindrance. The Second Symphony has just three movements, the first in a mood of despair with a note of defiance, the second laden with lamenting. The third movement starts in agitation, and develops into what one might take to be the march of storm-troopers' boots. Then as from afar, ris-ing like a prayer over the din, is heard a trumpet nobly intoning Bach's chorale "How brightly shines the morning star." The contrast is dramatically effective, and the symphony ends with a brief burst of hope and light.

Herbert von Karajan's famous recording, paired with Symphony No. 3, is currently and maddeningly out of the catalog, but there is solace in the brilliant new recording by Mariss Jansons listed above. At mid-price, the classic early '60s version by Charles Munch is still viable, with very generous couplings at mid-price. The age of the recording is the only drawback, and it is a slight one.

> **Jansons, Oslo Philharmonic Orchestra.** EMI 55122 [DDD] + Symphony 3, *Pacific 231*
>
> **Munch, Boston Symphony Orchestra.** RCA Gold Seal 60685 [ADD] + Symphony No. 5; Milhaud: *La Création du Monde, Suite Provençale* (mid-price)

Charles Ives (1874-1954)

Ives was not only one of the great eccentrics in the history of music; he was, on the face of it, one of the most unlikely eccentrics. If I were to greet the first visitors from Mars and tell them that one of the greatest, possibly the most original, of American composers of symphonic and vocal and chamber music was the originator of "estate planning" and headed one of the nation's largest and most successful insurance agencies, I would probably be hustled aboard ship and have my tonsils removed (of course, that might happen anyway).

He was born in Danbury, Connecticut, the ninth generation from one of the original settlers of New Haven and descendant and relative of several successful business people. The major exception was Ives's father, who followed a musical career; General Ulysses S. Grant is reported to have remarked to President Lincoln that the George Ives band was the best in the entire Union Army. This remarkable man experimented in his spare time with every kind of sound combination, including polytonality and quarter-tone music, and this in the last quarter of the nineteenth—not the twentieth—century.

The elder Ives died at age forty-nine. Charles often spoke in later years of his devastation, and it is reasonable to suppose that he had a strong desire to expand on his father's efforts. Bored with the orthodoxy of his music classes at Yale, the young Ives tried out his iconoclastic ideas on the organ of the New Haven church, where he played Sunday service.

After college he married and went into the insurance business, finding it to accord with his humanitarian impulses. For twenty years, from 1898 until he suffered a severe heart attack in 1918, he composed in the evenings and on weekends. His activities were restricted thereafter, although he did not retire until 1930, and he lived to the age of seventy-nine.

Beginning in about 1922, some of Ives's music began to circulate among interested musicians, and gradually some of the works received performances and critical acclaim. In 1945 he was elected to the National Institute of Arts and Letters, and two years later his Symphony No. 3 was awarded the Pulitzer Prize—forty-two years after it was composed! (He gave the money away, commenting that "prizes are for mediocrity.")

By the 1960s his reputation had raised him to almost cult status. His works were extensively recorded and programmed and books were written about his extraordinary life, colorfully flavored with his pithy and often pungent Yankee observations. When a man in the audience booed at a concert of modern music, Ives stood up and shouted, "Stop being such a God-damned sissy!"

Much of his own music was truly decades ahead of its time in its exploration of atonalism, aleatoric ("chance") techniques, polytonal writing, and other means of expression, and by the time Ives was appreciated, all of these had become common currency through the work of other composers. Although he belatedly received the admiration he was due, many critics caution that much of his work was by nature naive and by necessity incomplete, unsophisticated, or arbitrary. It has been discovered also that some of the "modernisms" in Ives's music were "tipped in" by the composer years after the original date of composition!

Symphony No. 2

This may be easy-listening Ives, but it painlessly introduces his wild and hyper-American imagination in palatable form under the cover of a Brahmsian orchestration. It is a stew of everything from *Turkey in the Straw* to *Columbia, the Gem of the Ocean,* seasoned with wrong notes, shocking chords, bad phrasing, and general nose-thumbing, but inexplicably endearing and even, by the end, deeply moving.

Leonard Bernstein's 1958 classic recording is incomparably rousing, and sells at mid-price. Michael Tilson Thomas has a well-known digital version with the same coupling, but at full price I would stick with Bernstein and his later digital reading.

Bernstein, New York Philharmonic Orchestra. CBS 47568 [ADD] + Symphony No. 3 (mid-price)
Bernstein, New York Philharmonic Orchestra. DG 429220 [DDD] + *Central Park in the Dark, The Unanswered Question,* four other pieces

Three Places in New England

Written between 1902 and 1914 but not performed until 1930, this "cycle" of three tone poems is one of Ives's few works to appeal even to Europeans, who seem to find most of his music incomprehensible. The three "places" are: *Boston Common; Putnam's Camp, Redding, Connecticut;* and *The Housatonic* [River] *at Stockbridge.* The most famous—or infamous—moment occurs in the second piece when Ives creates the illusion of two brass bands passing each other while playing at different tempi!

Appropriately enough, the Orchestra of New England turns in an all-out Ives sampler, using the 1929 small-orchestra version of the *Three Places.* The sonics are superior; the label is not carried in every store, however. Having bumped maestro Tilson Thomas from the preceeding listing, I welcome him back here for his mid-price recording joined by other Ives works conducted by Seiji Ozawa.

Sinclair, Orchestra of New England. Koch 7025 [DDD] + other short works (many recorded for the first time)
Tilson Thomas, Boston Symphony Orchestra. DG 423243 [ADD] + Symphony No. 4, *Central Park in the Dark* (with Ozawa conducting) (mid-price)

Leoš Janáček (1854-1928)

Janáček was past sixty when he began to achieve acclaim. His opera *Jenůfa* had finally had a successful production, and his creative vigor was renewed by a love affair with a much younger woman. The diverse strands of his career now came together in one fair cloth, and at an age when many are ready to retire, he created a string of masterpieces including the Sinfonietta, two string quartets, four operas, and the *Glagolitic Mass.*

The climb to success had been not only long, but arduous. Janáček was the ninth of fourteen children born to a Moravian village schoolmaster. He eked out a living for years as a teacher and conductor, attracting little notice as a composer. He had one son and one daughter, each of whom died young. His first six decades comprised a history of personal tragedy and professional obscurity.

His boyhood training had taken place under a priest who wrote music, and he later studied organ at the College of Music in Prague; in spite of this, Janáček was at best an agnostic, and his Mass is a pantheistic celebration of nature. One critic thought that Janáček, "now that he is old and a firm believer," must have mended his ways, but the enraged composer (then seventy-two) sent the critic a postcard: "No old man, no believer." A couple of years later, near death, he augmented the statement with "till I see for myself." He refused to grow old, and one of his freshest, finest works is a wind sextet titled *Youth,* which he wrote at the age of seventy.

Janáček's unique style and sound world were formed to a great extent out of the Moravian countryside and its folk music. "I want," he once wrote, "to be in direct contact with the clouds; I want to feast my eyes on the blue of the sky; I want to gather the sun's rays into my hands, I want to plunge myself in shadow, I want to pour out my longings to the full: all directly."

He was provincial in the best sense, his personal language flowering by virtue of being isolated from the musical currents of his time. The composers who did interest and affect him were those who strove hardest to bring everyday reality into their esthetic: Leoncavallo, Mascagni, and above all Mussorgsky. These were in turn filtered through his own psyche, which was characterized by a nervous irascibility tempered by a tender compassion for the earth and its creatures.

Only in recent years has Janáček, much like his spiritual forebear Mussorgsky, been recognized for the originality and genius of his music: modern, yet eminently accessible; "primitive," yet subtle and sophisticated; romantic, yet angular and astringent. His dramatic flair blazes powerfully in his amazing operas, ranging from *The Cunning Little Vixen,* in which half the characters are animals, to *The Makropoulos Affair,* the tale of a three hundred-year-old woman, to *From the House of the Dead,* an uncompromising transcription of Dostoyevsky's portrait of life in a Siberian prison.

Sinfonietta

First performed in 1926, the work was inspired by fanfares that Janáček heard at a military band concert in a park. It is a five-movement suite with a brilliantly original and effective construction, and one of the most striking openings in all of music. These fanfares will get your attention! (And hold it.)

Virtually all major critics are uncharacteristically unanimous about the greatness of the Charles Mackerras recording, interpretively and sonically. In sound alone it stands near the top of the thousands of London recordings made over many years, and it is now at mid-price.

Mackerras, Vienna Philharmonic Orchestra. London Jubilee 430727 [DDD] + *Taras Bulba;* Shostakovich: *Age of Gold* Suite (mid-price)

Aram Khachaturian (1903-1978)

Khachaturian is the best-known composer of Armenian origin or ancestry, and yes, there are others, Richard Yardumian and Alan Hovhaness being reasonably well-known examples. And we could discuss the life and works of Gomidas Vartabed, but that definitely belongs to another book.

Khachaturian was a nationalist, folk-oriented composer who followed the Soviet party line (one of his less-loved works in the West is his *Ode to Stalin*) but managed not to have all of his creativity smothered by its restrictive demands. That alone should be cause for admiration.

He was born in Tiflis, son of a bookbinder, and had almost no formal music training until age nineteen, when he was able to enroll in a school in Moscow; he had been listening, however, even as a child, to the indigenous music surrounding him. He studied cello and composition at the Gnessin School and was subsequently admitted to the Moscow Conservatory. He was in his thirties before gaining international recognition for his single piano and violin concerti. Khachaturian's forms are loose and rhapsodic, his melodies long and sinuous, his orchestrations barbarically colorful—thus arousing the wrath of musicologists, but making a direct and welcome appeal to the average listener.

Gayne: Suite

One of the best-known modern ballets, *Gayne* (or *Gayaneh,* as it often appears in an alternative transliteration), was first performed by the Kirov Ballet in 1942. The scenario presents morally edifying themes as enacted by peasants on an Armenian collective farm. The dictates of Socialist Realism are now grist for parody, but the music continues to delight. The *Saber Dance* is only the most famous of numerous highly enjoyable dances.

Vivid recording enhances lively performances by Neeme Järvi of the ballet music, along with the delightful *Masquerade* Suite and the well-known Piano Concerto, with Armenian soloist Constantine Orbelian.

Järvi, Scottish National Orchestra. Chandos 8542 [DDD] + *Masquerade* Suite, Piano Concerto (with Orbelian)

Zoltán Kodály (1882-1967)

Kodály has been overshadowed in music history by his friend Béla Bartók, but like him he was an avid scholar of Hungarian folk music and incorporated his discoveries into original works in a colorful and memorable way. He was not as intellectual or original as Bartók, but he had plenty to offer on his own more modest terms.

Kodály spent his childhood and youth in rural Hungary, his ears catching the indigenous music of the countryside. His serious study began at age eighteen when he entered the Budapest Conservatory. It was here that he made friends with Bartók, and subsequently joined him in rummaging all over Hungary, collecting and publishing the native folk music. Kodály later wrote that "The vision of an educated Hungary, reborn from the people, rose before us." The influence of this music changed Kodály from a neo-Brahmsian composer to one of striking neo-primitivism, though of a far more genteel brand than Bartók's.

His output was relatively sparse, but it spanned nearly the whole of his venerable life. His first performed work was an overture he wrote in elementary school, and he wrote a symphony at the age of eighty. His many years of researching, teaching, and composing made him a major cultural hero in Hungary, where he was, for a long period, more honored than his expatriate colleague Bartók, not least because of his warmer and more avuncular personality. Kodály also developed a method of music education which is now used in many countries.

During World War II, Kodály, who was married to a Jew, worked for the anti-Nazi underground in his occupied country. His activities helping Jews to escape were discovered by the Gestapo, but because of his eminence and popular esteem he was left relatively unhindered. The Nazis feared a general uprising if Kodály were arrested.

Háry János: Suite

Háry János is a kind of Hungarian Baron Munchausen—an eccentric old gentlemen who vividly recalls marvellous exploits he never actually committed. His story is told in a colorful opera which is almost never heard outside of Hungary except in the orchestral suite extracted from it. The six movements showcase nearly every good quality Kodály had to offer: tenderness, humor, bracing rhythms, memorable tunes, exotic orchestration. It is an endearing memorial to a noble and intelligent artist.

The classic recording by George Szell is not likely to be surpassed, if equalled. Even though it is analog, at mid-price I would not counsel complaining. Szell seems to have had a real feeling for his fellow Hungarian conservative.

Szell, Cleveland Orchestra. CBS 38527 [ADD] + Prokofiev: *Lt. Kijé* Suite (mid-price)

Darius Milhaud (1892-1974)

Milhaud became, at the death of Ravel, the most famous French composer. He was also the most prolific (writing some six hundred works) and, in the words of his fellow composer and fervent admirer Virgil Thomson, "one of the most completely calm of modern masters."

Born in Aix-en-Provence, a beautiful and ancient town on the Mediterranean, Milhaud showed musical precocity at an early age, and studied at the Paris Conservatory with Widor and Dukas and at the Schola Cantorum with d'Indy. He became friends with the poet Paul Claudel, who was also a diplomat, and joined him for over a year as an attaché to the French legation in Brazil. There he became entranced by the tango and other indigenous music, whose spirit and form he often integrated into his later compositions. Another strong influence was American jazz, incorporation of which into concert works became a kind of specialty which enhanced his reputation in the 1920s.

After returning to France he was anointed as one of "The Six," that notorious but artificial group of composers who stood for insouciant insubordination in the world of music. He was distinguished from the others not only by his incredible industry, but by his melodic and technical fluency, personal charm, and effective use of polytonality (another specialty, as it turned out). He was, said Arthur Honegger, "the most gifted of us all." He was also noted for his wide culture and deep religiosity.

Milhaud, who proudly described himself as "a Frenchman from Provence, and by religion a Jew," fled the Nazi invasion of France with his wife in 1940, joining the faculty of Mills College in California. Although returning to France after the war, he regularly returned to the U.S., teaching at Mills and, in the summers, at Aspen, Colorado. He maintained a rigorous and active career over a long life, despite being confined to a wheelchair for more than thirty years due to severe arthritis. He is buried, as he wished, in his beloved Aix, under the Mediterranean sun.

La Création du Monde

A work for eighteen instruments, including saxophone, "The Creation of the World" is a chamber ballet telling an African story of first things. The original stage design and costumes were by Fernand Léger. The music was directly modeled after New Orleans-style jazz that Milhaud heard and closely studied while visiting Harlem.

The classic Charles Munch recording is already recommended under Arthur Honegger; a virtuoso reading at mid-price. Leonard Bernstein delivers plenty of *élan vital* on his more recent full-price recording, which also offers two characteristic Brazil-inspired works of Milhaud.

Munch, Boston Symphony Orchestra. RCA Gold Seal 60685 [ADD] + *Suite Provençale;* Honegger: Symphonies 2, 5 (mid-price)

Bernstein, National Orchestra of France. Angel 47845 + *Le Boeuf sur le toit, Saudades do Brasil*

Carl Nielsen (1865-1931)

Nielsen is one of the best examples in music of a "progressive conservative." He was not opposed to modernisms, but he saw no reason to reject the past; he cherished his freedom to use all the materials and styles that music has offered and bend them to his will. And that he was able from the humblest beginnings to rise in today's estimation to one of the great symphonists is testament to a will that was powerful indeed.

He was born of peasant stock on the Danish island of Funen, in the same year as another great Scandinavian composer, Jean Sibelius. As a youth he picked up the rudiments of music, and at eighteen enrolled in the Copenhagen Conservatory. His best instrument was the violin, which he played in the Royal Opera Orchestra until 1905, three years before he became its conductor. He also taught at the Royal Danish Conservatory, becoming its director one year before his death.

As a composer, his early influences were the German Romantics, especially Brahms. He subsumed the treasury of Danish folk music as well, but can hardly be called a nationalistic composer in the usual sense. As much as anything, he built his esthetic on his experiences with nature. He avoided schools, movements and isms; his guide was not a manual of composition, but his inner self. He mastered the tools of his trade and employed them however necessary to communicate his message.

What he had to say was essentially optimistic. His own life was as well-adjusted as any composer's ever was; he had a model marriage (no pun intended—his wife was a sculptor), many friends, and a marvelous wit which is often reflected in his music. Although there is plenty of conflict in his work, it is nearly always underpinned by a glowing faith in nature and life.

Nielsen's international recognition came well after his death, as it gradually dawned on music lovers that here was not a mere provincial, but a composer for the ages, perhaps most memorably in his six symphonies. These are works of tremendous structural integrity and often raw emotional power.

Symphony No. 4, Op. 29, "Inextinguishable"

Second only to No. 5 in fame, the Fourth Symphony consists of four movements played without break, symbolizing the perpetual overlapping growth of all life implied in the subtitle, and celebrated in the music. It was first performed in 1916.

A perfectly balanced digital recording, excitingly played under the baton of Herbert Blomstedt, leads the field. At mid-price, the clear favorite is Simon Rattle, coupled with a Nielsen tone poem and the Sibelius Fifth Symphony; a generous disc.

Blomstedt, San Francisco Symphony Orchestra. London 421524 [DDD]
+ Symphony No. 5
Rattle, Philharmonia Orchestra. Angel 64737 + *Pan and Syrinx;* Sibelius:
Symphony No. 5 (mid-price)

Symphony No. 5, Op. 50

Only two movements comprise this unique—many would say greatest—Nielsen symphony. The first encapsulates a virtual "war" between the side drum and the rest of the orchestra, a portrayal of conflict wholly original and once heard, quite unforgettable; the second movement is a foil to the first, moving on to vigorous affirmation.

The Blomstedt recording recommended just above is all one needs to start on this symphony.

Blomstedt, San Francisco Symphony Orchestra. London 421524 [DDD]
+ Symphony No. 4

Carl Orff (1892-1982)

Orff is known to the general public for only one composition, *Carmina Burana,* but it is one of the most popular works written by anyone in the twentieth century. Despite this, and the fact that he developed one of the most distinctive and instantly recognizable styles in the history of music, he has been one of the most critically reviled composers.

Orff was born in Munich and spent virtually his entire life there, scion of a family with generations of military and scholarly connections. His music studies, largely self-didactic, led him to concentrate on teaching, research, and conducting for the first half of his life. He was one of the founders of a music school in Munich in 1925, and is noted for his series *Schulwerk,* which sought to teach music to children by leading them through the evolution of Western music, starting with simple scales and rhythms. He continued teaching this method after founding the Orff Institute in Salzburg in 1961, and the system is still widely used today.

He did compose music in earlier years, mostly in imitation of other composers—particularly Schoenberg and Richard Strauss. In his early forties he repudiated these derivative works, withdrawing or destroying most of them, and abandoning the line he had previously followed from Wagner to the twelve-tone school. He looked now to the Renaissance and Baroque, especially Monteverdi and Bach, for inspiration, although he also professed admiration for Stravinsky.

In addition to *Carmina Burana* (with which, he said, "my collected works begin"), Orff wrote a number of operatic and stage works which uniquely feature large percussion ensembles and much spoken dialogue. His later style emphasizes driving, repetitive rhythms and a blend of old folk idioms with modern or even jazzy elements.

The undeniably catchy rhythms and clear melodies of Orff's music have not endeared him to classical music academics, who generally feel he panders too much to popular taste. Another complaint is that his scholarly theories are little more than simple-minded commonplaces dressed up in fancy language (his style was once characterized as "neo-Neanderthal"). Orff was further tainted in many minds by his celebrity during the Nazi period in Germany, although he denied being political and was generally considered rehabilitated after World War II.

Perhaps the fairest estimate of the composer was written in a 1956 *New Yorker* article by Winthrop Sargeant: "I am not sure how great a composer Mr. Orff is. There are times when he seems to me a sort of rich man's banjo player. But one thing about his music strikes me very forcibly; it is never tiresome or dull."

Carmina Burana

First produced in 1937, Orff's big hit was designated a "scenic cantata," and he intended it not just to be sung, but pantomimed as well with scenery on stage. The text is adapted from poems unearthed in an old monastery in the nineteenth century, revealing the monks to have been rather more worldly than their vows should allow. The title means simply "Songs of Burana," that being the old Latin name of the Bavarian town where the monastery was situated. The work itself is in three sections: "In Springtime," "In the Tavern," and "The Court of Love."

Although André Previn, Eugen Jochum, and Seiji Ozawa have all led outstanding versions, this work cries out for spectacular sonics as well as good interpretation, and the current standout must be Herbert Blomstedt in digital. If you are scrimping, the least painful way is to get Eugene Ormandy's outstanding 1960 version, remastered, at budget price. It is one of that maestro's best recordings out of hundreds.

Blomstedt, San Francisco Symphony Orchestra and Chorus. London 430509 [DDD]

Ormandy, Philadelphia Orchestra, Rutgers University Choir. Sony 47668 [ADD] (budget)

Francis Poulenc (1899-1963)

Poulenc was called by a friend, in a bit of French overstatement, "part monk, part guttersnipe." Certainly he was a mass of contradictions—one moment deeply religious and serious, the next frivolously impudent—both in his life and music; his compositions ranged from the *Four Motets for a Time of Penitence* to a song cycle called *Banalités*. The fastidious and the ludicrous were equal components of his manner and method.

Born into a well-to-do family, Poulenc showed outstanding musical ability as a youth and studied piano with Ricardo Viñes, the most famous interpreter of Debussy's keyboard works. His formal training after that was spotty, but he began to attract notice with his piquant compositions and his association with the group of *enfants terribles* known as "Les Six," which also included Milhaud and Honegger.

His dog face and droll wit endeared him to French high society, among whom he spent many evening hours at parties, where he absorbed that heightened sense of the ridiculous which peeks out from so many of his works. On the other hand, the death of a dear friend in a car accident in 1936 led Poulenc to a revival of his childhood Catholic piety, which informs other of his compositions, most notably his moving opera *Dialogues des Carmelites*.

He wrote little in the way of purely orchestral or symphonic works, preferring the marriage of words and music, which he called "an act of love." He wrote a large number of songs, almost all for his friend, the baritone Pierre Bernac, and they are among the finest written in the twentieth century. He also excelled in short piano works, choral music, and ballet.

His often casual and breezy style was looked at askance by many critics. "When he has nothing to say," wrote David Drew of Poulenc, "he says it." But this composer was seldom seeking to utter profundities. He looked upon himself as an entertainer, and said that in his opinion, music "should humbly seek to please." Those who can appreciate an art devoid of bombast and enlivened by irreverence, always accessible to the lay listener, may find a kindred soul in Poulenc.

Concerto in G Minor for Organ, Strings, and Timpani

Popular, oddly enough, almost everywhere but France, Poulenc's Organ Concerto was written in 1938. It was commissioned, as were other works, by a notable patron of the arts, the Princesse Edmond de Polignac (who was, more prosaically, an heiress of the Singer Sewing Machine Company fortune). It is neo-Baroque in concept.

A recent digital release with organist Peter Hurford, conducted by Charles Dutoit, brings out the sonic splendor to the full, and presents Poulenc's piano concerti with the outstanding Pascal Rogé. The classic Maurice Duruflé performance, conducted by Georges Prêtre, is aptly coupled with the "basic" Gloria and another choral work, but a 1963 recording is not wholly justifiable at full price.

Hurford, Dutoit, Philharmonia Orchestra. London 436546 [DDD] + Piano Concerto, 2-Piano Concerto (with Rogé)
Duruflé, Prêtre, ORTF Orchestra. EMI 47723 [ADD] + *Gloria, 4 Motets for a Time of Penitence*

Gloria in G

The Koussetitzky Foundation commissioned this work, a twentieth-century tribute to Vivaldi. It is distinguished by melodic beauty, rhythmic variety, and a unique atmosphere comprising both gaiety and mystery. Few moments in music are more spontaneously joyful than the *Laudamus Te* section of the Poulenc *Gloria*.

There is no adequate low-price version of this work, so the choices are between Leonard Bernstein's very good performance with highly desirable couplings, or the older but even better-played and sung Prêtre recording. Both are analog.

Bernstein, New York Philharmonic Orchestra. CBS 44710 [ADD] + Stravinsky: *Symphony of Psalms;* Bernstein: *Chichester Psalms*
Prêtre, ORTF Orchestra and Chorus. EMI 47723 [ADD] + Organ Concerto (with Duruflé), *4 Motets for a Time of Penitence*

Serge Prokofiev (1891-1953)

By one measure, Prokofiev could be considered the greatest composer of the twentieth century, for he wrote at least one acknowledged masterpiece in most of the standard forms:
Symphony (Nos. 1 and 5)
Piano Concerto (No. 3)
Piano Sonata (No. 6)
Violin Concerto (No. 1)
Violin Sonata (No. 2)
Ballet *(Romeo and Juliet)*
Opera *(War and Peace)*
Orchestral suite *(Scythian Suite)*
to suggest a few. And just for an encore, he created some of the greatest film scores (e.g. *Ivan the Terrible, Alexander Nevsky*), turning those into great cantatas as well, and topping it all off by writing a masterpiece of children's music, *Peter and the Wolf.* Although few musicologists would actually rate Prokofiev above Stravinsky or Bartók, I would suggest that despite his fame and popularity, he is still not taken as seriously as he deserves.

Paradox and irony were virtually life principles for Prokofiev. He was one of the first major artists to leave the Soviet Union after the 1917 revolution, and one of the few to return of his free will. After he returned he was widely regarded in the West as a Russian propagandist, while in his homeland he came under severe censure for creating "cacophony" and for appealing to "distorted tastes." He was one of the few great composers since Mahler to invest his music with humor, but he could match anyone in the evocation of poignant sorrow. He could be one of the most uncompromisingly dissonant of composers, or one of the most lyrical and romantic.

Prokofiev was born in comfortable circumstances in Ukraine and was a happy, gifted child. He wrote his first work, called "Hindu Galop," at age five, and by nine had completed two (!) operas in piano score. He was admitted to the St. Petersburg Conservatory at age thirteen, studying there with Liadov, Rimsky-Korsakov, and Tcherepnin, the last-named giving his young pupil a taste for many styles, from Haydn to the moderns.

He began to experiment with modern harmonies and orchestration, finding in them a distinctive language in which to express his vein of fantasy and irony, often veering towards the acerbic (one of his piano suites is frankly titled *Sarcasms*). Some of the more avant-garde works, such as the Symphony No. 2, are hard on the ears even today; John Michel, music director of Minnesota Public Radio, once called listening to it "like going around in a washing machine with a bunch of rocks." At the premiere of the *Scythian* Suite (1916), conservative composer Alexander Glazunov ran from the hall, his hands over his ears, and one of the violinists in the orchestra told a friend, "My wife is sick and I have to buy medicine; otherwise I would never agree to play this crazy music."

Prokofiev left Russia in 1918 to undertake a U.S. tour. His brilliant piano playing was applauded, but his compositions were condemned as "Bolshevism in music." He spent the 1920s in Paris, where his style was found far more acceptable, even chic. After fifteen years abroad he returned to the Soviet Union, where he remained until his death, mixing and matching his output—i.e., composing works of originality and integrity alongside frankly jingoistic garbage designed to placate the Soviet censors.

At its best, Prokofiev's sound is distinctive, his melodies and rhythms being especially memorable. He possessed both wit and warmth, despite his early reputation for acidic irony and grotesquerie. And in an era when so many composers were preoccupied with theories, messages, and attitudes, he composed prolifically as one who simply felt and understood music instinctively and had a natural communicative power.

Alexander Nevsky, Op. 78

Sergei Eisenstein's classic 1938 epic historical film was scored by Prokofiev, who later created this cantata from various elements in the original, augmented by a text drawn up by Prokofiev and a collaborator. It is written for mezzo-soprano, chorus and orchestra, and is a work of truly cinematic power. The final chorus, "Alexander's Entry into Pskov," is thrilling enough to make you into a Russian patriot, at least for a few minutes.

Claudio Abbado's digital recording brings out the epic qualities vividly. A budget two-disc set by Leonard Slatkin is also a fine performance, and offers in addition Prokofiev's other "film cantata," *Ivan the Terrible*. Both recordings add the *Lt. Kijé* Suite.

Abbado, London Symphony Orchestra and Chorus. DG 419603 [DDD] + *Lt. Kijé* Suite

L. Slatkin, St. Louis Symphony Orchestra and Chorus. Vox Box 5021 (2) [ADD] + *Lt. Kijé* Suite, *Ivan the Terrible* (budget)

Concerto No. 3 in C for Piano, Op. 26

Bravura and sophistication characterize Prokofiev's most popular concerto, which had its premiere in Chicago about the same time as his ill-fated opera, *The Love for Three*

Oranges, in 1921. It is recognizably Russian in its lyricism, fervor and drama, although without the more extravagant gestures of the Romantics.

The outstanding digital recording is by pianist Santiago Rodriguez, not yet a household name. Nor is his label, Elan, but a search is worth it, as well for the coupling. Gary Graffman's late-60s recording with George Szell is a classic at mid-price, rivaled only by Martha Argerich under Claudio Abbado, though this analog recording, not even remastered, is still at full price.

Rodriguez, Tabakov, Sofia Philharmonic Orchestra. Elan 2220 [DDD] + Rachmaninoff: Piano Concerto No. 3
Graffman, Szell, Cleveland Orchestra. CBS 37806 [ADD] + Piano Concerto No. 1, Piano Sonata No. 3 (mid-price)
Argerich, Abbado, Berlin Philharmonic Orchestra. DG 415062 [AAD] + Tchaikovsky: Piano Concerto No. 1 (with Dutoit conducting)

Lieutenant Kijé Suite, Op. 60

A misplaced punctuation mark accidentally "creates" a (fictitious) Lieutenant Kijé, whose existence must then be documented to avoid embarrassing the Tsar. Such is the droll conceit of a 1933 film for which Prokofiev was perfectly suited to write the music. The suite takes the imaginary hero from birth to death, all tongue in cheek.

The two recordings recommended above under *Alexander Nevsky* are useful here, plus the George Szell disc listed under Zoltán Kodály. But one cannot omit one of Eugene Ormandy's finest recordings, with generous "basic" couplings, at a budget price.

Abbado, London Symphony Orchestra. DG 419603 [DDD] + *Alexander Nevsky*
Ormandy, Philadelphia Orchestra. CBS Odyssey 39783 [ADD] + *Love for Three Oranges* Suite, Symphony No. 1 (budget)
Szell, Cleveland Orchestra. CBS 38527 [ADD] + Kodály: *Háry János* Suite (mid-price)
L. Slatkin, St. Louis Symphony Orchestra. Vox Box 5021 (2) [ADD] + *Alexander Nevsky, Ivan the Terrible* (budget)

The Love for Three Oranges: Suite, Op. 33b

The full-length satirical fairytale opera from which the suite derives was written in America, premiering in Chicago in 1921 to booing and hissing. It is still seldom heard today, quite unjustly, for it is filled with wonderful music. Ironically, the famous *March* of this patriotic Soviet composer served for many years in the U.S. as the theme of the popular radio and television show, *The FBI in Peace and War.*

The Ormandy disc listed just above is choice here, but another bargain is the three-disc set of music of Prokofiev and Stravinsky conducted outstandingly by Stanislav Skrowaczewski.

Ormandy, Philadelphia Orchestra. CBS Odyssey 39783 [ADD] + *Lt. Kijé* Suite, Symphony No. 1 (budget)

Skrowaczewski, Minnesota Orchestra. Vox Box 3016 (3) [ADD] + *Romeo and Juliet* (sel.), *Scythian Suite;* Stravinsky: *Firebird* Suite, *Petrushka, Le Sacre du printemps* (budget)

Peter and the Wolf, Op. 67

The famous tale of heroic Peter and his animal friends (and enemy) was written by Prokofiev himself. A narrator speaks between and over the musical parts, in which each character is labeled with a signature theme and further identified by a specific instrument or group of instruments: Peter is a string quartet, the cat is a clarinet, the wolf is three French horns, and so on.

Sir John Gielgud is the distinguished narrator on a recent disc conducted by Richard Stamp and designed for a young audience; proceeds of the album benefit handicapped children. Another good digital choice is the André Previn disc, with the conductor narrating. Double duty also falls to Leonard Bernstein on his classic 60s version, now at mid-price.

Gielgud, Stamp, Academy of London. Virgin Classics 59333 [DDD] + Saint-Saëns: *Carnival of the Animals;* Mozart: *Eine Kleine Nachtmusik*

Previn, Royal Philharmonic Orchestra. Telarc 80126 [DDD] + Britten: *Young Person's Guide to the Orchestra, Courtly Dances* from *Gloriana*

Bernstein, New York Philharmonic Orchestra. CBS 37765 + Saint-Saëns: *Carnival of the Animals* (mid-price)

Romeo and Juliet, Op. 64

Prokofiev actually arranged and conducted the suites before the complete ballet was ever staged. It had been written for the Kirov Ballet but was unaccountably shelved for several years. Finally, in 1940 it achieved a production followed by international fame, and today it is generally acknowledged as the greatest full-length ballet composed since Tchaikovsky.

For a single digital disc of highlights, the consensus falls on conductor Esa-Pekka

Salonen. At a budget price, the Skrowaczewski recommended elsewhere is not only a bargain, it is also a superior performance.

Salonen, Berlin Philharmonic Orchestra. Sony 42662 [DDD]

Skroweczewski, Minnesota Orchestra. Vox Bos 3016 (3) [ADD] + *Love for Three Oranges* Suite; Stravinsky: *Firebird* Suite, *Petrushka, Le Sacre du printemps* (budget)

Symphony No. 1 in D, Op. 25, "Classical"

Prokofiev's intention here was to create a work that might have been written by Haydn had he been born in Russia in the twentieth century. Its bracing instrumentation and lively synthesis of old and new have made it a concert favorite.

Herbert von Karajan's recording comes with the Symphony No. 5, which is the headliner of the disc. The others listed below have been previously recommended for their couplings. The Orpheus Chamber Orchestra version is to be preferred for both performance and sound if the couplings please. André Previn's well-known recording, coupled with Symphony No. 5 like Karajan's, is currently unavailable.

Orpheus Chamber Orchestra. DG 423624 [DDD] + Bizet: Symphony in C; Britten: *Simple Symphony*

Ormandy, Philadelphia Orchestra. CBS Odyssey 39783 [ADD] + *Lt. Kijé* Suite, *Love for Three Oranges* Suite (budget)

Solti, Chicago Symphony Orchestra. London Jubilee 430446 + Mussorgsky: *Pictures at an Exhibition;* Tchaikovsky: *Overture 1812* (mid-price)

Karajan, Berlin Philharmonic Orchestra. DG 437253 + Symphony No. 5 (mid-price)

Symphony No. 5, Op. 100

Written during World War II, the Fifth Symphony is a broad and heroic work inspired by the self-sacrifice of the Russian people. Basically noble in tone throughout, its progress is colored with occasional melancholy, but concludes in jubilation.

The Herbert von Karajan recording mentioned above under Symphony No. 1 is the best, and indeed only, choice I could offer here, the Previn version being out of print at this time. It is a classic reading.

Karajan, Berlin Philharmonic Orchestra. DG 437253 + Symphony No. 1 (mid-price)

Sergei Rachmaninoff (1873-1943)

Rachmaninoff is the best possible illustration of how unsatisfactory it is to lump all the composers of the twentieth century into the "modern" category. Although his creative career encompassed all the discoveries and revolutions of Debussy, Stravinsky, Schoenberg and the rest, he completely ignored them. Every bar of his music could have been written by a contemporary of Tchaikovsky, and hardly anyone would notice the difference. For this reason he has never been a favorite of critics, who are paid to notice people who do completely new and outrageous things, although he has become one of the most beloved composers of the general public.

The fifth of six children, Rachmaninoff at first grew up pampered by a doting mother and an aristocratic father who was an excellent pianist. However, hard times came when Sergei was only nine; his parents separated, and only a year later he was enrolled in the St. Petersburg Conservatory. In two more years he was off to the more prestigious Moscow Conservatory, where he made rapid progress in piano and composition while often chafing under the drudgery of routine lessons and rigid discipline.

At first he struggled at trying to make a living at music. A success here and there would be more than offset by a fiasco, such as that which greeted his first symphony. He often sank into depressions which interrupted his work (Stravinsky once described him as "six feet of gloom"). He had to undergo three months of hypnosis before he could resume work on his great Piano Concerto No. 2. He did, however, manage to sustain a lifelong happy marriage.

In 1918 Rachmaninoff and his family sailed for America, leaving behind a Bolshevik society with which they had no sympathy. From then until his death, Rachmaninoff would be especially active as a concert pianist—one of a handful of the greatest of all time. He recorded all of his performances of his own concerti and continued composing, although his muse seemed to wane in later years.

In 1931 he bought a house in Switzerland, on Lake Lucerne, where he was able to enjoy his passion for speedboats and fast cars. He sent money to causes he supported in Russia and eventually was "forgiven" by the Soviet authorities for writing "decadent bourgeois" music.

Despite his often unfavorable reputation among musicologists which was caused by his utter lack of interest in inventing anything new, Rachmaninoff was a more than competent musical architect, an inspired melodist, and a great orchestrator. He set high standards for himself, and although his music may be conservative relative to that of his contemporaries, it is not trivial or weak in any way.

Fifty years have passed since the experts were predicting a swift oblivion for Rachmaninoff. "Artificial and gushing," was the description of his music in one edition (now revised) of the venerable *Grove's Dictionary of Music and Musicians*. "The enormously popular success some few of Rachmaninoff's works had in his lifetime is not likely to last," the author droned on. But half a century later, Rachmaninoff is more popular than ever, and has taken his place in the pantheon of great composers as firmly as most of the Old Masters.

Concerto No. 2 in C Minor for Piano, Op. 18

"Full Moon and Empty Arms" was the 1940s hit pop song cribbed from the last movement of this most romantic of all piano concerti. Nevertheless, it has survived all efforts to water it down, and despite its melodic prodigality and lush scoring, it has enough integrity to keep the vultures well away from its long-predicted demise. If you do not want to leap to your feet cheering at the last dramatic bars of this music, you are probably not cut out for Rachmaninoff's world.

There are so many superlatively great analog recordings of this work that for a digital recording, one must turn to a relatively unknown artist on the budget Naxos label for a worthwhile recording; but Jenö Jandó is more than respectable and holds his own with the more august names.

The Byron Janis, Earl Wild, and Vladimir Ashkenazy recordings are particularly attractive at mid-price. The Van Cliburn and Artur Rubinstein performances are legendary, but the record companies are going to charge you for that well-known fact.

Janis, Dorati, Minneapolis Symphony Orchestra. Mercury 432759 [ADD] + Piano Concerto No. 3, Prelude in C-sharp Minor, etc. (mid-price)

Wild, Horenstein, Royal Philharmonic Orchestra. Chandos 6507 [ADD] + Piano Concerto No. 3 (mid-price)

Ashkenazy, Previn, London Symphony Orchestra. London Jubilee 417702 [ADD] + *Rhapsody on a Theme of Paganini* (mid-price)

Cliburn, Reiner, Chicago Symphony Orchestra. RCA 55912 [ADD] + Tchaikovsky: Piano Concerto No. 1

Rubinstein, Reiner, Chicago Symphony Orchestra. RCA 4934 [ADD] + *Rhapsody on a Theme of Paganini*

Jandó, Lehel, Budapest Symphony Orchestra. Naxos 8.550117 [DDD] + *Rhapsody on a Theme of Paganini* (budget)

Concerto No. 3 in D Minor for Piano, Op. 30

The composer was the soloist at the premiere in New York City in 1909. Walter Damrosch conducted on that occasion, but a month later the orchestra was led by no less than Gustav Mahler. As fervent as anything by Rachmaninoff, the third piano concerto is actually quite similar to the second, only denser and more difficult to play. Incidentally, the composer stopped playing it after he heard Vladimir Horowitz, seeing that he had been beaten at his own game.

There is a fully recommendable digital version for this one in the person of Santiago Rodriguez, recommended earlier under Prokofiev. Analog editions include two from the list just above, with the addition of Vladimir Horowitz in his 1951 recording with Reiner, to be preferred over the disappointing 1978 Ormandy recording.

Rodriguez, Tabakov, Sofia Philharmonic Orchestra. Elan 2220 [DDD] + Prokofiev: Piano Concerto No. 3

Horowitz, Reiner, RCA Symphony Orchestra. RCA 7754 [ADD] + Piano Sonata No. 2, three short pieces (mid-price)

Janis, Dorati, London Symphony Orchestra. Mercury 432759 [ADD] + Piano Concerto No. 2, Prelude in C-sharp Minor, etc. (mid-price)

Wild, Horenstein, Royal Philharmonic Orchestra. Chandos 6507 [ADD] + Piano Concerto No. 2 (mid-price)

Rhapsody on a Theme of Paganini, Op. 43

Rachmaninoff took the 24th Caprice for solo violin of Niccolò Paganini as the theme for this set of twenty-four variations, in which the theme is frequently contrasted with the *Dies Irae* melody from Gregorian Chant. This ostensible tribute to the violinist/composer who was often alleged to be the Devil, with reference to the end of the world as described in the medieval Requiem liturgy, is actually one of Rachmaninoff's more light-hearted compositions! Perhaps only a man so naturally lachrymose could make dismal things seem so cheerful. The 18th variation, by the way, is the "famous" one, and there truly is no passage of Romantic music more Romantic.

Three recordings already listed under Piano Concerto No. 2 should suffice here for the beginning collector:

Ashkenazy, Previn, London Symphony Orchestra. London Jubilee 417702 [ADD] + Piano Concerto No. 2 (mid-price)

Rubinstein, Reiner, Chicago Symphony Orchestra. RCA 4934 [ADD] + Piano Concerto No. 2

Jandó, Lehel, Budapest Symphony Orchestra. Naxos 8.550117 [DDD] + Piano Concerto No. 2 (budget)

Symphony No. 2 in E Minor, Op. 27

The composer conducted the first performance in 1908. The symphony was an instant success, and remains one of the most beloved in the standard repertoire. Often suffused with melancholy, it is resplendent with hard-won affirmation at the end.

Two richly rewarding digital versions are on slightly hard-to-find labels, conducted by Andrew Litton and Gennady Rozhdestvensky. The André Previn classic, his first and best of three recordings, is easy to find and mid-price besides.

Litton, Royal Philharmonic Orchestra. Virgin Classics 59548 [DDD] + *Vocalise*

Rozhdestvensky, London Symphony Orchestra. IMP PD 904 [DDD]

Previn, London Symphony Orchestra. RCA Silver Seal 60791 [ADD] + *The Rock* (mid-price)

Maurice Ravel (1875-1937)

Ravel was the most elegant composer of the century; maybe of all time. His dapper wardrobe and wavy hair were a perfect foil to his finely-wrought music, which Stravinsky called the product of "a Swiss clockmaker." Indeed, Ravel openly sought technical perfection, fully aware that no one ever achieves it. His music is as meticulously chiseled as were his own Basque cheekbones, but the oft-heard implication that his music is therefore dry and unfeeling is disproved by a few minutes' listening.

The son of a railway engineer, Ravel began piano lessons at age seven. He spent fifteen years at the Paris Conservatory, studying with Gabriel Fauré among others. By 1905 he had composed several fine works, including the *Pavane for a Dead Princess* and his Quartet in F, yet four years in a row he was passed over for the prestigious Prix de Rome which he had hoped to win. Finally there was such an uproar from prominent musicians across France that the Conservatory's director, Théodore Dubois, was forced to resign (he was replaced by Fauré).

Two years later, scandal again put Ravel in the spotlight when a song cycle he had written stirred accusations that he was plagiarizing Debussy, a charge long since dropped by the jury of history. In any case, Ravel was now famous, and lived up to his reputation by turning out a succession of masterpieces. By World War I he was widely acknowledged as France's greatest composer—even though he was wholly Basque and Swiss by descent.

Ravel was hardly over five feet in height. He was emotionally reserved; he never married, but loved children and animals, seeming to be more comfortable with them than with adult humans. His small villa was filled with tiny curios and mechanical toys which he loved to show off to a select circle of friends. He loved good food and strong cigarettes.

In 1932 he suffered a slight injury in a taxi accident. Within a few months he began experiencing strange symptoms: his muscles seemed to atrophy, he could barely hold a pen, and eventually he was paralyzed. Suspecting a brain tumor, surgeons operated on him. No tumor was found, but in a few days Ravel was dead.

Alborada del gracioso

Somewhat clumsily translated as "The Jester's Morning Song," this virtuosic evocation of strumming guitars and bursting sunrise is Ravel's orchestration of one of five pieces for solo piano originally published as *Miroirs,* a word somewhat clumsily pronounced by English speakers.

Charles Dutoit leads the pack in digital in one of his very finest recordings (which is going some), but is admirably challenged by Jesus Lopez-Cobos in brilliant sound on Telarc, with the same program plus one extra piece of music. The mid-price list is topped by great performances from Fritz Reiner and Paul Paray in analog.

Dutoit, Montreal Symphony Orchestra. London 410010 [DDD] + *Boléro, Rapsodie espagnole, La Valse*

Lopez-Cobos, Cincinnati Symphony Orchestra. Telarc 80171 [DDD] + *Boléro, Rapsodie espagnole, La Valse, Valses nobles et sentimentales*

Reiner, Chicago Symphony Orchestra. RCA Gold Seal 60179 [ADD] + *Pavane for a Dead Princess, Rapsodie espagnole, Valses nobles et sentimentales;* Debussy: *Ibéria* from *Images pour orchestre* (mid-price)

Paray, Detroit Symphony Orchestra. Mercury 432003 [ADD] + *Pavane for a Dead Princess, Rapsodie espagnole, La Valse, Le Tombeau de Couperin;* Ibert: *Escales* (mid-price)

Boléro

"Yes, it is my masterpiece," an exasperated Ravel once snapped to Honegger, "unfortunately, it contains no music." *Boléro* was written to be danced by Ida Rubinstein, who starred in the balletic premiere of 1928. It was premiered two years earlier as a concert piece by Arturo Toscanini and brought the audience cheering to its feet. Since then it has remained at or very near the top of the Classical Hit Parade, and has become associated in the popular mind as the ultimate in chic sensuality.

The current general catalog spread out before me shows seventy-three recordings of *Boléro* currently in print. Naturally, there are many worthy discs among them, but it is fairly easy to pick out three or four of particular merit on musical, sonic, and repertoire grounds. Charles Dutoit has two recordings at different prices depending on couplings, and his *Boléro* is the equal of any in very brilliant sound. The digital Lopez-Cobos disc listed above returns here, and is joined by the classic Herbert von Karajan recording from the mid-60s at mid-price. You may buy any *Boléro* you wish, but I am trying to keep it simple!

Dutoit, Montreal Symphony Orchestra. London 430714 [DDD] + *Daphnis et Chloe* Suite No. 2, *Pavane for a Dead Princess, La Valse* (mid-price)

Dutoit, Montreal Symphony Orchestra. London 410010 [DDD] + *Alborada del gracioso, Rapsodie espagnole, La Valse*

Lopez-Cobos, Cincinnati Symphony Orchestra. Telarc 80171 [DDD] + *Alborado del gracioso, Rapsodie espagnole, La Valse, Valses nobles et sentimentales*

Karajan, Berlin Philharmonic Orchestra. DG 427250 [ADD] + *Daphnis et Chloe* Suite No. 2; Debussy: *La Mer, Prelude to the Afternoon of a Faun* (mid-price)

Concerto in G for Piano

French clarity is joined here with jazzy riffs to create a piano concerto with two crisp outer movements enclosing a nocturne that ripples like a moonlit lake. Ravel conducted the first performance in 1932, with Marguerite Long at the piano.

The current goddess of this work is Spanish pianist Alicia De Larrocha. Her current in-print digital version is conducted by Leonard Slatkin.

De Larrocha, L. Slatkin, St. Louis Symphony Orchestra. RCA 60985 [DDD] + Concerto for the Left Hand, *Valses nobles et sentimentales,* Sonatine

Daphnis et Chloe

Premiered in 1912, Ravel's masterpiece was commissioned by the impresario Serge Diaghilev as a vehicle for his ballet superstar, Vaslav Nijinsky. The book is based on the Greek myth of two rustic lovers who are separated, then reunited by the god Pan. The work's proportions are as elegant as any Greek temple, its orchestration the most shimmering of Ravel's career, the flow and surge of evocative harmony and melody irresistible, and the finale, in which sheets of sound crash over the consciousness like Aegean tidal waves, is overwhelming. Ravel created two suites from the complete score, of which No. 2 is most often heard as an independent concert piece.

Charles Dutoit is in first place again, both with the complete ballet and the suite. The complete recording was one of the great early digital recordings. The sound and performance are still entrancing. Another choice for the Suite No. 2 is Herbert von Karajan, on a mid-price disc already listed under *Boléro* and elsewhere.

Dutoit, Montreal Symphony Orchestra. Suite No. 2, London 430714 [DDD] + *Boléro, Pavane for a Dead Princess, La Valse* (mid-price)
Dutoit, Montreal Symphony Orchestra. Complete ballet, London 400055 [DDD]
Karajan, Berlin Philharmonic Orchestra. Suite No. 2, DG 427250 [ADD] + *Boléro;* Debussy: *La Mer, Prelude to the Afternoon of a Faun* (mid-price)

Pavane pour une infante défunte (Pavane for a Dead Princess)

As with many Ravel orchestral hits, this one started life as a piano solo, written when he was only twenty-one. It was orchestrated in 1910 and was an immediate success. When asked the significance of the title, Ravel replied that he just liked the way it sounded. In response to a student who played the piano version too slowly, he is reported to have said "Please remember that I have written a pavane for a deceased princess, not a deceased pavane for a princess."

All of the listed recordings have been recommended elsewhere, so I shall just list them:

Reiner, Chicago Symphony Orchestra. RCA Gold Seal 60179 [ADD] + *Alborada del gracioso, Rapsodie espagnole, Valses nobles et sentimentales;* Debussy: *Ibéria* from *Images pour orchestre* (mid-price)

Paray, Detroit Symphony Orchestra. Mercury 432003 [ADD] + *Alborada del gracioso, Rapsodie espagnole, Le Tombeau de Couperin, La Valse;* Ibert: *Escales* (mid-price)

Dutoit, Montreal Symphony Orchestra. London 430714 [DDD] + *Boléro, Daphnis et Chloe* Suite No. 2, *La Valse* (mid-price)

Giulini, Philharmonia Orchestra. DG 419243 [DDD] + Fauré: *Requiem*

Bernstein, New York Philharmonic Orchestra. CBS 37769 [ADD] + Dukas: *Sorcerer's Apprentice;* Saint-Saëns: *Danse macabre, Bacchanale from Samson et Dalila;* Chabrier: *España;* Offenbach: Overture to *Orpheus in the Underworld* (mid-price)

Quartet in F

Despite charges that Ravel copied Debussy, this Quartet is one of his few works to betray any direct influence. In any case, he dedicated it not to Debussy, but to Fauré. It is a work of ingenious refinement; the critic Roland-Manuel proclaimed it "a miracle of grace and tenderness."

The best-known recording is by the Italian Quartet (Quartetto Italiano), a 1965 classic now at mid-price. The Guarneri Quartet are an excellent alternate at the same price level, and with a bonus piece by Debussy. The best digital recording is by the Alban Berg Quartet. All are coupled with the Debussy Quartet.

Italian Quartet. Philips Silver Line 420894 [ADD] + Debussy: Quartet in G Minor (mid-price)

Guarneri Quartet. RCA Silver Seal 60909 [ADD] + Debussy: Quartet in G Minor, *Suite Bergamasque* (with Alexis Weissenberg) (mid-price)

Alban Berg Quartet. EMI 47347 [DDD] + Debussy: Quartet in G Minor

Rapsodie espagnole

Published in 1907, this work established Ravel as a master of orchestration as well as an authentic Spanish style, endorsed by no less an expert than Manuel de Falla (q.v.). The four sections are labeled *Prelude to the Night, Malagueña, Habañera,* and *Festival.*

Four fine recordings have already been recommended above:

Dutoit, Montreal Symphony Orchestra. London 410010 [DDD] + *Alborado del gracioso, Boléro, La Valse*

Lopez-Cobos, Cincinnati Symphony Orchestra. Telarc 80171 [DDD] + *Alborada del gracioso, Boléro, La Valse, Valses nobles et sentimentales*

Reiner, Chicago Symphony Orchestra. RCA Gold Seal 60179 [ADD] + *Alborada del gracioso, Pavane for a Dead Princess, Valses nobles et sentimentales;* Debussy: *Ibéria* from *Images pour orchestre* (mid-price)

Paray, Detroit Symphony Orchestra. Mercury 432003 [ADD] + *Alborada del gracioso, Pavane for a Dead Princess, Le Tombeau de Couperin, La Valse;* Ibert: *Escales* (mid-price)

La Valse

One of Ravel's most popular orchestral works, the exact intent of the piece is uncertain. It is usually interpreted as a kind of remembrance of the Viennese waltz in a lovely but gradually more disturbed dream, then brutally shattered at the end as, presumably, World War I breaks out with the crack of a gun.

Superior versions listed below have all been recommended elsewhere above:

Dutoit, Montreal Symphony Orchestra. London 430714 [DDD] + *Boléro, Pavane for a Dead Princess, Daphnis et Chloe* Suite No. 2 (mid-price)

Dutoit, Montreal Symphony Orchestra. London 410010 [DDD] + *Alborada del gracioso, Boléro, Rapsodie espagnole*

Lopez-Cobos, Cincinnati Symphony Orchestra. Telarc 80171 [DDD] + *Alborada del gracioso, Boléro, Rapsodie espagnole, Valses nobles et sentimentales*

Paray, Detroit Symphony Orchestra. Mercury 432003 [ADD] + *Alborada del gracioso, Pavane for a Dead Princess, Le Tombeau de Couperin;* Ibert: *Escales* (mid-price)

Ottorino Respighi (1879-1936)

Respighi was the leading exponent of Impressionism in Italy, although his talent was not comparable to Debussy's. He was the author of a great deal of music that borders on the tawdry, but at his best he was a brilliant orchestrator and arranger.

Respighi was born into a musical family, studied at first with his father, and later on with both Max Bruch and Nikolai Rimsky-Korsakov. Eventually he became a professor of composition at the famous Academy of Saint Cecilia in Rome, and was appointed its director in 1923.

He was among the few Italian composers who emphasized symphonic music over opera, although he wrote several of those as well. He was a talented scene painter, as his three famous tone poems attest, but also a wonderful transcriber of other people's music, as in the *Ancient Airs* and his colorful ballet *La Boutique fantasque*, after Rossini.

Respighi would be more comfortably numbered among the Late Romantics than among the Moderns, had he not been born so late. He had little interest in twentieth century techniques of composition. "Why," he once asked an interviewer, "should I use new techniques when one still has so much to say through the language of conventional music?" To be sure, one does find in Respighi the occasional snippet of avant-gardism, but it never forms an essential part of his style. For the most part that is a result of blending the influences of Richard Strauss, the Impressionists, and the Russian nationalists. Eclectic perhaps, but often vastly entertaining.

Ancient Airs and Dances

In Respighi's day, most of the Italian Renaissance composers were entirely unknown to the general public, and preserving their work through modern orchestral transcriptions could be seen as a perfectly reasonable act of homage. Many such arrangements have disappeared in recent years as the original music has been restored and performed on authentic instruments, yet Respighi's three suites of *Ancient Airs and Dances* have survived quite vigorously. This is because they are transcriptions of a very high order, and can stand as independent, interesting works right alongside the originals.

If you can find it, the Omega recording (from Vanguard Records) is an amazing "sleeper," featuring the Australian Chamber Orchestra conducted by Christopher Gee. Every major critic has raved about the charming performance and the superior sonics of the disc. Easier to obtain and very well done is the Jesus Lopez-Cobos version. Antal Dorati is superb at mid-price, noting that there is no filler.

> **Gee, Australian Chamber Orchestra.** Omega 1007 [DDD] + *The Birds:* Suite
> **Lopez-Cobos, Lausanne Chamber Orchestra.** Telarc 80309 [DDD] + *Botticelli Tryptych*
> **Dorati, Philharmonia Hungarica.** Mercury 434304 [ADD]

Fountains of Rome; Pines of Rome; Roman Festivals

Respighi's three famous tone poems were written at different times, but form a natural tryptych and are often recorded as a group. These works clearly echo Respighi's lessons with Rimsky-Korsakov. *The Fountains of Rome* is the earliest piece, first performed in 1917, and remains the most popular. It was inspired by four of Rome's many beautiful fountains, whose names are attached to each of the movements of the music. *The Pines of Rome*, conceived as a sequel to the earlier work, was first heard in 1924 and has similar pictorial associations. Arturo Toscanini led the first performance of *Roman Festivals*, an evocation of Ancient Rome, in 1929. It has been somewhat less popular than the other two, the writing being rather more harsh (but then, how can you write otherwise when describing Christians being ripped to pieces by the lions?).

Charles Dutoit's recording, recently reissued at mid-price, brings the authentic Impressionist flavor that is so often forgotten in these pieces. Riccardo Muti is thrilling in the more cinematic vein, while Marriner opts for a breezy neo-Classical air in al fresco sound. Enrique Bátiz supplies a highly competitive version at budget price.

Dutoit, Montreal Symphony Orchestra. London 430729 [DDD]
Muti, Philadelphia Orchestra. Angel 47316 [DDD]
Marriner, Academy of St. Martin-in-the-Fields. Philips 432133 [DDD]
Bátiz, Royal Philharmonic Orchestra. Naxos 8.550539 [DDD] (budget)

Joaquin Rodrigo (1901-)

Rodrigo is alive and well at ninety-two as I write these words, and let us salute him. He is basically one of those one-horse composers, known worldwide for his *Aranjuez Concerto*, but falling off rapidly after that. He can, however, be considered one of the best of the minor composers of the twentieth century.

He was born in Sagunto, Spain, and became blind at the age of three. He studied music, from an early age, eventually with Dukas at the Schola Cantorum in Paris. He was encouraged to compose by Manuel de Falla, and developed a suave and melodious style based on colorful Hispanic idioms.

He has written a number of concerti for various instruments, but his name is most intimately associated with the guitar. During the Spanish Civil War he lived in France and Germany, but returned to Madrid in 1939. Spain has awarded him many honors, and he has successfully toured the world with his music.

Concierto de Aranjuez

Perhaps the most famous of all guitar concerti, this work, inspired by the Aranjuez region of Spain, is highly impressionistic and evocative, especially in its celebrated Adagio movement. It liberally employs jazz idioms.

Charles Dutoit's mid-priced digital disc with guitarist Carlos Bonell offers inspired musicianship all around and very attractive couplings, in warm, well-balanced sound. Guitarist John Williams has recorded this piece several times; I suggest the version conducted by Daniel Barenboim, coupled with the Villa-Lobos Guitar Concerto. Julian Bream has a desirable version at mid-price, conducted by John Eliot Gardiner, coupled with Rodrigo's second-best composition and some "basic" pieces by Villa-Lobos; or, alternatively, in a different package with different couplings.

Bonell, Dutoit, Montreal Symphony Orchestra. London 430703 [DDD] + Falla: *El amor brujo, Nights in the Gardens of Spain* (mid-price)

J. Williams, Barenboim, English Chamber Orchestra. CBS 33208 + Villa-Lobos: Guitar Concerto

Bream, Gardiner, Monteverdi Orchestra. "Basic 100, Vol. 26," RCA 61724 [ADD] + *Fantasia para un gentilhombre* (with Brouwer conducting); Villa-Lobos: Five Guitar Preludes, *Bachiana Brasiliera* No. 5 (with Moffo, Stokowski) (mid-price)

Bream, Gardiner, Monteverdi Orchestra. RCA Gold Seal 6525 [ADD] + Villa-Lobos: Guitar Concerto (with Previn conducting), Five Guitar Preludes (mid-price)

Erik Satie (1866-1925)

Satie was one of the most unconventional of all the composers, even for a Frenchman. His influence on a younger generation of his confreres was ultimately more significant than his own compositions; composer and author Eric Salzman deftly described Satie as "a remarkable innovator with a great deal of genius, if little talent."

As a youth he studied at the Paris Conservatory but, impatient with academia, dropped out after a year. He began writing piano pieces with peculiar titles such as *Flabby Preludes for a Dog, Sketches and Exasperations of a Big Boob Made of Wood,* and *Dessicated Embryos.* Unnoticed by most critics amongst the whimsy were harmonies which anticipated those of Debussy.

Satie earned a living playing popular tunes at the Black Cat Cafe in the Montmartre district, dismissed by the musical establishment as a charlatan. He came under the influence of the Symbolist poets, as well as the Rosicrucians. He started his own religion, called The Metropolitan Church of Jesus the Leader, and held services in a dingy room furnished with rotting chairs.

Only a few musicians, notably those who came to be known as the Group of Six (and who came to regard Satie as their spiritual godfather), understood that his purpose was to deflate the pretensions of the German Romantic school with its giant structures and somber philosophical gestures. Satie wanted to return music to a simpler, more economical esthetic, shorn of all empty rhetoric and leavened by wit.

Past age forty Satie realized that his message was impaired by his lack of technical prowess. He therefore enrolled in the Schola Cantorum and studied for three years with Vincent d'Indy and Albert Roussel. Subsequently he composed works larger in scope than heretofore.

In his last years he sought both solitude and poverty. He took rooms in a Paris suburb where he became affectionately known as "le bon maestro d'Arcueil." He lived in total squalor, preferring to identify with the disenfranchised of the world. And he continued to write his unique music, naughty and sardonic and impudent and just a little mad. It is no accident that Satie became a hero to the counterculture of the 1960s, for whom the first Gymnopédie was almost a theme song.

Trois Gymnopédies

Written originally for piano solo in 1888, the first and third of these pieces were later orchestrated by Debussy. The title refers to dances that were performed by naked boys as part of rituals at ancient Greek festivals. The melodies have a distinctly "timeless" quality, and the harmonies are most original.

For the orchestral versions, Leonard Slatkin's digital disc contains other great music of similar mood and tone in great sound. For the piano versions I suggest a wonderful compilation of French piano music by Cristina Ortiz on the IMP label from England, found in larger stores. (There is a classic series of Satie's complete piano music by Aldo Ciccolini, but this may be a bit much for starters.)

(Orchestral) **L. Slatkin, St. Louis Symphony Orchestra.** Telarc 80059 [DDD] + Barber: *Adagio for Strings;* Vaughan Williams: *Fantasia on a Theme by Thomas Tallis;* Fauré: *Pavane,* etc.
(Piano) **Ortiz.** IMP PCD 846 [DDD] + Debussy: *Clair de lune,* six other pieces, and pieces by five other French composers

Arnold Schoenberg (1874-1951)

Schoenberg did more than any other composer to single-handedly change the sound of twentieth-century music. He was the most significant theorist of his age and the founder of the so-called Second Viennese School, made up of the atonal or twelve-tone composers.

Schoenberg's father ran a shoe shop in Vienna and sang in a choral society. Although there was little money for lessons, Arnold learned to play violin, viola, and cello as a child, learning mostly through a friend. His father died when Arnold was sixteen and he took a bank job to support his mother and younger sister. At twenty-one he decided to somehow make his living in music. He got a job conducting a chorus, and in so doing met the composer Alexander von Zemlinsky, who became a lifelong influence, introduced him to Wagner's music, gave him the only formal training he ever had, and in 1901 became his brother-in-law.

Schoenberg and his wife moved to Berlin, where the composer received moral and monetary assistance from Richard Strauss. The couple, now with a daughter, went back to Vienna in 1903, where Schoenberg began his teaching career. Alban Berg and Anton Webern were among his first students; they were to become, with Schoenberg, the Unholy Trinity of Atonalism. Gustav Mahler also befriended Schoenberg, and his departure for American in 1907 was a blow to the budding young composer.

More disappointments, however, were in the offing. In 1908 his wife ran off with a mutual friend, and although she was persuaded to return, the friend committed suicide. Schoenberg now began to write his "atonal" works (a misnomer, as they are not without tones or pitches, but simply do not follow the conventional tonal system) and immediately suffered critical abuse, which in turn had a negative effect on his teaching income. He was also the victim of anti-Semitic propaganda (despite the fact that he had converted to Protestant Christianity in 1898), and was almost murdered by a neighbor.

These difficulties led the Schoenbergs to return to Berlin, where fortunes improved, again aided by Richard Strauss, who got Schoenberg a teaching position. World War I interrupted his career as he was called to military service. At the end of the war he settled in Vienna once more and soon began to develop his "twelve-tone method," an abitrary system of tonal relationships whose main advantage was to provide an escape hatch from the perceived bondage of the traditional major-minor key system.

Schoenberg's first wife died in 1923, and he remarried. The pair, who were to have three children together, moved back to Berlin, where Schoenberg wrote several important works and taught at the Prussian Academy. This very successful interlude was shattered by the advent of the Nazis in 1933. Schoenberg fled to Paris, where he returned proudly to his original Jewish faith prior to moving on to the U.S., where, within a year, he was appointed a professor at UCLA. He became an American citizen in 1941.

Although Schoenberg was in a very real sense the "father of modern music," he was well-grounded in the past. When asked who his teachers had been he liked to answer "Haydn and Mozart." But he also knew his Brahms and Wagner, and even Johann Strauss (he reorchestrated some of the famous waltzes). He insisted that his music was a natural outgrowth of the Late Romantic tradition, and justifiably argued that his new technique should be called not "atonal" but "pantonal." This new music was highly complex, dissonant, melodically jagged, and rhythmically asymmetrical, and has never won the affections of the public, who generally find it ugly and disagreeable. It has remained almost exclusively the domain of musical cognoscenti.

Chamber Symphony No. 1 in E, Op. 9

Scored for fifteen solo instruments, five strings and ten winds, this work is still only midway between the older diatonic tradition and Schoenberg's simmering atonalism. Although difficult to play with good balance, it is a fast and exciting piece which has become one of the composer's most-recorded works.

The outstanding recording is digital and features the conductor-less Orpheus Chamber Orchestra, coupled with the much less famous Chamber Symphony No. 2 and the very famous *Verklärte Nacht*.

Orpheus Chamber Orchestra. DG 429233 [DDD] + Chamber Symphony No. 2, *Verklärte Nacht*

Five Pieces for Orchestra, Op. 16

When this work was first heard in London in 1912, Schoenberg provided a program note that said "This music seeks to express all that swells in us subconsciously like a dream." One critic wrote the next day that it was, perhaps, music of the future, "and we hope, of a distant one." Trying to drum up enthusiasm, Schoenberg gave in to the public demand for pictures with their music and gave the movements subtitles such as "Yesteryears" and "Summer Morning by a Lake." That made it all better.

James Levine's outstanding digital disc, virtually a "sampler" of the Second Viennese School, includes comparable works by each of the Atonal Big Three. Antal Dorati is conductor of an early 60s reissue at mid-price, extremely well done in every regard.

Levine, Berlin Philharmonic Orchestra. DG 419781 [DDD] + Berg: Three Pieces for Orchestra; Webern: Six Pieces, Op. 6

Dorati, London Symphony Orchestra. Mercury 432006 [ADD] + Berg: 3 Pieces for Orchestra, *Lulu* Suite; Webern: 5 Pieces for Orchestra, Op. 10 (mid-price)

Variations for Orchestra, Op. 31

Dating from 1928, this is a full-fledged twelve-tone composition, and actually beautiful once you adjust your ears to the style. The nine variations are easy to follow as they are each in a different mood and tempo. It was premiered under the baton of the great Wilhelm Furtwängler and caused quite a row (no pun intended) in the audience.

The classic recording is by Herbert von Karajan, coupled with *Verklärte Nacht*, a performance of intense power.

Karajan, Berlin Philharmonic Orchestra. DG 415326 [ADD] + *Verklärte Nacht*

Verklärte Nacht, Op. 4 (Transfigured Night)

Schoenberg was twenty-five when he wrote this post-Wagnerian Expressionist tone poem for string sextet. Later he arranged it for string orchestra. It is inspired by a poem of Richard Dehmel, recounting the confession of a woman to her lover as they stroll in the moonlight; she is having a child by her unloved husband.

Although hardly typical of Schoenberg's mature style (there is not a single "tone-row" in it), it remains his most popular work, basically Late Romantic in style, but beautiful and affecting, whatever it is.

The two recordings recommended above with this work as coupling stand as first choices here:

Orpheus Chamber Orchestra. DG 429233 [DDD] + Chamber Symphonies Nos. 1, 2
Karajan, Berlin Philharmonic Orchestra. DG 415326 [ADD] + Variations for Orchestra, Op. 31

Dmitri Shostakovich (1906-1975)

Shostakovich was among the greatest twentieth-century composers, but also among the most variable. His works range rather incredibly from sublime masterpieces to unredeemable junk. Partly this was a result of the need to tapdance around the shifting demands of the Communist arbiters of taste, but it was also due to a natural tendency in Shostakovich to veer from the noble to the trivial and back again. It was just as well, for his vulgar impulse often resulted in some minor masterpiece of light music, such as his whimsical transcription of "Tea for Two;" on the other hand, it could produce a symphony as vapidly bombastic as No. 12.

Shostakovich was born in St. Petersburg to a well-off family. His father was a mining engineer, his mother a talented pianist who trained Dmitri and his two sisters in the basics of music. By age twelve it was obvious that the boy was extraordinarily gifted, and he auditioned successfully before Alexander Glazunov, then director of the St. Petersburg Conservatory.

Upon graduation he completed his First Symphony, which made him instantly famous; the "boy genius" was hailed around the world. In fact, the symphony was no mere harbinger of coming greatness—it was already great. But the young composer was dissatisfied with it, and gave up composing for a while to follow a career as a pianist. The urge to compose returned in less than two years, however, and he proceeded to turn out symphonies, operas, chamber music, and solo piano works at a healthy pace.

In 1936 he had his first serious run-in with Soviet authorities, when his grimly satirical opera *Lady Macbeth of Mtzensk District* was excoriated as a "muddle instead of music…the music quacks, grunts, growls and suffocates itself" (so said a *Pravda* article that appeared shortly after Joseph Stalin had seen the opera). The composer, the article warned, "could end very badly." Shostakovich quickly backtracked, withdrawing his Fourth Symphony, which was close to being premiered. Thenceforward he was ever on the alert against going too far for the liking of the Socialist Realism crowd.

He redeemed himself, at least temporarily, with the Symphony No. 5 in 1937. In this tour-de-force Shostakovich created a great work that satisfied officialdom in its exterior qualities but at the same time reached poetic depths within. He did so well with this juggling act that instead of "ending very badly" he won the Stalin Prize in 1940 for his Piano Quintet. (History repeated itself when Shostakovich was condemned in 1948 for "ideological weakness," then won the Stalin Prize again for an oratorio praising the dictator's reforestation program.)

The artistic atmosphere lightened somewhat after Stalin's death in 1953, but Shostakovich continued for another twenty years to balance his more intellectual productions with jolly patriotic drivel, just to be safe. The dichotomy is even more noticeable when one compares his sardonically witty works, written à la Prokofiev, with those that express a profoundly tragic despair; it is sometimes difficult to believe the same person wrote them, but the paradox may be chalked up to his Jekyll and Hyde existence.

Four years after the death of Shostakovich, a book of his purported memoirs as "told to" one Solomon Volkov was published in New York. In it the author claims that his capitulations to the Soviet system were a subterfuge, and that his music was a disguised protest against a murderous regime. However, there is good reason to believe that the book is a hoax, and so, even in death, the mystery of which was the real Shostakovich persists.

Concerto No. 1 for Piano, Trumpet, and Orchestra, Op. 35

One of the composer's lighter works, this unusual concerto for two oddly paired soloists brims with cheerfulness—even exhilaration—from beginning to end. It was premiered in 1933 in St. Petersburg, and in America a year later under Leopold Stokowski.

A young Evgeny Kissin is the smart-alecky pianist, perfectly cast in this saucy work in its best digital recording. At mid-price, the early-60s Bernstein version (he is both soloist and conductor) wears well and has apt couplings.

Kissin, Kan, Spivakov, Moscow Virtuosi. RCA 7947 [DDD] + Chamber Symphony, Op. 110a, Preludes

Bernstein, New York Philharmonic Orchestra. Sony 47618 [ADD] + Piano Concerto No. 2; Poulenc: 2-Piano Concerto (mid-price)

Quartet No. 8 in C Minor for Strings, Op. 110

Shostakovich wrote fifteen string quartets, of which this is by far the best known for its intense expression of anguish. It was inspired by the destruction of Dresden in World War II, leading the composer to dedicate it to "the memory of the victims of fascism and war." When it was first played for him he is said to have buried his face in his hands and sobbed.

The great Borodin Quartet from Russia has recorded all of the Shostakovich string quartets. The disc containing No. 8 offers two additional quartets, all played with depth and breadth. The popular Kronos Quartet includes this work in a typical Kronos program of intriguing variety. Although analog and full price, the Voces Intimae String Quartet on the Swedish import label Bis has great sound, a fine performance, and a perfect coupling—the melancholy and moving Piano Trio No. 2.

Borodin Quartet. Virgin Classics 59041 [DDD] + Quartets Nos. 3, 7

Kronos Quartet. Nonesuch 79242 [DDD] + Crumb: *Black Angels;* Ives:
They Are There; Martá: *Doom;* Tallis: *Spem in Alium* (arr. quartet)
Voces Intimae String Quartet. Bis 26 [AAD] + Piano Trio No. 2, 7 Romances

Quintet in G Minor for Piano and Strings, Op. 57

A neo-Classical work in five movements of considerable expressive variety, this work
speaks from the heart and is written with great skill and sensitivity. It is considered by some
the composer's finest chamber work, and possibly the best written in Russia in the twentieth
century.

The Borodin Trio (and two helpers make five) offers an expressive performance, well
recorded, and coupled with the "basic" Piano Trio No. 2.

Borodin Trio, Zweig, Horner. Chandos 8342 [DDD] + Piano Trio No. 2

Symphony No. 5, Op. 47

The symphony that saved the composer's neck in 1937 has become not only his greatest hit, but one of the most popular symphonies ever written, surely the most beloved of
the twentieth century. It is similar in atmosphere to Beethoven's Fifth, with its majestic
opening, followed later by an intensely introspective slow movement, exploding into a brilliant finale that comes up like a sunburst. Most listeners take the finale as triumphantly
life-affirming, but the dubious Memoirs claim it actually symbolizes "fate crushing the
brave."

Vladimir Ashkenazy and Neeme Järvi both offer splendiferous digital recordings, with
additional music. The Ashkenazy version features the only recording of the *Five Fragments* for
Orchestra, Op. 41; Järvi has the more familiar suite from the cynical ballet, *The Bolt*. Both
Leonard Bernstein and André Previn conduct famous performances from the early stereo era,
now at mid-price. Bernstein's truly historic version was Shostakovich's own favorite.

Ashkenazy, Royal Philharmonic Orchestra. London 421120 [DDD] + *Five
Fragments* for Orchestra, Op. 42
Järvi, Scottish National Orchestra. Chandos 8650 [DDD] + Ballet Suite
No. 5 from *The Bolt*
Bernstein, New York Philharmonic Orchestra. CBS 37218 [ADD]
(mid-price)
Previn, London Symphony Orchestra. RCA Gold Seal 6801 [ADD] +
Rachmaninoff: *The Rock* (mid-price)

Symphony No. 10 in E Minor, Op. 93

Not so popular as No. 5, the Tenth Symphony is nevertheless considered by many connoisseurs to be a more significant and powerful work. It is imbued with an almost constant nervous energy, culminating in a grand peroration. It was written in 1953. One of its attractions is that it seems to be "saying something"—one is compelled to believe that there is an underlying program. But just what that might be, the composer never lets on.

Herbert von Karajan was the classic interpreter of this symphony, and both his digital and analog recordings top the list of recommendations, the older (1966) version at mid-price.

Karajan, Berlin Philharmonic Orchestra. DG 413361 [DDD]
Karajan, Berlin Philharmonic Orchestra. DG Galleria 429716 [ADD] (mid-price)

Trio No. 2 in E Minor for Piano, Violin and Cello, Op. 67

Shostakovich is often at his best in his chamber works. This trio, written in 1944, was prompted by the death of a close friend and is largely somber in tone. Its four movements sustain melancholy for nearly half an hour without ever losing the listener's attention, so vivid is the work's expressive power.

The digital recording by Isaac Stern, Yo-Yo Ma, and Emanuel Ax was a 1990 Grammy nominee. The Borodin Trio and the deeply probing trio from Sweden both offer more "basic" couplings, the Piano Quintet and Quartet No. 8, respectively.

Stern, Ma, Ax. CBS 44664 [DDD] + Cello Sonata, Op. 40
Borodin Trio. Chandos 8342 [DDD] + Piano Quintet
Palsson, Tellefsen, Helmerson. Bis 26 [AAD] + Quartet No. 8, Seven Romances

Jean Sibelius (1865-1957)

Sibelius made a reputation as a symphonist and tone poet, but above all as the Finnish national composer-laureate. He was able to capture the distinctive national idiom and transmit (and transmute) it to a worldwide audience hanging on his every note.

His father, a medical doctor, died of cholera when Johan was only two. (I say "Johan" because that was his birth name. He adopted "Jean" from a sea-captain uncle who had Frenchified his name while abroad.) He started piano at nine, but much preferred the violin, which he began at fifteen. As a youth he sometimes sat from dawn to dusk beside a lake, experimenting on his fiddle and burning with the dream of becoming a great virtuoso. His first composition, written at age ten, was entitled *Water Drops*.

Still a teenager (this was before television, remember) he read the epics of Homer in ancient Greek and the odes of Horace in Latin. He was interested in astronomy and proficient in mathematics. His mother wanted him to study law at the University of Helsinki, but after a year there he was certain that music was his destiny and enrolled in the Conservatory, where he was an outstanding student. A scholarship took him on to Berlin and later Vienna, where he studied composition.

Returning to Finland, Sibelius steeped himself in the old myths and the national epic, the *Kalevala* (with whose meter we are familiar from Longfellow's *The Song of Hiawatha,* which borrowed it outright). At age twenty-six he won nationwide recognition with his giant tone poem *Kullervo,* based on the ancient legends. Soon he was producing outstanding works of nationalistic inspiration and teaching violin and theory at the Conservatory.

In 1897 the Finnish government provided him with a stipend which enabled him to devote all his time to composing, and in 1899 the publication of *Finlandia* made him the international cultural spokesperson for his country.

Many in those days assumed that the music of Sibelius was built on authentic folk melodies, but the truth is that every melody was completely original. As with most of the great nationalist composers, Sibelius was so imbued with his native culture that he could evoke it without copying literally from source material. In his great tone poems he obviously called on literary inspiration, but his symphonies are "pure" music; in the symphony, he once said, "music begins where words leave off."

The "folk" strain of his muse began to fade after the turn of the century, and his works took on a more inward and personal nature. At the same time, he was overindulging in cigars and liquor and struggling with constant debt. An illness in 1908 darkened his outlook and forced him to give up his addictions for a while, but his concentration on work increased. His financial problems gradually faded as he toured the major music centers, conducting his works and receiving numerous honors along the way.

World War I seriously interrupted his career, and the Finnish civil war in 1918 forced Sibelius temporarily from his home. His output declined precipitously, and by the mid-1920s he was essentially a recluse, back on tobacco and booze.

He lived on for another thirty years in silence, holed up in his lakeside home, hinting regularly that he was writing an Eighth Symphony, but more likely struggling with the bottle. Asked what he was doing all those years, he answered "Creating my masterpiece." But when he died in his ninety-first year, there was nothing. He was buried in the garden, next to his beloved wife of more than sixty years.

Concerto in D Minor for Violin, Op. 47

In his earlier years, Sibelius was himself a violinist, but it was only long after he had stopped playing that he wrote his only concerto for the instrument, and as it turns out it is one of the finest composed in the twentieth century. The first movement is rhapsodic, the middle lyrically emotional, and the last a vigorous dance—Tovey called it "a polonaise for polar bears."

The consensus leader in digital versions is that by Cho-Liang Lin, with the Finnish conductor Esa-Pekka Salonen. The violin playing is perfection, and the apt coupling is another great, but lesser-known, Scandinavian violin concerto by Carl Nielsen. This recording was a Grammy winner in 1989. Budget-lovers are in luck with an excellent performance by young Korean violinist Dong-Suk Kang at a very low price, and digital too.

Lin, Salonen, Philharmonia Orchestra. CBS 44548 [DDD] Nielsen: Violin Concerto

Kang, Leaper, Czechoslovak Radio Symphony Orchestra, Bratislava. Naxos 8.550329 [DDD] + short pieces by Svendsen, Sinding, Halvorsen (budget)

Finlandia, Op. 26

Easily the most impassioned, inspiring piece of national music ever written, *Finlandia* was written as the finale to a historical tableau. Its famous chorale is one of the best-known melodies in the world, and fitted out with words, it has become the Finnish national song.

Vladimir Ashkenazy leads a great program on the best digital disc, and at mid-price besides. Analog mid-price versions well worth having are by Herbert von Karajan (famous especially for *Finlandia*) and Sir Colin Davis, one of the greatest Sibelius conductors. An excellent choice at even lower price is the budget recording well-conducted by Horst Stein.

Ashkenazy, Philharmonia Orchestra. London Jubilee 430737 [DDD] + Symphony No. 2, *Karelia* Suite (mid-price)

Karajan, Berlin Philharmonic Orchestra. DG Galleria 427222 [ADD] + Liszt: *Les Préludes;* Tchaikovsky: *Overture 1812, Capriccio italien* (mid-price)

C. Davis, Boston Symphony Orchestra. Philips 420490 [ADD] + Symphony No. 2, *Swan of Tuonela, Valse triste* (mid-price)

Stein, Suisse Romande Orchestra. London Weekend Classics 417697 [AAD] + *Swan of Tuonela, En Saga, Night Ride and Sunrise, Pohjola's Daughter* (budget)

Swan of Tuonela

Like *Finlandia* originally part of a larger work, *The Swan of Tuonela* is best known now as an independent tone poem. It describes a mythical swan said to sing as it floats down the dark river of Tuonela, the Hell of Finnish folklore.

The Colin Davis and Horst Stein recordings mentioned just above fill the bill here:

C. Davis, Boston Symphony Orchestra. Philips 420490 [ADD] + *Finlandia*, Symphony No. 2, *Valse triste* (mid-price)

Stein, Suisse Romande Orchestra. London Weekend Classics 417697 [AAD] + *Finlandia, En Saga, Night Ride and Sunrise, Pohjola's Daughter* (budget)

Symphony No. 2 in D, Op. 43

Despite the composer's protestations about "pure" symphonic music, the suspicion is inescapable that this beloved symphony was inspired by northern winds howling through pine forests and mighty waves breaking over granite crags, so vividly does it "speak." Sibelius freely admitted that the rugged climate and scenery of Finland was one of his innermost creative stimuli.

Vladimir Ashkenazy's fine digital disc at mid-price, with *Finlandia* and the *Karelia* Suite, is surely a winner for all-around value. Sibelius expert Sir Colin Davis, also at mid-price, but analog, has even more "basic" couplings. Herbert von Karajan's highly rated recording is digital and mid-price, but offers no couplings. Perhaps the greatest performance on record, that by Sir John Barbirolli, is still available and in refurbished sound, but at a high price with no couplings, on a label not carried in some stores.

> **Ashkenazy, Philharmonia Orchestra.** London Jubilee 430737 [DDD] + *Finlandia, Karelia* Suite (mid-price)
> **C. Davis, Boston Symphony Orchestra.** Philips 420490 [ADD] + *Finlandia, Swan of Tuonela, Valse triste* (mid-price)
> **Karajan, Berlin Philharmonic Orchestra.** Angel Studio 69243 [DDD] (mid-price)
> **Barbirolli, Royal Philharmonic Orchestra.** Chesky 3

Symphony No. 5 in E-flat, Op. 82

Broad in scope and noble in tone, the Fifth Symphony radiates a serene power. Its famous ending, with huge brass chords evoking a giant striding over mountains, is one of the composer's most arresting inspirations.

Simon Rattle entices here with a wonderful performance at a wonderful price, and with very apt and generous couplings. I would leave it at that for a first spin; the Colin Davis version is available only in the four-disc set of the complete symphonies, and the esteemed Herbert von Karajan recording is in early 60s sound which has not been remastered, and is still at full price, with a "non-basic" coupling that is not a great performance.

> **Rattle, Philharmonia Orchestra.** Angel 64737 + Nielsen: Symphony No. 4, *Pan and Syrinx* (mid-price)

Valse triste

Sibelius's brother-in-law Arvid Järnefelt wrote a play called *Death* for which the composer contributed incidental music. The haunting "sad waltz" is danced by a dying woman in her last dream.

This piece is handily included in the fine Sir Colin Davis recording, recommended three times already for its couplings:

C. Davis, Boston Symphony Orchestra. Philips 420490 [ADD] + *Finlandia, Swan of Tuonela,* Symphony No. 2 (mid-price)

Igor Stravinsky (1882-1971)

Stravinsky was, if not the greatest (and many would call him so), certainly the most famous composer of the twentieth century. He was to music as his friend Picasso was to painting— the dominating figure of his art, the icon of Modernism, a symbol and a signpost of the times. But there is a peculiar phenomenon about his career: the works for which he is best known were written mostly between the ages of twenty-eight and thirty. He continued to compose for nearly sixty more years, revered and deferred to by Academia, but hardly any of these more "advanced" works have won affection from the public.

Although Stravinsky, son of an opera singer, loved music from childhood, there was little in his first years to indicate the famous composer to come. He studied piano as a child, but at his father's insistence undertook a course in law at St. Petersburg University. Not until age twenty did he firmly decide on a career as a composer. He studied with Rimsky-Korsakov for six years, producing such works as a very conventional symphony. Stravinsky had four children by his wife, who was his first cousin.

The big break came in 1910, when the impresario Serge Diaghilev turned to Stravinsky after another composer had defaulted on a commission to write a ballet on the Russian legend of the fire-bird. Stravinsky wrote the score hurriedly; it was a sensation, made the composer world-famous, and tormented him the rest of his life by remaining his most popular work.

There followed another successful ballet, *Petrushka,* and then in 1913 a famous scandal with the highly dissonant and primitivistic *Le Sacre du printemps* (always called in English *The Rite of Spring,* but more properly *The Consecration of Spring*). There was a near-riot in the hall as apostles of the avant-garde shouted at—and came to blows with— defenders of the old traditions.

Stravinsky and his wife were in Switzerland when the Russian Revolution broke out, and they decided not to go home. Diaghilev lured Stravinsky back to his Ballets Russes for another commission, *Pulcinella,* but the composer was changing his style, turning away from his Russian nationalist roots to the more pan-European idiom of neo-Classicism. This remained his style between the two World Wars, and there was a great deal of carping that he had abandoned his original manner.

Burdened with debt, Stravinsky began touring in the 1920s as a pianist and conductor to make money. His travels took him all over Europe and to North and South America. He became a French citizen in 1934, and soon after published an autobiography. Within the next five years his mother died and his wife and one daughter succumbed to tuberculosis. On top of these tragedies, war was on the horizon, so Stravinsky accepted an invitation to lecture for a year at Harvard University and moved permanently to the U.S., where he re-married and changed citizenship once again. The couple soon settled in Hollywood.

During World War II Stravinsky wrote little of importance, and up until 1953 his chief product was the opera *The Rake's Progress,* on which he worked for three years. Then he became friends with Robert Craft, a young musician who was to become (and is in part to this day) his shadow, alter ego, and prime minister to the world, acting as a secretary, advisor, conductor, interpreter of his works, biographer, and general apologist.

It was Craft who introduced Stravinsky to the methods of the twelve-tone composers which he had previously ignored. Stravinsky was particularly taken with the spare purity of Anton Webern and soon he had forsaken neo-Classicism to become a serial, or "atonal" composer. This was even less popular with the general public than his neo-Classicism had been, but Stravinsky calmly forged ahead. He was denounced by many of his previous admirers for capitulating to the "enemy," while leading composers of the newer avant-garde, such as Pierre Boulez, now ridiculed Stravinsky as a poseur and opportunist.

Stravinsky was a precisionist in everything he did, and the often cool detachment and streamlined logic of his music tends to appeal most to those who are of his temperament. His inspirations did not flow, as Beethoven recommended, "from the heart to the heart," but from the brain to the brain. However one feels about him, he was one of the most influential composers of the past century, and despite his three changes of style, his works are stamped with a distinctive individuality. Only Schoenberg matches him in historical significance, and between them they managed to think up the majority of techniques which have made the Moderns clearly different from the Romantics.

Today, a quarter of a century after his death, Stravinsky occupies very nearly the same position he did for much of his life: venerated by most of the intelligentsia but, except for the early neo-Romantic ballets, avoided by the average listener.

Firebird Suite

The suite of highlights is much more often heard in concert than the complete ballet, for all the really "good music" is in the short version. The point has been made, however, that the glorious final flight of the fire-bird can seem unprepared if what precedes it is too short. Nevertheless, it is traditional to start with the Suite, and my recommendations are so restricted.

Robert Shaw's early digital recording remains a first choice to show off the splendor of the *Firebird,* coupled with colorful music of an earlier Russian, Alexander Borodin. A half-price two-CD set with Bernard Haitink and Igor Markevitch variously conducting offers all three famous Stravinsky ballets, plus the striking neo-Classical ballet *Apollon musagète*. In the budget category, Stanislav Skrowaczewski is conductor on a three-CD set of the three "great" ballets and selections from Prokofiev as well.

> **Shaw, Atlanta Symphony Orchestra.** Telarc 80039 [DDD] + Borodin: Overture and *Polovtsian Dances* from *Prince Igor*
> **Haitink, London Philharmonic Orchestra; Markevitch, London Symphony Orchestra.** Philips Duo 438350 (2) [ADD] + *Petrushka, Le Sacre du printemps, Apollon musagète* (mid-price)
> **Skrowaczewski, Minnesota Orchestra.** Vox Bos 3016 [ADD] + *Petrushka, Le Sacre du printemps;* Prokofiev: *Romeo and Juliet* (sel.), *Love for Three Oranges Suite* (budget)

Petrushka (complete)

Petrushka is a wooden puppet. All the puppets in a show are regularly brought to life by a magician, until Petrushka is slain by one of the other characters. At the end of the ballet, his ghost returns to terrorize the magician. The music, laden with folk tunes authentic and simulated, is full of atmosphere. Unlike *The Firebird, Petrushka* is almost always heard complete, although in the composer's 1947 revision instead of the 1911 original. Take note of which recording you are buying, since they are substantially different; you may prefer one over the other, or wish to have both if it becomes a favorite work.

The best digital recording is easily that conducted by Claudio Abbado, coupled with Mussorgsky's *Pictures at an Exhibition.* The Haitink/Markevitch and Skrowaczewski sets recommended under *The Firebird* are continued here, with the addition of the famous Pierre Boulez recording from the late 1960s, coupled with *Le Sacre du printemps,* but unfortunately still being sold at full price.

> **Abbado, London Symphony Orchestra.** DG 423901 [DDD] + Mussorgsky: *Pictures at an Exhibition*
> **Haitink, London Philharmonic Orchestra; Markevitch, London Symphony Orchestra.** Philips Duo 438350 (2) [ADD] + *Firebird* Suite, *Le Sacre du printemps, Apollon musagète* (mid-price)
> **Skrowaczewski, Minnesota Orchestra.** Vox Box 3016 (3) [ADD] + *Firebird* Suite, *Le Sacre du printemps;* Prokofiev: *Romeo and Juliet* (sel.), *Love for Three Oranges* Suite (budget)
> **Boulez, New York Philharmonic Orchestra.** CBS 42395 [AAD] + *Le Sacre du printemps*

Le Sacre du printemps *(The Rite of Spring)*

In this case there is no question of revisions or versions; the complete, unexpurgated ballet that shocked the first audience and the world back in 1913 remains untouchable. Stravinsky claimed to have dreamed the scenario, "a solemn pagan rite: wise elders, seated in a circle, watching a young girl dance herself to death." Imitation of Russian folksong is again an important element, but this time the presentation overwhelms the senses. A huge orchestra pummels the listener with screaming dissonances and bone-breaking rhythms. It was terribly Modern in 1913, but by 1941 had been domesticated by Walt Disney as music for cartoon dinosaurs. Our ears are well-used to these sounds by now, but *The Rite of Spring* remains both a historical signpost in the development of music and a vivid, exciting composition.

There are so many extraordinary choices here in analog that I don't see any real advantage to listing digital titles. There are dozens of recordings of this work; if you must have digital, you are on your own in this case, since I can't come up with one that I would spend money on before any of the following.

Given that understanding, the Herbert von Karajan recording claims special attention—a great reading with a great coupling at mid-price. Recordings recommended above recur below, with the addition of Riccardo Muti's wonderfully wild performance at mid-price, perhaps the best version if you want to reenact *Fantasia* in your rumpus room.

Karajan, Berlin Philharmonic Orchestra. DG 429162 [ADD] + Mussorgsky: *Pictures at an Exhibition* (mid-price)

Haitink, London Philharmonic Orchestra; Markevitch, London Symphony Orchestra. Philips Duo 438350 (2) [ADD] + *Firebird* Suite, *Petrushka, Apollon musagète* (mid-price)

Skrowaczewski, Minnesota Orchestra. Vox Box 3016 (3) [ADD] + *Firebird* Suite, *Petrushka;* Prokofiev: *Romeo and Juliet* (sel.), *Love for Three Oranges* Suite (budget)

Muti, Philadelphia Orchestra. Angel 64516 + Mussorgsky: *Pictures at an Exhibition* (mid-price)

Boulez, Cleveland Orchestra. CBS 42395 [AAD] + *Petrushka*

Symphony of Psalms

It isn't easy to get beyond Stravinsky's "Russian period" when trying to introduce people to his music, but I wanted to include at least one of the best works from his neo-Classical (middle) period. The most famous of these is surely the *Symphony of Psalms,* a setting of Biblical passages in Latin with an atmosphere of ancient times. Hard to get more "Classical" than that.

Leonard Bernstein's recording of three twentieth-century choral masterpieces, including his own *Chichester Psalms,* makes a great introduction to this music. Stravinsky himself conducted and recorded most of his major works; some consider these definitive, others think his approach is too dry and objective for complete enjoyment. In addition, the recordings are, of course, not recent, and they continue to sell at full price, so I have been reluctant to recommend them for a beginning collection; however, this would be the time to try one. The composer's version of the *Symphony of Psalms,* coupled with his two orchestral symphonies, is considered one of his most successful discs, and you can branch out from there. (Once again, I feel there is no advantage here in slapping in a digital recording.)

Bernstein, New York Philharmonic Orchestra. CBS 44710 [ADD] + Bernstein: *Chichester Psalms;* Poulenc: *Gloria*

Stravinsky, CBC Symphony Orchestra, Toronto Festival Singers. CBS 42434 [ADD] + Symphony in Three Movements, Symphony in C

Virgil Thomson (1896-1989)

Thomson was one of America's most stimulating, thoughtful, original, and long-lived composers and critics. He created the first really distinctive American opera; he composed distinguished film scores; he wrote witty and perceptive critiques of the American musical scene for many years; and he was still active at age ninety-three.

Thomson's ancestors went west from Virginia as pioneers in the nineteenth century. Southern Baptists, they fought on the Confederate side in the Civil War. Virgil was born in Kansas City, Missouri into a morally strict family of modest cultural attainments. Somehow he gravitated to music, and was composing piano pieces with names like *The Chicago Fire* at age four.

As he developed into a young man, his music abilities were augmented by a precocious talent for crafting prose. After serving briefly in World War I, he enrolled at Harvard University and came under the spell of Erik Satie's music. Soon he was an enthusiastic Francophile and studied with Nadia Boulanger in Paris for a year. He was thrilled to meet Satie and to discover the music of the Group of Six, who followed the same path of overthrowing Romantic orthodoxy by mixing jazz and dance-hall tunes with serious compositional techniques. It was a perfect fit for Thomson, who found a unique style by blending the French classical tradition with his heritage of nostalgic middle-Americana.

In the mid-1920s he returned to Paris and became friends with the poet Gertrude Stein and her circle of progressive artists whom she named "the lost generation." Their collaborative opera, *Four Saints in Three Acts,* enjoyed a major success in 1934, despite its avant-garde text and deceptively simple music. Thomson's fame was secured. The production, coordinated by John Houseman, choreographed by Frederick Ashton, and designed by the painter Florine Stettheimer, with an all-black cast, became a legend in American theatrical history.

From 1940 to 1954 Thomson was chief music critic of the New York *Herald Tribune,* contributing brilliant insights on American concert life and composers and championing contemporary music. His wit was incisive, and he was not averse to turning it on himself: he defined a music critic as one who "seldom kisses, but always tells."

During this period he continued to compose, producing the ballet *Filling Station,* film scores for the documentaries *The Plow that Broke the Plains* and *The River,* and a mythical opera about the early crusader for women's rights, Susan B. Anthony, called *The Mother of Us All.* Another admired work is his score to the film *Louisiana Story,* which won the Pulitzer Prize in 1949. His fascinating autobiography was published in 1966.

A surprising number of music histories give little space to this venerable and lovable genius, treating him as a marginal figure with no distinctive profile. Nothing, in my opinion, could be farther from the truth. His melodiously deceptive surfaces, like Mozart's, merely overlie an ocean of refined sensibility. His music is eleganty crafted, yet warm and human. It is richly evocative of an America half-real, half-imagined, but vividly recreated out of nostalgia and sincere affection.

The Plow that Broke the Plains

The 1936 documentary film gave Thomson his first chance to write for the cinema, and it was revelatory. Instead of the plush, sleazy imitations of Late Romantic composers that were common up until then, Thomson provided clean, lean music of simple dignity and unvarnished sincerity. Bits of jazz and blues jostle with cowboy songs, banjo chords, and even a few thumps on the old washtub to help tell the story of the Way West.

Sir Neville Marriner's fine mid-price recording has been recommended earlier for its couplings.

Marriner, Los Angeles Chamber Orchestra. "American Miniatures," Angel 64306 + *Autumn;* Barber: *Adagio for Strings;* Copland: *Fanfare for the Common Man,* three short pieces (mid-price)

Ralph Vaughan Williams (1872-1958)

Vaughan Williams could be a bit deceiving. His gentle nature was disguised behind a frame as big and burly as a bear, and his genius as a symphonist—one of the greatest in the twentieth century—was sometimes obscured by a perception that he was but a provincial composer of folk-inspired idyllic landscapes.

He did belong in part to the English "pastoral school," which was not necessarily a bad thing, although most of its composers are considered of secondary importance. But if he was one, he was the greatest one. And he went far beyond the merely nationalistic by seeking out the universal message latent in his native idiom.

Vaughan Williams (for that was his surname, British style) grew up in a cultured household and was introduced to art music at an early age. He studied at the Royal College of Music with Sir Hubert Parry, and later abroad with both Max Bruch and Maurice Ravel. By age nineteen he had published his first composition.

By 1901 he had become intensely interested in the English folksong tradition and resolved to incorporate it into his creative work. With his friend Gustav Holst he traveled around the countryside collecting indigenous music and writing it down. He also lectured and contributed scholarly articles on the subject. In 1906 he edited the *English Hymnal.* He served in World War I, then returned to the Royal College of Music as an instructor. In 1921 he added conducting the London Bach Choir to his already busy schedule, which had become crowded with composing ever more successful works—symphonic, vocal, choral, and operatic.

His career simply expanded with a slow, tranquil grace straight through to his eighty-sixth year, when he died shortly after completing his Ninth Symphony. Long before the end he had become the "grand old man of English music," the most important British composer between Elgar and Britten.

Vaughan Williams developed his own distinctive style, blending the folk traditions with a more advanced type of rhythm and harmony. He was a modern composer, but conservative, uninterested either in Schoenberg's atonalism or Stravinsky's neo-isms. Up until 1935 his style favored the folk-pastoral idiom; after the Fourth Symphony, however, a more rugged and abstract vein was often apparent in his music.

Fantasia on a Theme by Thomas Tallis

First written in 1910, later twice revised, and not published until 1921, this work for double string orchestra and solo quartet was well worth the wait. The original tune, taken from one of Tallis's psalter settings of 1567, is treated in a beautifully evocative manner, overwhelming in emotional power. Along with the shorter and simpler *Fantasia on "Greensleeves,"* it is probably the most internationally beloved work by an English composer.

André Previn is well-regarded in recordings of Vaughan Williams; his is undoubtedly the best digital version, especially desirable since it is coupled with his outstanding Fifth Symphony. Leonard Slatkin's really outstanding disc has already been recommended earlier; in this piece it compares favorably with the classic analog recording by Sir Adrian Boult from the early 70s, still available at mid-price. Bernard Haitink's digital recording is also highly recommendable, and is coupled with the best digital version of the "basic" Symphony No. 2.

Previn, Royal Philharmonic Orchestra. Telarc 80158 [DDD] + Symphony No. 5

L. Slatkin, St. Louis Symphony Orchestra. Telarc 80059 [DDD] + Barber: *Adagio for Strings;* Satie: *Trois Gymnopédies;* Fauré: *Pavane,* etc.

Boult, London Philharmonic Orchestra. EMI 64017 [ADD] + Symphony No. 2 (mid-price)

Haitink, London Philharmonic Orchestra. EMI 49394 [DDD] +
Symphony No. 2

Symphony No. 2, "London"

Although not the greatest Vaughan Williams symphony, the "London" makes a most
attractive introduction to the other eight. It is frankly programmatic, each of its four movements being almost an independent tone poem. The first suggests the city coming to
vibrant life after a foggy dawn. Vaughan Williams described the second as "Bloomsbury
Square on a November afternoon." The third movement evokes Westminster Embankment
at night, with the sounds of the Strand heard from a distance. The finale is in two sections,
the first a solemn march which works up to a powerful climax, the second (after an expec-
tant interlude in which we hear Big Ben chiming) a cruise down the rippling Thames, ending, apparently, at dawn, with the music which opened the symphony.

This sorts out quite neatly: Bernard Haitink's digital recording is a clear favorite, with
Sir Adrian Boult's mid-price analog version being one of that conductor's greatest perfor-
mances. Both recordings include Vaughan Williams's most popular work, the *Tallis
Fantasia*, and both are played by the same orchestra (on the same label!).

Haitink, London Philharmonic Orchestra. EMI 49394 [DDD] + *Fantasia
on a Theme by Thomas Tallis*
Boult, London Philharmonic Orchestra. EMI 64017 [ADD] + *Fantasia on
a Theme by Thomas Tallis* (mid-price)

Symphony No. 5 in D

The composer dedicated this serene yet expansive symphony to his fellow-composer,
Jean Sibelius, whom he greatly admired. It belongs to the "pastoral" part of his work, but is
in no way wispy or weak. The last movement, a passacaglia, ends in quiet ecstasy.

As mentioned above, André Previn is something of a Vaughan Williams
specialist/expert, and both of his recordings of this symphony are in print and top the list.
The earlier analog one is probably the greater performance, and is cheaper, but has less
"basic" couplings and, of course, older sound.

Previn, Royal Philharmonic Orchestra. Telarc 80158 [DDD] + *Fantasia on
a Theme by Thomas Tallis*
Previn, London Symphony Orchestra. RCA Gold Seal 60586 [ADD] + Bass
Tuba Concerto, Three Portraits from *The England of Elizabeth* (mid-price)

Heitor Villa-Lobos (1887-1959)

Villa-Lobos was at least as colorful a man as was his music. One of the few composers to favor having his picture taken in a pin-striped suit with a fat cigar jutting from his jaw, looking like a 30s movie gangster, Villa-Lobos was the most famous Brazilian classical composer, and probably the most prolific composer of the twentieth century. Counts of his compositions range from 1,600 to more than 2,500; no one is absolutely sure of the figure, since he was prone to give a manuscript away as a souvenir and toss off a new one to replace it.

His father was Spanish, his mother Indian. The father, a schoolteacher, was an amateur musician who tutored his son in cello and clarinet, but died when Heitor was only eleven. The boy continued as best he could, teaching himself to play an old piano, figuring out the guitar, naively playing the violin by holding it upright like a cello. (Years later he was asked what instruments he could play. "I can't play the oboe," he answered remorsefully.)

Villa-Lobos spent much of his youth on the streets, taking in the sounds and rhythms of Afro-Brazilian musicians. He started writing his own music at twelve, and made money playing guitar in theaters and coffee houses. At eighteen he set out across the country to discover "the Brazilian soul" in music, from jungle chants to urban popular song. Among his many adventures he claimed to have narrowly escaped being boiled alive by cannibals.

In 1919, pianist Artur Rubinstein was touring South America. Rubinstein was quite the movie buff and took in the cinema one evening in Rio. He was intrigued by the music accompanying the silent film. Discovering it to be the work of a young native musician, Rubinstein sought him out. A few days later Villa-Lobos showed up at the pianist's hotel room with a group of friends and put on a concert of his works.

Rubinstein was so impressed that he arranged to send Villa-Lobos to Paris for professional study; but when he got there, in typical style, he put on a concert of his music instead of attending to his studies. "I didn't come here to learn from you," he proclaimed, "I have come to show you what I have done!"

Villa-Lobos returned to Brazil internationally famous, and was made director of the Department of Artistic and Musical Education. Among his more notorious pedagogical projects was a choir of over thirty thousand schoolchildren singing patriotic music in a soccer stadium, Villa-Lobos conducting them with a Brazilian flag. The composer was becoming equally well-known as an educator and national icon, as well as for his almost superhuman energy (he founded his own music conservatory, and in his leisure time became the billiards champion of Rio de Janeiro).

In subsequent years he traveled frequently to France (and occasionally the U.S.) to conduct his works, and of course continued composing assiduously, seeking ever more unusual combinations of instruments and sonorities (one work is scored for soprano, three metronomes, and orchestra). He invented two characteristic musical forms, the *Bachiana Brasileira,* a suite in which Brazilian folk elements are treated as if composed by Bach, and the *chôro,* a kind of serenade evoking music of the Brazilian street bands.

Mostly self-taught, but imbued with a wide-ranging musical culture from bird calls to

Bach, Villa-Lobos was one of those rare composers who created a style so personal and unique that few have dared to copy it.

Bachiana Brasileira No. 5 for Soprano and Eight Celli

The two movements of this piece were written several years apart, from 1938 to 1945. The opening Aria, a conception perhaps of how Bach would have written the Air on the G String if he were a Brazilian, immediately became Villa-Lobos's signature composition. Its Portuguese text describes the moon rising through lustrous clouds at midnight.

Barbara Hendricks is the lustrous soprano with Enrique Bátiz conducting on the best digital version, coupled with two more of the most attractive of the *Bachianas Brasileiras*. A classic of analog days is the version by Leopold Stokowski with Anna Moffo singing, now available at mid-price with excellent couplings as indicated:

Hendricks, Bátiz, Royal Philharmonic Orchestra. Angel 47433 [DDD] + *Bachianas Brasileiras* Nos. 1, 7

Moffo, Stokowski, American Symphony Orchestra. "Basic 100, Vol. 26," RCA 61724 [ADD] + Five Guitar Preludes; Rodrigo: *Concierto de Aranjuez, Fantasia para un gentilhombre* (with Julian Bream) (mid-price)

Concerto for Guitar and Orchestra; Preludes (5) for Solo Guitar

Villa-Lobos wrote a large body of great music for classical guitar. The Concerto was created as recently as 1951. It nostalgically recalls the composer's days playing in the street bands of Rio. The melodic, colorful preludes speak for themselves.

Two recordings earlier recommended under Joaquin Rodrigo and under the listing just above fill the bill here, with the addition of another Bream record with a different assortment:

(Concerto and Preludes on one disc.) **Bream, Previn, London Symphony Orchestra.** RCA Gold Seal 6525 [ADD] + Rodrigo: *Concierto de Aranjuez* (with Gardiner conducting) (mid-price)

(Preludes only.) **Bream.** "Basic 100, Vol. 26," RCA 61724 [ADD] + *Bachiana Brasileira* No. 5 (with Moffo, Stokowski); Rodrigo: *Concierto de Aranjuez* (with Gardiner conducting), *Fantasia para un gentilhombre* (with Brouwer conducting) (mid-price)

(Concerto only.) **J. Williams, Barenboim, English Chamber Orchestra.** CBS 33208 + Rodrigo: *Concierto de Aranjuez*

William Walton (1902-1983)

Walton may be said to have continued the tradition of Elgar in British music up to the present. In developing an original voice, neither radical nor unduly conservative, he managed to remain both distinctively personal and English. Although he wrote relatively few works (except for his two symphonies, just one in each genre), an unusually high proportion of them are frequently performed and widely admired.

Walton's parents were singing teachers from Lancashire, from whom the boy naturally picked up a great deal about music: he once said he could sing Handel's *Messiah* before he could talk. At age ten he won a scholarship to Christ Church Cathedral Choir School. As an undergraduate at Oxford he became friends with the colorful Sitwell family of literati: Sacheverell, Osbert—and Edith, whose *Façade* poems led to Walton's *succès de scandale* in 1923 with his jaunty musical setting.

Walton's academic career was cut short by failure in algebra; he later said this contributed to his avoidance of the "slide-rule school" of composition. Nevertheless, his unusual musical talent attracted the attention and encouragement of composer Ferruccio Busoni, conductor Ernest Ansermet, and musicologist Edward Dent.

His first important composition, a Piano Quartet, was published when he was seventeen, and his String Quartet was performed at an important festival of modern music when he was still only twenty-one. A succession of fine works followed, including concerti for viola and violin, two symphonies, the cantata *Belshazzar's Feast,* the opera *Troilus and Cressida,* and scores for several films including Shakespeare's *Hamlet, Richard III,* and *Henry V.*

Walton was knighted in 1951, and the next year contributed two stirring, neo-Elgarian marches for the coronation of Elizabeth II. In his later years he and his wife lived on the Mediterranean island of Ischia, where he continued even more leisurely his slow, meticulous creation of fine music.

Belshazzar's Feast

Walton's early choral training stood him in good stead for this cantata, one of the most vivid and memorable of its kind. The Biblical verses, compiled by Osbert Sitwell, recount the fall of Babylon and the "handwriting on the wall." It was first performed in 1931, and while occasionally sniffed at by critics for its conservative idiom, has only grown more popular with the years.

As with Vaughan Williams, André Previn is one of Walton's greatest interpreters, and there are two of his readings of this work in the catalog. The digital one is available either on his orchestra's own label (imported) or on an American equivalent. Its coupling is the suite from Walton's great film score for Shakespeare's *Henry V.* The analog version adds two characteristic overtures and a piece in tribute to Benjamin Britten. Robert Shaw's digital recording is also outstanding, and offers a coupling of Leonard Bernstein's great choral piece *Chichester Psalms,* a most apposite choice.

Previn, Royal Philharmonic Orchestra and Chorus. RPO 7013 or MCA 6187 [DDD] + *Henry V* Suite
Shaw, Atlanta Symphony Orchestra and Chorus. Telarc 80181 [DDD] + Bernstein: *Chichester Psalms*
Previn, London Symphony Orchestra and Chorus. EMI 64723 + *Portsmouth Point* Overture, *Scapino* Overture, *Improvisations on an Impromptu of Benjamin Britten* (mid-price)

Symphony No. 1 in B-flat Minor

Brooding or conflicting for most of its length, this work finally wins through to affirmation in the great symphonic tradition, but its sound-world is uniquely Waltonian: nobly "English," but tonally ambiguous, unified by an undercurrent in the bass. The effect is compellingly dramatic.

Once again Previn tops the charts, his digital performance being marginally less effective than the 1968 analog version, but in far more brilliant sound. It must be pointed out that British conductor Vernon Handley had a digital recording that many critics thought surpassed everyone's, Previn's included, but apparently lack of name recognition quickly forced this disc from the American catalogs.

Previn, Royal Philharmonic Orchestra. Telarc 80125 [DDD]
Previn, London Symphony Orchestra. RCA Gold Seal 7830 [ADD] + Vaughan Williams: Overture to *The Wasps* (mid-price)

Anton Webern (1883-1945)

Webern enables me to draw this survey of the history of classical music and its recordings to a close almost in silence; not because Webern was unimportant, but because his music was so brief, his output so miniscule, his life so uneventful, and his demise so pitiful.

He was born in Vienna and received a doctorate from the University in 1906, thus becoming the first composer to start out with a degree in musicology. At first he was a devoted Wagnerian, even composing a piece for soprano and orchestra called *Siegfried's Sword* (unfinished).

But in 1904 he met Arnold Schoenberg. He signed on as his first pupil, and so he remained the rest of his life, turning into the most single-minded follower of the atonal, and later, twelve-tone, school. Those who find this music harsh or difficult might contemplate the fact that Webern had a pathological fear of noise, and the slightest deviation from perfection of pitch or volume was torture to him.

He was active most of his life as a conductor, ironically often giving outstanding performances of light music such as Johann Strauss waltzes. He was a fanatical perfectionist in every detail of his life; a different conductor had to be engaged to lead the premiere of Berg's Violin Concerto after Webern had used up two of the three allotted rehearsals preparing just the first eight bars of the music! He was neurotically tidy and neat, wrapping his manuscripts in ribbons, and once pointing out about one hundred printing errors in a Schoenberg score, all marked in color-coded pencil.

He was a small man with poor eyesight, unprepossessing in appearance at first, but with a charisma born of dedication when he spoke of his ideals or sat at the piano to demonstrate. He wrote few works, and they are famous for their extreme economy, seldom lasting more than a few minutes. They have been called the musical equivalent of Japanese *haiku* poetry.

Webern's music—austere, uncompromising, unadorned, anti-Romantic—was ridiculed by all but the most intellectual and avant-garde musical sophisticates. After Austria was annexed by the Nazis, his music was forbidden, his books burned, and he was allowed only enough students to survive. He only escaped slave labor by agreeing to do proofreading for his former publisher.

One evening in 1945, visiting his son-in-law, who had been secretly dabbling in the black market, Webern stepped outside the house to smoke a cigarette. American soldiers were just arriving to arrest his son-in-law, and one of them, perhaps seeing Webern reach into his pocket—no one knows for sure—fired three shots at the shadowy figure. The composer staggered back into the house and died shortly afterwards.

So ended a life of suffering and rejection, but also of high idealism, with (to rewrite T. S. Eliot) a bang *and* a whimper.

Five Pieces for Orchestra, Op. 10

This entire work, with five precisely designed sections, takes less than five minutes to play. In this short space Webern puts a large number of instrumental soloists (not really a true "orchestra") through a variety of tempi and moods. Anything that could possibly be considered superfluous to the central thesis is stripped away. Webern gave each tiny piece a tiny name: Prototype, Transformation, Return, Memory, and Soul.

Two outstanding recordings are both happily at mid-price: Herbert von Karajan with an all-Webern program, and Antal Dorati's with representative companions by Berg and Schoenberg.

Karajan, Berlin Philharmonic Orchestra. DG 423254 [ADD] + Five Movements for String Quartet, op. 5, Passacaglia for Orchestra, Symphony for Chamber Orchestra (mid-price)

Dorati, London Symphony Orchestra. Mercury 432006 [ADD] + Berg: Three Pieces for Orchestra, *Lulu* Suite; Schoenberg: Five Pieces for Orchestra, Op. 16 (mid-price)

Six Pieces for Orchestra, Op. 6

The pieces here are longer than in the previous work, but still quite brief by normal standards. This is Webern's only work scored for large orchestra. The variety of mysterious and striking effects is astonishing.

A great digital disc conducted by James Levine offers three works, one by each of the three leaders of the Atonal School. Each is a good introduction to its composer.

Levine, Berlin Philharmonic Orchestra. DG 419781 [DDD] + Schoenberg: Five Pieces for Orchestra, Op. 16; Berg: Three Pieces for Orchestra

A Minimal Epilogue

Among the many tides and currents washing over the world of music in the last generation, one has become especially notable. Minimalism, as it is called, relies on establishing patterns which are then repeated continually, but with slowly evolving alterations. An offshoot of Primitivism (see Carl Orff), this music is a reaction against the overly-cerebral music of many twentieth-century avant-garde composers, and often borrows idioms from ethnic and popular music.

It is, in my opinion, too early to give this school full measure in a book such as this, which is designed to concentrate on the tried and true; nevertheless, so much has been recorded of, and written about, this music, and it has developed such a large audience, that a brief consideration of some of its leaders is in order.

John Adams (1947-)

Adams is the composer of this school considered Most Likely to Succeed by many critics; that is, they see his music as definitely lasting beyond the mere fad stage. Partly this is because he stretches the definition of Minimalism to include more elements of the musical palette, and thus enrich his expressive range.

The Chairman Dances

Catchy dance music for Chairman Mao may sound a bit outré, but so it goes in the Adams opera *Nixon in China,* one of the most talked-about compositions of recent years.

The opera is available on a complete recording, but for an introduction, stick to this excerpt on a fine "sampler" disc of Adams's music containing a number of items, very well conducted by Edo De Waart.

De Waart, San Francisco Symphony Orchestra. Nonesuch 79144 [DDD]

Shaker Loops

The title has a double implication, referring both to the religious practices of the American Shakers and to the musical mechanisms of trills and shakes.

De Waart and his forces are excellent here again, coupled with a work by one of the pioneer Minimalists, Steve Reich. There is strong competition, however, from conductor Christopher Warren-Green on a British import offering additional works by Philip Glass, Steve Reich, and one of the newer and most striking Minimalists, Dave Heath.

De Waart, San Francisco Symphony Orchestra. Philips 412214 [DDD] + Reich: Variations for Winds
Warren-Green, London Concert Orchestra. Virgin Classics 59610 [DDD] + Glass: *Company, Facades;* Reich: *8 Lines;* Heath: *The Frontier*

Philip Glass (1937-)

Glass is the best known, most recorded, and most orthodox of the Minimalists, sticking to the repetitive pattern concept to create a hypnotic effect.

Glassworks

The title is, to put it mildly, self-explanatory, as well as forgivably self-serving. An impulse to roll the eyes becomes harder to resist when the performers turn out to be the Glass Ensemble, but the disc is still a good compendium of this composer's art. A veritable glass menagerie, one might say.

Glass Ensemble. CBS 37265 [DDD] (mid-price)

Piano Music

Another compilation delineating the Glass style, this music is played, authoritatively one must think, by the composer himself.

Glass. CBS 45576 [DDD]

Henryk Górecki (1933-)

Górecki is the oldest of this group and shows the closest links to the Primitivists. His works make few demands on listeners, stressing direct themes and rich harmonies.

Symphony No. 3

Subtitled "The Symphony of Sorrowful Songs," the lyrics comprise the lament of a mother for her dead son. The work was premiered in 1977.

The symphony has been recorded twice, with the newer version, featuring the beautiful voice of soprano Dawn Upshaw, becoming one of the most surprising commercial successes in the record business. It was at the top of the classical charts for thirty-five weeks, and in 1993 alone sold over four hundred thousand copies.

Upshaw, Zinman, London Sinfonietta. Nonesuch 79282 [DDD]

About the Author

Bill Parker has been a classical music broadcaster, author, and record executive for over thirty years.

He was an announcer and producer for several radio stations, principally Minnesota Public Radio where he worked for seventeen years, producing both regional and national classical music programs.

Mr. Parker has written three previous books, numerous liner notes for record albums, and many newspaper and magazine articles. He has also worked in the record business as the manager of six record stores, and as midwestern sales manager for a large classical record distributor. Currently, he is senior buyer of classical recordings for a major national retailer.

His favorite quotation is from Sergei Rachmaninoff: "Music is enough for a whole lifetime—but a lifetime is not enough for music."

Public Radio Stations

Alabama

Birmingham: WBHM-FM
(90.3Mhz)
Huntsville: WLRH-FM (89.3Mhz)
Mobile: WHIL-FM (91.3Mhz)
Troy/Montgomery: WTSU-FM
(89-Mhz)
Tuscaloosa: WUAL-FM (91.5Mhz)

Alaska

Anchorage: KSKA-FM (91.1Mhz)
Barrow: KBRW-AM (689kHz)
Bethel: KYUK-AM (640kHz)
Dillingham: KDLG-AM (670kHz)
Fairbanks: KUAC-FM (104.7Mhz)
Haines: KHNS-FM (102.3Mhz)
Homer: KBBI-AM (890kHz)
Juneau: KTOO-FM (104.3Mhz)
Ketchikan: KRBD-FM (105.9Mhz)
Kodiak: KMXT-FM (100.1 Mhz)
Kotzebue: KOTZ-AM (720kHz)
McGrath: KSKO-AM (87.0kHz)
Petersburg: KFST-FM (100.9Mhz)
Sitka: KCAW-FM (104.7Mhz)
Valdez: KCAW-FM (104.7Mhz)
Wrangell: KSTK-FM (101.7Mhz)

Arizona

Flagstaff: KNAU-FM (88.7Mhz)
Phoenix: KJZZ-FM (91.5Mhz)
Tucson: KUAT-AM (1550kHz)
KUAT-FM (90.5Mhz)
KXCI-FM (91.7Mhz)
Yuma: KAWC-AM (1320kHz)

Arkansas

Fayetteville: KUAF-FM (91.3Mhz)
Jonesboro: KASU-FM (91.9Mhz)
Little Rock: KUAR-FM (89.1Mhz)
KLRE-FM (90.5Mhz~

California

Arcata; KHSU-FM (90.5Mhz)
Berkeley: KPFA-FM (94.1Mhz)
Chico: KCHO-FM (91.7Mhz)
Fresno: KSJV-FM (91.5Mhz)
KVPR-FM (89.3Mhz)
Long Beach: KLON-FM (88.1Mhz)
Los Angeles: KPFK-FM (90.7Mhz)
KUSC-FM (91.5Mhz/
Los Angeles)
KFAC-FM (88.7Mhz/
Santa Barbara)
KCPB-FM (91.1 Mhz/
Thousand Oaks)
KPSC-FM (88.5Mhz/
Palm Springs)
Northridge: KCSN-FM (88.5Mhz)
Pacific Grove: KAZU-FM (90.3Mhz)
Pasadena: KPCC-FM (89.3Mhz)
Sacramento: KXPR-FM (90.9Mhz)
Salinas: KHDC-FM (90.9Mhz)
San Bernardino: KVCR-FM
(91.9Mhz)
San Diego: KPBS-FM (89.5Mh)
San Francisco: KALW-FM
(91.7Mhz)
KQED-FM (88.5Mhz)
San Luis Obispo: KCBX-FM
(90.1 Mhz)
San Mateo: KCSM-FM (91.1 Mhz)
Santa Cruz: KUSP-FM (88.9Mhz)
Santa Monica: KCRW-FM
(89.9Mhz)
Santa Rosa: KBBF-FM (89.1Mhz)
Stockton: KUOP-FM (91.3Mhz)

Colorado

Boulder: KGNU-FM (88.5Mhz)
Colorado Springs: KRCC-FM
(91.5Mhz)

Denver: KCFR-FM (90.1Mhz)
KUVO-FM (89.3Mhz)
Fort Collins: KCSU-FM (90.5Mhz)
Grand Junction: KPRN-FM
(89.5Mhz)
Greeley: KUNC-FM (91.5Mhz)
Ignacio: KSUT-FM (91.3Mhz)

Connecticut

Fairfield: WSHU-FM (91.1 Mhz)
Middlefield: WPKT-FM (90.5Mhz)
WNPR-FM(89.1 Mhz/Norwich)

District of Columbia

WAMU-FM (88.5Mhz)
WDCU-FM (90.1 Mhz)
WETA-FM (90.9Mhz)
WPFW-FM (89.3Mhz)

Florida

Fort Myers: WSFP-FM (90.1Mhz)
Fort Pierce: WQCS-FM (88.9Mhz)
Gainesville: WUFT-FM (89.1Mhz)
Jacksonville: WJCT-FM (89.9Mhz)
Miami: WLRN-FM (91.3Mhz)
Orlando: WMFE-FM (90.7Mhz)
Panama City: WKGC-FM (90.7Mhz)
WKGC-AM (1480kHz)
Pensacola: WUWF-FM (88.1Mhz)
Tallahassee: WFSU-FM (88.9Mhz)
WFSQ-FM (91.5Mhz)
Tampa: WMNF-FM (88.5Mhz)
WUSF-FM (89.7Mhz)
West Palm Beach: WXEL-FM
(90.7Mhz)

Georgia

Athens: WUGA-FM (91.7Mhz)
Atlanta: WABE-FM (90.1Mhz)
WCLK-FM (91.9Mhz)
WWET-FM (91.7Mhz/Valdosta)

WUNV-FM (91.7Mhz/Albany)
WJSP-FM (88.1 Mhz/Columbus)
WXVS-FM (90.1 Mhz/Waycross)
WDCO-FM (89.7Mhz/Macon)
WACG-FM (90.7Mhz/Augusta)
WABR-FM (91.1 Mhz/Tifton)
Savannah: WSVH-FM (91.1Mhz)

Hawaii

Honolulu: KHPR-FM (88.1Mhz)
　　KKUA-FM
　　　(90.7Mhz/Wailuku/Maui)

Idaho

Boise: KBSU-FM (90.3Mhz/Boise)
　　KBSM-FM (91.7Mhz/McCall)
　　KBSWFM (91.7MhzlTwin Falls)

Illinois

Carbondale: WSIU-FM (91.9Mhz)
Chicago: WBEZ-FM (91.5Mhz)
DeKalb: WNIF-FM (90.5Mhz)
　　WNIU-FM (89.5Mhz)
Edwardsville: WSIE-FM (88.7Mhz)
Glen Ellyn: WDCB-FM (90.9Mhz)
Macomb: WIUM-FM (91.3Mhz)
Normal: WGLT-FM (89.1Mhz)
Peoria: WCBU-FM (89.9Mhz)
Rock Island: WVIK-FM (90.1Mhz)
Springfield: WSSU-FM (91.9Mhz)
Urbana: WILL-AM (580kHz)
　　WILL-FM (90.9Mhz)

Indiana

Bloomington: WFIU-FM
　　(103.7Mhz)
Evansville: WNIN-FM (88.3Mhz)
Fort Wayne: WBNI-FM (89.1Mhz)
Indianapolis: WAJC-FM (104.5Mhz)
　　WFYI-FM (90.1 Mhz)
Munice: WBST-FM (92.1Mhz)
Vincennes: WVUB-FM (91.1Mhz)
West Lafayette: WBAA-AM
　　(920kHz)

Iowa

Ames: WOI-AM (640kHz)
　　WOI-FM (90.1Mhz)
Cedar Falls: KHKE-FM (89.5Mhz)
　　KRNI-AM (1010kHz/
　　　Mason City)

KUNI-FM (90.9Mhz)
KUNY-FM (91.8Mhz/
　　Mason City)
Cedar Rapids: KCCK-FM (88.3Mhz)
Council Bluffs: KIWR-FM
　　(89.7Mhz)
Fort Dodge: KTPR-FM (91.1 Mhz)
Iowa City: KSUI-FM (91.7Mhz)
　　KSU l-AM (91 0kHz)
Sioux City: KWIT-FM (90.3Mhz)
Waterloo: KBBG-FM (88.1Mhz)

Kansas

Hutchinson: KHCC-FM (90.1Mhz)
Lawrence: KANU-FM (91.5Mhz)
Manhattan: KKSU-AM (580kHz)
Pierceville: KANZ-FM (91.1Mhz)
　　KZNA-FM (90.5Mhz/Hill City)
Pittsburg: KRPS-FM (89.9Mhz)
Wichita: KMUW-FM (89.1Mhz)
　　KSOF-FM (91.1Mhz)

Kentucky

Bowling Green: WKYU-FM
　　(88.9Mhz)
Highland Heights: WKNU-FM
　　(89.7Mhz)
Lexington: WBKY-FJ (91.3Mhz)
Louisville: WFPK-FM (91.9Mhz)
　　WFPL-FM (89.3Mhz)
Morehead: WMKY-FM (90.3Mhz)
Murray: WKMS-FM (91.3Mhz)
Richmond:WEKU-FM (88.9Mhz)

Louisiana

Baton Rouge: WRKF-FM (89.3Mhz)
Hammond: KSLU-FM (90.9Mhz)
Lafayette: KRVS-FM (88.7Mhz)
New Orleans: WRBH-FM
　　(88.3Mhz)
　　WWNO-FM (89.9Mhz)
Shreveport: KDAQ-FM (89.9Mhz
　　KLSA-FM (90.7Mhz/Alexandria)
　　KBSA-FM (90.9Mhz/
　　　EI Dorado, AR)

Maine

Bangor: WMEH-FM (90.9Mhz)
Portland: WMEA-FM (90.1Mhz)

Maryland

Baltimore: WBJC-FM (91.5Mhz)
　　WEAA-FM (88.9Mhz)
　　WJHU-FM (88.1Mhz)
Salisbury: WSCL-FM (89.5Mhz)

Massachusetts

Amherst: WFCR-FM (88.5Mhz)
Boston: WBUR-FM (90.9Mhz)
　　WGBH-FM (89.7Mhz)
　　WUMB-FM (91.9Mhz)
Worcester: WICN-FM (90.5Mhz)

Michigan

Ann Arbor: WUOM-FM (91.7Mhz)
Bay City: WUCX-FM (90.1Mhz)
Detroit: WDET-FM (101.9Mhz)
East Lansing: WKAR-AM (870kHz)
　　WKAR-FM (90.5Mhz)
Flint: WFBE-FM (95.1Mhz)
Grand Rapids: WGVU-FM
　　(88.5Mhz/Allendale-
　　　Grand Rapids)
Interlochen: WIAA-FM (88.7Mhz)
Kalamazoo: WMUK-FM
　　(102.1Mhz)
Marquette: WNMU-FM (90.1Mhz)
Mount Pleasant: WCMU-FM
　　(89.5Mhz)
　　WCUL-FM (91.7MHZ/Alpena)
　　WUCX-FM (90.1Mhz/Bay City)
Twin Lake: WBLV-FM (90.3Mhz)
Ypsilanti: WEMU-FM (89.1Mhz)

Minnesota

Colleqeville/St. Cloud: KSJR-FM
　　(90.1Mhz)
Duluth: KUMD-FM (103.3Mhz)
　　WSCD-FM (92.9Mhz)
　　KBPR-FM (90.7Mhz/Brainerd)
　　WGGL-FM
　　　(91.9Mhz/Houghton)
　　WIRR-FM (90.9Mhz/Bulh)
　　KQMN-FM (91.5Mhz/
　　　Thief River Falls)
Grand Rapids: KAXE-FM (91.7Mhz)
Mankato: KMSU-FM (89.7Mhz)
Minneapolis: KBEM-FM (88.5Mhz)
　　KFAI-FM (90.3Mhz)
Minneapolis/St. Paul: KUOM-AM
　　(770kHz)

Moorhead: KCCM-FM (91.1Mhz)
    KCRB-FM (88.5Mhz/Bemidij)
Northfield: WCAL-FM (89.3Mhz)
Rochester: KLSE-FM (91.7Mhz)
    KZSE-FM (90.7Mhz)
    KGAC-FM (90.5Mhz/St. Paul)
    KLCD-FM (89.5Mhz/
    Decorah, IA)
St. Paul/Minneapolis: KNOW-AM
    (1330kHz)
    KNSR-FM
    (88.9Mhz/Collegeville)
    WSCN-FM (100.9Mhz/Dulth)
    KSJN-FM (91.1Mhz)
Worthington/Marshall: KRSW-FM
    (91.7Mhz)
    KRSU-FM (91.3Mhz/
    Appleton, MN)
    KRSD-FM (88.1Mhz/
    Sioux Falls, SD)

Mississippi

Holly Springs: WURC-FM
    (88.1Mhz)
Jackson: WJSU-FM (88.5Mhz)
    WMPN-FM (91.3Mhz/Jackson)
    WMAB-FM
    (89.9Mhz/Mississippi
    WMAE-FM
    (89.5Mhz/Booneville)
    WMAH-FM (90.3Mhz/Biloxi)
    WMAO-FM
    (90.3Mhz/Greenwood)
    WMAU-FM (88.9Mhz/Bude)
    WMAV-FM (90.3Mhz/O-ford)
    WMAW-FM (88.1Mhz/Meridian)
Lorman: WPRL-FM (91.7Mhz)

Missouri

Columbia: KBIA-FM (91.3Mhz)
    KOPN-FM (89.5Mhz)
Kansas City: KCUR-FM (89.3Mhz)
Maryville: KXCV-FM (90. Mhz)
Rolla: KUMR-FM (88.5Mhz)
Springfield: KSMU-FM (91.1Mhz)
St. Louis: KDHX-FM (88.1Mhz)
    KWMU-FM (90.7Mhz)
Warrensburg: KCMW-FM
    (90.9Mhz)

Montana

Billings: KEMC-FM (91.7Mhz)

Missoula: KUFM-FM (89.1Mhz)

Nebraska

Lincoln: KUCV (90.9Mhz)
    KTNE-FM (91.1 Mhz/Alliance)
    KHNE-FM (89.1 Mhz/Hastings)
    KLNE-FM (89.7Mhz/Lexington)
    KXNE-F, (89.3Mhz/Norfolk)
Omaha: KIOS-FM (91.5Mhz)

Nevada

Las Vegas: KCEP-FM (88.1Mhz)
    KNPR-FM (89.5Mhz)
Reno: KUNR-FM (88.7Mhz)

New Hampshire

Concord: WEVO-FM (89.1Mhz)

New Jersey

Lincroft: WBJB-FM (90.5Mhz)
Newark: WBGO-FM (88.3Mhz)
Trenton: WWFM-FM (89.1Mhz)

New Mexico

Albuquerque: KUNM-FM
    (89.9Mhz)
Las Cruces: KRWG-FM (90.7Mhz)
Pine Hill: KTDB-FM (89.7Mhz)
Portales: KENW-FM (89.5Mhz)

New York

Albany: WAMC-FM (90.3Mhz)
    WCAN-FM
    (93.3Mhz/Canajoharie)
    WAMK-FM (90.9Mhz/Kingston)
    WANC-FM
    (103.9Mhz/Ticonderoga)
Binghamton: WSKG-FM
    (89.3Mhz/Binghamton)
    WSQG-FM (90.9Mhz/lthaca)
    WSZC-FM (91.7Mhz/Oneonta)
Buffalo: WEBR-AM (970kHz)
    WNED-FM (94.5Mhz)
    WBFO-FM (88.7Mhz)
Canton: WSLU-FM (89.5Mhz)
New York City: WBAI-FM
    (99.5Mhz)
    WFUV-FM (90.7Mhz)
    WNYC-AM (820kHz–
    WNYC-FM (93.9Mhz)
Oswego: WRVO-FM (89.9Mhz)

Rochester: WXXI-FM (91.5Mhz)
    WXXI-AM (1370kHz)
Schenectady: WMHT-FM (89.1Mhz)
Syracuse: WAER-FM (88.3Mhz)
    WCNY-FM (91.3Mhz)

North Carolina

Asheville: WCOS-FM (88.1 Mhz)
Chapel Hill: WUNC-FM (91.5Mhz)
Charlotte: WFAE-FM (90.7Mhz)
Davidson: WDAV-FM (89.9Mhz)
Fayetteville: WFSS-FM (89.1Mhz)
New Bern: WTEB-FM (89.3Mhz)
Spindale: WNCW-FM (88.7Mhz)
Wilmington: WHQR-FM (91.3Mhz)
Winston-Salem: WFDD-FM
    (88.5Mhz)

North Dakota

Belcourt: KEYA-FM (88.5Mhz)
Bismarck: KCND-FM (90.5Mhz)
    KMPR-FM (89.5Mhz/Minot)
    KPPR-FM (89.5Mhz/Williston)
    KDPR-FM (89.9Mhz/Dickinson)
Fargo: KDSU-FM (91.9Mhz)
Grand Forks: KFJM-AM (1370kHz)
    KFJM-FM (89.3Mhz)
New Town: KMHA-FM (91.3Mhz)

Ohio

Athens: WOUB-FM (91.3Mhz)
    WOUC-FM
    (89.1Mhz/Cambridge)
    WOU L-FM (89.1 Mhz/l ronton)
    WOUB-AM (1340kHz)
Cincinnati: WGUC-FM (90.9Mhz)
    WXVU-FM (1.7Mhz)
Cleveland: WCPN-FM (90.3Mhz)
Columbus: WCBE-FM (90.5Mhz)
    WOSU-AM (820kHz)
    WOSU-FM (89.7Mhz)
    WOSV-FM (91.7Mhz/Mansfield)
Kent: WKSU-FM (89.7Mhz)
Oxford: WMUB-FM (88.5Mhz)
Toledo: WGTE-FM (91.3Mhz)
    WGLE-FM (90.7Mhz/Lima)
Yellow Sprintgs: WYSO-FM
    (91.3Mhz)
Youngstown: WYSU-FM (88.5Mhz)

Oklahoma

Edmond: KCSC-FM (90.1Mhz)

Norman: KGOU-FM (106.3Mhz)
Stillwater: KOSU-FM (91.7Mhz)
Tulsa: KWGS-FM (89.5Mhz)

Oregon

Ashland: KSOR-FM (90.1Mhz)
  KSMF-FM (89.1Mhz/Ashland)
  KSJ K-AM (1230kHz/Talent)
  KSKF-FM (90.OMhz/
    Klamath Falls)
  KSBA-FM (88.5Mhz/Coos Bay)
Corvalis: KOAC-AM (550kHz)
Eugene: KLCC-FM (89.7Mhz)
  KWAX-FM (91.1Mhz)
Portland: KBOO-FM (90.7Mhz)
  KOPB-FM (91.5Mhz)
  KOAB-FM (91.3Mhz/Bend)
  KRBM-FM (90.9Mhz/Pendleton)
  KBPS-AM (1450kHz)

Pennsylvania

Erie: WQLN-FM (1.3Mhz)
Harrisburg: WITF-FM (89.5Mhz)
Philadelphia: WHYY-FM (90.9Mhz)
  WRTI-FM (90.1Mhz)
  WXPN-FM (88.5Mhz)
Pittsburgh: WDUQ-FM (90.5Mhz)
  WQED-FM (89.3Mhz)
Scranton/Wilkes-Barre: WVIA-FM
  (89.9Mhz)

Puerto Rico

Hato Rey: WIPR-FM (91.3Mhz)
San Juan: WRTU-FM (89.7Mhz)

South Carolina

Charleston: WSCI-FM (89.3Mhz)
Columbia: WLTR-FM (91.3Mhz)

South Dakota

Porcupine: KILI-FM (90.1Mhz)
Vermillion: KUSD-AM (690kHz)
  KTSD-FM (91.1 Mhz/Reliance)
  KUSD-FM (89.7Mhz/Vermillion)
  KESD-FM (88.3Mhz/Brookings)
  KDSD-FM (88.3Mhz/Pierpont)
  KBHE-FM (89.3Mhz/Rapid City)
  KQSD-FM (91.9Mhz/Lowery)
  KPSD-FM (97.1 Mhz/Faith)

Tennessee

Chattanooga: WUTC-FM (88.1Mhz)

Collegedale: WSMC-FM (90.5Mhz)
Johnson City: WETS-FM (89.5Mhz)
Knoxville: WUOT-FM (91.9Mhz)
Memphis: WKNO-FM (91.1Mhz)
Murfreesboro: WMOT-FM
  (89.5Mhz)
Nashville: WPLN-FM (90.3Mhz)

Texas

Austin: KUT-FM (90.5Mhz)
Beaumont: KVLU-FM (91.3Mhz)
College Station: KAMU-FM
  (90.9Mhz)
Commerce: KETR-FM (88.9Mhz)
Corpus Christi: KEDT-FM
  (90.3Mhz)
Dallas: KERA-FM (90.1Mhz)
El Paso: KTEP-FM (88.5Mhz)
  KXCR-FM (89.5Mhz)
Harlingen: KMBH-FM (88.9Mhz)
Houston: KPFT-FM (90.1 Mhz)
  KUHF-FM (88.7Mhz)
Killeen: KNCT-FM (91.3Mhz)
San Antonio: KPAC-FM (90.9Mhz)
  KSTX-FM (89.1Mhz)

Utah

Logan: KUSU-FM (91.5Mhz)
Park City: KPCW-FM (91.9Mhz)
Provo: KBYU-FM (89.1Mhz)
Salt Lake City: KRCL-FM (90.9Mhz)
  KUER-FM (90.1Mhz)

Vermont

Colchester: WVPR-FM (89.5Mhz)
  WVPS-FM
    (107.9Mhz/Burlington)
  WRVT-FM (88.7Mhz/rutland)

Virginia

Harrisonburg: WMRA-FM
  (90.7Mhz)
Norfolk: WHRV-FM (89.5Mhz)
  WHRO-FM (90.3Mhz)
Richmond: WCVE-FM (8.9Mhz)
Roanoke: WVTF-FM (89.1Mhz)
  WVTU-FM
    (89.3Mhz/Charlottesville)
  WVTR-FM (91.9Mhz/Marion)

Washington

Granger: KDNA-FM (91.9Mhz)

Pullman: KWSU-FM (1250kHz)
  KFAE-FM (89.1 Mhz/Richland)
  KRFA-FM (91.7Mhz/Moscow,lD)
Seattle: KUOW-FM (94.9Mhz)
Sopkane: KPBX-FM (91.1Mhz)
Tacoma: KPLU-FM (88.5Mhz0

West Virginia

Charleston: WVPN-FM (88.5Mhz)
  WVPB-FM (91.7Mhz/Beckley)
  WVPW-FM
    (88.9Mhz/Buckhannon)
  WVWV-FM
    (90.9Mhz/Huntington)
  WVNP-FM (89.9Mhz/Wheeling)
  WVPG-FM
    (90.3Mhz/Parkersburg)
  WVEP-FM
    (88.9Mhz/Martinsburg)
  WVPM-FM
    (90.9Mhz/Morgantown)

Wisconsin

Hayward: WOJB-FM (88.9Mhz)
Kenosha/Racine: WGTD-FM
  (91.1Mhz)
La Crosse: WLSU-FM (88.9Mhz)
Madison: WERN-FM (88.7Mhz)
  WHLA-FM (90.3Mhz/La Crosse)
  WHRM-FM (90.9Mhz/Wausau)
  WHWC-FM
    (88.3Mhz/Menomonee)
  WHBM-FM (90.3Mhz/Park Falls)
  WPNE-FM (89.3Mhz/Green Bay)
  WHSA-FM (89.9Mhz/Brule)
  WLBL-AM (930khz/Auburndale)
  WHAD-FM (90.7Mhz/Delafield)
  WHHI-FM (91.3Mhz/Highland)
  WHA-AM (970kHz)
  WGBW-FM (91.5Mhz/green Bay)
  KUWS-FM (91.3Mhz/Superior)
  WORT-FM (89,9Mhz)
Milwaukee: WUWM-FM (89.7Mhz)
  WYMS-FM (8.9Mhz)
Rhinelander: WXPR-FM (91.7Mhz)

Wyoming

Laramie: KUWR-FM (91.9Mhz)

Index